# What Others Are Saying About the "Hallelujah Diet" and the Teachings of Dr. George Malkmus

"I have received your teaching series on Back to the Garden and the success that you have had with your modified raw diet. The tape lectures that I have reviewed were inspiring to me. I am a research scientist retired from the FDA/NIH. I am currently working on nutrition and oxygen therapy. Our research has shown that when we eat natural nutrients (at least 65% raw fruits and vegetables) there is an energy explosion within our body. This gives the body the necessary tools it needs to rebuild strong cells that it takes to gain control of the body... We have had great success with our program... This we believe is or will be the beginning road map to return to the Garden of Eden... I would like very much to meet with you."
    John H. Norris, Ph.D., Maryland

"For the past 15 years I suffered from acute colitis, with constant pain and much bleeding. It drained me physically – I was always tired. A year ago I got desperate before the Lord, praying, *Lord, I can't minister to this huge congregation and keep all these ministries to the needy going unless You heal my bowels. I am at my wits end; I'm too weary to go on.* The Holy Spirit directed me to nutrition for healing. I always made fun of **health nuts** and all the claims being made for alternative health plans. The Holy Spirit taught me what to do: I got off sugar. I drink the juice of carrots and apples daily. I drink Barleygreen... I have been completely healed! I have more energy than I had at thirty years of age, and I have never felt better in my life..."
    David Wilkerson, President, World Challenge

"I was diagnosed with fibromyalgia in 1995 and was on several different medicines. None of the drugs helped me and I spent most of 18 months in bed. Through our church I heard about a seminar on 'Diet for Healing' and was introduced to the book ***God's Way to Ultimate Health***. I started on the Hallelujah Diet full force and within three weeks I knew I was getting better. I made a complete life change and now I am able to exercise. I have more energy and walk six miles a day plus bicycle riding. I didn't have a severe weight problem but in the last 14 months I have lost 25 lbs. and I feel wonderful. My family is as happy as I am and have made diet changes also. My 84-year old father is taking Barleygreen and juicing carrots. HALLELUJAH!"
    Judy Boling, Florida

"We are so glad we found your book. We started on the Hallelujah Diet and have lost nearly 70 lbs. between the two of us in two months. Not to mention how much better we feel. We are ordering more books to pass around to the people in our church. Some have already started the diet without reading the book but want to read it when we can get more copies..."
    Pastor Mike and Cathy Hoover, Arizona

"... we have more good news for you. We went to the doctor for a check up. The blood profile was beautiful. Blood pressure for George was 127/70. EKG good, urine good, etc. Then we asked the doctor for an extra test for the bladder cancer without going into the bladder and poking around. He said yes. He sent George to the cancer lab... They sent this to a special cancer testing place... it came back – no cancer! Praise the lord!!"

    Erna and George Rizzotto, Florida

"I gave a set of your books to my doctor and told him that I wanted to try eating this way. He said it looks good to me, so go ahead and try it. In six weeks I was off Zocor and the chol/tg were way down from the last two years. Thank God and you."

    Bossie Carlsen, Florida

"Three months ago I saw your video and read your book *God's Way to Ultimate Health* and it changed my life. Praise God! I was crippled with arthritis in my knees, right shoulder, and degenerative joint disease in my right ankle due to an auto accident in 1989 which broke my ankle in eleven different places. I thought I was headed for a wheelchair. The pain was so severe... God heard my cry and through your ministry I have lost 32 lbs, walk a mile a day or ride my stationary bike for 30 minutes. We had a foot washing service at church Saturday and praise God I was able to kneel and wash my partners feet. Haven't been able to do that since the accident in 1989. I also can walk on the sole of my feet instead of my toes. I am so excited and telling everyone. Haven't had this much excitement since I was saved in 1977. I will keep you in my prayers as I am a believer in your teachings. Thank you."

    Marian Duffield, Kentucky

"When I heard Dr. George H. Malkmus on the 700 Club I sent for a copy of the *Back to the Garden* magazine. After reading it, I ordered all the back issues, plus *Why Christians Get Sick* and *God's Way to Ultimate Health*... We bought a juicer, Barleygreen, and Herbal Fiberblend. I went cold turkey on the Hallelujah Diet. It has been six months and I have lost 31 lbs. which I needed to lose... As a child of God I cannot sit down to food that I know to be poison to my body and ask God's blessing on it... I am 76 years old."

    Dorothy Johnson, Minnesota

"... I am a great fan of George Malkmus, and about a year ago I went on his diet and changed my life... a year ago I was crippled to the point of pulling myself out of bed each morning on a wire after hurting my back two years prior... Then I learned of George's diet. After starting George's diet, only three weeks later I was bouncing out of bed like a 16-year old. I am a professional Christian Country Singer from Nashville..."

    Steve Hamby, Tennessee

"Today I thought I would write to let you know I have been working on the new way of eating (Hallelujah Diet) and living. Overweight, I have had high blood pressure for over 30 years and taking medication every day. I went to the doctor the fifth of this month after making the (diet) change only two months ago and for the first time my blood pressure went from 140/80 to 120/60. He couldn't believe this and was almost angry when I told him how I changed my food intake. He told me it will never go down and stay down. He told me I would always have high blood pressure. Besides this, here are the other changes that have taken place. Smooth as silk skin; no more pain in legs and feet and arms; rest better; lost 17 lbs. Thank you."

    Carrie Leiphart, Pennsylvania

# GOD'S WAY
## TO ULTIMATE HEALTH

*A common sense guide for eliminating sickness through nutrition*

**Dr. George H. Malkmus**

WITH

**Michael Dye**

**God's Way to Ultimate Health**

The nutritional and health information in this book is based on the teachings of God's Holy Word, the Bible, as well as research and personal experiences by the authors and many others. The purpose of this book is to provide information and education about health. The authors and publisher do not offer medical advice or prescribe the use of diet as a form of treatment for sickness without the approval of a health professional.

Because there is always some risk involved when changing diet and lifestyles, the author and publisher are not responsible for any adverse effects or consequences that might result. Please do not apply the teachings of this book if you are not willing to assume the risk.

If you do use the information contained in this book without the approval of a health professional, you are prescribing for yourself, which is your constitutional right, but the author and publisher assume no responsibility.

*However, you are encouraged to quote this book liberally, so that as many people as possible may hear about these ideas and Biblical truths to the ultimate end that somehow, some day, in some way, the whole world may be reached with the knowledge and message, "YOU DO NOT HAVE TO BE SICK!!!" You are also encouraged to read this book out loud to your, family, friends, acquaintances and even total strangers. May pastors proclaim it from their pulpits. May doctors share it with their patients. Take this book to foreign lands and share it. In fact, please do anything you can to make the world a better place to live, and the people in it happier, healthier and more loving. *It is the goal of Hallelujah Acres to try to bring the people of today back to the simple lifestyle and natural diet that God originally planned for mankind ... a peaceful, happy life, free from stress and sickness.*

**Library of Congress Cataloging in Publication Data**
Malkmus, George H.
    *God's Way to Ultimate Health*
    1. Christian  2. Health  3. Food, Raw - Therapeutic use.

*Visit our web site at:*
*http://www.hacres.com*

Library of Congress Catalog Card No. 94-096534
ISBN 0-929619-02-1

| | | | | |
|---|---|---|---|---|
| First Printing 1995 | Third Printing 1996 | Fifth Printing 1997 | Seventh Printing 1997 | Ninth Printing 1998 |
| Second Printing 1995 | Fourth Printing 1996 | Sixth Printing 1997 | Eight Printing 1997 | Tenth Printing 1998 |
| Eleventh Printing 1999 | Twelfth Printing 1999 | Thirteenth Printing 1999 | | |

Printed in the United States of America
All Bible quotations are taken from the authorized **King James Version**
Cover art by Michele Warner. Inside art work by Tata Andres.

Published and Distributed by:

HALLELUJAH ACRES PUBLISHING
P. O. BOX 2388
SHELBY, NC  28151

# Introduction

We want to begin this book with a very special *thank you* to the thousands of people who have put the teachings of Hallelujah Acres to work in their lives. These people have been able to show others with their own life that indeed "You do not have to be sick." So many of these people have become a light of inspiration for others to follow. We have found so many times that when just one person who is suffering from heart disease, cancer, diabetes, etc. changes his or her diet and lifestyle to the principles taught in this book and becomes well, the lives of dozens or even hundreds of other people are touched.

So often we have seen when just one person makes these dietary changes, before long people in his or her family are so impressed that they are soon on the same diet. This pattern can continue with friends, church members and co-workers. It is a wellness that becomes contagious and can quickly spread to everyone with the desire to eliminate sickness, pain and suffering from their lives.

Also, a very special *thank you* to more than 300 people whose testimonials and letters are used on the pages of this book as an "amen" to our teachings ... and to the evangelist, medical doctor, chiropractic physician and doctor of nutrition who wrote forewords to this book. We feel honored to have a prominent evangelist and three well-known health professionals endorsing these Biblical-based dietary teachings.

But even more important are the results from the masses. The bottom line is results. What do other people who have tried this diet have to say?

What these people have to say is so important to us that the layout of this book allows their words to flow down the sides of the pages – along with quotes from medical doctors, scientists, researchers, Biblical scripture, famous philosophers, ministers, etc. – as an "amen" to the book's text.

If you find something in the text of this book a little hard to swallow, then start paying closer attention to the testimonials of people who have actually put these teachings to practice. These are real people with real testimonials. Again, the bottom line is results.

But many people may choose to ignore these results and the scientific evidence, simply to conclude that this book is too radical, or possibly even outlandish, in its dietary recommendations. That is an unfortunate and inaccurate conclusion, and it says a lot about the illogical "normalcy" that is now accepted by mankind on the subject of diet, nutrition and health care.

Yes, there will be some people who feel a diet based on raw fruits and vegetables – given to us by the divine providence and wisdom of our Creator – is radical and outlandish. These same people feel it is perfectly normal to eat a meal oozing with fat and cholesterol to clog up their arteries, and dozens of man-made chemicals that can drastically alter their body chemistry. We have become so brainwashed that we think it is "normal" to eat a meal of processed, adulterated foods from a tin can, cardboard box or frozen dinner with man-made chemical ingredients that can't even be pronounced by most people ... but that someone who insists on eating food exactly as it was created by our Creator is a radical!

A close look at what we consider "normal" and acceptable foods will reveal that there is something badly wrong with this commonly-accepted normalcy. With this in mind, we ask that you not be too quick to reject this book as radical, outlandish or heretical.

We must consider the consequences of accepting a diet of artificial, nutritionally-void foods grown, flavored and preserved with man-made chemicals. And then look at the additional price we pay when these foods make us sick and we seemingly have no choice but to turn to commonly-accepted medical procedures such as surgery, prescription drugs, radiation and chemotherapy.

When we look at the warped logic and sad outcome of all this, we must recognize that most foods people eat today and the costly medical procedures we incur were never a part of God's original plan for mankind. Our artificial modern diet and high-paid, inefficient medical establishment have become prime examples of the world's way of doing things. In fact, those who profit from the processed food industry and medical procedures would like for us to think that there is no other way of sustaining our bodies and maintaining health.

But there is another way.

From the very beginning of Creation, the Lord gave mankind everything we need to sustain our bodies in perfect health. He made no mistakes and no omissions. Read this book and you will end up with a whole new perspective on the consequences of going the world's way ... and why we should instead choose God's Way to Ultimate Health.

# God's Way to Ultimate Health

## Contents

## Part III: An "Amen" From People Who Have Tried the Hallelujah Diet

## Part IV: Recipes and Tips on How to Prepare Natural Foods

# Foreword by Dr. J.C. House, Doctor of Divinity

In the divine providence of God, there are times in life when a person appears on the scene and it seems as if that person was "called into the Kingdom for such a time as this." That individual then has such an impact in certain areas of life, that things are never the same again.

I believe that Rev. George Malkmus is that kind of an individual in the field of Bible Nutrition. His premise, "YOU DON'T HAVE TO BE SICK," is more than a premise. It's a promise.

George Malkmus does not teach theory ... He teaches fact, based on Bible truth and 19 years of research and personal experience. Rev. Malkmus' personal experience is that he switched to the diet he now advocates 19 years ago and healed himself of colon cancer and several other problems, ranging from high blood pressure to hemorrhoids. On this diet, Rev. Malkmus has enjoyed outstanding health, free of all illnesses, for the past 19 years.

George Malkmus' writings have circled the globe; his lectures on "How to Eliminate Sickness"

> *This book, God's Way to Ultimate Health, is the most complete treatise on the subject of Biblical Nutrition I have had the privilege of reading. I consider it must reading for any concerned person in today's society. – Dr. J.C. House*

have been heard by thousands; and his quarterly publication, *Back to the Garden,* is going into more than 34,000 homes at this time, and growing rapidly. Countless testimonies are on file sharing remarkable recoveries from all types of illnesses.

This book, *God's Way to Ultimate Health,* is the most complete treatise on the subject of Biblical Nutrition I have had the privilege of reading. I consider it must reading for any concerned person in today's society.

We live in a day when the masses are sick ... when a so-called National Health Care Plan is a paramount issue among politicians on the national level ... when individuals often find themselves bankrupt after illnesses and hospitalization ... and when businesses find it necessary to completely restructure financially because of rising health care costs. The answer to it all is found in this book. George Malkmus presents a simple, inexpensive, Bible-based plan to good health and longevity that is absolutely profound in its simplicity.

George Malkmus stands alone in the field of Bible Nutrition. I personally shall be eternally grateful for the truths that he shared with me that changed my life forever in the area of health.

Read this book, put it to practice and benefit from its truths.

Dr. J.C. House, Evangelist
Joshua, Texas
March 1995

# Foreword by Dr. David A. Darbro, Doctor of Medicine

Americans are becoming aware that much of what we have been told by those we rely upon for healthcare is not true. In fact, powerful political and economic forces exist throughout the land which thrive upon the public's health misfortunes. These vested interest groups, because of financial reasons, do not wish to see these people freed from disease and pain. They hire expensive lawyers, influence the media and bitterly oppose those who say there is a better way.

*God's Way to Ultimate Health* is a book offering freedom to people enslaved by the shackles of chronic degenerative disease. Some of those who make a living from other people's ill health would certainly not want you to read this book.

Why should I, a practitioner of medicine for 30 years, encourage anyone to read a book on health written by a protestant pastor? The answer to that question is because this book gives the reader the keys which can unlock the doorway to health. I believe these pages are must reading for anyone who seeks the truth and wants to lead a healthier life.

> *God's Way to Ultimate Health is a book offering freedom to people enslaved by the shackles of chronic degenerative disease. Some of those who make a living from other people's ill health would certainly not want you to read this book. – David Darbro, M.D.*

Just a word about my credentials. After graduating from the Indiana University School of Medicine I went into family practice. Shortly thereafter I became a Charter Fellow of the American Academy of Family Physicians and received my specialty board certification as a Diplomate of Family Practice. I spent my first 15 years in medicine treating symptoms by using various pharmaceutical approaches. During that time I almost never saw anyone cured of arthritis, diabetes, hardening of the arteries, hypertension, cancer, multiple sclerosis, etc. Although I gave my patients the best AMA-approved care available, and referred many of them to appropriate specialists, practically nothing was done to slow the rapid downhill slide of their chronic degenerative diseases. The suffering of these people ended only in the grave.

My motive for going into medicine was to help people get well. Although I was able to manage some symptoms by using pharmaceuticals, I was unable to reverse any serious disease process or see my patients return to genuine wellness. The problem hit close to home when my mother developed an erratic heart rhythm that would not respond to her cardiologist's treatments. Her doctors gave her no choice other than to live with her problem. Because of mom's deteriorating condition I was open to alternative approaches which lay outside the boundaries set by orthodox medicine. I began attending seminars on alternative means of treatment, given by a Mayo Clinic-trained internist. I found merit in some of these alternative treatments, despite attacks and allegations by the medical hierarchy claiming these were "unproven" forms of treatment. Then I learned that the Office of Technological Assessment of the United States Government had shown that 80 to 90 percent of the therapeutic approaches which were accepted by the medical profession as standard care *were actually unproven!* No wonder I wasn't seeing anyone cured! I suddenly realized that 80 to 90 percent of what I had been taught in medical school was UNPROVEN! This information brought me to a painful crossroads in my medical career. Was I to continue the rest of my professional life, secure in the safety of organized medicine and peer review, but be untrue to myself, my patients and the truth? Or was I to seek the truth and become a pioneer different from my colleagues because I was willing to abandon the diagnose-

*In my humble opinion, this book should be on every doctor's desk and serve as a primary reference to be used daily with patients. – David Darbro, M.D.*

and-treat-the-symptom way of thinking, and instead use innovative approaches which could restore health to my patients? My 15 years of frustration with the lack of medical results ended when I changed my thinking and headed 180 degrees in the opposite direction toward alternative medicine.

The last half of my career has been spent studying principles that underlie much of alternative medicine. After practicing a few months in my new area of specialty, I at last began to see the long-sought-for results in my patients. Some hypertensives were able to stop their drugs, some angina patients ceased having chest pains, some diabetics could get off their insulin, some arthritics began to freely move without pain, and even an occasional cancer patient went into remission. To my delight, even mom's heart problem soon disappeared and she was able to stop her prescription medicines.

These 15 years have been precious learning experiences filled with valuable lessons that have taught me how to make wise health choices. However, I have found the price is often high when one does not follow the "usual and customary" medical practices. Many of my colleagues in alternative medicine have lost their licenses to state medical review boards, and others have been threatened with loss of licensure if they continue practicing forms of alternative therapy. But regardless of the painful casualties that occur during this process of change, the public is becoming aware of available options, and is assuming greater and greater responsibility for their individual health. In this way the noble profession of medicine changes for the better.

My adventure in alternative medicine has rewarded me with an 80 to 90-percent success rate when the patient has done his part. Could this rate be improved? Something more was needed to bring my success rate to maximum attainable levels. What were the missing pieces to the puzzle?

I believe these missing pieces have been provided by the life and ministry of a pastor with no medical training. This pastor has learned, through his own trials and tribulations, the importance of eating food the way our Creator originally intended. My staff and I attended a weekend of intensive training at Hallelujah Acres in the small, rural community of Eidson, Tennessee, where Rev. George Malkmus taught us the Back to the Garden Health Ministers program. We found answers to questions about diet, live foods, what is and is not nutrition, how to exercise, etc. This program was learnable, livable, do-able and can be adopted into anyone's lifestyle who sincerely seeks a healthy existence, free of sickness, pain and premature death.

At this seminar we heard testimonials about P.S.A. levels dropping from 227 to normal. (P.S.A. is a measure of prostate cancer.) A lady shared that her breast cancer which had metastasized to her bones had remarkably diminished since beginning the Hallelujah Diet. Some found their chest pains from hardening of the arteries were gone. Others had lost weight, increased their energy level, found new hope, and on and on. My conclusion after talking personally to those people is that Rev. Malkmus' program works! I find his approach is unique because it is based on a combination of Biblical teachings, the very best nutritional information available to modern science and nearly 20 years of personal experience by Rev. Malkmus. I am convinced that the conclusions contained in this book provide the answers to the vitally important health questions of our day. I urge you to read this book carefully, because it can save you many years of personal research in the jungle of conflicting health claims. It could also save your life!

### • A word to fellow health professionals:

May I now say a word to my M.D. and D.O. colleagues who are also in the noble profession of medicine? Doctor, have you ever asked yourself why people are turning away by the droves from orthodox medicine and seeking alternative care? Our honored profession once provided the public with a security blanket they could depend upon, but somehow this blanket has now become thread bare, stained and full of holes. People are realizing that we doctors do not have the answer to the basic question of why they lost their health to begin with, much less can we tell them how to regain it. For those of you who have sold your soul to orthodox textbook medicine, my remarks will probably not make much of an impression. For others, however, who sincerely seek the truth, there will be something of value for you in this book. I urge you to read it with an open mind. A few days of reading this book will provide you with vital knowledge we didn't receive during our years of medical school training.

Doctor, if you or a loved one is suffering or dying from one of the serious degenerative diseases, I also encourage you to read this book. Are you truly convinced that pharmaceuticals, radiation, chemotherapy or surgery are the best option if your own wife, son, daughter or parents are diagnosed with cancer? A.M.A.-approved pharmaceuticals, radiation, chemotherapy and surgery are not treatments that restore health. Indeed, these are treatments that would make a healthy person sick! Doctor, how can you justify giving cancer patients a treatment that we all know is weakening their immune system at the very time when it is most important to strengthen their immune system? My colleague, there *is* a better way than we have been taught. If health is restored, cancer disappears. Healthy people don't have cancer.

If you are a cardiologist or heart surgeon, and are eating the **S**tandard **A**merican **D**iet (appropriately called the SAD diet), you are as susceptible as anyone else in the nation to be struck down with sudden death from a heart attack. If you apply the principles in this book to your own life you will greatly diminish your risk of suffering either a heart attack or stroke.

Physician: Are you embarrassed by patients who know more about nutrition than you do? Are you dismayed because HMOs not only dictate how you are to practice medicine but also goad you into herding huge numbers of patients through your office like cattle each day to hand them a prescription for the latest drugs? There is a better way that can deliver you and them from the disease management trap. In fact, this book may give you ideas of how to practice traditional medicine as it was originally intended by Hippocrates, the Father of Medicine. Hippocrates taught that the body is capable of healing itself, and that a doctor's aim should be to promote the general well-being of the patient so the "physician within" can get on with this healing. In fact, the word "physician" comes from the Greek word "physis," which was coined by Hippocrates himself. Explaining the concept of "physis," Hippocrates wrote that it is the tendency of nature "though untaught and uninstructed … to preserve a perfect equilibrium … to re-establish order and harmony." He taught that it is the duty of the physician to merely assist this tendency of the body to achieve its own equilibrium, harmony and health. The cardinal rule of Hippocrates for the physician was "First, do no harm." Doctor, do I have to remind you that you took the Hippocratic Oath before you were allowed to treat your first patient? So, how can you in good conscience administer potentially harmful radiation and drugs and then brand George Malkmus as a radical and a heretic for promoting healing through healthy diet and lifestyle? Hippocrates said, "Let your food be your medicine and your medicine be your food." From this viewpoint, *God's Way to Ultimate Health* becomes a textbook of traditional medicine. In my humble opinion, this book should be on every doctor's desk and serve as a primary reference to be used daily with patients.

The public wants us to lead them to safety. We physicians are to lead by example. Thus we must first heal ourselves and in so doing regain the right to be heard by others. So I urge you to engraft these principles into your own life, find that they work, and then confidently share them with your patients. And do not worry about losing business if all your patients become healthy. You will always be busy with new referrals if you teach people how to become healthy and maintain a state of wellness.

### • A word to pastors:

Are you frustrated because the members of your congregation suffer from the same diseases as the world? Could it not be true that we must return to God's original diet for mankind in order to radically decrease the concentration of destructive man-made poisons in our food chain in order to regain our health? These bodies we live in were not designed for foods saturated with preservatives, antibiotics, artificial flavors, chemical fertilizers, pesticides, hormones and other hazardous chemicals. Nor were we designed for foods whose molecular structure has been ruined by irradiation, microwave cooking, deep frying or scalding high temperatures. As if that weren't enough, we were also not designed for foods containing refined sugar, chemicalized salt, and the excessive fat and protein from the flesh of animals. Our bodies were designed for a simpler fare of live foods given to us by our Creator.

The bottom line is: OUR DIET IS KILLING US! Many of those who follow Christ say with their lips that they bend the knee to Christ in the spiritual realm. But do they really, if they persist in polluting these magnificent bodies with what we know is harmful? Are we not guilty of wrongdoing and hypocrisy if we knowingly put dead, refined, man-made garbage into our body – the temple of God – which is not our own but was "bought with a price?"

These bodies are the dwelling place of that which is sacred and must not be defiled. We are made in the image of God and we must care for these bodies in reverence to our Creator. The Christian of today must show the world that we honor God by eating natural foods as they are provided by God, rather than gorging ourselves with man-made, adulterated junk food, so we can live an abundant, wholesome, productive and disease-free life. Rather than bringing glory to the name of Christ, church potluck dinners full of artificial, dead, refined food, soda pop and coffee bring only paunchy, overweight bellies, disease and drug addiction. (Yes preacher, the caffeine in coffee and soft drinks served at your church is a "drug" and anyone who has to have it every day is an "addict.")

I beseech you, pastor, read this book and consider well these truths. We *can* throw off the shackles which so easily beset us. Your ministry can be a living example of encouragement to your pastorate as your ideal waist size reveals the fruits of your commitment to loving obedience.

### • A word to the general public seeking a better life:

You are important and have a mission and purpose in life which only you can fulfill. You are responsible for your own health status. It matters not whether you are a doctor, a pastor, a lawyer, a maintenance engineer, a common laborer or a housewife. Regardless of your occupation, your health depends on whether you are obedient to natural law or whether you violate it. If you violate natural law by insisting on putting toxic foods into your body, how can you expect to ever be well? What performance would you expect from your car if you insisted on filling it with cheap, low-grade, junk fuel, contrary to the recommendations of its manufacturer? The same principles apply to our bodies. If you trust the manufacturer of your car to determine what grade of fuel should be put in its gas tank, then how can you not trust the Creator of your body as the authority over – and provider of – what should go into your stomach? I urge you to learn God's natural laws for health and apply them in your life so these natural laws can *benefit* you with the blessings of health, high spirits and longevity rather than allowing these natural laws to make you downcast with sickness, disabilities and a premature death. The scriptural references in this book will help you to better understand the value of the foods created by our Creator to nourish our bodies. And you will see the personal testimonials and the scientific evidence to give even more support that God's original diet for mankind, specified in Genesis 1:29, does indeed work! Take this advice seriously by applying these principles to your life so that healthful living can be yours. Much expense, anguish and suffering can be avoided if you do.

## • A word to the youth of this country:

Yours is the future. When I was a boy growing up in the 1940s, America used to be the healthiest nation on earth. Now in the 1990s, we have fallen to 100th place. Your elders are sick and have been deceived in so many ways. For one thing, they have believed in the "Four Basic Food Groups," which taught that meat was our primary source of protein and that we need milk to build "strong healthy calcium-filled bones." Research has found this is not so! Dr. Mary Ruth Swope, internationally known health educator, calls the Four Basic Food Groups nothing but a clever advertising ploy primarily designed to benefit the meat and dairy industries. The bottom line is this: You must decide for yourself what is truth and what is fiction in many realms, for your very lives depend on it. Read this book. Help those you love attain optimal health by learning the truth and then sharing what you have learned with others. Armed with this information you can become a beacon of light and hope to those who so badly need this information.

May *God's Way to Ultimate Health* provide you with the key to a fascinating new way of life that can unlock your personal doorway to health.

Dr. David A. Darbro, M.D.
Indianapolis, Indiana
March 1995

# Foreword by Dr. Rowen S. Pfeifer, Doctor of Chiropractic

I have known Rev. Malkmus for only little more than one year, yet I feel a real kinship with him – a kindred spirit. We began our search into health, nutrition, diet and exercise approximately the same time (I began in 1974). Although my search and Rev. Malkmus' search were totally independent from one another, we arrived at virtually the same conclusions. This is rather amazing considering all the misinformation, conflicting studies, biased reporting and confusion there is in these areas. But it's not so amazing when we realize the Master's hand was on both of us, guiding us, as willing seekers, to the truth. The Lord spoke to each of us through adversity and proclaimed victory over what seemed like utter defeat.

In my case, even though I had been studying nutrition for about 10 years by the time I went to Palmer Chiropractic College in Davenport, Iowa, I was not practicing all I knew to do. With the added stresses of working full-time, an extremely heavy class and study load, not enough time or money to eat right and predisposing chronic constipation, I developed a severe case of colitis. This was complete with heavy blood and

> ## *We as Christians need to avoid "the world's" dietary habits in favor of God's design for our dietary needs.*
> ## *– Dr. Rowen S. Pfeifer*

mucus discharge, bloating and gas, etc. This could be very embarrassing and I didn't dare stray far from a bathroom. I saw a couple of medical doctors who didn't seem too concerned and they offered no treatment. Shortly after I graduated from Palmer and moved back to Nashville, Tennessee, the problem got much worse. This time I went to a so-called preventative M.D. who misdiagnosed me with Candida Albicans Yeast Infection, and gave me a prescription for Nystatin. I then developed a severe case of diarrhea and I was so out of it I didn't realize just how close to death I was getting. I couldn't go to the office; I just laid at home waiting and hoping, and getting weaker every day.

Fortunately, my wife recognized how bad off I was and forced me to go to the emergency room. I spent seven days in the hospital on IV's to replace fluids and electrolytes lost to the bleeding and diarrhea. Later, as I sat in the office of my internist, a very sharp, young doctor, I asked him, "What can I do nutritionally that will help you help me to get well?" His response floored me! He said (and remember, this is a well-educated, relatively new medical doctor with all the latest scientific knowledge), "What you eat will have no effect on your colitis." I thought to myself, "WHAT??? How could anyone say that? Didn't he know that all the food we eat ends up passing through the colon, and the quality (or toxicity) of that food could definitely affect the health of the colon (along with every other cell in our body)?"

Well, I kept quiet. I was still in real rough shape and my confidence level wasn't at its peak. I followed his instructions and took the high-powered and very dangerous Prednisone off and on for a year or so. Every time we tapered off the Prednisone and onto the "maintenance drugs" (Azulfadine, Dipentum, etc.), the problem returned. I was getting frustrated. I wanted answers! I knew enough about drugs, especially these drugs, to know *there was no way I was going to take them for the rest of my life!* I sought the Lord earnestly. Personal and private prayer, intercessory prayer with some prayer warriors, and alter calls – a lot of each of these. I was looking for the "instant healing" (without any responsibility or action on my part). It didn't come.

Then one day while singing with the choir, as had happened so many times before, the pastor had an alter call. Only this time I didn't feel led to go down for prayer. Instead, I got a word from the Lord standing right there. He said, "Do what you already know to do." Could it be that easy? But *was* it that easy? What that meant to me was stopping all medications, going on a short fast (five to seven days on nothing but distilled water), then on a raw food diet! But what did conventional wisdom say? If you have a colon problem, you are not supposed to eat any roughage (raw fruits and vegetables) since it would further irritate the colon. But I knew in my heart that what I needed was the nutrients that could *only* be derived from raw foods. So I started immediately on a six-day distilled water fast with plenty of rest and relaxation to allow for healing. Then I went on raw fruits and vegetables with lots of carrot juice – very similar to what Rev. Malkmus teaches. (This was several years before I met him or knew anything about Barley Green.)

Within two months, all symptoms were gone. That was almost five years ago, and since that time, none of these symptoms have re-occurred. Interestingly, I recently came across some statistics which helped me to explain the reason for my rapid success. What I learned was that *it takes only five days for the cells on the inner walls of the colon to be replaced with brand new cells.* So, after the six-day fast, the ulcerations and inflammation in my colon were virtually healed. I was then able to easily tolerate the "roughage" and therefore was able to extract the nutrients I needed for continued healing and repair. This was the impetus I needed to redouble my efforts to learn the truth about healing, nutrition, diet, lifestyle, exercise, weight management, etc.

With an open mind, lots of prayer for guidance, a desire for the Lord to use me in whatever way He chose, a willingness to be available for any direction He would lead, and a deep desire to find a *purpose* and a *mission* I could gladly follow because it was something I just genuinely loved to do, He has led me to the discovery of some very simple, basic truths. Truths which Brother Malkmus and I share, for I believe the Lord led him through a similar journey, just a different set of circumstances. Now we want to share what we have been shown with all who are prepared to listen. To understand this information and to then apply it to your life will require a major paradigm shift. We've been looking at health from a *Disease Model* for many, many years now. The time has come for a paradigm shift to a *Wellness Model.*

Please keep in mind that our Standard American Diet (S.A.D.) has badly perverted our taste buds for most, if not all, of our lives (ever since we were force-fed store-bought formula and cooked, dead baby foods as infants). So in the switch to fresh, raw fruits and vegetables, give yourself a little time for your system to cleanse itself and become accustomed to the wonderful new taste delights of this way of eating. You will be pleasantly surprised. I was the fussiest of all eaters; I ate almost no fruits or vegetables as a child. In fact, I'm 44 years old now, and it has only been in the past five to six years that I have really begun to appreciate natural foods. Once you've experienced this, the old fatty, cooked, sugary foods lose most, if not all, of their appeal.

Rev. Malkmus has put together a wonderful program and ministry. When I came across one of his newsletters (by Divine Providence, I am convinced), and then read *Why Christians Get Sick,* it was sweet music to my ears. He had put together very concisely all the principles I had learned in my research, complete with Scriptural references. I was ecstatic! I thought I was quite alone in my quest for biblically sound health teachings, which I felt were so sorely needed in America and its Churches. Now, with *God's Way to Ultimate Health,* Brother Malkmus takes another giant step forward in presenting the Christian health message in an understandable, scientifically-backed and scripturally sound manner. This is a "must read" for every Christian! We don't need to be sick!!! We, as Christians, need to avoid "the world's" dietary habits in favor of *God's design* for our dietary needs. Carefully consider what Rev. Malkmus has to say in this book. Then put it into practice and experience the vibrant new life that comes from eating the foods God created to nourish our bodies, which are indeed the temple of God.

Yours in Christ For Vibrant Health!

> Dr. Rowen S. Pfeifer, D.C.
> Nashville, Tennessee
> February 1995

# Foreword by Dr. Mary Ruth Swope, Doctor of Nutrition

The first intuitive thought I had after reading George and Rhonda Malkmus' manuscript of this book was the recollection of a statement made in my hearing by a famous preacher, years ago. This pastor was under a heavy barrage of criticism by his superiors for practicing child-like faith. In defense of his position before the church tribunal he said, "A man with an experience with God is never at the mercy of a man with a theory or a doctrine." I believe that. And I believe it applies to this book today.

Following close behind was a second thought from the past. Dr. Robert Mendelsohn, M.D., of Chicago made an eloquent speech titled "WHO ARE THE REAL QUACKS?" He spoke of a report of The Office of Technology of the U.S. Congress pointing out that only 10 to 20 percent of all American medical remedies have ever been subjected to the controlled study necessary to prove safety and efficacy. In other words, from 80 to 90 percent of medical remedies have never been proven. To quote Dr. Mendelsohn, "Unproven remedies is a way of saying 'Quack Medicine.' " We therefore are faced with the challenge of deciding for ourselves the plan we will follow to produce optimal health and prosperity in our lives.

*It is obvious that there is a major difference between the Genesis 1:29 diet and the typical American diet, including what trained nutritionists offer as a choice.*
*– Dr. Mary Ruth Swope*

As we look at the contrast between a diet recorded in the Scriptures in Genesis 1:29 and what our scientists, including the medical profession, offer us today as the alternative, I believe a prudent person would do well to opt for the treatment which is least likely to harm him or kill him. That makes sense. It is obvious that there is a major difference between the Genesis 1:29 diet and the typical American diet, including what trained nutritionists offer as a choice.

To quote a third person who has influenced my thinking and beliefs, "A medical profession which doesn't know who God is or, worse yet, denies that God exists, is certainly unable to define what health is – thus would be likely to center itself upon disease management rather than health attainment." The idea that nutrition doesn't matter to U.S. physicians has its basis in fact. The average doctor in his four years of medical school receives about 2.5 hours of study in nutrition. Controlled illness through drugs verses health and wellness through proper diet has, therefore, been the tragic result of this.

I believe and want you to believe that God through Nature is the one who heals, cures, mitigates, relieves and treats a symptom or disease. I believe and want you to believe that God gave Adam and Eve specific directions for what to eat for optimal health. Count on it: the formula is immortal.

A famous doctor who espoused this philosophy was Hippocrates (460 - 377 B.C.). His statement "Food is your best medicine and the best food is the best medicine" is timeless, in addition to being famous. His theory was, if a medical procedure works, use it again and again – not needing to know why or how it works.

I totally agree with the Malkmus' that nutrients are agents of healing and that healing comes from inside us – the DNA working with intelligence and precision, with relentless energy day and night, always in our best interest.

Let me make a summary statement. My own experience in raising experimental animals in the laboratory, first at Ohio State University's Medical School Nutrition Research laboratory, gave me overwhelming evidence to believe like Hippocrates. To make an animal ill, just remove any single nutrient from his rations. Continue the denial of the required life-force and the animal dies. Before his crisis illness, however, he could be fed the denied nutrient and in a few days look like the healthy mice who had never been ill. Yes, there is such a thing as a "Mr. Food Doctor." And the Malkmus' have proven this same principle works for humans too.

Lastly, Dr. Charles Mayo, of the famous Mayo Brothers in Rochester, Minnesota (1900), made this statement for public consumption: "We are all afraid of germs … but what we should be afraid of is lowered resistance which comes from within … normal resistance to disease is directly dependent upon adequate food … It never comes out of pill boxes … adequate food is the cradle of normal resistance, the playground of normal immunity, the workshop of good health and the laboratory of long life."

May Hallelujah Acres gain momentum exponentially and roar through the land with the power of a Niagara! I pray for your strength, your health, your prosperity and your ministry success.

> Dr. Mary Ruth Swope,
> Scottsdale, Arizona
> February 1995

In *Green Leaves of Barley,* Dr. Mary Ruth Swope writes: "If it could be expected that all scientists in the world agreed on a single fact, I believe they would agree … 'Life begins, is maintained and ends at the cellular level.' The health of a single cell holds the key to the health of the whole organism." Her book adds, "Cells made strong through good nutrition will go a long way in giving you an immune system that will resist the illnesses so prevalent in our society."

# Introduction:

# The Hallelujah Acres Story

*"Some may retort that the work of winning souls is more important than helping people stay or get well physically or than prolonging their lives. But unless men who know the Word of God and who have the riches of experience stay well and alive physically, how can they tell the message of man's redemption?*
– Quoted from *God's Key to Health and Happiness*, by Elmer A. Josephson (Ordained Baptist Minister)

Hallelujah is a Biblical word used to express praise, joy and thanksgiving. It was chosen by Rev. George Malkmus as an expression of gratitude to God after he was healed of not only colon cancer, but *all* physical problems, following his change to a more natural diet and lifestyle in 1976. Acres was added to the name of his ministry in 1986 when Rev. Malkmus purchased a 50-acre mountain farm in Eidson, Tennessee. On April 11, 1992, Rev. Malkmus married Rhonda Jean at the farm, and today they own and operate **Hallelujah Acres.**

Hallelujah Acres actually began as a dream after Rev. Malkmus' research and experience revealed that sickness – including cancer, heart attacks, diabetes, arthritis and most other illnesses – are created by our diet and lifestyle, and are totally unnecessary and avoidable! He also learned that if we will but change our diet and lifestyle, these physical problems will usually go away and stay away!

From his background of 20 years pastoring churches from New York to Florida, Rev. Malkmus felt a compelling need to share this life-saving information with fellow Christians and anyone else who would listen. Much was being discovered in medical and scientific research

***The best dietary information now available to medical science only serves to substantiate the wisdom of the original diet of raw fruits and vegetables handed down to mankind by God in Genesis 1:29.***

about the advantages of a vegetarian diet of mainly raw fruits and vegetables. For several decades, there has been strong evidence that meat, dairy, eggs, sugar, salt, white flour, processed foods and chemical additives are creating and worsening the devastating, degenerative diseases that are robbing so many people of their life and health. This same evidence has shown a diet that eliminates these harmful substances and nourishes our bodies with living foods can prevent and actually reverse these diseases.

But this information was not getting out to Christians and other people whose diets and lives were under the firm control of fast food joints, manufacturers of processed foods and junk-food television commercials.

The unique approach of Rev. Malkmus shows that the best dietary information now available to medical science only serves to substantiate the wisdom of the original diet of raw fruits and vegetables handed down to mankind by God in Genesis 1:29. So the message of Rev. Malkmus has been to encourage people to return to the diet that God gave us in the first Chapter of Genesis, and to remind Christians that our bodies are "the temple of God."

In an effort to share his knowledge and healing experience with as many people as possible, Rev. Malkmus wrote his first book, *Why Christians Get Sick,* in 1989. It has been very well-received – as letters from all over the world attest – and is now in its ninth printing. Rev. Malkmus also holds seminars in churches and before civic groups all over the United States and into Canada, and has made numerous radio and television appearances. It has been very exciting in recent years to see Rev. Malkmus' teachings substantiated by new studies in how nutrition and lifestyle relate to our wellness.

But in the early years of Hallelujah Acres, walking into churches with a message encouraging people to give up their meat, junk food, etc., and switch to a vegetarian diet of mainly raw foods was just not a very popular proposition. In those early years of his ministry, Rev. Malkmus' message was shunned by most Christians, even those in poor health who so badly needed to make these dietary changes. He won very few converts.

But those few converts who did listen, change their diet and heal themselves of heart disease, cancer, arthritis, diabetes and other serious diseases soon became powerful testimonials for all around them to see. *Their wellness became contagious.* In the small town of Rogersville, Tenn., throughout the country and around

**Rev. George and Rhonda Malkmus
at Hallelujah Acres**

the world, wherever people who were sick began sincerely applying the dietary program taught by Hallelujah Acres, they often regained their health and other people saw the results.

Rogersville (population 5,000) is a good example of how word travels fast in a small town. Rev. Malkmus opened Hallelujah Acres restaurant and health food store in Rogersville on Feb. 12, 1992, first in a small store front, 11 feet wide, that had a seating capacity of 16 people. People came in ever-increasing numbers, not only to obtain better food, but to hear the health message, so the restaurant and health food store had to be relocated March 1, 1993 into a larger building, with a capacity of 56 people. The Hallelujah Acres restaurant was successful because it showed people a diet that is healthy can also taste good.

In fact, the restaurant was so successful that Rev. Malkmus closed it on

March 28, 1994. The problem was that while he was reaching thousands of people by conducting seminars all around the country, writing a new book and publishing *Back to the Garden,* the enterprise that was taking up the majority of his time was running the restaurant.

After closing the restaurant, Rev. Malkmus and Rhonda relocated Hallelujah Acres back to their 50-acre farm in Eidson, about 12 miles northwest of Rogersville. From there they refocused their goal on reaching the masses through seminars, books, *Back to the Garden* newsletters, video and audio tapes, radio and television appearances, and Back to the Garden Health Ministries. People involved in this exciting ministry came to Tennessee from all over the country to learn more about God's way of eating and healing sickness, and taking that information back to their communities to reach even more people.

Dr. Malkmus' second book, *God's Way to Ultimate Health,* published in 1995, is the most complete compilation of information we have ever seen on how to maintain or regain your health in accordance with God's natural laws. Almost 100,000 copies are in print!

Because of the tremendous growth of his ministry, in November of 1997, Dr. Malkmus and Rhonda relocated Hallelujah Acres to a former Bible college on 17 beautiful acres in Shelby, North Carolina.

The results Rhonda and Rev. Malkmus are seeing in people's lives have been extremely gratifying as they receive daily testimonies from those who have been helped.

The Hallelujah Acres' ministry dreams of reaching the world with the knowledge and message, "YOU DON'T HAVE TO BE SICK!!!"

# Part I:

# A Biblical Foundation

# for Health

"Know ye not that
ye are the temple of God
and that the spirit
of God dwelleth
in you?  If any man
defile the temple of God,
him shall God destroy:
For the temple of God
is holy, which temple
ye are."
– I Corinthians 3:16-18

# Chapter 1

# God's Way to Ultimate Health

*By Rev. George H. Malkmus*

The year was 1976. I was 42 years old and I was told I had colon cancer. A tumor about the size of a baseball had been found underneath my left rib cage where the transverse and descending colon come together. I was devastated! I asked, "Why me Lord?" I didn't understand!

It was because of this – what appeared to be a tragic event in my life, and the research and personal experiences that followed – that I was taught GOD'S WAY TO ULTIMATE HEALTH.

Let me elaborate a little more on how it all happened. In 1976 I was the pastor of a Baptist Church, near Glens Falls, New York, a church I founded in 1970. It was a very successful ministry. Membership in this church grew from nothing to over 600 members. In addition to the church, we had a Christian School, grades K through 12, along with a Bible Institute, both of

*In the almost 20 years since I recovered from colon cancer, one of the most basic and important things I have learned is that there is a vast difference between God's ways and man's ways!*

which I also founded. Five large busses brought people to the services, while my radio broadcast, *America Needs Christ,* was heard on many radio stations each week. Over a dozen young people from our church and school were in college preparing for full-time ministry. Truly, this seemed to be the high point of my ministry and God was certainly blessing.

Just prior to all this, I had watched my mother die of colon cancer. Mom was a registered nurse, and she believed her doctors when they told her that chemotherapy, radiation and surgery were her only hope of surviving. Mom submitted to these treatments and died a horrible death! At the time of her death, I felt it was the treatments she received at the hands of the medical doctors that ultimately caused her death rather than the cancer itself.

What was I to do? Should I submit my body to the same medical treatments mom had? What I had seen my mother go through was so horrible! Also, as a pastor for 20 years, I had sat at the bed-side of so many people and watched the devastating effects of chemotherapy, radiation and surgery experienced by others in the treatment of their cancers. I had also conducted the funerals for many of them.

Another thing that bothered me was that in so many cases prayer didn't seem to make any difference. I had seen some of the most dedicated Christians, even after great faith, personal prayer as well as collective prayer, get sicker and sicker and often die after going the medical route. What should I do? I had a family and a church that needed me. Many people told me I should go the medical route and some were putting pressure on me to do just that.

It was during this time of uncertainty that I turned to an Evangelist friend in Texas by the name of Lestor Roloff for help. Brother Roloff was one of those "health-nuts." We often

**Rev. George Malkmus**

affectionately referred to him as "Carrot Juice Roloff." I was really in a dilemma as to what I should do for my cancer when I called Brother Roloff. His advice to me sounded strange. He advised me not to go the medical route of chemotherapy, radiation and surgery, as mom had gone … BUT TO SIMPLY CHANGE MY DIET TO RAW FRUITS AND VEGETABLES, AND DRINK LOTS OF FRESH CARROT JUICE!

Wow! That sounded too simplistic! But it sure sounded better than the medical route which I had pretty well decided not to pursue. So, overnight I changed from a meat-centered, cooked and processed food diet with plenty of sugar desserts, to an all-raw diet with lots of carrot juice. I stayed on this total raw diet for approximately one year. I didn't eat any cooked food during that year … just raw fruits, raw vegetables and one to two quarts a day of freshly extracted, raw carrot juice.

*The results were spectacular! Almost immediately I started to get well!* In less than one year, my tumor had totally disappeared. It simply got smaller and smaller until it was gone. But that was not all. In less than one year, every physical problem I had been experiencing also disappeared! Such physical problems as hemorrhoids, hypoglycemia, severe allergies and sinus problems, high blood pressure, fatigue, pimples, colds, flu … even body odor and dandruff were *gone! Totally healed!*

In the years that have followed – and I am over 60 years old at this writing – I have not experienced as much as a cold, sore throat, upset stomach, been to a doctor or taken as much as an aspirin. It is so thrilling, at my age, to still be able to play football, basketball and softball with the boys, jog five miles

*From the Hallelujah Acres mailbag:*

"I am so excited about what you folks are doing. For so long I have looked for a place where health and nutrition were being preached from the only one foundation of truth: God's Word. May His blessings shower on you and doors be opened and the enemy pushed back. Keep on keeping on … God bless you all!"
– Mary Anne Komar, Illinois

with ease, and have more energy, endurance and stamina than I had when I was 20 years old.

With that as a little background, let me share how God used this experience in my life to create Hallelujah Acres Ministries and the writing of this book. You see, ever since that day in 1976 when I was told that I had cancer, I have been researching nutrition, healthy lifestyle and how it all relates to the Bible. Also, I have been experimenting on my own body to see how it reacted to various foods. Along with all this, I have also been watching and listening to the testimonies of thousands of others who have made similar dietary changes.

My conclusion after all these years of research and experience is that WE DO NOT HAVE TO BE SICK!!! Disease and sickness are self-inflicted! Almost every physical problem, other than accidents, is *caused* by improper diet and lifestyle! All we have to do to be well is eat and live according to the way God intended!

In the almost 20 years since I recovered from colon cancer, one of the most basic and important things I have learned is that there is a vast difference between God's ways and man's ways! I have found that while most good Christians want to go God's way, and have tried to protect themselves from the sins of the world, they have accepted the world's teachings in almost every area of life concerning how to care for our physical bodies, which are the temple of God.

A tragic example of this is when you look at the two ways to approach cancer, one of the most devastating and horrible diseases in history. My mother went the world's way (the orthodox medical route) in an attempt to rid herself of her cancer. She accepted the drugs, radiation and surgery of her doctors, and as far as I am concerned, these treatments were what caused her death! I rejected the world's way and went God's way. I turned to the Bible, adopted God's original diet as found in Genesis 1:29 and every physical problem simply went away, including my cancer.

And my experience was not unique! My wife Rhonda came to a Health Seminar I was conducting in 1991. (We were married April 11, 1992.) She was wearing a size 20 dress at that time and was almost crippled with arthritis. Within approximately one year after changing her diet and lifestyle, she had lost over 80 pounds, reduced her dress size to a 10, and her arthritis was totally gone. Even a degenerated spine, the result of a bout with spinal meningitis at age 7, had healed. Yes, X-rays revealed her spine was totally healed, degeneration gone in less than two years after changing her diet and lifestyle.

Another example is a dear friend of mine who was a diabetic when I first met him in 1989. At that time he was trying to control his blood sugar with pills prescribed by his doctor. I encouraged him to change his diet in 1989, which he did not do. Two years later the doctor told him that the pills were not adequate any more and that he must be admitted to a hospital to adjust and stabilize his blood sugar and start him on two daily shots of injection insulin. Again I told him he needed to change his diet. And again he paid no heed.

After another two years had elapsed, the doctor told him that he needed

*From the Hallelujah Acres mailbag:*

Eunice Jordan

"I bought one of your books *Why Christians Get Sick* here in Chattanooga during the Southside Baptist Church Fellowship. I was very impressed with the information in this book. I have been interested in nutrition for 37 years and have been searching for a better way of treating my body. I have bought many books but find yours the very best. We have a church book store that I manage. I would like to stock your books and tapes."
– Eunice Jordan, Mississippi

to put him into the hospital and cut off his foot, which is not an uncommon occurrence for those who go the orthodox medical route in the treatment of diabetes. Only this time he said "no" to his doctor. Instead he came to one of our seminars and immediately adopted God's Natural Diet. In less than two weeks he was off insulin and his blood sugar was in normal range. That was over two years ago. Today, he is still off all medication and still has both his feet!

We have received thousands of testimonies as dramatic as these, and some even more so, from people who have switched from the world's way of eating and treating physical problems to God's way. As you continue to read through this book you will read many of their testimonies.

What we need here in America and around the world is a HEALTH REVOLUTION! We must turn away from the world's way of dealing with physical and emotional problems and turn to God's way! The world's way is bankrupting us, costing Americans over a trillion ($1,000,000,000,000.00) dollars a year while the physical and emotional condition of our population – Christian and non-Christian alike – continues to decline.

In order to make intelligent changes, we must realize there are alternatives to the world's approach to health and how to deal with physical problems. We must understand both ways … and why one works and why the other does not. Sadly, very few people, including most pastors, preachers and evangelists, have been aware of God's way, when it comes to the physical body. Thus we have been programmed only in the world's way, even from the pulpits in our churches.

Because of this programming, most people, when they first hear of God's ways, think them strange and "far out." So in order to help understand the differences, let's look at a few physical problems being faced by many people today and compare the two ways of dealing with these problems.

Take cardiovascular problems, which result in heart attacks and strokes. Heart disease is the number one killer (50% of all deaths) in America today. Every 34 seconds, someone in America dies from physical problems associated with this disease. The cost to those who go the medical route for the treatment of heart disease is over $110 billion per year.

The first approach usually taken by medical doctors in an effort to control this problem is to prescribe drugs. It is not uncommon for a person with high blood pressure to be given as many as three or four drugs. One of these drugs will chemically force the blood vessels to dilate (get bigger), thus lowering blood pressure. But this drug causes the heart to speed up. In an effort to control the speeding up of the heart caused by the first drug, the doctor usually prescribes a second drug to slow it down. Each of these drugs is capable of causing the body to retain fluid. Thus the doctor often prescribes a third drug, a diuretic, which is designed to chemically force the body to release the extra fluid being retained in an effort to try and keep all these drugs (poisons) from doing more harm.

Almost all of these drugs can cause impotence in males. The diuretics can cause dizziness, headaches and even depression … while at the same time

*raising cholesterol levels!* Then there are the "beta blockers" that can cause not only depression, but insomnia, as well as liver and kidney damage. The world's approach of using drugs just causes more and more problems within the body while never dealing with the *cause.* To top it all off, there is the devastating financial costs of going this medical route.

In an effort to reduce cholesterol, doctors prescribe over two billion dollars ($2,000,000,000.00) worth of drugs a year, and frankly, they don't do the job. Yet the side effects from these drugs can cause liver damage, headaches, diarrhea or constipation and are now being linked to depression, violence and even suicide.

Angioplasties (balloon therapy) is another way the world tries to deal with clogged arteries. The average cost of this procedure is $15,000, not counting the drugs and follow-up. And yet a study in the *Journal of the American Medical Association* in 1992 showed that half of the angioplasties in the United States were probably unnecessary. Studies also show that for those who underwent this procedure, 57 percent have their arteries clog back up.

Then there is by-pass surgery. The average cost of this operation is $45,000. It is a very dangerous operation, that finds most patients back on the operating table within three to five years (because their arteries have clogged back up again), if they are not dead. About 5 percent of by-pass surgery patients die on the operating table.

One of the latest of the *new* technologies for cleaning out the arteries is called *atherectomy.* This procedure is something like a Roto-Rooter. They take a tiny, high-speed rotating knife, insert it in the arteries and ream out the cholesterol. This also is a very risky surgery.

Now compare all the above efforts by medical doctors (the world's way) of treating cardiovascular problems with God's way. Here at Hallelujah Acres, we have testimony after testimony from people who had experienced high blood pressure, high cholesterol and clogged arteries who were able to totally reverse these problems, usually in a very short time, by something as simple as changing their diet and lifestyle. How can this be?

Well, it all goes back to our failure to eat and live the way God intended. The world's diet is full of fat, salt and other contaminates that clog up our arteries and produce all sorts of physical problems. Yet, in most instances, all people have to do to correct a physical problem is change their diet and lifestyle! When they do this, the body will usually cleanse the arteries by itself and the problem will usually simply disappear in a very short time. And furthermore, studies show that if a person stops consuming animal products, they will reduce their chances of ever having a heart attack or stroke by over 96 percent!

What is the cost of going God's way? Probably a reduced grocery bill and a long healthy life. While the cost of going the world's way can be continued physical problems and thousands and thousands of dollars in medical bills for treatments that never get to the root cause – namely diet and lifestyle.

I have found that the world's way (accepted medical procedures) for dealing with physical problems is *almost always wrong!* Take diabetes as another example. Compare the world's way of treating adult-onset diabetes with

God's way in the case of the friend we just read about. Going the doctor/drug route, my friend had continued to deteriorate for years as his doctor increased his insulin while using antibiotics and other drugs to treat infections in his feet, which the doctor told him were being caused by his diabetes.

By the time the doctor told him that he needed to amputate his foot, my friend had already spent over $40,000 treating his diabetes! But he refused to let the doctor cut off his foot. He simply changed his diet and lifestyle, and in less than two weeks he was off insulin and his blood sugar level was in normal range.

As I write this, it has now been two years since my friend changed his diet and lifestyle from the world's way to God's way. He has taken zero drugs during these two years and he still has both feet. He also had heart problems which have totally disappeared.

Take arthritis as another example. The medical profession still says that the cause of arthritis is not known. The only thing they tell their patients is that they can expect it to get worse and worse and that there is no way to reverse it. They also treat arthritis with drugs and surgery while the patient's physical condition usually continues to decline. Cortisone and similar drugs are often administered to try and help relieve the pain, but it doesn't last long and when the pain returns, it is usually worse than ever. The side-effects from these drugs can include high blood pressure, diabetes, cataracts, bone loss (osteoporosis), ulcers and more.

Now compare the orthodox medical approach to the testimony of my wife Rhonda with her arthritis and what happened

*From the Hallelujah Acres mailbag:*

"Doing great! Blood sugar is down and now taking less than 50 units of insulin per day - had been taking 200 units per day. Praise the Lord! … I am thankful to the Lord for letting me come across your magazine *(Back to the Garden)* about four or five months ago. I weighed about 240 then. I'm now about 210."
– Pastor E. G. Holzback, Faith Baptist Church, South Carolina

***What is the cost of going God's way? Probably a reduced grocery bill and a long healthy life. While the cost of going the world's way can be continued physical problems and thousands and thousands of dollars in medical bills for treatments that never get to the root cause (diet and lifestyle).***

when she changed from the world's way to God's way. She was crippled up with arthritis for over 10 years, unable to walk a block without extreme pain. She took pain pills by the handfuls. Within one year after changing her diet, she went from not being able to walk a block without severe pain and exhaustion to speed-walking four miles in less than an hour! Her arthritis was totally gone and she has not had a pain pill since. Not even an aspirin. What did she do to bring about this total elimination of arthritis from her body? She simply changed from the world's diet and lifestyle to God's diet and lifestyle, and all her physical problems simply and quite quickly disappeared.

Compare my mom's experience with mine in the treatment of cancer. Mom went the world's way and accepted the doctors' chemotherapy, radiation and surgery … treatments that I felt ultimately caused her death. I refused the world's treatments, adopted God's diet as He gave it in Genesis 1:29, and my cancer simply disappeared. I have been totally free of all physical problems since 1976.

On God's Ultimate Diet, almost every physical problem usually disappears in a comparatively short period of time! Weight normalizes.

*Until someone personally experiences it, they cannot fully comprehend the total scope of the benefits of living and eating God's way. It improves the physical, as well as the emotional and psychological well-being of a person. People become happier, depressions go away, problems don't seem so monumental. Our whole outlook on life improves. Even the spiritual part of us becomes more attuned.*

"We do not degenerate because we grow old ...We grow old because we degenerate!"
– Ross Horne

Emotional problems disappear. Life takes on a whole new glow and becomes exciting. Until someone personally experiences it, they cannot fully comprehend the total scope of the benefits of living and eating God's way. It improves the physical, as well as the emotional and psychological well-being of a person. People become happier, depressions go away, problems don't seem so monumental. Our whole outlook on life improves. Even the spiritual part of us becomes more attuned.

Most doctors mean well, but all of their training is in the world's way. In fact, the average doctor knows practically nothing about nutrition because the typical doctor has received less than three hours of nutritional training in his / her entire preparation to become a doctor. And the nutritional training they do receive is the world's way, not God's way, so what they have learned about diet is not able to help our bodies to strengthen their immune system and heal disease by creating healthy new living cells.

"If you are a patient, you may know more about nutrition than your doctor. Nutritional information is beginning to sweep the world like a prairie fire because it does make sense. People are becoming well as a result. They are looking for a doctor who understands the nutritional concept. There are practically none. If you are a doctor and if you will catch up with the demands of the public, your future will be far more assured than ever before. You will again achieve that image of respect once accorded you in yesteryear. You will satisfy the requirements of your Oath of Hippocrates. Best of all, you will get, and keep, most of your patients well. Your services will be in great demand. I know, because it happened to me."
– Alan H. Nittler, M.D., *A New Breed of Doctor*

Sadly, most doctors are just as sick as their patients! If doctors cannot keep their own bodies well and functioning properly, how in the world can they help anyone else?

However, we are thrilled to find that more and more doctors are starting to question their indoctrination in medical school as they see the devastating consequences of their drugging, burning and cutting patient after patient. Many are allowing their eyes to be opened and are moving in God's direction. Pray for them. The peer pressure and controls on them by their union, the American Medical Association, is very powerful. In many states, a doctor can lose his license if he recommends or treats his patients' physical problems with anything other than drugs, radiation and surgery.

The key to preventing heart attacks, cancer, diabetes, arthritis and a host of other physical problems is in our own hands. We can literally control whether we are going to be sick or not and how long we are going to live by simply choosing how we live our lives ... the world's way or God's way! God's way leads to a long, happy, pain-free, sickness-free life! While the world's way usually leads to a short, unhappy, sickness-filled life with lots of pain and suffering, to say nothing of the financial costs. This book sets before you two very different paths, one a broad road (the world's way) that leads to destruction and the other a narrow road (God's way) that leads to life! I trust that you will very carefully consider both roads as you continue to read through this book ... and that you will choose "GOD'S WAY TO ULTIMATE HEALTH!"

*"...I have set before you life and death, blessing and cursing: therefore choose life, that both thou and thy seed may live:"* (Deuteronomy 30:19)

# Chapter 2

# Rhonda Malkmus Heals Arthritis and A Degenerated Spine ... and Loses 80 Pounds

Rhonda's physical problems began at the age of 7 when her parents rushed her to the doctor, not knowing what was causing her to have an extremely high fever. The doctor immediately put her into the hospital. Within hours she lapsed into a coma and for days lingered very close to death.

The diagnosis was spinal meningitis. Fortunately, Rhonda recovered, and from then on her doctor would refer to her as "my miracle girl." The doctor had no explanation as to how or why she recovered and thus he felt it had to have been a miracle.

Rhonda's physical problems did not end with her spinal meningitis. In the fall of 1981, while driving down a country road, on a dark, rainy, and foggy night in Iowa, her car was struck by a freight train. As her car approached an unmarked railroad crossing, she could not see a train that was fast approaching the crossing. When she did see it, it was too late and the train struck her small foreign car!

*"Some people think if you change your diet to what George teaches, you will be hungry all the time. What I found was that when I changed my diet and began exercising, the hunger went away ... You have to realize, it's a lifestyle change. It's not a fad and it's not just a diet," Rhonda emphasized.*

There were two impacts – the first when the train, which was traveling at approximately 35 m.p.h., hit her car, and the second when the car landed. Rhonda remembers when she first saw the train, just moments before impact, knowing there was no escape. She thought, "OK Lord, thy will be done!" It was in that brief moment that she fully expected to die. But she didn't die! The car, after flying through the air, finally landed upside-down in a big mud puddle. Stunned, but still conscious, her first thoughts were of a Bible verse which says, "In everything give thanks for this is the will of God, in Christ Jesus, concerning you!" (I Thessalonians 5:18).

Hesitantly she gave thanks and was able to get herself and her passenger out of the car safely while the engineer of the train stood by and watched, too much in shock to offer any assistance. Upon arrival at the hospital, no one could believe she and her young lady passenger friend had been able to walk away from a car that had been struck by a freight train traveling 35 m.p.h.

At the hospital, X-rays were taken and although they did not reveal any broken bones, they did reveal severe deterioration of her spine which the doctors attributed to her bout with spinal meningitis some 30 years earlier. And although she had not suffered any broken bones, she did experience multiple cuts, abrasions, contusions, a concussion and more. The impact was so powerful that every filling in her mouth had been jarred loose and required replacement.

The weeks, months and years that followed were extremely painful. The medical doctors could offer nothing to help her, other than drugs for the pain. They told her that she would have to learn to live with that pain probably the rest of her life. She did find some relief from a chiropractic physician, but as time went by she developed very severe, debilitating arthritis in nearly every joint in her body.

As the years went by, her condition deteriorated to the point that she couldn't walk without severe pain. She had to put hot water on her hands to get them to function each morning. She couldn't stand up without assistance after being seated, and her neck was almost immobile. During these years, it was not uncommon for her to take as many as four Ibuproffin as often as every two hours a day. As a result of her pain, she moved her body as little as possible, and this caused Rhonda to put on many unwanted pounds. Before too long, she found herself carrying more than 200 pounds on her 5-foot, 3-inch frame. Excess weight had always been a problem for Rhonda and now her situation seemed hopeless. She knew she must exercise in order to remove the excess weight, but it was too painful for her to even think about moving around any more than necessary.

Fortunately, in the fall of 1990, Rhonda's life started to turn around when she moved to Rogersville, Tennessee after a series of events that showed God's hand directing her life. She had only planned to visit friends in Rogersville to consider it as a possible site for relocation because the severe winters in Wisconsin were making her arthritis unbearable. Four years prior to this trip she had placed her home on the market. When she returned home, to her surprise, there was a buyer offering her exactly what she had been asking for her house all those years. She took that as an indication from the Lord that she was to move to Rogersville – which she did!

In January of 1991, shortly after she arrived in Rogersville, Rhonda attended a "How to Eliminate Sickness" seminar conducted by Rev. George Malkmus at the Hale Springs Inn in downtown Rogersville. This seminar was to forever change her life! "As soon as I got home from the seminar, I started

"And the Lord God planted a garden eastward in Eden and there he put the man whom he had formed. And out of the ground made the Lord God to grow every tree that is pleasant to the sight and good for food..."
– Genesis 2: 8-9

changing my diet and walking like George recommended," Rhonda recalls. "At first I could only walk a block, and that with lots of pain. But I was persistent and slowly as my diet and exercise improved – so did my arthritis! It took a few months, but I was gradually able to walk a mile in 15 minutes and ultimately four miles in an hour."

"George had told me, 'When you change your diet and start walking, you'll notice a difference.' but at first I was only losing inches and not pounds. I would go back to George and he just kept telling me 'Be patient, it will happen if you do not quit.' "

"And it did happen just as George said. It was gradual at first but finally the pounds started to go and I lost over 80 pounds and was able to reduce my dress size from a 20 to a 10 in about two years," she said.

Another benefit Rhonda said she noticed after changing her diet and lifestyle was almost an immediate lessening of her arthritic pain. "I noticed I wasn't as sore when I got up in the morning. Previously I had to run hot water on my hands to get them to work, but now that was no longer necessary. As time went by, the more I walked and was careful about my diet, the better I felt, and within less than two years, all my arthritic pain was gone."

"Some people think that if you change your diet to what George teaches, you will be hungry all the time. What I found was that when I changed my diet and began exercising, the hunger went away. I just started substituting live (raw) food for dead food. I gradually added more raw foods and left out meat. I found it very easy to make these dietary changes and I certainly do not miss the meat. Once you change your diet, you can listen to your body, and it tells you what is good food and what is not by the way you feel after eating different things. You have to realize it is a lifestyle change – not a fad or just another diet." Rhonda emphasized.

After being on the Hallelujah Diet, including Barley Green and carrot juice, for about two years, Rhonda had an almost unbelievable surprise when new X-rays were made of her back. To her utter amazement, the doctor told her that there was no sign of the the deterioration in her spine which had been so evident in 1981. Rhonda couldn't believe what she was hearing and asked to see the X-rays herself. When she saw them, could hardly believer her eyes – the deterioration was GONE! Rhonda said if she had not seen both sets of X-rays, she would not have believed it could be true.

Another unexpected benefit from the new diet has been an improvement in her eyesight. "I have worn eyeglasses since I was in junior high school, and almost every year my eyesight had gotten worse, requiring stronger lenses. Yet after only a few years on the Hallelujah Diet, one day I was working on a quilt square for my parents' 50th wedding anniversary and was frustrated by my sloppy work. When I took off my glasses to rub my eyes, I found I could see this close work better without my glasses then with them. So now, as a result of my new diet and lifestyle, I had to replace my eye glasses with weaker ones."

Rhonda's energy level also increased to the point that she is now able to work 12 and 14-hour days without exhaustion, whereas before, after only 5 or 6

"And ye shall know the truth, and the truth shall make you free."
–John 8:32

hours she would be extremely tired. Rhonda, however, will be the first to tell you that the greatest blessing she has received from her new lifestyle is the day George asked her to become his wife. George and Rhonda were married April 11, 1992 at the Hallelujah Acres Farm.

"One of the fringe benefits of working at Hallelujah Acres" Rhonda says, "is that I have the privilege of seeing the miraculous changes taking place in so many people who have applied the principles that George teaches. I wish the whole world could see and hear what I have seen and heard. It is incredible the way lives are being changed. George is right, God truly has given us a miraculous body that will heal itself of almost anything if conditions are made right for healing. We see it happen day after day." Rhonda said.

Today, Rhonda spends most of her time at Hallelujah Acres helping Rev. Malkmus in keeping the ministry running smoothly. It is a task that grows with each passing day as more and more people learn of the ministry and the ministry expands around the world. In her "spare time," Rhonda raises canaries, joins Rev. Malkmus in the garden and creates porcelain dolls.

*From the Hallelujah Acres mailbag:*

"I thank God for putting your book *Why Christians Get Sick* in my hands. I know it's only been a couple of months that we have been using Barley Green. It has already done wonders for us in every way..."
– Carrie Donaldson, Michigan

# Chapter 3

# Why Christians Get Sick

(Note: *Why Christians Get Sick* was Rev. Malkmus' first book, and was first published in 1989. This chapter includes a summary of that book. To order *Why Christians Get Sick,* see the form at the end of this book.)

After a bout with colon cancer, Rev. George Malkmus discovered the same "secret" that many others have found: The way to enjoy good health and prevent or cure cancer, heart disease and other ailments is with proper exercise and a diet of natural foods – specifically raw fruits and vegetables.

But that's hardly *new* news. Rev. Malkmus was not the first person – and he is working diligently to ensure that he will not be the last – to get excited over the discovery that people can change their health and the way they feel, simply by changing their diet and lifestyle. Nor is it new for some – including Rev. Malkmus, who was diagnosed with colon cancer in 1976 – that this discovery can actually mean the difference between life and death.

*But what is unique about the message of Rev. George Malkmus is that he has taken the very latest scientific knowledge of health, nutrition and diet, verified these theories through his own personal experience . . . and then shown that this modern-day knowledge is the same as God's original plan for man as taught in the Bible.*

In his book, *Why Christians Get Sick,* Rev. Malkmus helps the reader to get a grasp on this latest scientific knowledge about health, which begins at the cellular level. Our body's approximately 100 trillion cells must constantly be cleansed and replaced. Rev. Malkmus notes that cells cannot properly cleanse or renew themselves when the body is full of toxins and has inadequate nutrients. He says the only food that can be used to rebuild a healthy living cell is live food – specifically raw fruits and vegetables. His book supports this position with the opinions of nutrition and medical experts, people who have tried the diet, and a bibliography of 70 books.

And Rev. Malkmus cites more than 150 Bible verses in *Why Christians Get Sick* to support these conclusions. In fact, he writes, "Yea, all that men need to know in order to live a healthy, happy, successful, spiritual life is found in the pages of the Bible!!!"

*From the Hallelujah Acres mailbag:*

"… I am overjoyed that your voice with the truth about keeping healthy is being heard in the Christian Community. The Christian Booksellers Convention just ended here in Atlanta. Usually someone selects a 'book of the year' … yours *(Why Christians Get Sick)* deserves to be honored as 'Book of the Century'! … Congratulations again on your forthright words and stance from a Biblical perspective."
Janet Bryan, Georgia

For example, he notes that only in relatively recent times has science learned what the Bible has been telling us for millenniums . . . that the human body is made from "the dust of the ground." It is easy to see that a body made up of living, natural elements from the Earth would require living, natural food from the Earth to renew its cells and sustain health.

As to the need for exercise, Genesis 3:19 commands: "In the sweat of thy face shalt thou eat bread . . ." After man sinned, "The Lord God sent him forth from the Garden of Eden to till the ground . . ." (Genesis 3:23).

Citing this verse, Rev. Malkmus writes: "Here is what I am getting at . . . the further man removes himself from the way God intended man to live, the more likelihood there is that man will experience problems!!!" We are "not only eating processed, packaged foods almost totally devoid of nutritional value, loaded with chemicals, but no physical exercise was required to obtain them."

Rev. Malkmus reminds us that the Bible warns of the consequences of defiling our body, citing I Corinthians 3:16 -18: *"Know ye not that ye are the temple of God and that the spirit of God dwelleth in you? If any man defile the temple of God, him shall God destroy: For the temple of God is holy, which temple ye are."* But he notes, "The average person uses more care in selecting the grade of gasoline to put into their automobiles than they do the food they put in their mouth."

He notes that since World War II, our food has been increasingly

**Rev. Malkmus reminds us that the Bible warns of the consequences of defiling our body . . . "the temple of God." But he notes, "The average person uses more care in selecting the grade of gasoline to put into their automobiles than they do the food they put in their mouth."**

contaminated with chemical pesticides and preservatives that weaken our immune systems and cause an array of physical problems. "There is no such thing as a safe chemical," he emphasizes. "Most Americans just take it for granted that if it is a product sold for food, that it is safe to eat. NOT SO!!! It's also amazing, but true, that the average person never associates his physical problems with what he eats or drinks." And then, when people get sick, instead of changing their diet or lifestyle that caused the problem, they turn to drugs offered by the medical profession.

Rev. Malkmus laments, "Christians are just as drug-oriented as non-Christians." He warns: "Health cannot be restored by taking drugs!!! Drugs cannot rebuild the cells of the body!!! The body is self-healing, when healthful practices are followed!!! Just as you are able to witness the healing of a cut . . . on the exterior as the body heals itself . . . just so it heals on the inside when conditions are made favorable for it to do so!!!"

He quotes Sir William A. Lane, a world authority on medical matters and regarded as England's foremost abdominal surgeon, addressing the John Hopkins Hospital and Medical College: "Gentlemen, I will never die of cancer. I am taking measures to prevent it . . . It is caused by poisons created in our bodies by the food we eat . . . What we should do, then, if we would avoid cancer, is to eat … raw fruits and vegetables; first, that we may be better nourished; secondly, that we may more easily eliminate waste products … We have been studying germs when we should have been studying diet and drainage … The world has been on the wrong track. The answer has been within ourselves all the time . . . Drain the body of its poisons, feed it properly, and the miracle is done. Nobody need have cancer who will take the trouble to avoid it."

But Malkmus shows the American Medical Association has played a major role in fighting against the recognition that what we eat is related to our health.

*After reading Why Christians Get Sick, it is clear there are two basic approaches to health care. One is to prevent disease by a more natural diet and lifestyle, and the second is to consume all the chemical food additives, processed foods, meat, sugar, salt, white flour and dairy that society has to offer, and then accept whatever drugs and surgical operations are prescribed as a cure.*

Statistics in the book reveal that one million Americans die from heart disease every year, while a half-million die from cancer. Cancer is killing more children between the ages of 3 and 14 than anything else. One out of every three Americans will develop cancer during their lifetime, and more than $200 billion a year is being spent on cancer treatment.

For Rev. Malkmus, these represent more than just numbers and statistics. His father died from a heart attack. His mother died from colon cancer. He was seeing dedicated Christian evangelists and pastors struck down at the height of their careers with disease. He was baffled as to why good Christians were sick and dying despite the passionate prayers of fellow Christians. And in 1976, Rev. Malkmus was diagnosed with colon cancer at age 42.

As he began an endeavor to heal his own body, Rev. Malkmus also began an intense search that would ultimately lead to an answer to his deeply heart-felt question: Why Christians Get Sick. He concludes that Christians get sick because they have violated the natural Laws of God and accepted modern society's diet and lifestyle. To solve problems caused by this, they seek man-made solutions in the form of prescribed drugs, rather than changing back to the diet and lifestyle that God originally intended.

In *Why Christians Get Sick,* Malkmus attempts to educate readers about the consequences of such a choice, but his emphasis is on the positive. He warns, "Many people in the world have shunned Christianity because they think it is only a religion of don'ts, and many of the Christians they come in contact with are anything but positive and happy. The world needs to see a consistent, positive Christianity!!! Christians need to accentuate the positive for their own mental and physical well-being as well as to show a negative old world something different! Something better!!! Christians ought to be the healthiest and happiest people on the face of this earth!!!"

Malkmus concludes his book with suggestions on how this can become a reality. It's enough to make you turn off your soap operas, give up your frozen TV dinners and walk outside in the fresh air to enjoy the full beauty of God's creation . . . and maybe even plant a row of carrots while you're out there.

*From the Hallelujah Acres mailbag:*

Robin Thomsen

"I cannot tell you what a blessing your book has been for me! After being ill for most of my life, plagued with allergies, asthma, no-name illnesses and with the modern-day medical world trying to treat symptoms instead of finding the causes, I gave up on them and I too looked for answers on my own . . . I have always believed in taking care of the body and eating healthy, but when I discussed it with fellow Christians they just dismissed it . . . With your book (*Why Christians Get Sick*) and its Biblical references I feel secure and have been able to get my (and the Lord's) point across . . . So well in fact that I am to do a class on Christians & Nutrition for our Women's Group . . . I think you have a wonderful ministry! Keep up the excellent work!"
– Robin Thomsen
Colorado

# What Others Are Saying About
## *Why Christians Get Sick:*

"I recently read your book *Why Christians Get Sick* and I wanted to let you know how much I enjoyed it. I will be recommending it to many of my clients to read."
> Vickie J. Karnos,
> Nutritional Consultant,
> California

"Thank you for writing *Why Christians Get Sick.* My studies in this area led me to similar conclusions."
> Pastor Paul R. Knierim,
> Ohio

"Our patients are really benefiting from your book (*Why Christians Get Sick*)"
> Dr. Michael Lebowitz,
> Colorado

"Your book *Why Christians Get Sick* has been a true blessing to me."
> Pastor G.S.,
> Canada

"I just finished reading your book *Why Christians Get Sick.* I thought it was excellent!...I've been a vegetarian for about one year now and my health has improved greatly. . . . Rev. Malkmus, I really enjoyed your book even though I'm not a very religious person . . . In closing, I want to thank you for writing this fantastic book and clearing up much confusion for me. I fully support what you are doing and wish you all the luck and God's will with your efforts to educate Christians and all people about diet and lifestyle changes to improve their health."
> N.P.,
> Ohio

"This past year I began an exercise program and began to eat better and lost 35 pounds. I feel better and have not had a single cold or flu this year! PTL! Your book (*Why Christians Get Sick*) seems to have put all of my thinking into a clear picture of what my spirit has been searching for."
> Dr. Stanley W. Gravely,
> Virginia

"I was thoroughly delighted by your book, *Why Christians Get Sick* . . . I am a nutritionist and have long had the dream of helping my fellow Christians with nutrition advice. You and I are in agreement on the ideal diet. You have weeded out the bad and kept the good. I commend you on your excellent work!"

Dr. Jana D. Bogs,
Hawaii

"I have just finished reading the book on *Why Christians Get Sick*. I agree that this is the greatest next to the Bible. It opened my eyes to many things.   I had been searching for a book like this for  a long time."

Rev. E.B.,
Pennsylvania

"Just finished reading your wonderful book, *Why Christians Get Sick*. I thank the Lord for a book that will explain what I have believed for the past 20 years. I will be sure to pass this book on. "

Carmen Acton
Indiana

"I was very pleased to read your book *Why Christians Get Sick*. My wife thought I had written it since our opinions and beliefs are so similar. It is interesting that a Minister learning of Science could mirror the same thoughts as a Scientist learning more about God. Actually I am a Christian. I attended Bethany College for my B.S. in Chemistry. My Ph.D work was in Organic Chemistry with further work in Biochemistry and Pharmacology. My area of interest and research was cancer. I intend to do my part in bringing the 'good news' of Christian health to Christians. I am ordering your book to use as one of my reference books for the course that I plan to teach..."

Dr. R. L. Coleman, Ph.D., D.N.H.,
Kentucky

"Read your book *(Why Christians Bet Sick)* in just a few hours - couldn't put it down. Loved it - thanks for caring about not just your own health but the health of others also! . . . I'll pray for you and the work ahead to let the world know 'Why Christians Get Sick.'"

Carol Reinart,
Wisconsin

"Your book *(Why Christians Get Sick)* came in the mail several weeks ago, and I have read, and reread, as I have marked it for future use.  I plan to present the summarized contents before my church in the very near future . . . Your raw food diet is not new to me, as I have heard of it, but never really got very interested in it. Perhaps as a therapist I have been overly AMA-indoctrinated.  After hearing your tape over the 3ABN Network, I, along with two patients, thought we should give it a try.  The two ladies that I have suggested try this way of eating, are very well pleased . . . Your book is well written, and brings out food for thought that even

*From the*
*Hallelujah Acres mailbag:*

Pastor David M. Helmic

"I read and reread everything you sent me. Thanks for writing such a revealing book *(Why Christians Get Sick)*. It is one every preacher should read. I would again invite you to come and speak to our church. ... I believe your message could be of help to many . . ."
Pastor David M. Helmic
Mississippi

*From the
Hallelujah Acres mailbag:*

Dr. Norman Piersma

"At last I've found the book *(Why Christians Get Sick)* I've been looking for these past 2 years. Praise the Lord! . . . We have just retired as missionaries to Colombia, South America. Two and a half years ago I was diagnosed with metastatic melanoma cancer and given 6 months to live. I opted, however, for the Gerson Therapy in Tijuana, Mexico. Next week I compete in the Michigan Senior Olympics!"
– Dr. Norman Piersma, Florida

people like me, who have spent many years treating the body, had not given consideration . . . Thank you again for the new (yet old) light you have brought to me."

> John McBride,
> Kansas

"An Elder in our fellowship gave me a copy of your book and I think it is great. I have studied a lot of information on different subjects, but what I like about your book *(Why Christians Get Sick)* is that it is addressed specifically to Christians. Keep up the good work and blessings to you from the Eternal Saviour ... "

> Pastor Jack Wedel,
> America's Future Christian Fellowship,
> Kansas

"I have just finished reading your book, *Why Christians Get Sick.* Our Bible Study Group is circulating it. I am very grateful for this book. Our group had this information before, but because it was not written from a scriptural perspective, our elders told us we could not circulate it through the church body. We can now!! Many still will not be interested because even Christians want to "have their cake and eat it too." Most still do not want to take responsibility for their health. They would rather abuse their bodies and expect God to heal them or blame the cause on a "spirit of infirmity." I am excited to learn that such a place as Hallelujah Acres exists. I applaud your efforts..."

> Candy Bernier,
> Pennsylvania

"I just finished reading your book *Why Christians Get Sick.* It is very well written ... I have been a vegetarian as well as my family for five years. We have also experienced better health and gotten rid of all health problems. We haven't had a need for a doctor in all that time. It is sad to see such unnecessary sickness and early death when the Bible clearly gives us a better way..."

> Dinah Johnson,
> New Mexico

"We want to thank you for all your efforts concerning our sick generation. We appreciate your book *(Why Christians Get Sick).* Have been able to use 50 copies and have another order for 50 more enclosed. This has been our way of living for more than 20 years and we need this to encourage us and to get more people to see it too. We know it works just like you say it does. Would you come to our community sometime and give a seminar..."

> Clara Troyer,
> Ohio

"We have just received *Why Christians Get Sick* and wish we had been able to read a book like this 50 years ago. I have just been diagnosed as having

Leukemia. My husband has parkinson. He is 78 and I am 71. We both thought we were watching our diets pretty good, but after reading your book we realize we didn't know anything..."

 E. G.,
 Oregon

"Dear Rev. Malkmus: Your book *Why Christians Get Sick* is terrific!

 Dr. Nathan M. Meyer,
 President, Bible Prophecy Association,
 Ohio

"I just read your book *Why Christians Get Sick* and it is very, very informative. I feel it is extremely important that this message of eating properly get out to the Body of Christ. I appreciate the fact that you tell people to take responsibility for what they put into their bodies and quit blaming God for their physical problems. God bless you as you get this message around the world! ... With our love,

 Nigel Buxton, M.R.C.S., L.R.C.P. (Royal College of Surgeons, Royal
 College of Physicians) & Elmira Buxton, M.D.,
 Ontario, Canada

"I picked up your book *(Why Christians Get Sick)* in a Christian Book Store in North Carolina. The fellow in the store recommended your book to me when I started talking about <u>health</u> ... and it is the <u>best</u> by far
that I have ever read - it says <u>everything</u> that I have been trying to say for 20 years!! ... I am giving your book to all my managers (25) and to every Pastor I know!!"

 Arlene Oostdyk, R.N., Natural Health Educator,
 New Jersey

*From the
Hallelujah Acres mailbag:*

"Your book, *Why Christians Get Sick,* has been sorely needed for a long, long time. Christians especially, it seemed to me, felt that any food downed after grace would do them all the good their prayers mentioned, or even if it weren't mentioned..."
Ruth Sargent,
Virginia

"I just finished reading your book *Why Christians Get Sick* and it has turned my life around. Thank you for such a caring and valuable message. May God bless you and your ministry!"
Doris Oldham,
South Carolina

# Chapter 4

# Our Statement of Faith:

**The Message of Hallelujah Acres is essentially . . .**
**Superior Health will exist if our**
**Living practices are in keeping with God's Natural Laws**

With superior health we are fit vessels for God's Holy Spirit and we are better able to serve God and proclaim our Saviour, the Lord Jesus Christ!

Good health is a necessary condition for the enjoyment of life and it is the Lord's will that we enjoy life. Jesus said: *"I am come that they might have life, and that they might have it more abundantly."* (John 10:10)

1) We believe and teach that God created man! (Genesis 1:26 - 27; 2:7)

2) We believe that God not only created man, but that He created a perfect body, with a capability of living without sickness *forever!* (Genesis 1:31, 3:22)

3) We believe that the body is the dwelling place or *temple* of God. Yea, the Holy Spirit literally dwells in the body of each believer. (I Corinthians 6:19 - 20). Christians often associate the *"fleshly nature"* with the body itself. This is not a proper interpretation of the Scriptures.

*"Know ye not that ye are the temple of God and that the spirit of God dwelleth in you? If any man defile the temple of God, him shall God destroy: For the temple of God is holy, which temple ye are."* **(I Corinthians 3:16 - 18)**

4) We believe that health is natural and normal and *will be* our portion if we will but observe God's Natural Laws in our daily walk through this life. (Galatians 6:7)

5) We believe that God does not want us to be sick. The Bible tells us in III John 2 that God wishes *"above all things that thou mayest prosper and be in health, even as thy soul prospereth."*

6) We believe that sickness comes *ONLY* when we violate the Natural Laws God gave us to live by. ***Disease is abnormal, unnatural and unnecessary!*** The only exception to this statement would be sickness for the *"glory of God"* or *"because of sin."* (I Corinthians 3:16-17)

7)   We believe that using drugs, radiation and the surgical removal of body parts in an effort to bring about healing is unnatural to the body and interferes with healthful body functions and the body's efforts to heal itself! (Mark 5:25 - 26)

8)   We reject the idea that sickness and disease are inevitable in our lives.  Rather, we contend that sickness and disease *will not occur unless there is sufficient **cause**!*  Proverbs 26:2 says, *" . . . the curse **causeless** shall not come."* We believe that no curse of sickness or ill health comes without a cause . . . and further, that if we will but ***eliminate the CAUSE, the curse (sickness) will usually go away and stay away!!!***

"Know ye not that ye are the temple of God and that the spirit of God dwelleth in you?  If any man defile the temple of God, him shall God destroy: For the temple of God is holy, which temple ye are."   (I Corinthians 3:16 - 18)

*"In my opinion, as long as our approach to healing (except in rare cases) involves the use of drugs, chemicals, radiation and scapels, we will never be successful. If we sincerely want to bring the American people back to health, or if we personally wish to reclaim our own perfect health, we must return to God and follow His ways - Nature's ways..."*
– Dr. Richard Anderson in his book *Cleanse & Purify Thyself*

# Chapter 5

# Where's God in Our Time of Sickness?

*By Rev. George H. Malkmus*

It has now been almost 40 years since I became a Christian and for most of these 40 years I have been involved in one way or another in various Christian ministries. Twenty of these years I spent pastoring various churches from New York to Florida.

As a pastor, I often experienced great difficulty understanding all the sickness I found within the Christian community. Why was it such a problem to me? Because as a pastor I saw that all too often, even though a person had all kinds of faith in God, prayed to God and even after much pleading with God, many, many Christians continued to be sick. Then they got sicker and sicker and often they died a very premature death.

*Why? Where was God?*

This dilemma reached its climax in 1976, when at the age of 42, I was told that I had a tumor the size of a baseball where the transverse colon turns downward into the descending colon. Just prior to being told this, I had watched my own mother die following treatments by the medical profession for colon cancer. At the time of mom's death I felt it had been the *treatments* that had caused her death rather than the cancer itself.

When I was told I had colon cancer, I didn't know a thing about nutrition and very little about the beautiful, self-healing body God had given me. The only thing I knew for certain was that I was *not* going to let the doctors treat me with the chemotherapy, radiation and surgery with which they had treated mom. I saw the devastating impact these treatments had on my mother and I feel they were a contributing cause – if not the *primary cause* – of my mom's death. So, on the advice of a friend, I did something as simple as change my diet and lifestyle, and immediately started to get well. In fact, in less than one year, not only had my tumor disappeared, but so had every other physical problem ... hemorrhoids, hypoglycemia, severe sinus and allergy problems, constipation, high blood pressure, fatigue, pimples, even body odor and dandruff! And for the past almost 20 years I have not experienced any sickness of any kind, not so much as a cold, sore throat, headache, upset stomach; nor have I been to a doctor or even taken so much as an aspirin. I'm now in my 60s and I can still play football with the boys, jog five miles and have more energy, stamina and endurance then I had at the age of 20. How do we account for this?

Since 1976 I have been studying everything I could get my hands on that relates to the human body, health, nutrition, lifestyle and how it all relates to the Bible. Also, since 1976 I have been experimenting on my own body and watching the results others got when they changed their diet and lifestyle. What I have found is so simple and yet so profound that I can't understand why we haven't seen it a long time ago. *God made a marvelous body!* He made it in such a way, that if properly nourished it would never get sick. But even if it did get sick, God programmed self-healing into the body so that if the offense (wrong foods or drugs) which had caused the problem was stopped and proper building materials (nutrition) were provided, the body would heal itself! It is all so very simple!

Let's look at how we treat sickness in this modern and so-called enlightened day in which we live: Those who believe in God will usually pray first ... then quickly run to the doctor. The doctor will ask what the symptoms are, then prescribe a drug that according to their training is supposed to relieve those particular symptoms. But how many, many church people do each one of us know who went this route only to find their health continuing to deteriorate? Often they died. Where was God? Many people have gone the vitamin, herb, mineral, protein supplement route with similar results.

As a pastor, something that really disturbed me was when I realized that almost half of all Americans die of heart attacks and strokes *and that the percentage of Christians and non-Christians that died of heart attacks and strokes was IDENTICAL!* Some 30 percent of the American population develops cancer *and the percentage is the SAME within the Christian community.* We could go on into all the other physical problems plaguing our country today, and find that the percentages of Americans who are experiencing diabetes, arthritis, asthma, ulcers, migraines, digestive disorders, obesity, allergies, mental illness, bad teeth, etc. ... *is the same within the Christian community as it is outside the Christian community. Where is God?*

Let me begin to answer that question by stating again that *God made a marvelous body!* He did not make any mistakes and He didn't make any junk, nor is He the One to blame when we get sick. It seems that Christians have been programmed into thinking that God is controlling everything ... including a person's health, and that the individual has no control. But nothing could be further from the truth. God gave each one of us a fabulous body *but then He*

> *God put within man the ability to self-heal, but only if we follow and abide by His natural laws! How sad it is that the Christian Community has gone outside of the Bible and God's ways and looked up to the medical profession as the teachers of health and the only ones capable of guiding our sick bodies back to wellness.*

"When I investigated hyperactive children, I found that many of them were 'wild and crazy' because they were sensitive to dairy products."
– Lendon H. Smith, M.D., *Dr. Lendon Smith's Low-Stress Diet*

"The answer to the question about how nutrition could possibly have anything to do with mental health is quite simple. What one eats, digests, and assimilates provides the energy-producing nutrients that the bloodstream carries to the brain. And any interference with the nutritional supply lines or with the energy-producing systems of the brain results in impaired functioning, which then may be called 'poor mental health.' "
– George Watson, Ph.D., *Nutrition and Your Mind*

"Schizophrenia is an example of a disease that has been linked to unmet, elevated nutrient needs. In one study, a group of schizoprhenics were found to have abnormal metabolism of vitamin C."
– Patrick Quillin, Ph.D., R.D., *Healing Nutrients*

*turned that body over to each one of us and told us to be good stewards or caretakers of that body.* *"What, know ye not that your body is the temple of the Holy Ghost ... therefore glorify God in your body ..."* (I Corinthians 6:19-20) and again *"If any man defile the temple of God, him shall God destroy ..."* (I Corinthians 3:16). *"Be not deceived; God is not mocked: for whatsoever a man soweth that shall he also reap."* (Galatians 6:7).

In other words, God gives each of us the freedom to choose what we do with our lives. We have the choice to accept Him as our Creator, Lord and Saviour or to reject Him. Then, even after we accept Him, we have the freedom to live for Him or not to live for Him. And when It comes to what we put into our bodies for nourishment and to sustain these body temples, we can choose to nourish our bodies with the foods God designed these bodies of ours to be nourished with or we can choose to put into them what the commercial interests of the world parade before us. My Bible says in Romans 12:1-2: *"I beseech you therefore, brethren, by the mercies of God, that ye present your bodies a living sacrifice, holy, acceptable unto God, which is your reasonable service. **And be not conformed to this world ..."***

Then after we get sick from putting into our bodies those substances which God never intended to enter these body temples, we run to a medical doctor as we have been programmed, hoping the doctor can help us. What most people do not realize is that the treatments administered by the doctor were never ordained by God, are literally poisons that will, in most cases, further complicate the problem. Here is what I am getting at ...

At Creation, God established certain universal laws that apply to the whole of His creation. These laws are perfect and eternal and no one can change them. The law of gravity is a good example. Get too close to the edge and you will pay the penalty for the violation of that law regardless of whether you have knowledge of that law, whether you like or dislike that law, or whether you are a Christian or not. The health laws are the same. God in His loving kindness gave them to us so that we might enjoy abundantly healthy lives. But any variance from them will cause problems within the body ... sickness! God gave us simple instructions in His Word, the Bible, for every situation we can have in life, but because most Christians haven't followed these teachings, they feel they need an "expert" from this world to tell them how to live, how to eat and how to deal with physical problems.

Man, thinking he knows more than God, has tried to improve on God's ways. Thus he has invented all kinds of treatments, potions, pills, ointments, drugs, chemotherapy, radiation, surgery and a host of others in an effort to cure illness, pains and discomforts. *Disease never has been and never will be cured this way, for all healing comes from within! Doctors do not cure, drugs do not cure, radiation does not cure, surgery does not cure, vitamin supplements do not cure, nor does any other man-made device. God put within man the ability to self-heal, but only if we follow and abide by His natural laws!* How sad it is that the Christian community has gone outside of the Bible and God's ways and looked to the medical profession as the teachers of health and the only ones capable of guiding our sick bodies back to wellness. But are they worthy of our trust? What is their track record?

The medical profession has always professed to be in possession of a true science of medicine, whose principles, applied to the various diseases, constituted the proper healing art. Yet how has the world profited from all this? How much better has the world been informed in how to maintain wellness by this medical profession? How much better is the health of the people of the world regardless of how much money is spent? The truth is that in the past *the medical profession has gone so far as to tell us that it doesn't matter what we eat, and that what we eat has nothing to do with the physical problems that we experienced.* The medical profession has been content to let people go on in their violations of the laws of life and health, and then, when disease occurs – which is the inevitable result of the violation of these laws – dose and drug our bodies with man-made elixers.

It is impossible for drug doctors to be health teachers because their whole system is in violation of every natural law that God gave that governs these bodies we possess. *Every drug in reality is a dose of poison, an outrage against nature and a war on the human constitution.* The false and absurd dogmas of the drug system never did and never can do anything for the people but further mislead them and further destroy their health. *"And a certain woman, which had an issue of blood twelve years, and had suffered many things of many physicians, and had spent all that she had, and was no better, but rather grew worse."* (Mark 5:25-26)

Drugs never cure disease. They only change the form and location of the problem – a process that leads to what are called *side-effects.* *Side-effects are also illnesses* … illnesses that are *caused by drugs!* Is it not illogical to use drugs in an effort to take away one physical problem while that same drug will produce other problems for which other drugs will need to be taken? Go to the library and look at the *Physician's Desk Reference,* for a listing of the devastating side-effects of drugs!

> "The combination of good natural foods plus the correct nutritional supplements could eliminate most of the mental health problems (as well as physical illness) and is inexpensive when compared to drugs and doctor bills."
> – Carl C. Pfeiffer, Ph.D., M.D., *Mental and Elemental Nutrients*

> *When It comes to what we put into our bodies for nourishment and to sustain these body temples, we can choose to nourish our bodies with the foods God designed these bodies of ours to be nourished with or we can choose to put into them what the world and commercial interests parade before us. My Bible says in Romans 12:1-2: "I beseech you therefore, brethren, by the mercies of God, that ye present your bodies a living sacrifice, holy, acceptable unto God, which is your reasonable service. And be not conformed to this world..."*

The crying need of today is for doctors who understand and have applied and experienced natural health principles in their lives to begin teaching and guiding others in these natural principles. Webster defines "doctor" as "originally a teacher or learned man." Webster's *third* definition is "specifically applied to physician or surgeon (MD)." I am not saying we do not need doctors. We need them desperately to do what a doctor is supposed to do: *teach* people how to live healthfully, according to God's natural laws, not with drugs, which merely sedate the nervous system, mask the symptoms and create additional health problems. Most medical doctors are very fine, sincere people and I am proud to be able to claim many of them as my friends. Here at Hallelujah Acres we have doctors contacting us daily from all over the world who want to know more about God's natural laws, what we teach and how they can apply these health principles in their practice. (Recently, we had a very prominent surgeon contact us. His mother had been diagnosed with colon cancer and he wanted her to pursue the natural healing route rather than the treatments employed by his profession.)

Many of these doctors are very disenchanted and distressed at the time, energy and money they invested and sacrifices they made to learn how to help others ... to only find they are contributing to the sickness and agony of the people with the treatments and methods they were taught to use. They find themselves in a very difficult dilemma because the laws protect them from the adverse side-effects and deaths that occur from the dispensing of drugs and the other accepted medical treatments. But if they prescribe God's Natural Laws and simple health principles to their patients, they can, in some states, lose their license to practice medicine, go to jail and be fined. May God help us!

***Here at Hallelujah Acres we teach a different way ... God's way!*** We teach that the only nourishment God ever intended to enter these body temples of ours is raw fruits and vegetables. Period! That's it!!! A quick look at the rest of God's Creation will reveal that all members of the animal kingdom other than man, eat their food raw! And except where the animal's environment has been polluted by man, there is no sickness in nature. Only man, in his great intellect, is foolish enough to destroy the nutritional value of the foods by cooking them before they are put into the body. In addition, man tries to manufacture all kinds of (so-called) foods that are simply poison to the body. That our bodies hold up to such abuse for such an extended period of time is a wonderful tribute to the marvelous body God gave each one of us. But there is a penalty to pay, eventually, if we persist in violating God's natural laws.

Here are some interesting things to consider regarding some common physical problems:

**\* HEART DISEASE, STROKE, HYPERTENSION & OTHER CIRCULATORY PROBLEMS** are primarily caused by the fat in animal products. Remove the animal products from the diet, the blood will thin and the arteries will in most cases cleanse and heal. In fact, if a person eliminates animal products from their diet, they reduce their chances of *ever* having a heart attack or stroke by over 96 percent. (Hydrogenated oils are also extremely hazardous.)

**\* CANCER.** There are over 100 different names given cancer, depending on what part of the body it is located. But all cancers are simply runaway cells, that is cells multiplying out of control. Every one of us has these maverick cells in our bodies constantly, but when our immune system is functioning properly, it recognizes these maverick cells for what they are, gobbles them up, digests them, spits them out, and that is all there is to it. But when our immune system is not functioning properly and when we have loaded our body with more toxins than our immune system can cope with, then we develop cancer. In fact, tumors are merely pockets of toxins and maverick cells our body is trying to dispose of. In 1976, when I changed my diet and lifestyle, the baseball-sized tumor in my colon area simply disappeared. Cancer literally feeds on animal fats and protein (and even high-fat and high-protein vegetable foods). When I stopped putting these types of foods into my body and changed my diet, my tumor just went away and has never returned. If a person doesn't smoke or eat animal products or consume sugar, their chances of ever developing cancer are practically nil.

* **DIABETES**. Adult-onset diabetes is usually not caused by a malfunctioning pancreas or sugar, but by the coating of the cells with cholesterol caused by the eating of animal products. Very often, all a diabetic has to do is remove animal products from his or her diet and the blood sugar problem will

> *If doctors, with all their knowledge of the human body, would merely become familiar with the principles of health and the simple Natural Laws that God established, and share them, they would be performing the greatest humanitarian service to mankind this world has ever known.*

simply disappear. It is this same fat (not the diabetes) that causes diabetics to develop glaucoma, blindness, circulation problems, etc.

* **ARTHRITIS** is caused by excess protein and fat in the diet which produce uric acid crystals in the joints. It is important to realize that high intake of vegetable protein and fats is just as capable of producing arthritis as animal protein and fats. Eliminating the causes of arthritis and giving the body some nourishing raw food, especially raw vegetable juices, will usually bring relief to the arthritic sufferer in a very short time

* **OSTEOPOROSIS** is just the natural reaction of the body trying to neutralize internal acidity caused by eating animal fat and protein and sugar. In an effort to try and neutralize this acidity, the body will rob teeth and bones of calcium. Thus osteoporosis can be avoided by eliminating animal fats and protein from the diet.

We could go on and on, naming one physical problem after another ... premenstrual tension, migraines, Alzheimer's, slowing mental acuity, failing eyesight, cataracts, skin problems, ulcers, hearing loss, gallstones and kidney stones, obesity, varicose veins, prostate inflammation, estrogen imbalance, etc. In almost every instance, these and most other physical problems can be stopped and usually completely reversed by something as simple as a diet and lifestyle change. Almost without exception, they all have their root cause in the consumption of substances that God never intended to enter the body. And the thrilling part is that even if the organs are left with only a fraction of their original capacity, when we stop the abuse (putting into our body the toxic, so-called foods) and give our body the proper building materials (raw fruits, vegetables and vegetable juices), the body can often perform that which borders on the miraculous.

*From the Hallelujah Acres mailbag:*

"Thank you ever so much for writing *Why Christians Get Sick*. The subject of your writing is near and dear to my heart. The Lord also led me to the Scriptures a number of years ago to find out what we should be eating. I was astonished to find out what the Word of God had to say on the subject, and how little the church has to say on the topic. Also, it should not be such a well kept secret between a very few Christians, but it should be shared with the world...."
– F. A. Buck, Maryland

*From the*
*Hallelujah Acres mailbag:*

"Thank you for a most delightful and informative seminar for our congregation. Our hallways are alive with conversation about better health and eating habits and my phone has not stopped ringing for tapes of the meeting and for additional information. Your presentation was such an encouragement to our people, and so Biblical. It just proves that when the truth is presented there is opportunity and power for change.

I suppose the most immediate benefit that I have seen among our people is HOPE! We have numerous people who are fighting cancer, heart conditions, high blood pressure, high cholesterol, severe arthritis, and a host of other ailments. Most of them had become resigned to live with medication and its side-effects, just hoping to get by. They had lost hope of ever feeling well again. Now that they have been exposed to a 'better way' they have hope again. The testimonies of how Barley Green and proper eating habits have changed lives in a few short weeks was nothing more than confirmation that the program works. When people hear how others are getting well by changing their diet, it is a tremendous encouragement

**Continued in the
Right Column of page 51**

## THE SOLUTION

*All one must do to keep from getting sick or to eliminate most physical problems even after they have manifested themselves, is to return to the original diet God gave to mankind ... raw fruits and vegetables.* That is all I did in 1976 when I was told that I had colon cancer. Overnight, I switched from the typical American diet of meat, dairy, sugar, table salt, white flour products, and predominantly cooked food to **raw fruits and vegetables with lots of freshly-extracted carrot juice.** Almost immediately, my physical problems started to leave me and within less than one year, all physical problems were gone and have stayed gone ever since!

But I am not alone and my experience is not unique. Here at Hallelujah Acres there is not a day goes by that someone does not tell us of fabulous improvements in their health that they personally have experienced when they did something so simple as change their diet and lifestyle. In fact, people get so excited that they want to share it with everyone they meet. And this is what must happen if we are going to change the health of Christian people and yea the health of the world. It is too good to keep to ourselves. Here at Hallelujah Acres, Rhonda and I are working literally seven-day weeks, often 16-hour days and putting the profits from our business into literature to reach as many people as possible with the message *"You do not have to be sick!"*

**Where's God?** He is right where He was when He created man and gave him the original diet in Genesis 1:29 which reads: *"And God said, Behold, I have given you every herb (vegetable) bearing seed, which is upon the face of all the earth, and every tree, in which is the fruit of a tree yielding seed; to you it shall be for meat."* Listen again as God speaks in Genesis 6:7 *"...I will destroy man whom I have created from the face of the earth ... for it repenteth me that I have made them."* And again in verses 11 & 12, *"The earth also was corrupt before God, and the earth was filled with violence. And God looked upon the earth, and, behold, it was corrupt; for all flesh had corrupted his way upon the earth."*

**Where's God** when it comes to physical problems? He is right there in the Scriptures and in each one of our lives trying to woo us back to Him and the diet that He originally gave to sustain mankind.

So my friend, there is a solution to this almost overpowering problem of disease, drugs, hospitals, surgery, astronomically high medical expenses and premature deaths, that has so many people both inside and outside the church in its grasp today. If doctors, with all their knowledge of the human body, would merely become familiar with the principles of health and the simple natural laws that God established, and share them, they would be performing the greatest humanitarian service to mankind this world has ever known. They would then be fulfilling their role as teachers of the true health message. Many doctors are already moving in this direction and beginning to incorporate more information regarding lifestyle changes in their recommendations to patients. Many pastors are starting to incorporate the health message into the teachings of the church.

The public is much more aware of the benefits of healthful living, and the message is growing every day. Won't you join us here at Hallelujah Acres and become a part of this great and exciting health revolution!

**Continued from the Left Column of page 50**

for them to do the same. I certainly do not believe our people will ever be the same again. It will be a wonderful day when 'Prayer Meeting' night is a time of praise and thanksgiving to the Lord instead of a place to air our aches and pains before God. I'm sure God will be more honored by our healthy bodies, living in fullness and peace, than with us always calling on him to heal.

Your message is certainly needed in the churches today. When God's people are remarkably different than the world then we can make progress in telling forth the truth. When we have something to give there will be hundreds seeking us out just to know what makes us different. If our health is better, and our quality of life is better than the world-at-large, then we have a tremendous opportunity to tell them about spiritual things. If we practice the laws of health then we shall start a revolution in this nation that could shake us to our spiritual foundations.

Thank you again for coming. We look forward to having you back again real soon."

– Tom Suiter, pastor Indian Springs Baptist Church, Tennessee

# Chapter 6

# The Healthy Cell Concept

*By Rev. George Malkmus*

Have you ever thought about where you came from, or where and how your life began? Oh, I know that in the beginning God created the original male and female. But . . . today, where do we come from? How are we made? What are we made of? Let's consider these questions!

Today, human life begins at conception, when the sperm of the male joins the egg of the female and a single cell forms. This single cell contains DNA, which is a blueprint of what the entire body will be like, including the sex of that individual . . . right on down to what the color of the eyes and hair will be.

*One year from this very moment, practically every cell in our body will have been replaced with a new cell. Scientists have confirmed that 98 percent of the atoms in our body were not there a year ago. Thus, one year from today, every one of us will have a new body!!! We should be struck with awe at what a marvelous self-regenerating and self-healing body God has given us.*

Now what happens after the sperm and egg unite is pretty awesome. That original cell divides into two cells (each with its own DNA) and the two cells become four cells, the four become eight, the eight become 16, the 16 become 32 and on and on these cells continue to divide and multiply at an unbelievable rate of speed for the next 11 months. At the end of approximately 11 months, two months after birth, the body has its full complement of cells . . . somewhere around 100,000,000,000 (one hundred trillion) of them, with each cell containing its own blueprint of the entire body!

At about two months after birth, this wild proliferation of cells stops and from here on and throughout life, there is not supposed to be any more wild proliferation of cells . . . only the replacement or recreation of cells. For example, throughout life, every four weeks or so, the entire outer layer of our skin is replaced with new cells. Approximately every two months, practically every cell in our heart muscle is rebuilt; and within a one-year period, our entire bone structure replaces. One year from this very moment, practically every cell in our body will have been replaced with a new cell. Scientists have confirmed that 98 percent of the atoms in our body were not there a year ago. Thus, one year from today, every one of us will have a new body!!! We should be struck

year from today, every one of us will have a new body!!! We should be struck with awe at what a marvelous self-regenerating and self-healing body God has given us.

The question arises . . . what kind of body will it be? Will this new body be weaker or stronger than the body we possess today?

The answer to that question is entirely up to each of us, because as the old cell dies and the new cell replaces, the new cell is totally dependent on the building materials we provide it . . . the foods we eat, liquids we drink and air we breath.

In *Green Leaves of Barley,* Dr. Mary Ruth Swope writes: "If it could be expected that all scientists in the world agreed on a single fact, I believe they would agree . . . 'Life begins, is maintained and ends at the cellular level.' The health of a single cell holds the key to the health of the whole organism." Her book adds, "Cells made strong through good nutrition will go a long way in giving you an immune system that will resist the illnesses so prevalent in our society."

If the cell's needs are properly met, each cell will live healthily and function properly, ultimately reproducing and replacing itself with a new, healthy, strong cell. That is how God made the body to function, and this is where the Healthy Cell Concept comes in. So, if we want to have abundant energy, good physical strength, and experience freedom from sickness, then we must take care of our cells so that they will function as God intended. But God will not interfere with this natural process of cause and effect, even if it is done in ignorance! The Bible warns in Galatians 6:7, ". . . for whatsoever a man soweth, that shall he also reap."

In his book, *The Golden Seven Plus One,* Dr. C. Samuel West writes: "The laws of nature are the laws of God. Nature is no respecter of persons. No matter how righteous a person is, if he breaks the mental, nutritional or physical laws of health, he will cause his own destruction."

To put it as simply as I know how: God created for us a marvelous, self-regenerating and self-healing body, along with the raw fruits and vegetables (see Genesis 1:29) we need to sustain ourselves in perfect health. Observing God's natural laws brings us superior health . . . while violating God's natural laws brings us sickness, suffering and often a premature death!

Proper cell care is the key to our health, energy, strength, mental stability . . . and, yea, to our very life!!! So it is vitally important that we learn all that we can about our cells. Here are some things to consider:

I. CELL ENVIRONMENT – In order for our cells to function properly, they must have a healthy environment. This includes maintaining a body

*From the*
*Hallelujah Acres mailbag:*

Wayne and
Marlene Brault

"...My not being able to sleep one night, getting up and turning the satellite on to 3ABN at midnight and hearing the interview with Rev. Malkmus was no accident! I am convinced that God wanted me to hear that interview and it was a new beginning for me...We love you, we pray for your ministry, we pass out free *Back to the Garden* issues, we follow your ministry closely...God bless you, we are 100% with you."
– Wayne and
Marlene Brault,
Oregon

*It is so exciting to realize that we can control the health of our body cells by proper diet and exercise!!! Based on what we put into our bodies . . . we determine what our body will be made of, and how well it will function. Thus, we can prevent sickness!!!*

temperature of 98.6 degrees; maintaining a proper acid / alkaline balance of about 7.4 pH; providing the cells with pure air and water, all necessary minerals, and keeping the cells free from stress. If we can keep the fluids surrounding our cells free of toxic waste, at proper temperature and pH, provide them with pure water, a sufficient and balanced supply of minerals, and keep them free from stress, the cells will live, function and re-create themselves without any problems. Dr. West concludes in *The Golden Seven Plus One* that ". . . if the fluid medium in and around the cells was right, it would be impossible to damage or kill cells."

II. CELL FOOD – Healthy cells require healthy food.  Healthy food is food eaten just as close to the way God made it as possible . . . and that means RAW!!!  Every step in the processing of food takes it further from the way God intended our cells to be nourished, and this includes the cooking of food! Man is the only member of the animal kingdom that destroys his food before he eats it!

Dr. Yoshihide Hagiwara, in his book *Green Barley Essence,* notes that on the cellular level, our bodies relive the "drama of creation millions of times every day, as the cells which form our tissue are reborn in countless succession in the life-sustaining chain." He says "the most delicate of conditions must prevail" for this constant recreation of life to be carried on, and that a "balance and maintenance of minerals is the key to health."

III. CELL EXERCISE – In order to ensure proper functioning of all cells, body fluids need to be kept moving. This can be accomplished only by exercise. Exercise is absolutely essential for building and maintaining healthy cells.  Exercise puts oxygen into the blood, keeps the lymph moving and helps maintain the general health of the entire body.  It strengthens and nourishes all the various organs and systems of the body. Many consider it the single, most important component in building superior health!  When exercise is neglected, all the cells – muscles, organs, glands,  the circulatory and respiratory

## Ten Simple Steps to Healthy Cells

1. **Eat foods just as close to the way they grow as possible!**
2. **Make at least 75 to 85 percent of your food intake raw!**
3. **Take at least three teaspoons of Barley Green daily!** (Rhonda and I take 3-4 Tablespoons daily.
4. **Drink only pure distilled water and never drink with a meal!** (It dilutes the digestive juices! Water filters *do not*  produce pure water!)
5. **Eliminate breakfast!** Have Barley Green. Eat some juicy fruit if you get hungry.
6. **Eliminate all meat and dairy products!**
7. **Eliminate all products containing white sugar!**  (Use a *little*  raw honey if desired).
8. **Eliminate all white flour and table salt!**  Use Braggs Aminos as a substitute for salt and whole grain flour instead of white.)
9. **Eliminate all products containing hydrogenated oil!**  (This would include all margarine, products containing Crisco type oils, peanut butter, etc.)
10. **Exercise vigorously every day and learn to breath deeply!**

*Barley Green is the most essential supplement (for lack of a better word) Rhonda and I take!  Barley Green is produced from organically grown barley leaves, harvested at their most nutritious stage.  The juice is extracted and then spray-dried at room temperature, thus retaining all of its nutrients, including enzymes.  Barley Green is the most "nutrient dense" food of which I am aware to provide the cells with the elements crucial to their optimal growth and functioning!  Within 5 minutes after it enters the body, Barley Green is in the blood stream feeding the cells and building the immune system.  Barley Green is a vital part of our daily nutritional program and I recommend it highly!  In fact, I consider Barley Green the single most important food I put into my body each day. (We do not recommend Barley Green in tablet form!  Nor do we recommend it be taken in juice . . . only in a small amount of distilled water or dissolved dry in the mouth!  Other companies have tried to imitate Barley Green but we do not find that their products give the same results!)

systems, etc. – become weakened and sluggish, and this leads to all manner of physical breakdown.

IV. CELL PROTECTION – God built into man's body a line of defense to protect him from being destroyed by an unfriendly environment. The body's defenses are skin, mucous membranes, friendly bacteria, tear glands, fever, lymphatic system, fighter cells, and the immune system. The immune system contains about a trillion cells called lymphocytes and about 100 trillion molecules called antibodies. These cells provide protection against all microscopic enemies seeking to enter the body. We build our immune system by eating raw food and drinking the juices of raw vegetables!!! We immobilize our immune system by putting harmful substances into our body! For example, white table sugar (which is literally a drug), paralyzes the immune system. Just nine teaspoons of sugar (one soda pop contains 10), in a day will immobilize the immune system by about 33% . . . while approximately 30 teaspoons of sugar will wipe out the immune system from even functioning that day. High fat intake seriously impairs the immune systems functioning as does white table salt. Caffeine suppresses the immune system by upsetting the delicate mineral balance, which deprives the immune system of essential minerals. All drugs and pain killers adversely affect the immune system . . . even aspirin.

V. POSITIVE MENTAL ATTITUDE – Ron Price, in his book, *The Healthy Cell Concept,* says: "A healthy cell attitude is the final ingredient of the HEALTHY CELL CONCEPT, and possibly the most important. All through history, attitude has been recognized as an important ingredient in the quality of life. The Bible says, 'As a man thinks in his heart, so is he.' Research has also documented that laughter and enjoyment can release substances in the body which enhance the immune system, while sadness, anger or worry can actually depress the immune system."

*From the Hallelujah Acres mailbag:*

"I would like your diet for healthier living. A friend of mine told me her son had throat cancer and she put him on your diet and the Doctors could not find any cancer..."
– Sue Bohnen, Florida

*If we want to know how to maintain wellness, we must first understand how we are made, how our body is designed to heal itself, and what foods God created for our bodies to function properly.*

My experience has shown that as we stop putting poison (which many of us call food) into our bodies and give our cells the proper building materials, our physical bodies as well as our mental and emotional faculties will restore themselves to wellness!

My personal conviction after almost 20 years of research is that if we could get people off the animal products (meat and dairy), sugar, salt, white flour products and drugs, and onto a raw food diet with lots of raw vegetable juices . . . that not only could we theoretically eliminate sickness from the world, but we could restore emotional and mental health to most people.

It is so exciting to realize that we can control the health of our body cells by proper diet and exercise!!! Based on what we put into our bodies . . . we determine what our body will be made of, and how well it will function. Thus, we can prevent sickness!!! And almost all sickness and disease can be corrected by simply cleansing the body of toxins and providing the cells with the proper

Kevin Elliot and Geraldine Gillenwater

"...I came to Hallelujah Acres and started taking Barley Green and carrot juice (in June 1993) ... For years I had a duodenal ulcer and spent a fortune on Doctor and Hospital bills, plus medicine which was so high - and it was only making my stomach worse. The gastritis was so bad a lot of nights I thought I would die ... Now I eat anything I want with no gas. My stomach seems to be completely healed. Two of my doctors said they didn't prescribe it (Barley Green and carrot juice), but they thought it was wonderful what it had done for me and for me to keep taking it ... My arthritis for years gave me a fit. I couldn't do anything without it getting me down and it was all over my body. I had so much misery in my back and legs I couldn't stand the pain. I also had slipped discs - two in my neck and two in my lower back ... But praise the Lord, since I got on Barley Green and carrot juice in June 1993, I have so much energy I painted the roof on my trailer, now mow over one acre of lawn, use a weedeater, push mower and riding mower. I bought a hoe, something I hadn't used in years and now I am helping my sister raise a big garden . . . I try to tell everyone about Barley Green and carrot juice. Some don't even believe me and some have followed my advice. Oh, I forgot to tell you I am 71 years young and I haven't felt so good in years and years. I will never be without Barley Green and carrot juice as long as it is on the market. Even though it is high it is still a lot cheaper than Doctor prescription medicine ... God bless you and Rhonda in your ministry."
– Geraldine Gillenwater,
Virginia

building materials. The sickness will usually disappear as the body rebuilds itself! The cause and cure of sickness is not a mystery . . . it is simply a matter of cause and effect!!!

Probably the greatest single thing I have learned in 18 years of research and personal experience is the only food that is "cell food" is raw food!!! And the quickest way to restore the body to wellness is by consuming large amounts of raw vegetable juices, especially Barley Green!

In 1976, I was told that I had colon cancer. At that time I was also suffering from hypoglycemia, hemorrhoids, severe allergies and sinus problems, high blood pressure, colds, pimples, dandruff, body odor, lack of energy, etc. Almost 20 years ago I switched overnight from the 'good-ol' American diet of meat, dairy, sugar, salt, white flour products, cooked food, etc., to an all-raw diet with large amounts of freshly extracted vegetable juices. What was the result? Within less then one year, every physical problem I had was gone . . . and has stayed gone to this present day!!!

# Chapter 7

# God's Marvelous Self-Healing Body

*By Rev. George H. Malkmus*

*In the beginning God created the heaven and the earth ... and the Lord God formed man of the dust of the ground, and breathed into his nostrils the breath of life; and man became a living soul."* **(Genesis 1:1 & 2:7)**

When God created man, He made no mistakes! In the beginning, everything God made was perfect, from placing the earth in proper orbit around the sun ... not too close lest we burn up and not too far lest we freeze. The percentage of oxygen was just right to sustain life. Even the food supply, picturesque scenery, tranquil setting, etc. It was all there in perfection. *"And God saw every thing that he had made, and, behold, it was very good."* (Genesis 1:31)

Then God placed man, His crowning creation, in the midst of this beautiful garden on planet earth. And God said to man *"Be fruitful, and multiply ..."* Every person reading these words, if they could trace their family tree back far enough, would find their ancestry originating *IN THE GARDEN!* Man has wandered far from this original Garden of Eden which God prepared for us. As a result of this wandering, we have suffered greatly. *It is the goal of Hallelujah Acres to try and bring people of today BACK TO THE GARDEN!* Back to the simple lifestyle, diet, freedom from stress and sickness, peaceful, happy life God originally planned for mankind.

*If we want to know how to maintain wellness, we must first understand how we are made, how our body is designed to heal itself, and what foods God created for our bodies to function properly.*

Maybe this sounds impossible or too simplistic. But we are seeing incredible results from multitudes all over the world who are making simple changes in their diet and lifestyle. Even in this stressful, polluted world in which we live, these people are seeing exciting things happening in their bodies and their lives: Healing of disease ... the return of a healthy glow, happiness and enthusiasm to their life ... and a heightened ability to serve God and appreciate His beautiful creation. All these benefits initiated by something as simple as a change to a more natural diet and lifestyle!

For most of the 2000 years since Jesus established His church,

Christianity has focused on the soul and spirit of man, while practically ignoring the body/temple. Church leaders often take scripture out of context by suggesting the physical body is wicked and evil. Yet my Bible says *"What? know ye not that your body is the temple of the Holy Ghost ... therefore glorify God in your body, and in your spirit, which are God's."* (I Corinthians 6:19-20) Romans 12:1 says we should *"... present your bodies a living sacrifice, holy, acceptable unto God, which is your reasonable service."*

Psalm 139:14 says *"We are fearfully and wonderfully made."* When we look at the anatomy of man we find this to be so. Right from the moment of conception, exciting things start to happen as the father's sperm penetrates the mother's egg, and genetic instructions from parents interact to begin a new individual.

On the very day of conception, the first cell divides into two, the two into four, and so on. Within five to nine days, the sex can be determined. By day 15 the heart is forming and by day 24 the heart is beating. In 42 days the skeleton is formed and the brain is coordinating movement of muscles and organs. Within eight weeks, every organ is present, the heart is beating steadily, the stomach is producing digestive juices, the liver is making blood cells and the kidneys are functioning. And so it continues until about nine months after conception, when the child is born.

How did the body know to do all this? There is only one answer my friend ... God programmed it all into the original couple, Adam and Eve, and it has been passed down to each of us today through the DNA and RNA of every generation since then. What is found in the DNA is awesome. But we are going to confine this treatise to the area of how we were designed to be nourished and healed.

The first thing we must realize is that the human body is a living organism, made up of approximately 100 trillion living cells. Every part of our body is made of cells ... our bones, blood, skin, muscle, eyes, heart, liver, etc. Each cell is a miniature generator that

*Just as a cut on the surface of our skin will heal itself, the rest of our body – from the cellular level to vital organs – is also designed to be self-healing. This self-healing will occur when we stop consuming the poisons that caused the problem and give our body the nourishment on which it was originally designed to live, prosper and heal. This ability to self-heal was programmed into our DNA by God at creation. Those who have made the change to a natural diet and lifestyle can see that God's original plan of self-healing works better than all the prescription drugs, chemotherapy, radiation and surgery modern medical science has to offer.*

requires fuel and oxygen to generate the electrical energy needed to power the body. The body also has a defense mechanism which we call the immune system. Then there is the nervous system which transmits impulses throughout the body. The endocrine system coordinates body functions of the glands. The respiratory system controls our oxygen intake. The circulation system involves movement of the blood. And there is so much more. Truly, "we are fearfully and wonderfully made."

*If we want to know how to maintain wellness, we must first understand how we are made, how our body is designed to heal itself, and what foods God created for our bodies to function properly.* These foods created by God as the original diet for man are described in Genesis 1:29, where we read: *"... I have given you every herb (vegetable) bearing seed ... and every tree, in which is the fruit of a tree yielding seed; to you it shall be for meat."*

On this original diet, man lived an average of 912 years, prior to the flood, without a single recorded instance of sickness. Following the flood, two changes were made in man's diet ... meat was added and man started to cook his food. Following these two changes in the way man ate, the lifespan rapidly declined in ten generations from an average of 912 years to 100 years. Today, we have moved even further from God's original diet by putting increasingly more toxic substances into our bodies so that today, by the age of 40, the average person already has serious physical problems. The average four-year-old already has plaque build-up in his arteries, and the average youth of today cannot even pass the President's minimal physical fitness requirements – a standard that has been lowered several times since 1940!

This generation is *sick*, and getting sicker by the day! The symptoms and signs of this sickness are the ever-increasing numbers of people afflicted by heart attacks, strokes, cancer, diabetes, arthritis, and a host of other degenerative diseases! But keep in mind that cancer, heart disease, etc. are not the problem itself, but merely symptoms of the problem. *The problem today is that we are putting into our bodies substances (poisons) God never designed these bodies of ours to have to deal with! And then we further complicate the problem by trying to treat the resulting symptoms with additional poisons (drugs).*

*Any successful approach to health must deal with the cause of the problem rather than merely the symptoms.* If we want to reverse our physical problems, we *must* get back to the basics ... to God and to an understanding of how He made us and how He intended us to be nourished and healed and how our bodies are designed to eliminate toxic substances.

Today, when we develop a physical problem, we have been programmed to believe that the problem is the result of some virus, germ, or bacteria that attacked our innocent body, or that we inherited the problem through our genes from parents, grandparents, etc. *Nothing could be further from the truth!!! Such teachings are designed to keep us from realizing the true cause of disease ... our own transgression of God's natural laws!* The truth is that almost every physical problem we experience (other than those caused by accidents), *we created* by violating the natural laws established by God at creation for the sustaining of our life, health and well being.

Then when we get sick, we try to treat the symptom of the disease with more poison (drugs), thinking this poison will destroy the physical problem. This only complicates the problem and actually creates new problems. What we must understand if we are going to restore our bodies to health is that *there are no cures!* My friend reading these words, I don't know how to say it strong enough: *THERE ARE NO CURES!!! The only way to restore the body to wellness is with a healthy diet and lifestyle!*

If we are going to restore the body to wellness, we must realize that drugs do not cure, chemotherapy does not cure, radiation does not cure, surgery does not cure, vitamins do not cure, herbs do not cure. The only way to restore the body to wellness is to eliminate what *caused* the physical problem in the first place and then give the body the building materials it needs to restore and rebuild itself. Programmed into each individual is *self-healing!*

*Just as a cut on the surface of our skin will heal itself, the rest of our body – from the cellular level to vital organs – is also designed to be self-healing. This self-healing will occur when we stop consuming the poisons that caused the problem and give our body the nourishment on which it was originally designed to live, prosper and heal. This ability to self-heal was programmed into our DNA by God at creation. Those who have made the change to a natural diet and lifestyle can see that God's original plan of self-healing works better than all the prescription drugs, chemotherapy, radiation and surgery modern medical science has to offer.*

The most important things needed for self-healing are fresh air, pure water, adequate rest, internal and external cleanliness, sunshine, a positive mental attitude, vigorous exercise and eating the foods created by God for our nourishment. And the *only* nourishment God ever intended for us to put into our bodies is pure water, fresh air, sunlight and fresh, raw fruits and vegetables. As long as these needs are met, the body is self-sufficient and will function properly in perfect health. But when we deviate from these basic biological needs, the body becomes clogged and poisoned, energy is depleted, physical problems result and life is shortened.

Rather than helping the body to restore itself to wellness by eliminating those things in our diet and lifestyle that created the problem, modern medicine seeks to aggressively fight the symptom. The way the medical profession deals with sickness today is wrong and it produces horrible results. Not a day goes by that I do not receive dozens of phone calls and letters from people from all over the world with the most horrible stories of the results they or their loved ones have experienced after going the traditional medical route for physical problems ... especially cancer.

Think about how we deal with cancer today. Cancer is caused in most instances by improper diet or lifestyle. Lung cancer caused primarily by cigarette smoking. Colon, breast, prostate and uterine cancer are caused primarily by animal products. In fact, animal products, excessive protein and fats are the cause of most of today's cancers. If we would but eliminate the causes, and give the body the proper building materials, most cancers would just disappear as the body's own self-healing mechanism would kick in.

Yet, the accepted first treatment for cancer today is usually chemotherapy. The basic chemical used in chemotherapy is similar to *mustard gas*!!! This chemical was used in World War I to kill soldiers on the battle field, and is such a hideous poison it has been universally banned from use in wartime through treaties. Yet this same poison is being injected into cancer patients today in hopes that it will kill some of the maverick cells, which it usually does. But it also kills the good cells and further weakens an already weak immune system. In fact, cancer would never have originated in the first place if the immune system had been functioning properly.

Radiation is another treatment used on cancer patients today. Recently we read of those who were exposed to radiation years ago in experiments conducted by the United States government. We were told these radiation victims needed to be compensated for the physical problems that arose because they were not told of the harmful effects of the radiation they received. Yet, today, *radiation* is used to treat cancer. It is supposed to destroy the maverick cells, which it often does. But in the process, it also kills good cells and destroys our ability to manufacture white blood cells, thus further weakening our immune system. How many cancer patients today are being told by their physicians of the dangers of radiation? **There is no safe use of radiation!** All radiation is dangerous, whether it be the treatment of cancer, microwave ovens or the radiation of food.

And then there is the surgery where they cut out the problem area. Chemotherapy, radiation and surgery all deal with the symptom … not with the **cause! The cause of almost all cancers is improper diet and lifestyle!** And that is why even after a person has gone through the above medical treatments, if they live through the treatments, the cancer will usually

> **Many people today believe they can dump anything they want into their bodies and that this garbage has nothing to do with their physical well-being. Then they believe when they get sick all they have to do is take some drug to take away that sickness.**

come back again. Why? Because only the symptoms were dealt with, not the underlying cause!

When I had my cancer problem in 1976 I refused medical treatment. I eliminated from my diet the things that had caused my tumor and my cancer just disappeared, as did every other physical problem that I had. And I have experienced no physical problems since that time.

Here at Hallelujah Acres we receive thousands of testimonies from people from all over the world who simply eliminated those things from their diet and lifestyle that were creating their physical problems, gave their bodies superior building materials … and they got well. One man recently told of 18 different physical problems that simply disappeared when he changed his diet. Several months ago, a Christian lady in Kansas City called to tell how she had gone the medical route, without success, for a huge tumor in her rectal area. She was in excruciating pain and couldn't even sit down. She called recently to tell us she had been on the Hallelujah Diet for just eight weeks and already the tumor and pain were gone and that she could sit without any discomfort. She was ecstatic! We share the testimonials and letters of dozens of such people in every issue of *Back to the Garden* and in the pages of this book.

So let's look at how we seek to nourish these bodies of ours and how we deal with physical problems in this present day.

## FOOD

The first thing we must establish is that our body is a living organism, made up of living cells and that *the only thing that is cell food is LIVING, RAW FOOD!* The body processes these raw building materials and transforms them into material for its own growth, repair and maintenance. At the same time, it rejects anything harmful that cannot be assimilated into the cell wall to be used to build new living cells.

---

*What we must understand if we are going to restore our bodies to health is that there are no cures ... The only way to restore the body to wellness is with a healthy diet and lifestyle!*

---

It must be remembered though, that food cannot do anything by itself. It can only provide us with the raw materials the body needs for growth, repair and maintenance.

*Only the body has the ability to heal itself when given the nourishment necessary to rebuild and restore its healing mechanism (immune system) and essential body organs!* Then as the body's healing mechanism starts to function at a higher level, it seeks out problem areas and heals them. It is so simple because all this was programmed into our DNA at conception.

So many people today are not aware that what they put into their bodies has anything to do with their health or well being. They think they can dump anything that tastes good into their body and it will continue to function properly. *This is simply not so* and a quick look at the general health of the people of today will verify this. So when the body starts to break down they attribute it to old age or some "bug" going around, rather than improper diet and lifestyle. In an effort to get rid of their physical problem, they usually turn to drugs.

## DRUGS

Drugs offer no nourishment, but are chemical poisons dangerous and destructive to the body. If taken long enough, drugs create new problems for which another drug is prescribed. All substances introduced into the body by injection, absorption, respiration or ingestion that cannot be utilized as food are poisonous. Then the poison is acted upon by the body in self-defense by accelerating its metabolism to remove the toxin. All such action by the body is damaging to the living organism, because much harm is done by interfering with its natural metabolism.

Medical doctors use a system called allopathy. Allopathy means "opposite disease." Rather than helping the body's immune system to fight the disease, the approach of allopathy is to introduce a foreign substance (drug) into the body to produce effects *different* from those of the disease itself, which often creates additional disease. Generally, allopathic doctors do not try to determine the cause of the illness, nor seek to remove the cause of the illness. What they do is treat the symptoms!

"Teach the people that its is better to know how to stay well than how to 'cure' disease."
– Ellen White, 1898

Allopathy is not an effective means of restoring health. But it has become the dominant means of health care today because it is the most profitable approach for doctors, hospitals and pharmaceutical companies. It creates repeat customers. For example, a drug company can make more money selling laxatives and antacids over and over again to the same people than it could by merely instructing these people to change their diet to prevent constipation or indigestion. A family doctor makes such a good living from families coming in regularly with colds, flu, ear-aches, etc., why would he want to encourage them to change to a healthier diet? And considering that a person can spend $20,000 to $100,000 or more in treating cancer, is it really surprising that the result of the medical establishment's "War on Cancer" has been an increase, rather than a decrease, in cancer?

### OTHER APPROACHES

VITAMINS, MINERALS, PROTEIN SUPPLEMENTS – These substances are often used to try to correct physical problems and sometimes help, but can also have a drugging and harmful effect on the body. God did not design our body to receive nutrients in pill form or as mega-doses of nutrients isolated from the form in which they are found in nature. It matters not what nutrients are listed on the label of a bottle of supplements. What matters is what nutrients reach the cellular level in a form that can be utilized by the body.

HERBS – Herbs are a milder and more natural approach to healing than allopathic drugs. Good results can be obtained for some ailments with the right herb. But herbs should not be looked upon as a cure-all for all our physical problems. If a person needs to treat symptoms with herbs on a regular basis, this is a sign that he needs to change his diet to correct the problem rather than continuing to take herbs to deal with the symptoms. Many practitioners of natural health recommend herbs as a natural means of working in conjunction with the body's immune system, as opposed to allopathic drugs, which work against the immune system. But an even better approach is to use natural foods (raw fruits and vegetables) to strengthen and rebuild the immune system, along with the body's 100 trillion living cells.

WATER FASTING – Water fasting is the quickest way to detoxify the body, but can be dangerous if not carefully supervised. Water fasting often produces severe cleansing reactions and usually leaves the body very weak, often taking months to restore the body's strength after the fast. During the fast, the body is forced to feed upon itself and its nutrient reserves, which are usually low to start with. Here at *Hallelujah Acres*, we find that when the body is sick, it desperately needs nourishment to provide the building materials to restore and rebuild the immune system and essential organs.

MACROBIOTIC DIET – Because it cuts out fats and

*From the*
*Hallelujah Acres mailbag:*

Lois Anderson and her father

"My dad who had two strokes when he was 68 and was partially paralyzed on the left side and his face disfigured came out of it by changing his diet. He is alive today at age 93 because he changed his diet. He encouraged me to make the change myself early enough so I wouldn't have to experience strokes like he did . . . Thanks so much for sending me your newspaper *Back to the Garden*! My hope and dreams are to help as many people as I can regain their health."
Lois Anderson
Wisconsin

*From the*
*Hallelujah Acres mailbag:*

"A good friend introduced me to your change of life-style and Barley Green after he became so concerned about my poor health. My blood pressure was 140/120. I was experiencing constant terrible headaches and blurred vision. My neurologist said that according to the MRI, I had experienced a mild stroke. Her treatment was a whole list of pills for all of the above mentioned problems. I was taking some to control my blood pressure, some to put me to sleep at night, some to wake me up and some to calm me down. As a result of all this medication I found it very difficult to function at all. During the time I was on all of this medication I had very little exercise and as a result I gained up to 221 pounds. At 42 years old I felt like I had just signed off and there was just not much hope for me ... I kept hearing about Barley Green and what it could do for me so I thought why not give it a try. I started with just Barley Green for a couple of weeks and started to feel some better. Next I bought a Champion juicer and started juicing carrots. By the end of the third week I cut my medication back by over 50% and started on raw

**Continued in the right column of page 65**

cholesterol, many people have experienced some initial benefits from the Macrobiotic Diet for some physical problems. But cooked foods make up over 95% of the Macrobiotic Diet, salt is promoted, while raw fruit is not recommended. Our research and experience shows that this diet will help some people in the short run but long-term use of this highly acidic diet actually promotes some physical problems, including arthritis and cancer.

PRITIKIN DIET – This diet also removes the animal products and consequently has produced wonderful results with heart-related problems and diabetes. But because of its heavy grain use, many followers of this program have developed arthritis and cancer. *Hallelujah Acres* does not recommend heavy usage of grains, as they create an acidic condition in the body, which leads to many serious physical problems, including, but not limited to arthritis, cancer, and osteoporosis.

GERSON DIET – Dr. Max Gerson developed this diet in 1919 to eliminate his own migraine headaches. He later learned that this diet not only eliminated migraine headaches, but most other physical problems as well, including diabetes, arthritis and even terminal cancers. The diet is very low in fat, protein and grain products, while using large amounts of fresh, raw vegetable juices and other raw foods. The results they are getting – even with terminal illnesses – are spectacular.

RAW FOOD DIET – God's original diet for mankind was raw fruits and vegetables and we must return to this diet if we are seeking health and wellness. Our bodies are living organisms, made of living cells that require living food to be nourished properly and function well. Although we believe the original diet consisted mainly of raw fruits, we find that if too much fruit is consumed, it can produce hypoglycemic problems. Therefore we recommend a balance between raw fruits and vegetables. We have also found that with today's degenerated bodies and depleted soil, it takes more than just the *eating* of raw food to restore wellness. This is where concentrated nutrients in raw vegetable juices come into play. Nutrients in the freshly-extracted juice of raw vegetables have been separated from the fiber or pulp, which means these nutrients can go directly into the blood stream and to the cellular level without the time-consuming and energy-consuming process of digestion. We do not recommend fruit juices as they are too high in concentrated sugar, even though they are natural sugars. Further, we do not recommend any juices that can be purchased in containers, as they have all been heated to destroy the enzymes so they will not spoil.

*Thus we conclude ...* that when the body is sick, the only substances that should be introduced into it are those substances that will help the body to heal itself. Our bodies are not the enemy with which we have to do battle, but an intelligent, living system that wants to be well ... and given favorable conditions, the body will in most instances heal itself, and usually quite quickly. ***When we get sick, it is because we have violated the natural laws God established at creation to govern this body/temple of ours!*** If we want to be well, we must stop the violation and cooperate with our body by giving it what it needs to rebuild and restore itself. ***We must remember that our bodies are*** *self-healing when given the chance!*

### OUR SELF-HEALING BODY

Many people today believe they can dump anything they want into their bodies and that this garbage has nothing to do with their physical well-being. They also believe that when they get sick all they have to do is take some drug to remove that sickness. If we are going to be able to eliminate our present physical problems and live in abundant health, we must turn away from this kind of thinking.

Sickness is the result of unhealthy living and if health is to be restored, we must remove the causes of the illness and supply the conditions for health. Healing is a normal biological process programmed into our DNA, but to make it happen we must remove the causes of our physical problems. No true healing can take place without first removing the cause and then providing the body with its simple, basic needs so it can restore itself.

Sickness is usually not God's judgment upon us nor simply bad luck, but something we created ourselves by failing to observe God's natural laws. If we desire abundant health we must do more than wish or pray for it. We must make a commitment to good health by applying a diet and lifestyle that will produce it. More and more Americans are realizing that the medical/drug approach does not produce health.

Almost every one of us knows someone who was diagnosed with cancer, went the chemotherapy/radiation/surgery route with horrible results, and often died after spending their life savings. Today, in spite of the billions of dollars being spent on blood pressure medication, by-pass surgery and other heart care by drugs and physicians, 50 percent of our population dies of heart disease.

***The time is ripe for a revolutionary change in the way we look at health care.*** And the answer is not the kind of a reform advocated by President Clinton's Health Care Plan. ***True health will come only when each individual learns how to take care of their own self-healing body! The crying need of today is a HEALTH REVOLUTION, which will happen only through education!***

If the people of our great nation would apply what Hallelujah Acres teaches, we could save hundreds of billions of dollars in medical costs. Insurance premiums would be drastically reduced as the only insurance needed would be for accidents. Productivity would increase in the workplace, as healthy people work better and produce more, and no one would lose time due to sickness. Tax savings from health care through Medicare, veteran hospitals, etc. would be enormous and the savings could be used to eliminate the national debt. Here at Hallelujah Acres we also find that emotional problems usually disappear and weight normalizes. And there is so much more.

The secrets to abundant health are known and are being experienced by many. However, most people do not know the simple truths to creating abundant health and they need to be told how they can take charge of their own body and

Continued from the
left column of page 64

vegetables and fruit. I have been on nothing but the natural diet now for approximately four months and as a result my blood pressure is a solid 120/80, my weight is down to 174 for a loss of 47 pounds, and I have stopped all twelve medications and I can't remember when I have had more energy. I have not had a headache since I started on this diet. Now I see other people who are suffering from all sorts of problems and try to convince them that they can feel better too if they will just change their life-style, but they do not want to give up on what they think they have. If they would just realize that they are just dragging themselves down mentally and physically maybe to the point of no return. I am so thankful that my good Christian friend introduced me to this life-style change..."
– D.R., Tennessee

"A diet high in saturated fat and cholesterol provides the building blocks for coronary atherosclerosis. The role of diet in heart disease has been studied for years. What's new is that we now know diet affects the heart very quickly, not just over a period of years. Even a single meal high in fat and cholesterol may cause the body to release a hormone, thromboxane, which causes the arteries to constrict and the blood to clot faster. ... The good news is that improvements also can occur very quickly. ... We can make different lifestyle choices to begin healing ourselves. In our research, we found that blood flow to the heart could begin to improve in just a few weeks."
– Dean Ornish, M.D., *Dr. Dean Ornish's Program for Reversing Heart Disease*

be responsible for their own well-being. As each individual realizes and applies this knowledge in their own life, they need to tell others, and it will not be long before the whole world will realize *"you do not have to be sick."* The purpose of Hallelujah Acres is to make this information available to as many people as possible. Please pray for us as we try to change the way the world deals with sickness.

Perhaps you would like to help people in your community through our outreach program, Back to the Garden Health Ministries, described in Chapter 26.

# Chapter 8
# A Letter to Hillary Clinton

**An Open Letter from Rev. George Malkmus to:**
**HILLARY RODHAM CLINTON**
**SUBJECT: THE HEALTH CARE PROBLEM IN THE UNITED STATES**
**AND PROPOSED LEGISLATION TO CORRECT IT**

I come to you as a citizen of these United States of America to offer a solution to a problem that is not only causing tremendous suffering to our people … but is also bankrupting our great nation. Mrs. Clinton, I believe you sincerely want an answer to this dilemma, therefore I submit the following for your consideration:

**1.** *"Health is the largest failing business in America,"* says Prof. E. Cheraskin, M.D. of the University of Alabama School of Medicine. The health care crisis is slowly bankrupting our citizens and our country. Costs for health care are climbing four times faster than the rate of inflation. In 1992 we spent $817 billion on health care while 1993 is expected to have cost $942 billion. During 1994 it is projected to reach $1 trillion and by the turn of the century $2 trillion. The plan advanced by you and President Clinton *will not stop this constant increase in medical costs!* Actually, it will accelerate the rise in health care costs as more and more people are brought into a system that has already proven to be a failure.

"Don't let Drug Companies and Out-of-Date Doctors keep you in the dark. Open your eyes! …Tradition-bound doctors are able to cure only about 25% of the ailments they treat. Most of what they do is relieve symptoms until your body's natural healing mechanisms and immune system can finish the job … Expand your choices . . . Join the tiny minority who have decided to take charge of their own health … Let Nature work for you, not against you … Avoid drugs when you can: They're blocking agents with side effects that often fight your body's normal healing process. In general, you'll discover your body is capable of healing itself if you give it the right stuff." – Dr. Robert C. Atkins, M.D., from the Fall 1993 issue of *Tomorrow's Health*

> *"We are a sick nation even though we are spending more to treat sickness per capita than any other nation on earth … If the health of the American people is to be improved and if the staggering cost of health care is to be curbed, we must look outside the current and established systems."*

**2.** *We are a sick nation even though we are spending more to treat sickness per capita than any other nation on earth!* If our present methods of treating disease worked, wouldn't our people be healthier? If our advances in medical technology were heading in the right direction, wouldn't we be winning the war against cancer, heart disease and other killers? Consider these horrible statistics from the Statistical Abstract of the United States 1992, as published by the U.S. Department of Commerce:

\* Cardiovascular diseases affect 80% of all Americans;

\* 33% of all Americans develop cancer and it is projected to reach 50% by the year 2000;

* 6.5 million Americans suffer from diabetes;
* 77% of the adult population suffers from arthritic and rheumatic disorders;
* Over 25 million Americans suffer from asthma, bronchitis or emphysema;
* 16 million suffer from ulcers;
* 10 million are migraine sufferers;
* Over 50% suffer chronic digestive disorders;
* 80 million suffer from allergies;
* 22 million suffer mental illness;
* 98.5% of our population have bad teeth, and 31 million have no teeth of their own;
* 70-80% are overweight and 80 million are classified as obese;
* Nearly 90% of our children cannot pass a minimum physical fitness test.

These somber statistics are strong proof that the health of the American people is not getting better regardless of how much money is poured into *so-called* health care. *Also, these statistics reflect the poor health of our population even though over 70% of Americans already possess health insurance. Obviously, possessing health insurance does not produce health!* Sadly, the very drugs and treatments administered by our health-care professionals are the cause of many problems. (Over 25 percent of all hospital admissions are the result of adverse reactions caused by drugs prescribed by medical doctors.)

*3. Calling your proposed legislation a "Health-Care Plan" is a misnomer!* It would be more accurate to call the proposed plan a *"Disease-Care Plan."* The plan you and President Clinton have advanced *will not produce health*. On the contrary it will continue to perpetuate the same status-quo of sickness and ill health

> *"Our present health-care system is geared to provide what is most profitable for physicians, drug companies and hospitals – not to what is best for the people of our great land. This, Mrs. Clinton, is what must be changed if you and your husband wish to implement any true health-care reform."*

we presently face while costing more and more money.

*4. Countries that have plans similar to the one you advocate (e.g., Canada, England) have found it to be an increasingly more costly plan that just doesn't provide quality health care for all citizens as you say you want for the United States.*

*5. Our present health-care system is geared to rewarding sickness and its treatment!* It allows people that create their physical problems by improper diet and lifestyle to be rewarded when they get sick by providing them with health care, often paid for by those who take care of their bodies so as to maintain health. Your plan would also allow the physicians, hospitals and drug companies to make even larger sums of money because your plan promotes and perpetuates the *treating* of *symptoms* rather than the *prevention* of *disease!*

Physicians' incomes average $130,000 per year; surgeons and radiologists make over $200,000; cardiovascular surgeons $500,000; while the pharmaceutical industry takes in $55 billion a year, making it the nation's most profitable business.

*6. The plan you and President Clinton advance will increase our taxes and put even more money into a failing health-care system that, by any standards, offers ridiculously high costs and pathetically poor results.* It would be hard to imagine another American institution that offers less value per dollar. This is a system we must reform rather than expand, if we truly want to improve the health of the American people.

**If we are going to correct the above problems, A RADICAL CHANGE IS NECESSARY** – and it must be radically different from the wasteful, profit-oriented program that currently governs our health-care system.

Here is what I propose:

*1. Shift our emphasis to prevention of disease rather than the current goal of merely trying to treat disease after it has occurred. The public must be told how to alter their diet and lifestyle so that disease is not created in the first place.* This would be true health-care reform! *The proposed health-care reform is doomed to failure because it is geared to treating the symptoms of sickness rather than the causes of sickness!*

Dr. John Knowles, president of the Rockefeller Foundation says: *"the next major advances in the health of American people will come from the assumption of individual responsibility for one's own health and a necessary change in lifestyle."* With knowledge, people would then be able to intelligently choose between a system that promotes wellness through proper diet and lifestyle versus a system that promotes disease and rewards an industry with a vested interest in sickness and disease. The Department of Health, Education and Welfare says: *"it has become clear that only by preventing disease rather than treating it later, can we hope to achieve any major improvement in the nations health."*

*2. Educate the people!* True health-care reform will not result by rewarding people who continue their disease-producing diet and lifestyles. *Any health-care plan that does not have as its primary goal the education of the American people as to what they should and should not eat to produce wellness will fail!* It will only produce more physical problems and larger

> **From the book *Health & Survival* by Ross Horne:**
> "The diseases of civilization pandemic in the Western world threaten to ruin everybody, while modern medicine is powerless to stop them. For instance, the death rate from heart disease and cancer currently in the USA is just on one and a half million *every year* which, in one year mind you, is five times the total number of US servicemen killed in battle in the entire four years of US participation in World War II. And modern scientific medicine can do nothing about it.
>
> "Like Communism, now abandoned by the Russians, 'scientific' medicine has proven to be a failure and therefore so too is the 'health-care' system that is designed around it, in the fallacious belief that health can be restored into a sick body by the administering of drugs. At least Communism works in theory if not in practice, but our health-care system is wrong both in theory *and* in practice, and only goes to prove the law of diminishing returns: the more you put into it, the more useless it becomes. A medical system that thrives on ill-health is an expensive millstone we cannot afford to carry, and if not soon curbed it will lead us into bankruptcy. Medical dogma with its empty promises is no better than Communist dogma and its empty promises so, as with Communism, the time has come to abandon it ...
>
> "But there is a change in the wind, a stirring of awareness, and there are signs that a new era of enlightenment has begun. In regard to health matters, perhaps Dr. Alexis Carrel's prediction of 1936 has started to come true: 'Unless the doctors of today become the dieticians of tomorrow, the dieticians of today will become the doctors of tomorrow.' But time is running out ..."

> "My studies have proved conclusively that untreated cancer victims actually live up to four times longer than treated individuals...Beyond a shadow of a doubt, radical surgery on cancer patients does more harm than good."
> – Dr. Hardin Jones, prominent cancer researcher.

"Excluding skin cancer, the average cure rate of cancer by medical doctors is 17%."
– Edward Griffin, author of *World Without Cancer.*

expenditures of money.

Almost all sickness and disease is caused by improper diet and lifestyle, not by bacteria, viruses or inheritance as we have been led to believe by the medical industry. *The way to restore wellness to the American people is to teach them how to eat and live so as to create wellness.*

Dr. Beverly Winikoff of the Rockefeller Foundation in New York said: *"...There is a widespread and unfounded confidence in the ability of medical science to cure or mitigate the effects of such diseases once they occur. Appropriate public education must emphasize the unfortunate but clear limitations of current medical practice in curing the common killer diseases. Once hypertension, diabetes, arteriosclerosis or heart disease are manifest,*

*there is, in reality, very little that medical science can do to return a patient to normal physiological function. As awareness of this limitation increases, the importance of prevention will become all the more obvious."*

3. **Any new health-care plan must be one that encourages health by rewarding wellness and those who maintain health!** Most disease is self-induced by improper diet and lifestyle, thus, almost all sickness and disease is preventable by a diet and lifestyle that produces wellness. *Any health-care plan that does not place the responsibility for maintaining health*

# Doctors speak out on the need for health-care reform:

*"The greatest medical discovery of our time is the awesome power within the human body to heal and rejuvenate itself! This tremendous discovery is destined to change the way we practice medicine in America. In the future, instead of cutting the body...instead of drugging it ...instead of working against its natural systems...doctors will strive to feed and enhance the body's amazing power to self-heal. We're starting to see the shift in awareness already ... The medical establishment still seems to believe that nutrition cannot prevent disease, and is practically useless in treating it. Yet, we now have scientific proof that diet is the single most powerful tool for the treatment of disease. More powerful than drugs. More powerful than surgery. More powerful than anything in the doctor's bag. And you can do it yourself ... The medical profession is too narrow-minded to admit the enormous value of nutritional healing."*
- Julian Whitaker, M.D. in *Wellness Today*, July 1993

*"As a nation we have come to believe that medicine and medical technology can solve our major health problems. The role of such important factors as diet in cancer and heart disease has long been obscured by the emphasis on the conquest of these diseases through the miracles of modern medicine. Treatment not prevention, has been the order of the day. The problem can never be solved merely by more and more medical care ... Our greatest bulwark against the interests that have helped to create the present problems is an informed public."*
– Dr. Philip Lee, Professor of Social Medicine and Director, Health Policy Program, University of California, San Francisco

*"When people learn and practice 'the art of right living,' physicians may go back to their farms and workshops!"* – Dr. Issac Jennings, 1830

*"Gentlemen, I will never die of cancer. I am taking measures to prevent it ... It is caused by poisons created in our bodies by the food we eat ... What we should do, then, if we would avoid cancer, is to eat ... raw fruits and vegetables; first, that we may be better nourished; secondly, that we may more easily eliminate waste products ... We have been studying germs when we should have been studying diet and drainage ... The world has been on the wrong track. The answer has been within ourselves all the time ... Drain the body of its poisons, feed it properly, and the miracle is done. Nobody need have cancer who will take the trouble to avoid it."*
– Sir William A. Lane, England's foremost abdominal surgeon

*"I can't imagine a system that's more dysfunctional than the one we have now – more expensive, not doing the job, with more waste ..."* – Dr. Phillip Caper, medical policy analyst at Dartmouth Medical School

*"Our health care system is in crisis, bordering on chaos."*
– Former Surgeon General C. Everett Koop

*on the individual will fail!* If you feel it is necessary to continue paying for the medical treatments of those who refuse to change their diet and lifestyle, then please reward those who maintain wellness. A voucher system would be a tremendous incentive. Allot every American citizen X number of dollars a year for health care. If they don't spend it, then send them a check each year for the amount not used.

*4. Products that produce ill health should be removed from the market place or heavily taxed.* Let those who manufacture these unhealthy products and those who consume them help pay for the physical problems they produce. Some examples:

* *Tobacco* products cause most of the cases of cancer in the throat, lungs and stomach as well as a multitude of other physical problems including emphysema. Second-hand smoke, according to Paul Harvey, kills 2,000 Americans weekly.

* *Beverage alcohol* in any form is a destroyer, an addicting drug and a killer. Alcohol poisons the body, damaging the brain, heart, nerves, lungs and liver to mention only a few. Thousands die yearly from cirrhosis while the influence of alcohol kills 25,000 people on our highways and maims multitudes. At the same time it disrupts homes while causing child and spousal abuse and lowers productivity in the business place.

* *Caffeine* is an addictive drug found in coffee, tea, chocolate, soft drinks and many over-the-counter remedies. It causes birth defects, cardiovascular disease, and has been linked to cancer of kidney, pancreas, breast, ovaries, and large intestines.

* *Saturated Fat* is linked to over 50% of all deaths in America. If a person eliminates saturated fat from their diet, they would reduce their chances of ever having a heart attack or stroke by over 96%. Animal protein and fat is the main cause or a contributing cause in many cancers, including breast, prostate, colon and uterine. Saturated fat is also the main cause of adult-onset diabetes. Dr. John McDougal, M.D. wrote you a few months ago suggesting: *"Tax all unhealthy goods. You propose more taxes on cigarettes and alcohol. Great! But how about a 'fat tax.' Saturated fat could be taxed at 1 cent a gram, and all fats purposely added to a product would be taxed at 2 cents a gram. Under this system, a Big Mac would be taxed 24 cents per ounce..."*

* *Sugar* is another item creating untold suffering among our citizens, including tooth decay and all kinds of physical, mental and emotional problems. The average American consumes 50 teaspoons of sugar per day. Just one can of soda pop contains 10 teaspoons of sugar, which can immobilize the immune system by 30% for a whole day.

If we are going to improve the health of our people, we must warn them of the consequences of eating things that harm them. Calling the public's attention to the harm these products are doing by placing a tax and warning labels on them certainly would be a step in the right direction.

*5. Government-controlled institutions and agencies must not be allowed to use their powers to promote sickness and disease!* Some examples would be:

"...There is a widespread and unfounded confidence in the ability of medical science to cure or mitigate the effects of such diseases once they occur. Appropriate public education must emphasize the unfortunate but clear limitations of current medical practice in curing the common killer diseases. Once hypertension, diabetes, arteriosclerosis or heart disease are manifest, there is, in reality, very little that medical science can do to return a patient to normal physiological function. As awareness of this limitation increases, the importance of prevention will become all the more obvious."
– Dr. Beverly Winikoff of the Rockefeller Foundation in New York

\* Of the 129 state-accredited medical schools in America, only 29 require a course in nutrition. Doctors receive an average of less than three hours of nutritional training in medical school. This is outrageous! Doctors must become promoters of health through diet and lifestyle rather than just treaters of disease! The American Medical Association must be required to prepare a curriculum to teach doctors the value of nutrition in the prevention and treatment of disease.

\* The American Dietetic Association (ADA) is responsible for preparing the diets and approving all meals served in our public schools, jails, hospitals and to the elderly. An evaluation of these meals would show that they are high in sugar, saturated fat, sodium chloride and white flour, while being of little nutritional value. Some schools have even brought fast food restaurants right into their school cafeterias with the approval of the ADA. An evaluation of the meals served in our nation's hospitals would reveal a menu that *produces* sickness rather than helping to heal those hospitalized. This poisoning of our citizens through Government mandate and control must be stopped and the ADA must be required to teach dietitians the TRUTH about what is and what is not nutrition!

\* Each year, the USDA buys $3 to $4 billion worth of surplus foods (with tax payers' money), which it donates to the nation's schools. In 1991, 90% of the USDA surplus foods were eggs, high-fat cheeses, butter, ground pork, ground beef and whole milk. If the USDA had gone out intentionally to obtain foods that would destroy the health of our children, they could hardly have done better. This use of taxpayers' money to produce sickness in the youth of America is intolerable and must be stopped if we want to improve the health of our children.

***\* We are spending taxpayers' money to subsidize farmers to grow tobacco instead of vegetables.*** Then we pay for anti-smoking public education campaigns and treatment of cancer and heart disease caused by smoking. Why are we funding both sides of the war on cancer? If we are

*"Two years ago, the New England Journal of Medicine reported that in 1984, standard hospital procedures damaged 98,609, and killed 13,451 in New York State alone! Projected on a national scale, this means medical mistakes and malpractice might have harmed 1.4 million Americans, killing about 186,000 in one year. Name another industry which kills and maims so many people annually! Never has it been so IMPORTANT for you to be aware of your alternatives to conventional medicine. They could SAVE YOUR LIFE! . . .*

*Modern medicine is a business and doctors and hospital administrators are business people facing tremendous economic pressures these days. The temptation to order unnecessary procedures and tests is very real. Critics claim many doctors generate extra business by prescribing additional and sometimes unneeded services to make economic ends meet. This is shameful! But, look at the evidence...*

*\* It is estimated that perhaps 30% of all non-elective surgeries performed in the U.S. are NOT NEEDED!*

*\* An estimated half-million unnecessary Caesarean sections are being performed yearly, reports the Washington Post.*

*\* Up to 90% of all hysterectomies performed in the U.S. may NOT be needed!*

*\* Up to 85% of all bypass surgery is performed on patients who do not meet the criteria for benefit. (The AMA admitted this in its official journal!)...*

*\* 'Patients can no longer count on physicians to put their welfare first.' This is the sad message of Dr. Arnold Relman, past editor of the New England Journal of Medicine. He maintains that commercialization has so distorted the health system that it has already become 'difficult or impossible' for doctors to practice in a way that puts patients first.*

*\*Doctors' fees, hospital charges, and drug prices are the FASTEST-RISING prices on the Consumer Price Index. The growing commercialization of medicine has turned health care into a market-oriented system spinning out of control! Yet, for all the money we spend on health care, Americans are NOT getting healthier - just poorer!"*

**– Dr. Julian Whitaker, M.D., from the December 1993 issue of *Wellness Today***

going to use government subsidies to encourage farmers to grow specific crops, these should be healthful products.

    \* Even the Food Stamp program needs to be re-evaluated. While not allowing Food Stamps to be used for the purchase of alcohol and tobacco, Food Stamps can be used to purchase products loaded with sugar and oozing with saturated fat. ***The Government of these United States has a responsibility to its citizens not to use its power to promote or subsidize products that harm its people!***

    ***6. Please consider my own personal experience and the testimonials of others who have regained their health by something as simple as a change in diet.*** Approximately 18 years ago I lost my mother to colon cancer. She was a registered nurse who believed her doctors when they told her that chemotherapy, radiation and surgery were her only hope. At the time of her death, I felt it was the treatments and not the cancer that ultimately caused her death.

    Shortly after Mom's death, I was told I had colon cancer at age 42. Refusing to go the traditional medical route after seeing what it had done to mom, I opted for a change in diet and lifestyle. In less than one year, every physical problem I had was gone! Not just the cancer, but also high blood pressure, hemorrhoids, hypoglycemia, severe sinus and allergy problems, fatigue, even body odor and dandruff. I have maintained a vegetarian diet of at least 75 to 85 percent raw food, with daily consumption of carrot juice and Barley Green as a nutritional supplement for the past 18 years and have experienced absolutely no sickness … not even a cold, sore throat, headache or upset stomach. I have not taken as much as an aspirin or gone to a doctor. I'm in my 60s and I can still play football with the boys, jog five miles, and have more energy and endurance than I had when I was 20 years old.

    What made this change in my health possible was learning – and acting on the knowledge – that our bodies are living organisms made up of living cells that require living food (raw food) to function properly. Cooked food is dead food and has very little nutritional value. Cooking destroys all enzymes, about 83 percent of vitamin content, changes the molecular structure of the protein and turns organic minerals into an inorganic form unusable by our bodies. Unlike drugs and synthetic vitamins, which are toxic substances to our body, the nutrients of raw foods work with the body to invigorate its own healing capabilities. We teach that TRUE HEALING IS SELF-HEALING as we give the body proper building materials to heal itself.

    And my personal experiences are not unique! Several years ago I started a ministry called Hallelujah Acres in an effort to make what I had learned from my personal experience and research available to others. My book titled *"Why Christians Get Sick"* is now in its 9th printing while our publication titled *Back to the Garden* presently has a circulation of over 30,000. We also hold seminars all over the United States. What has been the results? Daily we receive testimonies from people who have applied our teaching and been made well from all kinds of physical problems by doing something as simple as changing their diet. Following are some testimonies. Please note that these are all real

*From the Hallelujah Acres mailbag:*

Pastor David Strong

"Keep on for Christ in your great ministry! You are giving folks *real Health Insurance*, instead of *Sickness* Insurance!! May the God of grace open His people's eyes!"
– Pastor David Strong, Calvary Baptist Church, New York

"Received your magazine *Back to the Garden* #6. It is just the best ever. George's letter to Hillary Clinton is just superb. I am so excited to see these facts being made available to so many people. I have so many friends and relatives that need to read this issue. Enclosed find check for …15 copies."
– R.B., Tennessee

people with real names and can be documented.

* *Dianne McKee* suffered for five years from severe abdominal pain. She had been to over 20 doctors, had four surgical operations, and was no better. Five days after changing her diet and lifestyle to what we teach here at Hallelujah Acres her pain was gone. Dianne changed her diet in early 1993 and has remained pain-free since that time.

* *Patsy Stockton,* a Pastor's wife on 130-140 units of injection insulin a day for her diabetes came to our seminar in January 1993. She also had high blood pressure, high cholesterol, sores in her mouth and she was overweight. Within three days after going on our program, her blood sugar had dropped from 371 to 112. In four months she was able to reduce insulin to four units, her blood pressure and cholesterol were normal, sores in her mouth were gone, liver spots on her hands and arms disappeared and she lost 48 pounds.

* *Rhonda,* my wife, (we were married in April 1992), came to my Seminar in January 1991. At that time she was overweight, wearing a size 20 dress, had severe debilitating arthritis and a degenerated spine and was unable to walk a block without severe pain. Since going on the nutritional program we teach here at Hallelujah Acres, she has lost over 80 pounds (down to a size 10 dress), her arthritis is gone, her degenerated spine is healed, she has had a dramatic increase in energy and speed walks four miles most every morning.

* *Becky McClellan* came to us six months ago after being debilitated by Multiple Sclerosis for seven years. She is now back to work, and takes care of her home and family. She said, "I feel like somebody handed me my life back this summer. I feel like I felt seven years ago."

* *Mary Payne* came to us in August 1992. At that time she was in extreme pain from rheumatoid arthritis, and her doctor had her on powerful pain medication. She could not get out of bed alone, could not dress herself alone. She was so ill that her husband had to comb her hair and brush her teeth. Her doctor told her she would be in a wheel-chair soon. She was also very overweight. Fourteen months after changing her diet and lifestyle to what we teach here at Hallelujah Acres, she has lost 105 pounds, is off all medication, all pain is gone and she says that all that remains of her arthritis is a little stiffness when she first gets up in the morning. Mary says she feels better than she has in over 20 years and is able to work in her garden again.

* *Carol Cover* had diarrhea for 22 months. She went the medical route for relief, which included many doctors, drugs and four trips to the Mayo Clinic. After 22 months of medical treatments she was down to 78 pounds and was dying. Within a few days after she changed her diet, her problem was gone!

These represent only a few of the testimonies from people who have adopted the program we teach here at Hallelujah Acres. And they continue to remain free of physical problems as long as they stay on this program.

*Mrs. Clinton, please investigate what I have shared.* Because of the financial profits from treating disease, you will find very limited support from those in the Medical Establishment for objective research into the benefits of preventative health care based on changes in diet and lifestyle. Modern science is learning much about the health benefits of eating fruits and vegetables, and the ways that vitamins, minerals and enzymes help our bodies to heal naturally. But still yet, most medical research is confined to looking for answers from pharmaceutical drugs, new surgical procedures, radiation, chemotherapy, etc. ... in other words, things from which the medical establishment can make a huge profit. It's sad to say, but the medical establishment has a tremendous financial incentive in keeping large segments of our population dependent on expensive surgical procedures, costly prescriptions and over-the-counter remedies consumed on a daily basis.

On the other hand, it's great when people are able to cure themselves simply by eating a natural diet and exercising. But this is an option discouraged in medical circles because there is no profit for doctors, hospitals, and drug companies. *Our present health-care system is geared to provide what is most profitable for physicians, drug companies and hospitals, not to what is best for the people of our great land. This, Mrs. Clinton, is what must be changed if you and your husband wish to implement true health-care reform.*

## CONCLUDING THOUGHTS

*If the health of the American people is to be improved and if the staggering cost of health care is to be curbed,we must look outside the current and established systems.* And I am not advocating the use of synthetic vitamins, herbs or homeopathic remedies as the solution. These substances, along with all drugs, only deal with symptoms caused by improper diet and lifestyle. What I am saying is that almost all physical problems are caused by putting into our bodies substances that they were never biologically designed to handle ... substances that are actually toxic to the body. Just as our automobile will not run properly if the wrong fuel is placed in the gas tank, neither will our bodies function properly if the wrong foods are put into them. *Almost all physical problems can be eliminated and perfect health can be maintained by proper diet and lifestyle!* My experience has even shown that when people adopt the diet and lifestyle we teach, most mental and emotional problems also disappear.

If I can be of assistance in any way, please do not hesitate to call on me. My life is committed to restoring our world to health and sane living.

Sincerely for a Healthy America,

Rev. George H. Malkmus
Eidson, TN
January 1994

"Many people already are aware that doctors are woefully ignorant in nutrition. Only about one-third of the nation's 125 medical schools require students to take courses in nutrition, and most of those courses are very brief. This is a shocking statistic, considering that 6 of the 10 leading causes of death are directly related to diet. Seven years ago, the National Academy of Sciences recommended that medical schools greatly expand their nutritional education, yet the number of medical schools requiring nutritional courses of any significant length is about the same as it was in 1980. Why is there such resistance to change? According to Dr. Marion Nestle, Chairwoman of the Department of Nutrition at New York University, the bottom line is money. Preventative health services such as nutritional counseling by doctors, are not reimbursable by the government or insurance agencies. Another factor is that new doctors need to make a lot of money to pay off the heavy expenses of medical school, so they gravitate to specialties that pay well. There are problems on other levels, as well. Because doctors aren't trained in nutrition, there aren't many physicians who are qualified to teach the subject – a self-perpetuating problem. ... According to one expert, the old guard is so firmly entrenched, improvement in the nutritional education of doctors cannot be instigated at the medical school level, but must be nationally mandated."
– Julian Whitaker, M.D., president of the American Preventative Medical Association

# Chapter 9

# Raw Food – God's Original Diet For Mankind

*By Rev. George H. Malkmus*

Confusion abounds as to what comprises the ideal diet. Many people are seeking a proper diet, but few are finding it – which is apparant from the tremendous number of physical problems people are experiencing today.

Why is there so much confusion? Why are so many suffering from so many physical problems? Part of the answer to these questions is because so much of the information concerning what we should be eating is contradictory! For instance, one voice says you need meat for protein and strength while other voices say meat causes heart attacks, strokes and cancer.

We have been told for years that cow's milk is a perfect food and is necessary for strong teeth and bones. Yet recently, Dr. Benjamin Spock and a large number of other medical doctors said cow's milk is not good for you and should never be given to children. How do we know what to believe or who to believe?

### What is the ideal diet???

When God created man, he placed him in a garden setting, and told him his diet was to consist of simply raw fruits and vegetables. Read Genesis 1:29. How did man fare on such a diet? He lived an average of 912 years without any recorded sickness. Following the flood in Genesis Chapter 7, meat was added to the diet (Genesis 9:3) and man started to cook his food. As a result of this change in diet, sickness entered the human race and man's life-span started to decline very rapidly ... from an average of 912 years prior to the flood to 100 years by the time you get to the end of the Book of Genesis!

In 1976, it

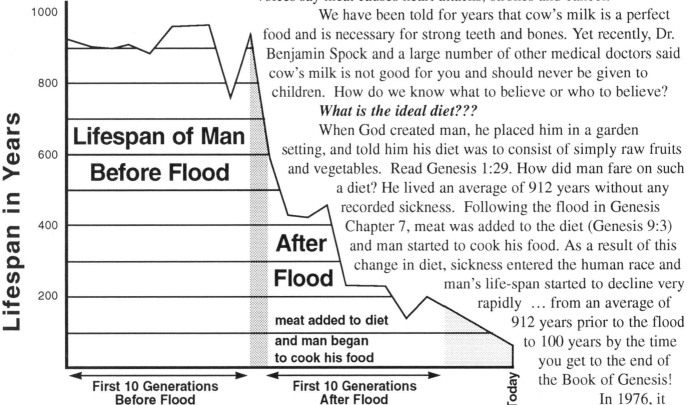

Lifespan in Years

1000

800

600 — Lifespan of Man

Before Flood

400

After

Flood

200

meat added to diet
and man began
to cook his food

First 10 Generations
Before Flood

First 10 Generations
After Flood

Today

76

was this same diet of raw fruits and vegetables – that God originally gave mankind in Genesis 1:29 – that saved my life and restored my health! And it has been this same diet that has kept me in perfect health with extremely high energy ever since!

So when people ask me, "What is the ideal diet?" I answer, "Based on all my personal experiences and research, without hesitation, I would have to say raw fruits and vegetables!"

This was the diet God originally gave to man. This was the diet that restored me to health in 1976, and has sustained me ever since. And this is the diet we see people turning to after they attend our seminars. Usually it takes only a short while before they return to tell us that their physical problems are "much better" or "totally gone."

Why did I and why do others experience such wonderful results after adopting a raw fruit and vegetable diet? Let me give an illustration that I hope will make it more understandable. Most people drive an automobile and realize they must put the proper grade of gasoline in the gas tank if it is going to run properly. If a low-grade fuel is used, it will ping and knock. If sugar is put in the gas tank, it will destroy the engine. Why? Because the engine was designed to run on a certain grade of fuel. We seem to understand that our car requires the proper grade of fuel in order to run properly, and so most people are very careful to put in good fuel.

Well, what about our body? Certainly, it is much more complex than any automobile engine. But what most people fail to realize is that God designed the human body to run on a certain grade of fuel also! If we give our bodies a low-grade fuel, or the wrong fuel, they won't run properly either.

Our body is made up of approximately one hundred trillion living cells. Each of these living cells has a DNA or blueprint of the cell that will be used to regenerate a new cell. As our cells die and are replaced by new cells, the new cell is totally dependent on the building materials available (the food we have been putting into our body). If the building materials have been poor, the new cell will be weaker than the cell it is replacing. If the building materials have been good, the new cell will be as strong as the cell it is replacing. If the building materials are superior, then the new cell will be stronger than the cell it is replacing. It is that basic and simple. We literally become what we eat!!!

Most people do not seem to realize that when food is cooked, almost all the nutritional value of the food is destroyed. All enzymes are destroyed by cooking. Approximately 83 percent of all vitamins are destroyed by cooking. The heat changes the protein into an unassimilable form, while the organic

---

*When God created man, He placed him in a garden and told him his diet was to consist of raw fruits & vegetables. On this diet, man lived an average of 912 years without sickness! Following the flood, meat and cooked food were added to man's diet. As a result, sickness entered the human race and man's life span declined from an average of 912 years to 100 years by the time you get to the end of Genesis!*

---

*From the Hallelujah Acres mailbag:*

"God bless you in your special ministry...We look forward to returning to the diet God originally planned for man."
– Rev. H.K., Alabama

"Medical fads and fashions come and go; thousands of new drugs are put on the market every year and thousands more taken off; but inner cleanliness and natural diet remain ever and always the most reliable ways to prevent and eliminate most diseases as well as maintain the best possible health... The raw foodist would enjoy a higher standard of living in a little hut than a junk food eater could in a palace. And raw foodism aids greatly in developing the spiritual maturity necessary for truly worthwhile achievements in life."
– Joe Alexander, author of *Raw Food Propaganda*

minerals our body so desperately needs are reduced to an inorganic, unusable form! Many put drugs in their body in the form of alcohol, nicotine and caffeine, all strong poisons! Then there are those who put drugs in the form of medicine into their bodies in an effort to try to correct physical problems caused by these low-grade fuels or poisons. But all these drugs do is mask the real problem and create new problems for which another drug must be taken. Every one of these drugs, even aspirin, is liver toxic – it damages the liver. It is a miracle our bodies survive as long as they do, with the improper fuel and the abuses we heap upon them.

Were our living bodies created to be sustained by dead, artificial food that has been cooked and radiated, processed, preserved with chemicals and adulterated with artificial flavors and sweeteners? And were our bodies meant to be repaired and healed by drugs, surgery, radiation, chemotherapy and other procedures of modern medicine?

If you wanted to know what type of fuel the automobile manufacturer intended to be used in your car, you might look in your owner's manual. Likewise, to learn what food God originally intended to be used as nutrition and sustenance for our bodies, let us look to the Bible.

Genesis 1:29 states, *"And God said, behold, I have given you every herb bearing seed, which is upon the face of the earth, and every tree, in the which is the fruit of a tree yielding seed; to you it shall be for meat."* Genesis 2:15 further states, *"And the Lord God took the man, and put him into the Garden of Eden to dress it and to keep it ... "*

I once saw a cartoon of a man and woman, each appearing to be in very poor health. The man was bald, and both had large protruding abdomens, wrinkles, arthritis, and were gross in appearance. The caption under the cartoon read: *"We've come a long way sweetheart."*

And yes, we have come a long way from the Garden of Eden where God first placed man. But it has been a journey in the *wrong direction!* God intended only good for man ... a long life on earth of love, health, peace and happiness while loving and serving his Creator and fellow man. And then ultimately to spend eternity with his Creator in Heaven. But is man experiencing this wonderful quality of life God intended? And if not, why not?

There are many theories as to what happened and why, and I have held several different thoughts myself down through the years. But the longer I observe the effects of various foods upon the human body, the more I am convinced that one of the greatest tragedies in history is the change in diet man made from the original raw vegetarian/fruitarian diet God gave to mankind in the Garden of Eden in Genesis 1:29 to one of meat and cooked and artificial foods.

When God created man, He designed him to run on only one kind of fuel – **RAW FOOD!!!** Man's body is a living organism, made of living cells, which require living food in order to be properly nourished and function well. When we put cooked food into our body, loaded with contaminants, the body starts to break down. It begins in the very young with colic, rashes, colds, earaches, upset stomachs, swollen glands and tonsils. As the child grows older, there may be tooth decay, pimples and the need for eye glasses. Then as we enter adult life there is arthritis, hypoglycemia, heart attacks, strokes, diabetes and cancers. *All this and a multitude of other diseases are unnecessary and are nothing but the result of improper diet and lifestyle!*

Those who profit from sickness have led us to believe these physical problems are natural, and that when we get sick we are just the innocent victims of some bacteria, germ or virus, or that we inherited these problems. They then tell us that the human body is a complex organism only they can understand so we must trust them and their expensive drugs, radiation and surgeries as our only hope for alleviating these problems. Yet their track record is horrible. We see people getting sicker and sicker. But Americans, including the Christian community, have accepted their teachings hook, line and sinker, while the state of health in America continues to decline and the cost of this so-called health care continues to escalate. The cost for "Health Care" in America in 1994 was over one trillion dollars ($1,000,000,000,000.00)!

So what is the answer? *At Hallelujah Acres we teach that the present approach to diet and health is totally wrong and completely contrary to the way God intended!* And that the only solution, if we are going to turn things around, is a return to God and a return to the *Garden* where God first created and placed man! Yes, we must get *Back to the Garden* where human life began and back to the way God intended us to live and be nourished. What I am suggesting is that we should put some thought into the types of food that God designed to nourish our bodies. There are only four substances that nourish our bodies. They are fresh, pure *air,* pure *water,* moderate amounts of *sunlight*, and *raw food! That's it! Anything else is a contaminate to the body and has an adverse effect on our health.*

The human body is a masterpiece, created by God! The Bible says *"We are fearfully and wonderfully made!"* (Psalm 139:14). The human body is a living organism made of living cells that are constantly in the process of dying and replacing. These living cells require proper building materials to function and reproduce themselves as God intended.

God provided the raw materials needed to sustain life all around us in nature. If we look at the rest of the animal kingdom that God also created, we see that every other animal, with the exception of man, feeds on raw food. Then further, when we look at the animal kingdom, except where contaminated by man, there is no sickness! Today, over 90 percent of the people die in America from three types of illness: heart disease (50% of all deaths), cancer (33% of all deaths) and diabetes (8% of all deaths). Is this the kind of life God planned for man? Or

is it the result of man deviating from God's plan? Our research and experience shows that God made no mistakes, but that man has made a colossal mistake by straying from God's ways and is thus paying a horrible price for this departure. *"My people are destroyed for lack of knowledge."* **(Hosea 4:6)**

We live in an age of almost total ignorance when it comes to the Laws of Life established by God at creation. The sad part of this is that most Christians are just as ignorant of these laws as the rest of the world. In fact, most Christians, in ignorance, have rejected God's laws and accepted the world's teachings in almost all areas that relate to physical life. Most Christians are living in ignorance and dying in distress rather than seeking knowledge and truth in this area. Most people today accept the teachings of this world's so-called authorities as gospel rather than searching the Scriptures to see *"whether those things be so"* (Acts 17:11). Today we accept and, in a sense, worship science and everything science teaches, never questioning whether their pronouncements are truth or not.

The other day I was watching the evening news and there was a scientist being questioned by a Senate sub-committee concerning the harmful effects of cigarettes. This scientist was asked if smoking was addictive. His answer was "absolutely not." He was asked if smoking caused lung cancer. Again his reply was "absolutely not." When a senator challenged his answers, this scientist stated that he only believed that which was scientifically verifiable.

---

**Excerpts from the article "Why Unfired Foods?"**
**by Dr. John Michael Douglas, from *Alive and Well On Planet Earth*, Issue I:**

"Thirty years ago, I went to medical school to study the healing principle. Only in 1990 did I finally learn it after having seen 100,000 patients, experimenting on myself for 19 years and reading tens of thousands of scientific books and articles...

"Hippocrates once said, 'The gods do not send illness to men. Men bring it on themselves.' If we take a minute to stop and analyze this statement, it becomes clear that barring natural catastrophes, man holds the key to his own health in his own hands. And firing (cooking) food makes the world and its inhabitants ill.

"When we eat what nature provides for us it serves us much better if we leave it alone. We must eat what nature gives us as close to 'as grown' as possible...I have spent my entire medical career studying how to be healthy and how to keep patients from falling prey to disease. It has been during these studies that I feel I have found the optimal way of eating for health maintenance, disease prevention and weight loss...

"When we treat food with thermal fire, we lose up to 97% of the water soluble vitamins (Vitamins B and C) and up to 40 percent of the lipid soluble vitamins (Vitamins A, D, E, and K). We also decrease the absorption of protein ... Heating also changes the lipids from cis, which is a curved form occurring in nature, to trans forms. Hydrogenated oils, such as margarine, shortenings and many of the other oils that are used in bakery products or to heat french fries, are in the trans form.

"These are incorporated into the cell wall and interfere with the respiration of the cell so that we find an increase in cancer and heart disease in those people eating the trans fats. The medical community has been continually collecting evidence to support what I discovered some years ago: *Cooked food is harmful to our bodies...*

"Wild animals know what to eat but it has become quite obvious that we do not. We might do better to take a lesson from nature's creatures. You won't see a lion eating cooked food, or a leopard dropping his kill of an antelope into a volcano before he eats it. The king of the beasts and all his underlings eat unfired/raw foods and that's all...

"The answer to the question, 'Why unfired foods?' Simple! Fired (cooked) foods are making each individual, our race and the world sick. Only by using unfired foods can we make ourselves, our race and the world healthy once again."

*Dr. John Michael Douglas, M.D., PhD., Dr.P.H., F.A.C.P. Dr. Douglas has practiced internal medicine for 19 years, with subspecialties in health improvement and engineering biomedicine. He holds two doctorates, in public health and philosophy in health principles. He has done 20 years of research on how lifestyle and nutrition can improve the health of people and the ecosystem.*

When the Senator asked him if he realized that there were very few who would agree with him, he simply replied "I am a scientist!" It often appears that scientists' findings are based upon personal philosophies or who is paying their paycheck rather than on truly scientific, verifiable fact!

As children in school, we accepted the four basic food groups as gospel, in the name of science. We accept as fact the teachings of government agencies who use supposedly scientific calculations to tell us of the nutritive value and the percentages we need of protein, vitamins, minerals, etc., never questioning whether this information could be just as false as that of the scientist who said smoking was harmless.

We also blindly accept the medical profession's teaching as to why we get sick. Then we accept their drugs, radiation, chemotherapy and surgery as the only means of dealing with sickness. Even though this medical approach is making us sicker and sicker, exhausting our savings and even killing people, we never seem to question the validity of these teachings. The Bible says in Romans 12:2 *"Be not conformed to this world,"* and yet the average Christian, in ignorance, has conformed to this world in almost every area that deals with physical life, and is paying an extremely heavy penalty.

> *Without realizing it, man has stepped into the arena in defiance of God and changed natural raw food made by God into a man-made, artificial, non-living, processed product we call "food." All this because man thinks he must improve on the way God made raw food.*

The Christian community of today is just as sick as non-Christians because they have accepted and practiced the teachings of the "authorities" of this world (government, science, medical, big business and even religion) as truth. As a result, the Christian community lives in constant violation of almost every fundamental principal of life God established when it comes to the body/temple God gave us and how we should live here on earth. We violate God's principles by what we feed our bodies and minds, and then when they break down, we violate God's principles in how to get well. Yes, sadly, the Christian community has conformed to the world to which God said *"be not conformed."*

Take an honest look at the world around you and see if what I am saying is not true. Look at the leaders of this world and you will see that these leaders, despite their political or religious philosophies, all have one thing in common: ***They are sick!*** Politicians and government leaders are sick! Scientists are sick! Educators are sick! Medical doctors are sick! Yes, just as sick as their patients! Business leaders are sick! Economists are sick! Even pastors, evangelists and missionaries are sick! All manifest every sort of physical problem and are dying premature deaths as a result of these sicknesses. How can we expect to have a healthy world when all our leaders, even the ones we look to for guidance in what to eat and how to take care of illness, are sick also? It is like the blind leading the blind.

Based on my personal experiences of living over 60 years, my conviction is that the two most important things we must learn in this life are: (1) How to

*From the Hallelujah Acres mailbag:*

"Praise God I heard you on 3 A.B.N. Immediately I went onto a raw foods only. Was tired, no ambition, pain, couldn't sleep, had to lift left leg into and out of car. Today is my 28th day of raw foods ... and my symptoms are gone!"
– Kathryn Cook, Oregon

nourish and properly care for this body/temple while here on planet earth, and (2) How to be properly prepared for the next life when this one has come to an end!

Yet, it was not until the age of 23, after attending church for most of my life, that I learned I must personally prepare for the life to come by receiving Jesus as my Lord and Saviour. And it wasn't until I was 42 years of age that I learned how to take care of my body/temple and control my physical health while here on earth.

One of the most thrilling things I ever learned was how to be healthy. For over 40 years I was in ignorance as to what I should eat and how I should live. I was thrilled at the age of 42 to realize I could control my health simply by how I lived and what I ate. How sad that it took me until I was 42 years old and experiencing a potentially life-threatening physical problem before I learned I could eliminate sickness and live free of disease if I would but simply obey God's natural laws concerning my body/temple.

God's natural laws are so simple that when the true nature of disease is understood, sickness is no longer a mystery. It is so thrilling to know that health can almost always be restored without drugs, chemotherapy, radiation and surgery, and that physical problems can almost always be eliminated by simply applying God's natural laws. If we experience sickness or disease, along with the resulting misery and suffering and financial cost, we have no one else to blame but ourselves. This is called personal accountability, something we shy away from in this present day, in which we want to blame someone or something else for all our problems.

After reading my books and other literature or listening to my seminars on health and nutrition, many people are adopting the diet of primarily raw foods that we teach here at Hallelujah Acres. The results are that multitudes have found almost every physical problem they were experiencing to simply disappear … from headaches and stomach disorders to arthritis, heart disease, diabetes and even cancer. Most of these were people who had applied the diet and healing methods of this world for years and some were even given up by doctors as terminal. Yet when they changed their diet and lifestyle they almost always get well, usually within a few short months. With the diet God intended for mankind, our bodies can become immune to almost all disease and we can look forward to a healthy life well past 100 years, free of disease and sickness as well as mental and emotional problems.

If we would but return to God's ways of nourishing the body, we could practically eliminate sickness from the face of the earth and man would die only of accidents or old age at about 120 years (Genesis 6:3). You see, when we cook our food, we destroy its nutritional value, and we force the organs of our body to work overtime to remove the toxic residue, which tires the body, produces illness, and shortens human life to only a fraction of what God intended.

Addiction to cooked food begins shortly after birth when mother tries to force cooked food (usually cereal) into the mouth of the young child. The child detests the taste of this cooked food and usually will attempt to reject this dead food by spitting it out. But, in ignorance, the mother will continue to force that cooked food into the baby's mouth until accepted (thinking this is nourishment the baby must have to grow and be healthy) ... and thus the cooked food addiction begins. This cooked food often produces crying by the baby as this unnatural food causes organs to be taxed to their limit trying to get rid of these toxic substances. Cooked food (especially pasturized milk) causes colic, restless nights, stomach ailments, fevers, rashes, swollen tonsils and glands and more as that tiny baby's body reacts to this unnatural food substance its DNA was never encoded to receive. One of the most cruel injustices we commit as parents is when we place cooked (pasteurized) milk, cooked cereal and cooked baby foods into the beautiful living body of little children designed by God to be nourished *only* with raw, living foods!

Today, most people accept cooked food as the normal means of supplying the body with nutrients, not realizing that the living cells of our bodies do not take nourishment from the dead and artificial ingredients found in cooked food. And so, after a typical meal of *cooked* meat, *cooked* potatoes, a *cooked* vegetable and a piece of *cooked* bread, followed by a *cooked* sugar desert, their stomach is full and they think they have satisfied the nutritional needs of their body. In reality, they have given their body practically no nourishment. And thus with a full stomach, they are slowly starving their body's cells.

Take the bread in that meal as an example. The miller takes the living grain of wheat and removes the outer shell called the bran (fiber) and it is either thrown away or sold in a health food store. Then he removes the germ (which contains all the nutrients) because it gums up his machinery. The germ also is often sold in a health food store. Then he takes what is left, which is called the endosperm, and grinds it into fine powder. But this powder is not pure white, so he bleaches it, often with a bleaching agent similar to Clorox. Now the flour is ready for the rest of the ingredients and baking ... *but it contains zero fiber and zero nutrition!* Knowing the public will not buy a product that does not have at least some nutritive values posted on its wrapper, the bread maker puts into this dead, fiberless, nutritionally-void substance, some artificial, coal-tar derived, vitamins and minerals which have been known to cause cancer. Now he can label it "enriched" and pass it on to the unsuspecting public as something that is supposed to be good food. Yet there is still no fiber and no real nutrition! And it is this type of so-called food we put into our beautiful body/temple that God created to be nourished only by living food. And I haven't even mentioned the other poisons added to that loaf of bread – sugar, salt, dough conditioners, preservatives, etc.

Then there are those who realize the miller has taken all of the goodness out of the flour, so they mill their own flour from organic wheat and other organic grains, thus believing they are leaving in the nutrients. They don't realize that when they bake that bread, the heat destroys almost all nutrients. Certainly, this is less harmful than the commercial product, but just as dead.

Without realizing it, man has stepped into the arena in defiance of God

*From the Hallelujah Acres mailbag:*

"I can see that the Lord has blessed you in so many ways to help others. In short, we are so very grateful for your ministry ... Since being at your place, we've gotten off meat. I'm also off all medicine and eating raw until the last meal of the day ... I am improving constantly from my candida problem" – Kurt and Jane Preuss, Missionaries to France

and changed natural raw food made by God into a man-made, artificial, non-living, processed product we call "food." Look at animals in nature and you will see they too have heart, lungs, kidneys, blood, flesh, bones, brain and so on, yet they are properly nourished and thrive on simple, raw foods provided by nature. The cow, horse and elephant eat grass or leaf and turn that raw material into everything they need to build and maintain a healthy, strong body. Yet man thinks he must improve on the way God made raw food.

*All food, as found in nature is* **RAW,** and consists of the same basic three elements: (1) naturally distilled water, (2) roughage or fiber, and (3) nutrients. The purest water known to man is found in raw fruits and vegetables, and water constitutes approximately 70% of our body. Roughage is necessary to keep the colon clean and functioning properly, while the lack of it causes constipation. Nutrients make up the smallest part of plant life, but when received into our body in raw, natural form provide *all* we need to be properly nourished.

*God made no mistakes when He created earth, nature and man. He did not fail to provide man with everything he needed to be properly nourished so we could experience perfect health. Man has erred by attempting to improve on what God made by cooking and processing food.*

This is just as true in man as with the rest of the animal kingdom.

All edible raw plants consist of almost the same elements, differing only in proportions, color, and taste. All plant and animal life is but an ongoing exchange and circulation of atoms. The seed sprouts, sends fourth a shoot, develops branches and leaves and ultimately bears the fruit (or vegetable). Then it is consumed by an animal or man and becomes skin, heart, liver, blood, etc., which eventually returns to the ground. It is an ongoing cycle that is repeated over and over again and has been since creation. But for this cycle to be complete and function properly, things *must be in a raw, living form.*

A scientist tries to analyze the nutrients, and tells us how many milligrams of each vitamin we need or how many grams of protein we need daily to be properly nourished. Then he takes these nutrients out of the natural foods or concocts similar nutrients artificially and sells them to us as vitamin, mineral or protein supplements. Then he tells us we need to take these manufactured, unnatural products in order to be properly nourished.

The difference between natural, raw foods versus cooked, processed foods and synthetic vitamins is the very difference between life and death. Raw foods are alive. Cooked, processed foods and synthetic vitamins are dead. But nowhere in any government nutrition table is there a distinction made between live foods and dead foods, or live nutrients and dead nutrients. Man cannot create life in a laboratory so scientists, nutritionists and medical doctors ignore the difference between food that is alive and food that is dead. The nonsense these scientists, nutritionists and medical doctors are presenting as fact is an absurdity. We must turn away from their foolish pronouncements and turn back to God and return *Back to the Garden* where God first placed mankind so we can learn how to be properly nourished and live in health as God intended.

*From the Hallelujah Acres mailbag:*

"... We get more excited every day as we listen, read and share your videos, tapes, book and *Back to the Garden.* Thank you! Thank you!! Thank you!!! We have a new motto: **TRUST THE RAW!** We are suggesting people may call us: **RAW TOTALLERS.** We are getting results in our own health, and in our patients. We are most thankful. All glory to God! Bless you for letting Him use you so powerfully for world betterment!"
– Nigel Buxton, M.R.C.S., L.R.C.P. (Royal College of Surgeons, Royal College of Physicians) & Elmira Buxton, M. D., Ontario, Canada

Take a look at the physical condition and health of the animals in the wild, feeding on natural raw nutrients as provided by God. Then look at the physical condition and health of man trying to live on tampered and altered food, and you tell me who is the smartest and who has the most common sense … the donkey who eats the raw grass or the man who eats cooked, artificial, poisoned foods and synthetic vitamin, mineral and protein supplements. Man is foolish to cast doubt on God's eternal wisdom. Every step man takes away from providing the human body with nutrition in its natural, living form is a step toward disease and an early grave.

What Hallelujah Acres teaches is a radical, yet simple change in the way mankind nourishes the body. This change, if adopted by all, would practically eliminate sickness from the earth. What we are teaching here at Hallelujah Acres is of such great humanitarian importance that it should be given immediate attention by political and religious leaders. If after basic and simple experiments, what I am proposing proves to be true, then all teachings to the contrary must be abandoned and this information must be made available to all mankind. If on the other hand, what I am teaching proves to be false … then it must be proclaimed that George Malkmus and Hallelujah Acres are wrong and our teachings are heretical.

Here is what I propose: After removing the drugs, place all the patients from just one hospital on the Hallelujah Diet for 90 days and compare the results with that of another hospital with an equal number of patients, using drugs and cooked food. Do the same thing in a mental institution and a jail. If those in authority would allow this to be done, and the results made public on the evening news, it would change the world in a very short time. This type of experiment could become a reality some day if our political and medical leaders sincerely wanted to help mankind, rather than to merely protect their political office and financial interests.

It is so sad that the only studies the medical establishment wants to conduct are those based on cooked food, drugs, radiation and surgery to deal with disease. Why do they hesitate to use raw food in their testing? Why do they then say there is not sufficient evidence of any benefit from a raw food diet, **when they are the ones who refuse to conduct any tests!** And they reject all independent research. Could it be that those who make tremendous profit from sickness know that if verifiable tests were conducted and this information made public, they would be out of business?

If what we teach here at Hallelujah Acres proves to be true, as it already has proven to be true to myself and the multitudes of raw eaters around the world who have experienced the removal of all sickness by simply applying

*From the Hallelujah Acres mailbag:*

"Thank you for your testimony. I have been on a raw diet for about 12 years and am a totally different person . . . I advocate it to all my friends."
– Betti Becker, California

## The Pottenger Cat Experiments On Raw & Cooked Food

One of the best-known studies of raw versus cooked foods with animals was a 10-year research project conducted by Dr. Francis M. Pottenger, using 900 cats. His study was published in 1946 in the *American Journal of Orthodontics and Oral Surgery*. Dr. Pottenger fed all 900 cats the same food, with the only difference being that one group received it raw, while the others received it cooked.

The results dramatically revealed the advantages of raw foods over a cooked diet. Cats that were fed raw, living food produced healthy kittens year after year with no ill health or premature deaths.

But cats fed the same food, only cooked, developed heart disease, cancer, kidney and thyroid disease, pneumonia, paralysis, loss of teeth, arthritis, birthing difficulties, diminished sexual interest, diarrhea, irritability, liver problems and osteoporosis (the same diseases common in our human cooked-food culture). The first generation of kittens from cats fed cooked food were sick and abnormal, the second generation were often born diseased or dead, and by the third generation, the mothers were sterile.

what we teach, then it must be given the very highest priority by all who have the means of disseminating this information to enlighten those who are killing themselves in ignorance.

God made no mistakes when He created this universe, planet earth, nature and man. He did not fail to provide man with everything he needed to be properly nourished so we could experience perfect health. It is man who has attempted to improve on what God made. It is man who has taken the natural food as served up to him by nature to meet our total nutritional requirements and corrupted these God-given foods. It is man who has doubted God's wisdom and provision and replaced it with his own folly. It is man who has corrupted God's ways, and it is man who is paying a very heavy penalty for the changes he has made.

Our bodies will usually literally heal themselves when we stop putting into them that which has caused our physical problems, and then provide the body with the proper building materials to rebuild. Here at Hallelujah Acres, we receive word daily, from all over the world, from people who have adopted the Genesis 1:29 diet, and have been healed … often problems they have had for 10, 20, 30 years or more, are better or gone in a few days to a few months.

Yes, God's

---

## The Great American Rat Experiment: Raw Food Vs. the Cooked, American Diet

The following is an account of an interesting three-part experiment comparing the effects of raw foods versus cooked foods with rats. This account is taken from a book titled *Goldot,* by Lewis E. Cook, Jr. and Junko Yasui:

"It has been found that a group of rats were fed diets of raw vegetables, fruits, nuts and whole grains from birth grew into completely healthy specimens and never suffered from any disease. They were never ill. They grew rapidly, but never became fat, mated with enthusiasm and had healthy offspring. They were always gently affectionate and playful and lived in perfect harmony with each other. Upon reaching an old age, equivalent to 80 years in humans, these rats were put to death and autopsied. At that advanced age their organs, glands, tissues and all body processes appeared to be in perfect condition without any sign of aging or deterioration.

"A companion group of rats were fed a diet comparable to that of the average American and included white bread, cooked foods, meats, milk, salt, soft drinks, candies, cakes, vitamins and other supplements, medicines for their ailments, etc. During their lifetime these rats became fat and, from the earliest age, contracted most of the diseases of modern American society including colds, fever, pneumonia, poor vision, cataracts, heart disease, arthritis, cancer and many more.

"Most of this group died prematurely at early ages but during their lifetime most of them were vicious, snarling beasts, fighting with one another, stealing one another's food and attempting to kill each other. They had to be kept apart to prevent total destruction of the entire group. Their offspring were all sick and exhibited the same general characteristics as the parents.

"As this group of rats died one by one or in epidemics or various diseases, autopsies were performed revealing extensive degenerative conditions in every part of their bodies. All organs, glands and tissues were affected as were the skin, hair, blood and nervous system. They were all truly total physical and nervous wrecks. The same conditions existed in the few which survived the full duration of the experiment.

"A third companion group of rats was fed the same diet as the second group to an age equivalent to about 40 years in humans. They displayed the same general symptoms of the second group – being sick and vicious so that they had to be separated to prevent them from killing each other and stealing one another's food.

"At the end of this initial period all rats in this group were placed on a strict fast, with only water to drink for a period of several days. Then they received the natural (raw) diet of the first group of rats. This diet was alternated with periods of fasting and within one month the behavioral pattern had changed completely so that the now docile, affectionate, playful creatures were once again able to live together in a harmonious society and from this point on *never suffered any illness.*

"Several rats were put to death and autopsied at the end of the initial period revealing the same general deterioration as that exhibited in the second group of rats. However, the remaining rats lived out the full duration of the experiment, to the equivalent of 80 years in humans, and when they were autopsied there were no signs of aging or deterioration or disease - just as those in the first group. The obvious disease, degeneration and deterioration of body parts evident in their first half of life had been completely reversed and excellent health restored.

"The same principles apply to human life as there is only one TRUTH! Thus it may be concluded that sick people may be restored to health simply by choosing the proper diet, fasting and observing the other rules of health. There is no mystery. There is no external force that will help - all healing being accomplished within the body by the body in accordance with the laws of organic life and health."

Original Diet does work!

So, what can you and I do to turn things around? First, if we have already experienced the benefits of raw eating in our own lives, we must share this information and our own personal testimonies with others. (Back to the Garden Health Ministries is an excellent means of doing this. See Chapter 26.) If you know these truths and yet have not been living this way, why not adopt this diet so that you can be an example to others? If you have not yet tried this way of eating, I challenge you to try it for 90 days. And then, let's all catch the vision of a world without sickness and do what we can to make it happen. May God help each of us as we seek to bring this world back to Him who created it all and **Back to the Garden** where man's life on earth began!

"The greatest change of the whole life of man and of all conditions and aspirations of his nature came with the discovery of fire...The taste of cooked food, once acquired, has proved the curse and the bane of mankind ever since. With the help of fire, man has been enabled to render edible things altogether foreign to his digestive apparatus...As the years went by, man became more and more short-lived, and more and more subject to disease and ailments."
– Dr. O.L.M. Abramowski in *Fruitarian Diet and Physical Rejuvination.*

# Chapter 10

# The Hallelujah Diet

*By Rev. George H. Malkmus*

In 1962, Dr. Frank Logsdon, former pastor of the famous Moody Memorial Church in Chicago, was a dinner guest in my home. At dinner, he told a fascinating story of how he had had cancer and, rather than going the medical route, had gone to the Page Institute in Tampa, Florida.

At this institute, he was told to remove five white foods from his diet, and to switch to a raw vegetarian / fruitarian diet. He had done this and his cancer disappeared! Dr. Logsdon was about 60 years old at the time he was in my home. Several years ago, I learned he was still preaching . . . which would put his age close to 90 now!

Interestingly, the five white foods he was told had caused his cancer are the same foods my research has shown to be causing most of our physical problems.

What are the five white foods causing our physical problems? I will list them, starting with the most dangerous substance we put into our body: MEAT!

MEAT contains white fat! The average American meat eater puts over 50 pounds of fat (cholesterol) into his body per year! This fat clogs the arteries, ultimately causing the heart attacks and strokes that will kill approximately 50 percent of our population.

Meat is also the culprit in causing colon cancer, breast cancer, prostrate cancer and other forms of cancer. Cancer is responsible for 33 percent of American deaths.

And meat is the primary cause of adult-onset diabetes, which kills 8 percent of our population. Meat also causes gout and arthritis and a host of other physical problems.

We are told that we need meat for protein and strength, but we are not told that the cooking of meat changes the molecular structure of the protein and renders the protein in meat unusable by the body. If we look to nature, we will find that there is not a single animal in the wild that cooks the flesh it eats! ***Eighteen years of research has revealed meat as it is produced today to be the*** *single most dangerous food that we put into our body.* I have not eaten any meat since 1976.

DAIRY is the second most dangerous substance we can put into our bodies for many of the same reasons. We are told milk is the perfect food and that it is needed for calcium. But we are not told that the pasteurizing of milk (heating it to temperatures of 160 degrees or higher) changes the calcium to an inorganic form, which cannot be assimilated by the body.

In nature, no animal pasteurizes its milk . . . and no animal drinks the milk of another animal, nor does it ever drink milk after the age of weaning. The only source of bad cholesterol (LDL) is animal products! *Animal products are not good food!!!*

SALT is another white substance that creates untold physical problems and suffering. The body needs sodium, but it must be in an organic form in order to be usable by the body. Table salt, sodium chloride, is an inorganic sodium compound formed by the union of sodium and chlorine that is extremely toxic to the body, causing it to retain fluid in an effort to keep this protoplasmic poison in suspension and out of the cells.

> **Why should any Christian be surprised to find that modern science and personal experience confirm that "God's Original Diet" of raw fruits and vegetables (Genesis 1:29) is the ideal diet for mankind?**

SUGAR is the fourth white substance creating our physical problems. Sugar is so denatured and concentrated from its original plant form that it is actually a drug! Just 10 teaspoons (approximately the amount found in one soft drink) will immobilize the immune system by about 33 percent. Approximately 30 teaspoons of sugar will shut down the immune system for a whole day.

WHITE FLOUR has had all the good substances (bran and germ) removed during processing. Then it is bleached, sometimes with a bleaching agent similar to clorox. Finally, they add some coal-tar-derived (carcinogenic) vitamins and it is sold to the unsuspecting public as "enriched." White flour is not good food; in fact it is hazardous to your health! It clogs up your intestines, creates excess mucus in your sinus passages and white flour depletes your nutrient levels as your body works to digest it.

In addition to these five white substances, we must also consider the impact of commonly used drugs on our bodies. Most people are aware of how dangerous alcohol and nicotine are to the body, but fail to realize that the caffeine in coffee, tea and soft drinks is also an extremely dangerous substance! Caffeine is called a stimulant because it excites all of the nerve endings in an effort to rid the body of this poisonous substance. If a person drinks over two or three cups of coffee a day on a regular basis, they will usually develop severe drug withdrawal headaches if they suddenly stop drinking it. Alcohol, nicotine and caffeine are dangerous drugs!

Now that we have briefly covered the substances that are creating most of our physical problems, let us look at the foods that nourish and heal our body.

The ideal diet for man is raw fruits and vegetables. This opinion is based

*From the Hallelujah Acres mailbag:*

"...I have only been on this diet (Hallelujah Diet) since the 4th of December 1993 but I have already felt such a difference. I have more energy and feel better than I have in 30 years ...God bless you - this is a real ministry. I thank God that He put me in contact with you."
– Bernie Veenkant, Florida

"Thank you! We heard your tape ... My husband lost one eye to diabetes and we are trying to save the other eye. As of August 3rd (after he went on the Hallelujah Acres Diet) ... from the first day it is the first time in 20 years his blood sugar has been in normal range and has stayed in normal range every day since. Thank you again."
– Charles & Retha Stewart, Texas

"Michigan will not be the same since we came to see you last week. We have gone cold turkey, no more meat in our diet. I am drinking my 4 glasses of carrot juice each day and 4 tablespoons of Barley Green ... I tell everyone about our new life, praise God. I feel 75% better already!"
– Don Shackelton, Michigan

on my scientific and nutritional research since 1976, Biblical study and the personal experiences of myself and others who have tried this diet. Much of what I say may sound radical to some, but why should any Christian be surprised to find that modern science and personal experience have confirmed that "God's Original Diet" of raw fruits and vegetables (see Genesis 1:29) is the ideal diet for mankind?

It has now been almost 20 years since I switched from a diet that was predominately made up of the five white substances previously listed, which caused me to have serious teeth and gum problems, hemorrhoids, hypoglycemia, high blood pressure, severe sinus and allergy problems, frequent colds, headaches, pimples, body odor, dandruff, low energy . . . and colon cancer at age 42! In 1976, at age 42, I switched to a totally raw vegetarian / fruitarian diet with large amounts of freshly extracted vegetable juices. In fact, for one year I never ate a piece of cooked food. During that year, not only did my colon cancer go away, but so did every other physical problem I had!

After that first year, I added some cooked food to my diet. Presently, my diet consists of approximately 85 percent raw foods, with the balance made up of freshly prepared cooked vegetarian food. My present diet is described on page 92.

I eat no meat, no dairy, no sugar and no white flour products, and haven't since 1976! My diet is usually raw until the conclusion of the day, with my only cooked food – if any at all – coming at the end of the evening meal.

The reason one should maintain at least a 75 to 85-percent ratio of raw foods is that when food is cooked, almost all its nutritional value is destroyed. All enzymes are destroyed by cooking. Approximately 83 percent of all vitamins are destroyed by cooking and the heat changes protein into an unassimilable form. Cooking also reduces the organic minerals our body needs into an inorganic, unusable form.

In addition to diet, a lifestyle that includes exercise is an essential element to healthy living. I almost always do stretching exercises, deep breathing exercises and at least an hour of aerobic exercise each day. This diet and lifestyle has sustained me in perfect health with high energy for nearly 20 years now!

The Bible says: "Bless the Lord . . . Who healeth all thy diseases; who redeemeth thy life from destruction . . . Who satisfieth thy mouth with good things; so that thy youth is renewed like the eagles." (Psalms 103: 1 – 5)

# The Hallelujah Acres Healthy Foods Pyramid

The original Basic 4 Food Groups that most of us were raised on has produced massive physical problems. Two of the four food groups were animal products. These animal products are producing heart attacks, which are the cause of 50 percent of all deaths in America today. Animal products are also the primary cause of most cancers and adult-onset diabetes, not to mention acid stomach, most allergies, etc. The Hallelujah Acres Healthy Foods Pyramid, by comparison, produces abundant health and a long life.

High-fat, high-protein & concentrated foods should be kept to a minimum. Extra-Virgin Olive Oil or raw Flax Seed Oil can be used on raw vegetable salads. Beans (including tofu and other soybean products) should not be relied upon as a regular staple of the diet because they are cooked and too high in protein. Small amounts of butter and honey can be used occasionally.

Minimize grains because most are acid-forming. Fruits and vegetables, by comparison, are alkaline. Cancer cells cannot survive in an alkaline environment. Limit cooked veggies to the evening meal. Remember, cooking destroys most nutrients.

Nuts & seeds are too high in fat & protein to eat regularly.

With the fiber removed, fresh vegetable juices are the most efficient way of getting nutrition to the cellular level.

In addition to great nutrition, eating raw vegetables & fruits are the best source of fiber.

If one eats a diet of at least 75 to 85 percent raw foods, this leaves 15 to 25 percent of the diet for cooked food. This 15-25 percent should not be junk! No meat, dairy, white flour, white sugar, salt, chemical preservatives or processed foods. If one avoids these harmful processed foods and animal products, the cooked food portion of the diet can satisfy cravings and offer a variation at the end of the day, with very little harmful effect on overall health. A cooked meal at the end of the day can be very satisfying, but remember, the only food that is cell food is raw food.

We recommend that at least 75 to 85 percent of one's diet be living (raw) food. This provides our living cells with the nutrition they need to function properly and to build healthy new cells. Living food is the key to a healthy life!

**High-Fat and High-Protein Concentrated Foods, Oils, etc**
flax seed & olive oil, butter, beans, honey, etc.
**eat very sparingly**

**Bread and Cooked Grains**
whole-grain bread, brown rice, millet, etc.
**eat moderately**

**Cooked Vegetables**
steamed vegetables and baked potatoes or sweet potatoes, vegetable soups and stews. **eat moderately and only at the evening meal**

**Raw Nuts and Seeds**
**High Protein & Fat – Consume Sparingly**

**Fresh Vegetable Juices** And, no, that does not include frozen, bottled or canned juice
Two to eight 8-oz. servings a day. Carrot juice should comprise at least 50% of any vegetable juice mix. Drink fruit juices sparingly.

**Barley Green**
Minimum of 3 teaspoons daily. For optimal nutrition, take 3 - 4 Tablespoons daily. Barley Green is a (convenient) form of vegetable juice. Take 30 min. before each meal.

**Raw Fruits**
Fruits are a cleansing food, and are very easy to digest, so they are ideal for the first meal of the day. Do not mix fruits with other foods, and do not mix different types of fruit improperly. (See pages 94-95 for more on food combining.) Generally one should eat more raw vegetables than fruits. Too much fruit can create hypoglycemic problems for some people due to its high content of natural sugars.

**Raw Vegetables**
You may eat **unlimited quantities** of raw vegetables. Raw vegetables are your best source of nutrition, and one should strive to eat a good variety of vegetables, especially greens and deeply-colored vegetables such as broccoli, spinach, carrots, beets, squash, etc. The deep colors indicate high quantities of beta-carotene and other vital nutrients. Eating a raw vegetable salad before a meal of cooked vegetables or grains will provide your body with living enzymes necessary to help digest the cooked food.

# The Hallelujah Diet

**by Rev. George H. Malkmus**

*People often ask me, "What do you eat?" Here is my answer:*

**BREAKFAST:** One tablespoon of BARLEYGREEN* powder either dry and let it dissolve in my mouth or in a couple of ounces of distilled water at room temperature. That is usually all I have until noon! If I do get hungry, then I may eat a piece of fresh juicy fruit later in the morning. Cooked food is an absolute no-no as my body is in a cleansing mode until about noon each day. (It is vitally important to me that the BARLEY GREEN powder I use comes from AMERICAN IMAGE MARKETING and that it contains kelp. There are other companies that have tried to imitate this product, but they are not processed the same way. I have tried other products, but they do not give the same results. Nor do the BARLEYGREEN caplets if swallowed. The caplets can be dissolved in the mouth like a lozenge, however. I enjoy them in this form, especially while travelling.)

**LUNCH:** One tablespoon of BARLEYGREEN* powder, as at breakfast. Sometimes I stir my BARLEYGREEN into 8 ounces of freshly extracted carrot juice**, which I find especially delicious and extremely nutritious. At least a half hour after the BARLEYGREEN, I prefer an all-raw fruit lunch. A banana, apple, dates, etc. Organic is always best when available. (Sometimes I have a vegetable salad for lunch instead of the fruit.) It is important that this be an all raw meal!

**SUPPER:** One tablespoon of BARLEYGREEN* powder either dry or in a couple ounces of distilled water or in carrot juice. Carrot juice must be *freshly* extracted, never canned, bottled or frozen. Then, at least 30 minutes after the BARLEYGREEN, I eat a large green vegetable salad of leaf lettuce (never head lettuce), broccoli, cauliflower, celery, carrots, etc. This is usually followed by some cooked food (baked potato, baked sweet potato, brown rice, steamed vegetables, whole-grain pasta, whole-grain bread, etc.) Later in the evening I often have a glass or two of organic apple juice or a piece of juicy fruit. (My diet consists of approximately 85 percent raw food, and 15 percent cooked food.)

To be sure I get the essential fatty acids needed by my body, I also have one tablespoon of Barlean's High Lignan Organic Flax Oil. I either have this on my evening salad or straight out of the bottle.

Exercise is also an essential part of my program. I do at least one hour of vigorous exercise daily. Additionally, I try to get some sunshine on as much of my body as possible every day.

*The reason I supplement my diet with BARLEYGREEN is that our food today is being grown for the most part in very deficient soils that often lack all the nutrients my body needs for building new, strong, healthy, vital, vibrant cells. BARLEYGREEN is grown organically and contains the widest spectrum of nutrients available today from a single source that I am aware of. It is also loaded with enzymes. I consider it the single, most important food I put into my body each day and always consume *at least* 3 tablespoons of it a day. Another AIM product we find very beneficial is Herbal Fiberblend, for added fiber, preventative maintenance of the colon and insurance against parasitic infestations. I take one tablespoon a day and Rhonda takes two tablespoons.

**The second-most important thing I put into my body each day is freshly extracted carrot juice made from large California juicing carrots. I try to drink at least 16 to 24 ounces each day. When I had my colon cancer ???? years ago, I consumed 32 to 64 ounces of carrot juice each day. If I had a serious physical problem today I would consume up to eight 8-ounce glasses of carrot juice each day in addition to my three to four tablespoons of BARLEYGREEN. The reason BARLEYGREEN and carrot juice is so important to me is:

1. Cooked food has practically no nutritional value.

2. A large percentage of the nutrients in raw food are lost in the digestion process, with only 1 to 35 % of nutrients reaching cell level, depending on the health of the digestive system.

3. When vegetable juices or BARLEYGREEN is consumed, up to 92% of the nutrients reach cell level. This is because the pulp has been removed and thus no digestion is necessary. Raw vegetable juices are the fastest way to nourish the cells and rebuild the body.

Many people seem to have a problem understanding what constitutes a nutritional diet. In an effort to clarify this, I have prepared a chart showing the IDEAL DIET, the TRANSITIONAL DIET, and the FOODS TO BE AVOIDED. I encourage people to work out of the FOODS TO BE AVOIDED column as quickly as possible. These are the *killer foods* that are creating most of our physical problems! Then add as much food as possible from the IDEAL DIET column. These are life-giving, cell-building and healing foods that will strengthen and rebuild the immune system. The TRANSITIONAL DIET column is OK for the cooked food portion of the diet, the 15 to 25-percent . . . if cooked food is desired.

| CATEGORY | IDEAL DIET | TRANSITIONAL DIET | FOODS TO BE AVOIDED |
|---|---|---|---|
| BEVERAGES | Freshly extracted vegetable juices & distilled water | Herb teas & cereal coffees. Organic bottled juices | **Alcohol, coffee, tea, cocoa, carbonated beverages and all other soft drinks, all artificial fruit drinks (kool-aid, gater-aid, etc.) and all canned juices** |
| DAIRY PRODUCTS | NONE | Non-dairy cheese, non-fat yogurt, low-fat cottage cheese & butter, all sparingly! | **All milk, cheese & eggs, ice cream, whipped toppings, non-dairy coffee creamers** |
| FISH | NONE | NONE | **Clams, oysters, shrimp, lobster, and all fish** |
| FRUIT | All fresh & unsulfered dried fruit | Stewed & unsweetened frozen fruit | **Canned & sweetened fruits (Commercial raisins are hazardous)** |
| GRAINS | NONE | Whole-grain cereals, bread, muffins, pasta, brown rice, millet, etc. | **All white-flour products, all hull-less grains (pasta, crackers, snack foods, white rice, cold cereals, etc.)** |
| MEATS | NONE | NONE | **All meat. Hot dogs, bacon, sausage, liver & luncheon meats are extremely hazardous** |
| NUTS & SEEDS | Raw almonds & sunflower seeds in small amounts | Other raw nuts & seeds in limited amounts | **All roasted and/or salted seeds & nuts (Peanuts and peanut butter are hazardous)** |
| OILS | Extra virgin olive oil & raw flax oil | Cold-pressed oils (e.g. canola, safflower) & cold-pressed mayo | **All lard, shortenings & margerines made w/ hydrogenated oils are extremely hazardous** |
| SEASONINGS | Herbs, garlic, parsley | Onions. Use Bragg Liquid Aminos in place of salt | **Salt, pepper** |
| SOUPS | Cold, raw soups | Soups made from scratch without fat stock or salt | **All canned & creamed soups** |
| SWEETS | NONE | Raw, unfiltered honey, rice syrup, unsulfered molasses, carob, pure maple syrup, date sugar (all in limited quantities) | **All refined white or brown sugars, syrups, chocolate, candy, gum, cake, cookies, donuts, pies, etc.** |
| VEGETABLES | All raw vegetables | Cooked fresh or frozen vegetables, baked white & sweet potatoes | **All canned vegetables, fried potatoes in any form, corn & potato chips** |

# Food Combining – Fruits

## Acid Fruits

Strawberries
Grapefruit
Oranges
Tangelos
Kiwi
Lemons*
Pineapple
Raspberries
Cranberries
Gooseberries
Tangerines
Limes
Kumquat
Sour Plums
Pomegranates

\* Lemons combine well with all plant foods and can be used to replace vinegar in recipes.

## Sweet Fruits

Bananas
Papaya
Thompson Grapes
Muscat Grapes
Persimmon
Dates
Figs
Raisins
Prunes
Other Dried Fruits

**Do Not Combine –**

⟷

**digests poorly together**

## Sub-Acid Fruits

Apples
Apricots
Blackberries
Blueberries
Cherries
Nectarines
Peaches
Pears
Mangos
Plums
Most Grapes
Passion Fruit
Guava
Papaya

**Combine –**
digests well together

**Combine –**
digests well together

### Do Not Combine Fruits with Vegetables or Grains

An exception to this rule is that you may combine leaf lettuce or celery with fruits to help deal with the excessive sugar.

## Melons

| Honey Dew | Casaba | Crenshaw |
| Cantalope | Watermelon | Persian |

Eat melons alone or leave them alone, as they do not digest well with other foods. Any of the melons can be combined with each other, however.

# Food Combining – Vegetables & Grains

## Starches
Potatoes
Parsnips
Corn
Pasta
Bread
Winter Squash
Lima Beans
Pumpkins
Coconut
Yams
Most Legumes
Whole-Grain Cereals
Brown & Wild Rice
All Grains

**Do Not Combine –**

← →

**digests poorly together**

## Proteins
Seeds*
Nuts*
Flesh Foods**
Dairy**
Soybean Analogs (fake meat)**
Sprouted Legumes
Lentils
Dried Peas & Beans
All other bean products

\* Best soaked 24 hours in distilled water before use.

** Included for clarity ONLY. Not recommended.

## Vegetables
Asparagus
Beets
Broccoli
Cauliflower
Carrots
Celery
Red, Yellow, Green Peppers
Leaf Lettuce & Endive
Cabbage
Kohirabi
Cucumbers
Beets
Eggplant
Spinach
String Beans
Kale
Parsley

*Tomatoes may be eaten with non-starchy vegetables*

**Combine – digests well together**

↖ ↘

## Fresh Vegetable Juice

Drink at least 30 minutes before a meal, and not with a meal. Barley Green is in the Vegetable Juice category.

**Combine – digests well together**

## Oils and Fats
Butter*
Avocados**
Olive Oil
Flax Seed Oil
Coconut
Almonds
Pecans
Pumpkin Seeds
Sunflower Seeds

\* Use very sparingly. Never use margarine or other hydrogenated oils.

** Avocado is best mixed with green vegetables or sub-acid fruits.

## A note on Food Combining

Various foods require different digestive juices and enzymes, and require different lengths of time for digestion. So, for optimal digestion and assimilation, it is best when foods are consumed in simple and compatible combinations. These food combining charts are included as a helpful guide, but are not absolute, and are not intended to be a set of unbending rules. Some recipes in this book do violate ideal food combining guidelines. For people on the Hallelujah Diet who are not fighting a serious illness, less than perfect combinations can be eaten on occasion.

"One farmer says to me, 'You cannot live on vegetable food solely, for it furnishes nothing to make bones with,' and . . . all the while he walks behind his oxen, which, with vegetable-made bones, jerk him and his lumbering plow along in spite of every obstacle."
– Henry David Thoreau

"Although we think we are one, and we act as if we are one, human beings are not natural carnivores . . . When we kill animals to eat them, they end up killing us because their flesh . . . was never intended for human beings, who are naturally herbivores."
– William C. Roberts, M.D., editor-in-chief of the *American Journal of Cardiology*

"You put a baby in a crib with an apple and a rabbit. If it eats the rabbit and plays with the apple, I'll buy you a new car."
– Harvey Diamond

# Chapter 11

# Meat, Dairy & Eggs

*By Rev. George H. Malkmus*

When the doctor told me in 1976 that I had colon cancer, I thought I was the innocent victim! I was told that because my mother had colon cancer, that was the reason I had colon cancer . . . "you inherited it," they said. Almost 20 years of research and personal experience have proved the fallacy of the "innocent victim" or "inherited it" reasoning.

I was not the "innocent victim,"nor did I "inherit it" from my mom. I had created my own colon cancer by eating meat!

In this chapter, we are going to look at meat, milk, cheese and eggs and how they relate to our health, quality of life and length of life.

To start with, let me say that we have not been told the truth by the meat, dairy and egg industries! And it is these very industries that provide the educational material for our public schools and even for the American Medical Association and American Dietetic Association. For years, the meat, dairy and egg industries, our doctors and most nutritionists have told us that we need meat and eggs for protein and strength, and dairy for calcium.

My research has revealed just the opposite: There is no usable protein in the meat and eggs we eat, nor assimilable calcium in the milk products we consume . . . but rather, meat, dairy and eggs sap our strength, do great harm to our body and shorten our lives!

The facts are that meat, dairy and eggs can be linked directly or indirectly to about 90 percent of all physical problems and deaths in America today!!!

### 50 percent of all Americans die from heart attacks and strokes

Heart attacks and strokes are caused primarily by the clogging of the arteries with fat (cholesterol). The average meat, egg and dairy consumer in America today puts into their body through the use of animal products over 50 pounds of FAT per year! It is interesting to note that the only source of bad cholesterol (LDL) is in animal products!

### 33 percent of all Americans die from Cancer

Cancer continues to take more and more lives . . . approximately 500,000

Americans die from cancer each year. One out of every three Americans will develop cancer during their lifetime. Colon cancer, breast cancer and prostate cancer are the fastest growing cancers in America today and the primary cause of these cancers is the consumption of animal products! The relationship between diets high in animal protein and cancer has been clearly established. Cancerous cells feed on animal protein, which triggers the abnormal proliferation of cells.

### 8 percent of all Americans die from Diabetes

Diabetes is becoming more and more prevalent each year! Yet adult-onset diabetes is usually not a sugar problem, nor a failure of the pancreas to produce enough insulin, but rather a fat problem! Adult-onset diabetes is usually caused by fat and cholesterol, which coats the cells and prevents the insulin from reaching the insulin receptor within the cell. Sadly, the high animal protein diet most doctors prescribe for their diabetic patients is the very thing that causes diabetes.

What animal products are doing to the people of America is a travesty! Let's look at a few statistics from *Diet for a New America*, for which author John Robbins was nominated for a Pulitzer Prize:

Someone in America suffers a heart attack every 25 seconds.

Someone in America dies from a heart attack every 45 seconds.

Most common cause of death in America: heart attack.

Risk of having a heart attack by average American: 50 percent.

Risk of having a heart attack by average American vegetarian: less than 4 percent.

Amount you reduce your risk of heart attack by eliminating meat, dairy and eggs from diet: over 90 percent.

Increased risk of breast cancer for women who eat meat compared to non-meat eaters: over 4 times.

Increased risk of fatal prostate cancer for men who consume animal products compared to vegetarians: 3.6 times higher.

Increased risk of fatal ovarian cancer for women who consume animal products, compared to vegetarians: 3 times higher.

The meat, dairy and egg industries tell us, "We are well-fed only with animals products." The meat, dairy and egg industries do not tell us that the diseases which are commonly prevented, consistently improved and often cured by a low-fat, vegetarian diet include: strokes, kidney stones, prostrate cancer, diabetes, peptic ulcers, hemorrhoids, obesity, salmonellosis, heart disease, breast cancer, pancreatic cancer, stomach cancer, hiatus hernias, gallstones, arthritis, trichinosis, osteoporosis, colon cancer, ovarian cancer, endometrial cancer, constipation, diverticulosis, irritable colon and gout.

"The beef industry has contributed to more American deaths than all the wars of this century, all natural disasters, and all automobile accidents combined."
– Neal Barnard, M.D., President, Physicians Committee for Responsible Medicine

*The facts are that meat, dairy and eggs can be linked directly or indirectly to about 90 percent of all physical problems and deaths in America today!!!*

"Science used to support the consumption of meat. It no longer does. It cannot. The facts are so overwhelming that the eating of animal flesh is doomed as the age of enlightened people is ushered in. One day mankind will look back in horror at the carnivorous habits of its predecessors. Habits of meat-eating will seem as barbarian and disgusting to future man as the eating of cat and dog meat now seems to the average American."
– Dr. Richard Anderson in his book *Cleanse & Purify Thyself.*

> "I have no doubt that it is part of the destiny of the human race in its gradual development to leave off the eating of animals, as surely as the savage tribes have left off eating each other when they came in contact with the more civilized."
> – Henry David Thoreau

Often in my seminars, Christians will challenge me by stating that people ate meat in the Bible. "That may be true," I answer., "but the meat in Bible days and the meat our forefathers ate was a totally different animal!" The meat in Bible days and the meat our forefathers ate was only about 3 percent fat. Beef, the way it is grown today is 20 to 30 percent fat, while pork is 40 to 60 percent fat! Nor was the meat our fore-fathers ate full of antibiotics, growth hormones, preservatives, toxins and cancer! Nor did they pasteurize and homogenize their milk or produce eggs in wire cages without benefit of daylight, green food, insects, etc.!

The effect growth hormones are having on the youth of America is producing a social tragedy that I find particularly distressing. This one will shock you. In the year 1950, the age of puberty for a young lady was around age 16 to 17. But something happened during the 1950's that has had a devastating effect on our young people. They started feeding animals growth hormones to make them ready for market sooner, and "fast food" restaurants came on the scene.

Because of these growth hormones and the increased consumption of meat by American youth, due to its easy availability through fast food restaurants, the age of puberty in the past 40 years has dropped from age 16-17 to age 10-11! One pediatrician reported recently that large numbers of girls as young as 7, 8 and 9 years old are now menstruating. This capability to reproduce is coming much too early in life and the young people are not mature enough mentally or emotionally to handle it. This is creating monumental problems for our youth, their parents, teachers, youth workers and society as a whole. These growth hormones have also found their way into our milk and dairy products.

Following are a few of the dramatic testimonies shared with us at Hallelujah Acres by people who have stopped their use of animal products and adopted a vegetarian diet with large amounts of freshly extracted vegetable juices and

### Cholesterol
*Rise in blood cholesterol from consuming one egg per day:* **12 percent**
*Rise in heart attack risk for 12 percent rise in blood cholesterol:* **24 percent**
*Average cholesterol level of people eating a meat centered diet:* **210 mg/dl**
*Chance of a male dying from heart disease if his blood cholesterol is 210/dl:* **Greater than 50 percent**
*Dietary cholesterol intake needed to support human health:* **None - the body makes its own.**
*Leading sources of saturated fat and cholesterol in American diets:* **Meat, poultry and dairy products**
*Amount of cholesterol in an average egg:* **275 mg**
*Amount of cholesterol in chicken:* **The same as beef, 25 mg per ounce**
*Main location of cholesterol in animal flesh:* **The lean portion**
*Cholesterol found in all grains, legumes, fruits, vegetables, nuts and seed:* **None**
*Chance of dying from heart disease if you do not consume cholesterol:* **Less than 4 percent**

### Protein Requirements
*Recommendations of the amount of daily calories to be provided by protein according to:*
*World Health Organizations of the United Nations:* **4.5 percent**
*Food and Nutrition Board of the USDA:* **6 percent**
*National Research Council:* **8 percent**
*Amount of total calories provided by protein in human milk:* **5 percent**
*(Period of most rapid human growth:* **Infancy)**
*Percentage of calories as protein in:* **Spinach 49 percent; Broccoli 47 percent; Lettuce 34 percent; Zucchini 28 percent; Tomatoes 18 percent**
*Health status of pure vegetarians from many populations of the world according to the Food and Nutrition Board of the National Academy of Sciences:* **Excellent**

### Calcium
*Documented cases of calcium deficiency caused by an insufficient amount of calcium in human diet:* **None**
*Disease linked to excess animal protein consumption:* **Osteoporosis**
*The average measurable bone loss of female meat-eaters at age 65:* **35 percent**
*The average measurable bone loss of female vegetarians at age 65:* **18 percent**

**(Excerpted from *Realities for the 90's*.)**

Barley Green:

F.C., a diabetic on injection insulin, stopped using animal products and in less than two weeks was off insulin with blood sugar normal! Heart murmur for over 60 years . . . gone! Was skipping every third heartbeat before changing diet . . . Doctor says this is also gone!

M.P. had rheumatoid arthritis, much pain, couldn't dress herself, had been on powerul arthritis medication and pain killers, etc. She stopped using animal products and in only eight weeks, her pain was almost gone, was off all medication, could dress herself and had lost over 30 pounds! Update: She has now lost over 80 pounds!

G.C. couldn't get cholesterol level below 300, even with medication. Eight weeks after eliminating animal products, cholesterol level was 176, nearly perfect! Triglicerides had dropped from over 500 to under 200 and had lost 28 pounds in the same eight weeks.

C.B. had been on drugs for high blood pressure for years. In less than 12 weeks, blood pressure was normal and was off medication!

> "... Whether industrialized societies ... can cure themselves of their meat addictions may ultimately be a greater factor in world health than all the doctors, health insurance policies, and drugs put together."
> – China Health Project (summary) 1983

---

> *We have not been told the truth by the meat, dairy and egg industries! And it is these very industries that provide the educational material for our public schools and even for the American Medical Association and American Dietetic Association.*

---

E.C. had a serious acid stomach condition, paying over $2,000 every few months for drugs that weren't helping that much. He was in such pain some days that he wanted to die. In three days after consumption of animal products stopped, the problem was gone!

Often people will say: "Oh, I don't eat red meat any more . . . I only eat chicken and fish." Somehow the American public has the misconception that chicken and fish are healthy. NOT SO! Chicken has the same amount of cholesterol as beef and is loaded with growth hormones. A chicken that used to take 15 weeks to mature is now ready for market in just six weeks. Sixty percent of all chicken is contaminated with salmonella. Then there are the antibiotics and other drugs. And when we look at fish, we find that in terms of calories consumed, fish has twice the cholesterol of pork or beef; has no fiber (as is the case with all other animal products), which promotes problems connected with lack of fiber, ranging from constipation to colon cancer; not to mention the risks associated with eating contaminated fish from polluted waters. Studies consistently show that when a person switches from a red meat diet to a diet high in chicken and fish, there is no drop in serum cholesterol levels!

Meat eating and the use of dairy products have not a single redeeming feature! There is no assimilable protein in meat or eggs, and no usable calcium in dairy! Why? Because the heating (cooking) of the protein deranges the molecular structure of the protein, making it unassimilable by the body. The pasteurizing of dairy products changes the organic calcium to an inorganic, unusable form. If we look to nature, there is not a single meat-eating animal in the wild that cooks the flesh it eats, nor is there an animal in the wild

*From the Hallelujah Acres mailbag:*

"I am writing to request a subscription to your newsletter. I have been vegetarian for a year now and have just recently cut dairy products out of my diet. I would like to learn more and make a fresh start on my sixteenth birthday, which is just a few days away."
– Misty Dawn McKee, Tennessee

"I heard you on 3ABN and did I ever enjoy the program...I am 92 years old and have been a vegetarian for over sixty years. ..."
– Edith Merritt, Washington

that pasteurizes the milk it feeds its young. Nor is there even an animal in the wild that drinks the milk of another animal, or drinks milk after the age of weaning.

In his book, *Don't Drink Your Milk!* Dr. Frank A. Oski, M.D. states that when the public is educated about the hazards of cow's milk, only calves will be left to drink it. "Cow milk has no valid claim as the perfect food. As nutrition, it produces allergies in infants, diarrhea and cramps in the older child and adult, and may be a factor in the development of heart attacks and strokes," Dr. Oski warns. Other disorders that he says are linked to milk include gastrointestinal bleeding, iron-deficiency anemia, skin rashes, atherosclerosis, acne, recurrent ear infections and bronchitis. And there's more: "Leukemia, multiple sclerosis, rheumatoid arthritis, and simple dental decay have also been proposed as candidates."

So who is Dr. Oski? He received his M.D. from the University of Pennsylvania; was appointed as an Associate in the Department of Pediatrics, University of Pennsylvania School of Medicine and assumed post of Professor and Chairman, Department of Pediatrics, John Hopkins School of Medicine and Physician-in-Chief, the Johns Hopkins Children's Center.

The facts are that meat, dairy products and eggs are not good food . . . but rather, dangerous substances that are *hazardous to our health!!!*

Personally I have not eaten meat or eggs, nor used dairy products for almost 20 years! Am I weak and sickly as a result? Anyone who knows me, knows that just the opposite is true. I am in my 60s and yet my strength, endurance and stamina is greater than when I was 20 years old. Few people, even young people, can keep up with me climbing the mountains. Since eliminating meat, dairy and eggs from my diet 19 years ago, I have experienced no sickness of any kind, not been to a doctor, not taken a drug . . . not even an aspirin! My diet is totally vegetarian and mostly raw.

Based on 19 years of research and personal experience, I can whole-heartedly recommend a vegetarian diet. *All the nutrients our body needs can be obtained from raw fruits and vegetables!!!* According to the Bible, this is the diet God originally gave man and the diet by which God intended his creation to be sustained!

"And God said: Behold, I have given you every herb (vegetable) bearing seed, which is upon the face of all the earth, and every tree, in which is the fruit of a treat yielding seed; to you it shall be for meat." (Genesis 1:29)

# Vegetarian Athletes

**Anyone who may be skeptical about the strength, endurance and general health of people choosing a vegetarian diet might consider these vegetarian athletes:**

Only man to win Ironman Triathlon more than twice: **Dave Scott, six-time winner**

World record 24-hour triathlon; swim 4.8 miles, cycle 185 miles, run 52.2 miles: **Sixto Linares**

Twenty world records in distance running, Nine Olympic medals: **Paavo Nurmi**

World's premier ultra-distance walker: **Robert Sweetgall**

World records, 400 and 1500-meter freestyle: **Murray Rose**

World records, distance butterfly stroke swimming: **James & Jonathon de Donato**

World record, cross country tandem cycling: **Estelle Gray & Cheryl Marek**

All-time major league baseball home run champion: **Henry Aaron**

Starting center for Boston Celtics, at age 36, 7'0", 240 lbs.: **Robert Parish**

World record, bench press: **Stan Price**

Mr. International body-building champion: **Andreas Cahling**

Mr. America body-building champion: **Roy Hilligan**

Eight national champions in Karate, including U.S. Karate Association World Champion: **Ridgely Abele**

World champion gymnast: **Dan Millman**

Excerpted from *Realities for the 90's,* published by EarthSave Foundation. *Realities* includes summarized facts from *Diet for a New America* by John Robbins and other sources.

# Chapter 12

# Oxygen and Exercise

*By Rev. George H. Malkmus*

As you read these words, your chest is softly, rhythmically and automatically rising and falling as air enters into and exits your lungs. You probably weren't even consciously aware of this until I called it to your attention. Yet, without this intake of air, which contains oxygen, your physical life would cease very quickly.

In the Bible, we read in Genesis 2:7: *"And the Lord God formed man of the dust of the ground, and breathed into his nostrils the breath of life: and man became a living soul."* Thus, God used two separate and distinct steps in the creation of man. First, he formed man of *"the dust of the ground."* At death, when a body is placed in the ground, it eventually reduces to the same ingredients from which man was originally formed ... mineral ash or *"dust of the ground."* This reduction to mineral ash is accomplished much more rapidly by cremation.

**"The greatest need of the body is 'pure air'! Approximately 96% of our nutritional need comes from the air ... while only 4% comes from the food we eat!"**
**– Rev. George Malkmus, in his first book, *Why Christians Get Sick***

So after step one in the creation of man, after "God formed man of the dust of the ground," God had nothing but a dead, lifeless body, similar to what we see when we visit a funeral home and look into that open casket. We do see a body, but it is motionless and it is lifeless. Why is it motionless and lifeless? What makes the difference between life and death?

Answering that question brings us to the most basic and important substance in man. An ingredient of such monumental importance that, without it, life is absolutely and positively impossible. My friend, the substance I am talking about is none other than oxygen! And so, God breathed into Adam the *"breath of life,"* and that dead heap of minerals sprang to **LIFE**! Just as oxygen was absolutely necessary to produce **LIFE** in Adam, it is that same oxygen that is absolutely vital and necessary to sustain **LIFE** in man today.

At birth, when a child slips from the womb and enters this world, its *first* and most basic **need** must be met, and it must be met quickly if life is to continue. What is that most basic need? Why it is that same *"breath of life,"* **oxygen,** that God breathed into Adam at creation. And so the baby takes into its little body that first breath and immediately we see the chest start to rise and fall as it rhythmically and automatically continues to take this *"breath of life"* into its lungs. This rising and falling of the chest as the lungs take in oxygen and give off carbon dioxide continues from birth throughout life. Most of the time we are not even aware that this process is taking place. Yet, if we were to cut off the oxygen supply for only a few moments, we would become quickly aware of our need for this life-giving and life-sustaining substance we call oxygen!

*After people have smoked for a period of time, their lungs take on the appearance of the inside of a wood stove chimney that is lined with black sticky creosote. This coating of the lungs restricts the intake of oxygen and the person slowly but surely suffocates the body cells, depriving them of their most important nutritional need.*

If a person finds himself in a smoke-filled room, he will automatically and rapidly seek fresh air as the body expresses an urgent need for oxygen. If the lungs cannot obtain fresh air (oxygen), the body soon suffocates and death quickly follows. Why? Because the oxygen supply has been shut off!

People who smoke slowly but surely cut off their oxygen supply as the tars in the smoke coat their lungs. After people have smoked for a period of time, their lungs take on the appearance of the inside of a wood stove chimney that is lined with black sticky creosote. This coating of the lungs restricts the intake of **oxygen** and the person slowly but surely suffocates the body cells, depriving them of their most important nutritional need. And if that isn't bad enough, tobacco smoke contains carbon monoxide, the same deadly substance found in automobile exhaust. Carbon monoxide combines with the hemoglobin in the blood and further reduces its oxygen carrying capacity. This decrease in oxygen causes the heart to pump faster to try and make up for the deficieny, constricts the blood vessels, thus creating poor circulation – and there is so much more. If you are a smoker, and love life, please stop smoking right now! And yes, you can if you really want to. Thousands are quitting every day.

Let's explore this subject of **"oxygen"** and see what we can learn. First, our body is a living organism, comprised of approximately 100,000,000,000,000 (one hundred trillion) cells. Each of these cells is its own entity and is capable of reproducing itself. However, in order to sustain life and reproduce itself, a cell has specific needs that must be met. The two basic needs are an adequate food supply and an efficient waste disposal system. The quality and quantity of the food supply along with the adequacy and efficiency of the waste disposal system determines the quality and length of our lives.

Yes, it s true that *"It is appointed unto every man once to die..."* (Hebrews 9:27) However, this is not saying that God has a pre-set time for each individual person to die ... but that every human being will die someday. The only exception to this is those believers who happen to be alive when Jesus returns for his own (I Thes. 4:16)  So, in reality, we have control over how long we will live on planet earth (barring accidents).  We also have control of whether we will get sick or not.

Sickness in the body can take many forms.  Most people think of cancer, heart attacks, strokes, diabetes, arthritis, the flu, colds, headaches, pimples, etc. as problems that are unavoidable.  People with these diseases often believe they are just the innocent victim, or it was fate, or it was inherited, or a bug or germ chose them as their breeding ground, or it was God's will, etc.  My friend, none of these excuses are the real cause of our physical problems.  Sickness, in whatever form it manifests itself, is the result of our failing to provide our cells with proper building materials and/or failing to adequately remove the toxic wastes from the cells.  This simply boils down to improper diet and life-style!

Sadly, our society has been programmed into thinking we can put anything we want into our bodies, abuse our bodies, neglect our bodies and then when our bodies break down, all we have to do is run to a doctor who will give us a miracle working drug and in a few days every-thing will be all right.  My friend, it just doesn't work that way, and man is realizing it a little more with each passing day.  Doctors do not have the answers to health, nor will health insurance policies, government programs or money make us well.  If we want to experience life here on earth as God intended, we must take control of our own health, and observe the natural laws given by God to mankind.  When these laws are observed, sickness will not come!  When we violate these laws, we will experience sickness.  It is that simple!

Whenever we start to experience a physical breakdown, such as a cold, sore throat, upset stomach, pimples, headaches or something more serious, like cardiovascular problems, heart attacks, stroke, arthritis, diabetes or cancer, we need to ask the question "WHY!"  We need to ask *"What did I do or fail to do that created this physical problem?  Which of God's natural laws did I violate?"*  Fortunately, in most instances, when we eliminate the cause of the physical problem, and give the body the proper nourishment, healing will usually follow naturally and quite rapidly.

Where does oxygen fit into all of this?  In my book, *Why Christians Get Sick*, I list God's seven natural laws for wellness.  And on page 105, I make this statement: *"The greatest need of the body is 'pure air'!  Approximately 96% of our nutritional need comes from the air … while only 4% comes from the food we eat!"*  Now, let's look at some additional facts about oxygen:

1. The quality of the air (its purity) we breathe affects the quality and length of the life we live.  Breathing good clean air increases the quality and length of our life!  Breathing polluted air decreases the quality and length of our life!

2. Increase the supply of oxygen to the brain (through deep breathing and exercise) and mental abilities will increase and the brain will become more alert!  Decrease the supply of oxygen to the brain (through smoking, air pollution and a sedentary life) and the brain's mental abilities will decrease and become

*From the
Hallelujah Acres mailbag:*

"… Keep up all the good and worthwhile work you are doing!  I just want you to know that since reading *(Why Christians Get Sick* and *Become Younger)*, I have gone completely raw vegetarian and fruits, and I feel so much better … I am 46 and don't look it.  I work out daily and watch what goes into my mouth!  It was difficult at first to make this total transition, but I can truly say I am bursting with energy now and feel mentally great.  In the past, I was always depressed and upset …  Thanks for everything you are doing to promote good health and mental well-being."
– Adrienne Carbetta, Texas

103

sluggish. Cut off the oxygen supply to the brain for only a brief moment (as during a stroke) and parts of the brain will die, producing paralysis in various parts of the body.

3. Increase the supply of oxygen to the body's cells and the body becomes full of energy and life! Decrease the supply of oxygen to the cells and the body fails to provide the energy necessary to perform properly, and we feel tired, sluggish and listless.

4. An increase in the supply of oxygen to the body's cells helps us mentally and emotionally, and we become happy and optimistic! Decrease the supply of oxygen to the body's cells and we become discouraged, depressed and pessimistic!

5. Increase the supply of oxygen to the body's cells and sickness cannot find a foothold! Decrease the supply of oxygen to the body's cells and it provides the breeding ground for sickness. *Sickness and disease cannot survive in an aerobic (oxygenated) atmosphere.*

---

***THE KEYS TO A LONG HEALTHY LIFE ARE: 1. PROPER NUTRITION; 2. ADEQUATE EXERCISE; AND 3. ABUNDANT OXYGEN! Most of man's miseries are caused by eating the wrong foods, failing to exercise sufficiently and not taking into the body abundant amounts of oxygen.***

---

We could go on, but the above should be adequate to show the importance, yea the imperative, of making sure our bodies receive an adequate supply of oxygen so we can experience life to its fullest. Jesus said: *"I am come that ye may have life, and that ye may have it more abundantly."* (John 10:10) Increasing the volume of air (oxygen) entering the lungs will increase the volume of oxygen being supplied to the cellular level of your body. This in turn starts a beautiful scenario of events to take place in our bodies. And the way we create this beautiful scenario is through exercise, which provides this oxygen to our cells in great abundance.

Exercise, in addition to providing oxygen to the body cells, also causes a flushing of the veins and arteries. This removes obstructions to the free flow of blood. As the arteries and veins become clearer and the oxygen supply entering the lungs increases, an increased amount of oxygen is transferred to the blood for dispersal. This oxygen-rich blood is then carried to the cells throughout the body. When the cells receive this increase in oxygen, they become energized and start vigorously cleaning house, rebuilding and rejuvenating the cells. As healthier cells are produced, they throw off debris and toxic wastes. An increased level of exercise is necessary to carry off this garbage for removal from the body. Couple this with a proper diet and it doesn't take long before we start to feel better. Life takes on a new glow, and many report feeling better than they have felt in years, if not better than they can remember ever feeling in their lives. It is all so very simple and exciting!

THE KEYS TO A LONG HEALTHY LIFE ARE: 1. PROPER NUTRITION; 2. ADEQUATE EXERCISE; AND 3. ABUNDANT OXYGEN! Most of man's miseries are caused by eating the wrong foods, failing to exercise sufficiently and not taking into the body abundant amounts of oxygen.

**So how do we change things? Where do we start?**

**1. START BY EATING RAW FOODS! Eating living (raw) foods is really the starting point. Living foods will start to normalize body weight and increase our energy. Increased energy will demand more exercise! Increased exercise will cause deep breathing! Deep breathing will bring copious amounts of oxygen into the body. Increased oxygen will oxygenate and stimulate the cells and thus produce abundant energy along with superior health! It is so amazingly simple!**

**2. THE NEXT THING WE NEED TO DO IS TO START EXERCISING, AND THE BEST WAY TO ACCOMPLISH THAT IS TO JUST START WALKING. Most people can at least do that much and it can provide wonderful benefits. Here is a simple way to get started: (a) Figure out a *measured mile* (Examples: Around the block four times, up and down the driveway 40 times, etc.) (b) Time yourself as you walk that mile at a comfortable pace and write down how long it took you. (c) Next day, walk that same mile again, only try to walk a little faster. Each day try to decrease the time it takes to walk that mile until you can walk a mile in 15 minutes. Each day, record the time it took. (d) After you can walk a 15-minute mile, stretch your walk to two miles and walk two miles each day until you can walk those two miles in 30 minutes (two 15-minute miles). (e) Then stretch it to three miles in 45 minutes and finally four miles in an hour. Then walk those four miles each and every day. If you will do that, along with an improved diet, it will change your life and quite possibly save it.**

The minimum amount of aerobic exercise recommended is 20 minutes every other day. Personally, I do not feel that is adequate. Rhonda and I strive to put in 60 minutes of aerobic exercise *every day*! Our workout begins with some easy walking and slow stretches for five to ten minutes. Then three to four miles of fast walking and often we interrupt the walking with slow jogging or sprinting. (After a person has been walking 15-minute miles over an extended period of time, it takes more vigorous movement to get the heart into the aerobic range.) Another way to help get the body into the aerobic range is through the use of ankle weights and hand-held weights. This not only increases the intake of oxygen but also helps build muscle mass.

Often, we will walk/jog on the nice days and work out on a mini-trampoline when the weather is bad. The mini-trampoline is a great form of exercise! One wonderful benefit is that it minimizes the jarring of the skeletal system and joints, compared to jogging on solid ground. Also, it promotes the

*From the Hallelujah Acres mailbag:*

"Dear Rev. Malkmus: I have already read your book and studied your tape and it has already made a difference in my life and body. I am 66 years of age and a former professional wrestler and football player who abused his body just about every way possible. I am becoming younger and stronger on a daily basis. I have eliminated meat from my diet and coffee. Am on distilled water and mostly raw foods. I have lost down to 185 pounds; which is the least I have weighed since I was 13 years old and feeling good. I am able to work out again and enjoy it. Energy is coming back to me. I teach a Bible study and I want to share this with them. I want to thank you for being such a blessing to my life!"
– Joe Blanchard, Texas

"Only 8% of Americans exercise enough to impact their physical condition in a positive way. Yet the benefits of exercise, and how it relates to diet, are well documented. For example, moderate exercise has been shown to lower 'bad' cholesterol and raise good cholesterol. It helps lessen the risk of diabetes, some types of cancer, and especially heart disease – the same diseases that can be lessened by building a good diet. The bottom line: Researchers now suspect that every hour of exercise adds two or three hours to your lifespan."
– Partners magazine, September 1993

moving of the lymph. This improves the body's ability to move and remove toxins. It is a great form of exercise and I recommend it highly. It is especially excellent for people living in an area where walking is not safe and for shut-ins.

We usually use light weights (one to three pounds in each hand) when working out on the mini-trampoline. We start with slow bouncing without removing our feet from the mat. Then slowly increasing the speed and height of the bounce and working into an easy walk. From there you can go into more vigorous movements of the legs ... going from a walk to a jog and then raising the knees higher while going to a more rapid pace. Then there are various exercises that can be performed on the mini-trampoline (jumping jacks, high jumps, etc.). A mini-trampoline can give a person an excellent aerobic work-out within the confines of their own home. An excellent book to read if you are interested in this form of exercise is *Rebound Exercise* by Al Carter.

As in our diet and life-style, we prefer to keep our exercise program simple and inexpensive. Certainly stretching, walking and jogging fit that criteria and, except for a good pair of walking shoes, costs nothing. If a person wants to go beyond that simplicity, the mini-trampoline would be an excellent next step if finances allow. Our next recommendation for anyone wishing to make an additional investment in exercise equipment would be the Nordic-Tract Ski Machine.

As we conclude these thoughts on oxygen and exercise, let me once again try to share the simplicity of what we teach here at Hallelujah Acres so that we can get the big picture. My friend reading these words, we are living in a world that has many voices crying out to us ... "This is the way, walk ye in it!" There is religion, big government, the medical establishment, science, education, the insurance industry and big business, just to name a few. Often their voices are contradictory and thus very confusing.

Let's look at a few of the voices we are hearing today:

Religion says that God is controlling our lives and that nothing happens to us unless it is the will of God. Thus, when we get sick, we pray to God. But too often this doesn't take away the sickness. So, next, we turn to the medical establishment, which says doctors are the only authority and that they alone are the ones who can help us when we get sick. In fact, they teach that any other means of dealing with physical problems is "quackery." If the doctor's drugs help take away the symptom of the illness, we thank God. Thus indicating that God has chosen the doctor and his drugs as His answer to our physical problems. If the doctor can't help us then we rationalize our sickness as simply "God's will."

Religion often teaches that because Adam and Eve sinned and thus fell, their sin is responsible for our physical problems. And thus, once again, we are not responsible, but just the innocent victims. That teaching is as false as Adam blaming Eve and trying to justify his own transgression.

Religion also often teaches that there is an "appointed time" to die, which God has fore-ordained for each one of us and that we have no control over how long we live. This also is absolutely untrue, but few people dare to question what religion teaches, thinking they would be questioning God. So they just blindly accept as truth what religion teaches.

My friend, there is usually a vast difference between what religion teaches and what is truth. Religion is usually the pronouncements of man, often under the influence of worldly teachings, clothed as the pronouncements of God. For a moment, just think of all the religions there are in the world today. What do they teach? Do they all teach the same thing, or do many of them contradict one another's teachings?

We have been trained to accept the teachings that come from the American Dietetic Association and the American Medical Association as truth. And the reason we should accept their teachings is because they are backed up by science. Thus science has become our god and we blindly accept and follow its pronouncements no matter how far-fetched their teachings may be.

Science and the medical profession tells us that we are the innocent victim of germs, viruses and bacteria when we get sick or that we simply inherited the problem through our genes from our parents or grandparents. Has it ever occurred to us that the pronouncements of science and the medical profession may not be truth at all, but simply the pronouncements of a group of people whose paychecks are being provided by those who stand to gain by their pronouncements? Recently I heard a scientist deny that nicotine is addictive or that cigarette smoking causes lung cancer. Almost all scientists' paychecks are provided by the industries who stand to profit from their findings ... the drug industry, tobacco industry, processed foods industry, etc.

There is hardly an evening goes by that we are not told of some new scientific finding on the evening news. They have just discovered a gene that *possibly* causes this problem or a new drug that *promises* hope for that problem. And thus the people are constantly being brainwashed that science and the medical industry – if provided with enough money and time – will ultimately come up with a magic bullet that will take away all our ills.

As a result of all the misinformation being disseminated today, the average person fails to realize that we can take responsibility for our own health and this beautiful body/temple God has given us. Too many people fail to realize that they don't have to be sick and thus most people die decades before they should or would if they took proper care of their body/temple. How different life would be if we took back control of these beautiful body/temples and started

*From the*
*Hallelujah Acres mailbag*

Ellen and Bob Brown

"Even though you are not pastoring a church, you *are* still pastoring we, the people. My husband and I have to write you about the wonderful 'change for the better' we made after hearing you at the Forest Lake Elementary Education Center (in Orlando)... We *both* enjoyed *so much* your lecture. We were sorry when you stopped. We started the next day by not eating 'til noon fresh fruit and not again until 6:30 or 7 p.m. when we eat fresh vegetables and then cooked vegetables. I have been on Barley Green many years, but my husband didn't like the taste. *Now* he takes it three times a day and likes it ... Now because of you ... Bob has lost 12 pounds in 12 days and half of his belly is gone. Everyone is telling him how good he looks! We both have more energy ... I have lost 4 1/2 pounds. We have read your book *Why Christians Get Sick* and it is fantastic! We're loaning 2 copies to people we love who are sick ... A million thanks for all you are doing to help us!"
– Ellen & Bob Brown, Florida

An update: "We are delighted you are providing the world with another book. An update on us is – it has now been five months since we met you, heard you and changed our eating habits. Bob has lost 36 pounds and lowered his cholesterol 81 points to 154. His blood pressure is now 110 over 70. I have lost 13 pounds. By the way, Bob's waist is seven inches smaller. No more big belly!"

providing for them the way God intended and taking care of them as God would have us. Sickness would practically vanish and death would only come as a result of old age ... not from cancer, heart attacks, strokes, diabetes, and the like.

My friend reading these words, 99 percent of our physical problems – as well as the aging process, to a great extent – are under our direct and personal control, and by following the guidelines we share here at Hallelujah Acres, we can practically eliminate sickness from our world. If you think this is too simplistic and pie-in-the-sky type of hype, I challenge you to try the Hallelujah Diet for 90 days, along with following a vigorous exercise program, and then you can personally determine who is right ... religion, the medical establishment, science, big government and all the rest, or this preacher.

In the Bible we read in chapter one of the Book of Daniel about Daniel and the three Hebrew children who exercised this power in their own bodies in their own lives against all odds when they refused to eat the meat and drink the wine that came from the king's table and chose only a vegetarian diet. What were the results? *"... their countenances appeared fairer and fatter in flesh than all the children which did eat the portion of the king's meat ... in all matters of wisdom and understanding ... he found them ten times better than all the magicians and astrologers that were in the realm."* Read the entire account in Daniel 1:8-20.

*We can maintain a healthy body, along with a young body and mind if we so desire. It is within our power because God has placed that power in our hands. And when we take care of God's creation (our bodies) as God intended we will not be sick or die young. "Whatsoever a man soweth that shall he also reap"* (Galatians 6:7) *"... I have set before you life and death, blessing and cursing: therefore CHOOSE LIFE, that both thou and thy seed may live."*

# Chapter 13

# PMS, Menopause and Diet

*By Rhonda Malkmus*

"The consumption of foods and beverages which are high in sugar content is associated with the prevalence of PMS."
– *Journal of Reproductive Medicine*, 1991

As George and I hold seminars throughout the country and even into foreign lands, the questions that women most frequently ask me as a woman are those which pertain to PMS (pre-menstrual syndrome) and menopause. This subject is an extremely important one to most women today because female problems can affect almost every hour of almost every day of a woman's life, physically, mentally and emotionally. In addition, PMS and menopause can affect those around us, our spouses, children and friends and thus, the whole world.

In my search for truth and knowledge on the subject of PMS and menopause, I have found that much of what is generally believed is false. It is often based on misinformation, horror stories and old wive's tales rather than on truth. Ladies, if we are going to find help for these problems, it is vitally important that we have an open mind and that we think positively about the natural changes taking place in our bodies. We must realize there is a vast difference between what women are

*It should be noted that the term PMS (pre-menstrual syndrome) did not appear on the scene until 1931 and did not become part of medical terminology until 1953. Why? What has changed in the past 50 years?*

experiencing today and what God intended! I would challenge you to put aside all the misinformation, old wive's tales and horror stories about PMS and menopause, and to consider some more positive thoughts about these beautiful body/temples God has given us and how God intended them to function and be cared for.

It is vitally important for us to consider that the very purpose of a woman's monthly cycle is to produce an egg so that mankind can reproduce and thus perpetuate the human race. This was designed by God so that man could fulfill God's command to "be fruitful and multiply" (Genesis 1:28). The purpose of the flow of blood is to shed the lining of the uterus. Susan Larkin, M.D. states that, "Each month the uterus prepares a thick, bloodrich cushion to nourish and house a fertilized egg. If conception occurs, the embryo implants itself in the uterine lining after six or seven days. If pregnancy does not occur, the egg does not implant in the uterus and the extra build-up of uterine lining is not needed. The uterus cleanses itself by releasing the extra blood and tissue so the build-up can recur the following month."

This monthly cycle was to be a normal and natural occurrence every 28 days during a woman's child-bearing years. Today, however, many women experience severe pain, cramping and heavy bleeding during their menstrual cycle, as well as during menopause. This is often accompanied by severe mood swings and depression. Is this normal? Is this what God intended? These are vitally important questions we must answer if we are going to enjoy life and if our bodies are going to function properly.

Often, women are told that all of this pain and bleeding and emotional trauma during PMS and menopause are the result of Eve's disobedience to God in the Garden. In ignorance, they base this belief on Genesis 3:16, where the Bible says, "Unto the woman he said, 'I will greatly multiply thy sorrow and thy conception; in sorrow thou shall bring forth children.' " What is the Bible teaching in this verse? Is it teaching that there will be pain, bleeding and emotional trauma during PMS and menopause or does it simply say that there will be some pain during childbirth?

For a few minutes, let's look at it from a different angle – *diet and lifestyle.* What we eat is usually the result of tradition, advertising and habit. During the early years of our lives, our dietary habits are usually very similar to those of our parents. As we grow up, we are introduced to new foods at a friend's house or a new product comes on the market and we give it a try and like it. Or a new offering is made at a fast food restaurant. It tastes good and before we know it, we have incorporated a new item into our diet. We do not seem to realize that what we put into our bodies can have devastating effects. How sad that we have never been taught to associate what we eat with our well-being or our physical, mental and emotional problems. Yet, the truth is that *we literally become what we eat! In reality, diet and life-style influence our lives probably more than any other factor in life.*

Prior to the 1950s most food was grown locally, without pesticides, fungicides and herbicides. Foods were not genetically altered, nor were they laced with preservatives, coloring agents, emulsifiers and other additives. Most of these toxic substances were added following World War II. Sadly, the average American of today, if he or she eats manufactured and processed foods, will put into their bodies over 10 pounds of these chemical additives every year!

It should be noted that the term PMS (pre-menstrual syndrome) did not appear on the scene until 1931 and did not become part of medical terminology until 1953. Why? What has changed in the past 50 years? What is causing more and more problems in this area with each passing year? I believe if we will take a long hard look at the "food" we have been putting into our bodies and the way we have been living, we will find some very interesting things – including most of the answers to the problems associated with PMS and

"Why do doctors give women Estrogen Replacement Therapy (ERT) at the end of menopause if estrogen is carcinogenic?...I believe that menopause is nature's way of decreasing estrogen formation in woman in order to protect her from cancer. Who are we to think that we know better than nature...I do not believe any woman needs estrogen unless she has had a hysterectomy at a very young age...Dr. Ray Peat believes that 10% or less of the women on ERT really need it, and these should surely take natural progesterone along with their estrogen to afford some measure of protection from carcinogenic effects."
– Lita Lee, Ph.D.

menopause.

***Growth hormones*** were first introduced by the meat industry in the 1950s so farmers could get their animals to market in less time, thus increasing their profits. Little did the women of America realize the significance of this change in the way their meat was being grown. An example of this would be that a chicken that in past years took sixteen weeks to be ready for market is now ready for market in six weeks due to these ***growth hormones***. When these animals are butchered, the growth hormones remain in the flesh of the meat and are consumed at our tables. Now if growth hormones can cause an animal to grow twice as fast as it normally would grow and cause an animal to mature in less than half the time God intended, what do you think these ***growth hormones*** do within our bodies?

***Growth hormones in meat*** are made of synthetic estrogen, similar to a hormone that is naturally produced in small amounts in a woman's body. Synthetic estrogen has been found to cause numerous problems, including cancer and emotional imbalances. Estrogen is the hormone, in its natural form, that God designed females to start producing in their bodies at the age of about 15 or 16. This is what initiates puberty. This is the hormone that regulates a woman's life and makes it possible for her to have children. This is the hormone that the body slowly stops producing after child-bearing years have ended. So, what happens in the body of a woman when these hormones are added to the meat she eats, thus causing the body to have larger quantities of estrogen than God intended?

One of the most horrible effects of these artificial growth hormones is what they are doing to young girls. If you look at the age of puberty 50 years ago, it was usually in the range of age 15 to 16. Then look at the age a young girl starts her menstrual cycle today and you will find it to be age 10, 11 and 12 on the average, and some even earlier. The capability of a young girl to be able to reproduce at this young and tender age is causing monumental problems in our society!

It is interesting to note that – even today – girls who are raised from birth on a vegetarian diet, excluding all animal products, commonly do not begin their menstrual cycles until about age 15 or 16. When a woman eats only the foods God intended, without the addition of artificial hormones, the blood flow is usually very light to non-existent, without pain, aches or mood swings. This is the way God intended it to be! Take for example the third-world countries of today, where meat and manufactured products are not a staple and where women are physically active. There you will find that the physical and emotional problems associated with PMS and menopause in this country ***are almost non-existent!***

***Ladies, we are creating our PMS and menopause problems ourselves, in ignorance, because we have adapted the diet and lifestyle of this world! Then when we experience the consequences of this wrong diet and lifestyle, we go to the medical doctors of this world for help and all they do is make things worse with their artificial hormones, drugs and surgery!***

"Estrogen Replacement Therapy places women at high risk."
– National Institute of Health Consensus Development Conference 1984

"A mounting body of evidence suggests that other sources of estrogen contribute to the background level of carcinogens in our food environment. Milk, commercial eggs and other dairy products often have traces of estrogen. Most commercial grade meat is laced with it. Birth control pills are based on it..."
– Betty Kamen, Ph.D. in her book *Hormone Replacement Therapy*

"Milk may add dietary estrogen and other hormones now used freely by the dairy industry."
– Dr. Susan M. Lark, M.D.

"Estrogen replacement increases the risk of cancer during use and for many years after it is discontinued."
– *Obstetrics & Gynecology,* 1990

"Evidence supporting estrogen's role in breast cancer comes from international studies."
– *Breast Cancer Research and Treatment* 1991

Have you ever considered that PMS and menopause are big business? Think of all the money being made selling medical prescriptions, and supplies, to say nothing of the doctor bills. Usually after only a few months on the Hallelujah Diet, the PMS symptoms, as well as those from menopause, simply disappear. Often ladies report no more cramps and only light bleeding as well as no more mood swings. That's pretty exciting!

Let's look at menopause. What is happening today to cause women, as they approach what should be a very special time in their lives, to be plagued by all these health and emotional problems? The answer is really quite simple. As the estrogen levels in a woman's body naturally decrease as they come to the end of their child-bearing years, usually in the late 40s, the hormone level drops. This can cause hot flashes, mood swings and other symptoms associated with menopause. Meat and dairy products, even without added growth hormones, can cause the body to increase the amount of natural estrogen being produced. The eating of animal products is the primary cause of these problems

> *Have you ever considered that PMS and menopause are big business? Think of all the money being made selling medical prescriptions and supplies to say nothing of the doctor bills. Usually after only a few months on the Hallelujah Diet, the PMS symptoms as well as those from menopause simply disappear.*

because this creates an even higher level of estrogen in the body. Then when the estrogen level begins to fall, it plummets, often causing even more severe problems. Add to this the side-effects caused by the recommended Estrogen Replacement Therapy and the body has a monumental task to try to deal with all of the outside influences placed upon it.

"Many women base their meals on meat and dairy...Unfortunately, large amounts of meat-based protein can increase the risk of osteoporosis. Meat protein is acidic. When a woman eats meat in excessive amounts, her body must buffer the acid load that meat creates. One way the body accomplishes this is by dissolving the bones! The calcium and other minerals released from the bones helps restore the body's acid-alkaline balance."
– Dr. Susan M. Lark, M.D.

We hear a lot about estrogen replacement therapy these days and that it is the answer for menopause and for menstrual problems. Let's examine it briefly. It has been in use since the 1960s. How safe is it? There is much controversy about this question and the side-effects that long-term use can cause the body. When I learned that Premarin is made from the urine of pregnant mares who have their foals removed during the 11th month of pregnancy so that their urine can be used to produce Premarin, I was repulsed. Then the foals are sold and slaughtered. Ladies, do we want to put horse urine in our bodies? I certainly do not.

Women who have had to undergo complete hysterectomies, have an even greater battle on their hands. Because they now have no ovaries to produce estrogen, the doctor prescribes artificial estrogen. These added hormones (estrogen replacement) can create many physical problems, including cancer and many side-effects including: bloating, bleeding, change in sexual desire, cramps, depression, irritability, breathing difficulties, cervical damage, eye damage and fibroid growths, just to name a few ... to say nothing of the increase in heart attacks of women during these years. Also, without ovaries the body begins to age more rapidly. One of the most hideous things a doctor can do to a woman is

112

to perform a complete hysterectomy, an operation that is almost always unnecessary.

Many reports are available showing that in countries where very few animal products are consumed and the diet is comprised mainly of fresh vegetables and fruits, passing through this "change of life" is of little consequence and hardly even noticed. Certainly, our Heavenly Father never intended for women to have to suffer as women suffer today! The simple truth is that we are creating these problems and experiencing all of the difficulties and suffering because of an improper diet and lifestyle and by putting into our bodies all these artificial hormones.

God designed our bodies to live and be nourished by fresh, raw fruits and vegetables ONLY! He also designed our bodies to be physically exercised on a daily basis. How many of us live according to His plan? Yet we don't seem to understand that when we "suffer," this suffering is usually simply the consequences of our wrong diet and lifestyle. It's high time for the women of America to *wake up* and take back their health and teach their daughters these forgotten and neglected truths.

At Hallelujah Acres we have found that simply by making some diet and lifestyle changes, we can usually eliminate almost all problems associated with PMS and menopause! Lets take a brief look at what we have found:

### THINGS TO AVOID

1. ANIMAL PRODUCTS. By removing all animal products from the diet, including fish, chicken, milk, cheese and eggs, the body will have fewer complications to deal with. By eliminating animal products, artificial hormones are also eliminated (unless taken into the body in the form of estrogen replacement or birth control pills). Flesh foods are also the primary cause of osteoporosis as they create an acidic condition within the body. This acidity causes the body to remove calcium from the bones in an effort to neutralize this acidity. We have also found that those who consume large amounts of soy products have many of the same problems associated with meat eating because of the high protein. Meat, without question, is the most dangerous substance we can put into our bodies!

Another problem associated with animal products is fat. The average American meat-eater consumes over 50 pounds of fat a year. This brings the current consumption of fat by the average American female to about 40 percent of her daily calorie intake. Here at Hallelujah Acres, we teach that the daily intake of fat should be approximately 5 percent of our total calorie intake. And this 5 percent can be found in the consumption of raw fruits and vegetables with very limited amounts of grain. Large amounts of grain in the diet produce fat as can be found in the animals that have been grain fed. The excess fat in the average American woman's diet adds to PMS and menopause problems. Raw seeds and nuts should be eaten very sparingly because of their high fat content.

"The major operation performed in 1985 was, you guessed it, hysterectomy. At $4,700 each, this adds up to $4.7 billion dollars per year. Coincidentally, this surgery generated the most income in 1985. There were 750,000 hysterectomies in 1985 not including those in federal/armed services hospitals or in public health clinics...Some other statistics will give you pause. Two in 1000 die on the table. Six hundred die from hysterectomies each year, not including those who die from other devastating effects later. Eight percent have life threatening complications before their release. Five percent require additional corrective surgery. It takes twelve months to recover from a hysterectomy. Yet only 4.7 to 5 percent are actually necessary (mainly due to cancer). Twenty percent are due to sterilization. Seventy-five percent are due to other ailments such as bleeding, fibroids, pelvic inflammation, chronic back pain, bladder infection. Regarding fibroids, only three to seven percent per 1000 become cancerous. These can be removed by a simple operation called myomectomy.
– From the *Health Freedom News* by Andrew and Cheryl Zupko, 1985.

2. SUGAR.  In the United States, the average woman consumes approximately 150 pounds of sugar per year!  Sugar immobilizes our immune system.  Just one can of soda pop contains almost 10 teaspoons … enough to immobilize the immune system by about 33 percent.  Sugar causes the pancreas to malfunction, leading to hypoglycemia and mood swings.  Sugar depletes the body's reserve of B vitamins and other vitamins and minerals.  Artificial sugar substitutes are not the answer. They can cause even greater problems and must be avoided if we want to experience good health.

3. TABLE SALT.  Our bodies receive all the natural sodium they need from fresh, raw vegetables and fruits.  When we add table salt to our foods, we create many problems within our body, including high blood pressure and water retention.  In countries where animal products and salt are not consumed, high blood pressure does not even exist.  Try to avoid all processed foods.  It is interesting to note that after food manufacturers have destroyed almost all nutritional value during processing, they almost always add sugar and salt.  Why?  Because without the addition of sugar and salt, there is practically no product on the supermarket shelf that would pass the taste test, and thus no one would buy their products. *Remember this well: After you leave the produce department in your supermarket, there is practically zero nutrition in the rest of the store!*  Yet the average American spends most of their food dollars in the "rest of the store."

4. WHITE FLOUR.   White flour products contain zero fiber.  As a child we used to make glue by mixing flour and water together.  Well, in our body, products made from white flour cause constipation, which leads to many other problems.  Try using whole grain flours instead of white flour.  But remember that all flour, after it has been baked in the oven, is devoid of almost any nutritional value … even organically grown, whole-grain flour products.

5. CAFFEINE.  Caffeine causes many problems for the body, including increased incidence of bladder and stomach cancer, raises blood pressure, increases heart rate, aggravates diabetes, etc.  Replace it.  Try an herb tea or Roma. Both are available at health food stores.  Also remember, caffeine in the diet increases menopausal and PMS symptoms.  Many women report that eliminating coffee, tea, caffeinated colas and chocolate relieves PMS breast tenderness.   A word of caution here: Reduce caffeine intake slowly to prevent withdrawal headaches.

6. TOBACCO.  It has been proven that women who smoke have an earlier menopause and greater calcium loss, which leads to brittle bones.  Smokers also suffer more symptoms through menopause and during PMS because smoking decreases the amount of natural hormones produced.  Smoking also constricts the arteries and impairs circulation.  Also, the tars in cigarette smoke line the lungs and slowly shut off the oxygen supply.  Women who smoke double their

risk of heart attacks and strokes. They also experience earlier menopause and more problems with brittle bones due to the loss of calcium. Smoking increases the risk of dying from lung cancer 8 to 12 times. The risks from smoking increase with age, including osteoporosis, glaucoma, heart disease and several other cancers.

7. ALCOHOL. Alcohol intensifies almost every PMS and menopausal symptom, including mood swings and hot flashes. Alcohol is a depressant creating depression and exhaustion. It also impairs the body's ability to absorb calcium. Alcohol has a diuretic affect on menopausal women, causing the loss of moisture from the skin. It dehydrates the body tissues, which carry vital minerals from the body. This loss of moisture from the skin also contributes to wrinkling of the skin.

## THINGS TO DO

1. EAT RAW FOODS. Make at least 75 percent to 85 percent of your diet raw! The closer a person follows the Hallelujah Diet, the less problems they will experience with PMS and menopause! Barley Green is a raw food and is the single most important food I put into my body each day. Personally, I take 3 to 4 tablespoons of Barley Green each day.

2. EXERCISE. Start a daily exercise program! This is extremely important. A good starting point is to find a measured mile – whether it be around the block four times or up and down the driveway 40 times. Then go out and walk that mile at a comfortable pace while timing yourself. Tomorrow go out and walk that same mile, only try to walk it just a little bit faster. Do that every day until you can do it in 15 minutes. Then go to two miles and continue to walk two miles until you can walk it in 30 minutes. Then step it up to three miles in 45 minutes and finally four miles in an hour. When you can walk four miles in an hour, maintain that each day. Daily, vigorous exercise will enhance your clarity of mind, physical stamina and give you a sense of well being. I personally try to speed walk four miles every day. I highly recommend it!

3. SUNSHINE. Sunshine produces Vitamin D in the body. It is important that we spend a little time in the sun, allowing the sun to fall on our exposed skin each day if at all possible. Do not get carried away and allow the skin to burn.

4. STRESS. Reduce stress and learn to go with the flow. That is often easier said than done. My personal experience has been that as I changed my diet to predominately raw and exercised regularly, I was able to handle stress much better. Many women have shared this same testimony with me.

5. LOVE. Take a little time for yourself and learn to love yourself as the Lord loves you so that you are able to love, help and give to others.

"Breast cancer develops in 1 of 9 American women, up from 1 in 20 in 1961. Breast cancer causes 32% of all cancers in women, with 175,000 diagnoses and 44,500 deaths expected in 1991. Also, in 1991, 20,500 women will be diagnosed with ovarian cancer and 12,400 are expected to die."
– National Institute of Health, Center for Disease Control, American Medical Association and others

"When menopause is created surgically, within a few minutes time, many problems arise. The sudden shock of the surgery causes the remaining organs to try frantically to take over some of the functions of the ones that were removed. I have observed: adrenal problems and pancreatic problems (such as diabetes), not to mention side effects of the surgery such as vaginal dryness and sudden hot flashes (for which estrogen is commonly prescribed). This seems such a dichotomy to me since estrogen excess and/or progesterone depletion is one of the primary causes of problems leading to hysterectomy (excessive bleeding, fibroids, endometriosis and cancer). The more research I read, the less inclined I am to think that women need supplemental estrogen, even after menopause, especially since we eat so many estrogenic foods and because estrogen can be produced in the human body, often increasing with age. This is so, even in women with hysterectomies. But in the case of surgery, sudden severe side effects often lead to estrogen therapy because it is not a gradual process and the woman believes she has no choice. However, I have never seen a menopausal women (whether natural or surgical) who did not successfully ameliorate hot flashes with progesterone treatment, sometimes (rarely) combined with homeopathic estrogen therapy. The only difference is time...But it does happen, sometimes in one month, and sometimes in six months."
– *Earthletter* Vol. 1, No. 2, June 1991

Remember, it is *your* body/temple and *you* can have control over it. You do not have to be sick! Take control! For too long, women have allowed others to control their bodies … advertisers, food merchants, fear, doctors, etc.

For the past year, I have been on a quest to find a natural hormone replacement to help women with menopausal problems. The basic and most important key is a natural diet of predominately raw food, exercise, etc., as mentioned earlier. This will usually all but eliminate menopausal symptoms as our body slowly stops producing natural hormones. But for those who need some help during this change of life, I have finally found a natural hormone replacement that will not harm us. Many experts in the field now agree that one reason behind the unsuccessful results and dangerous side-effects of estrogen replacement therapy is that estrogen is the wrong hormone to take. Progesterone is a better choice because natural progesterone can help the body to produce its own estrogen. Natural progesterone has been found in about 5,000 different plants, but the best source known today is found in a specific type of wild yams. A wild yam-based cream that we sell at Hallelujah Acres has helped many woman facing problems from menopause and P.M.S.

# Part II:

# An "Amen"

# from Modern Science

"If you have been looking for an easy way to have more energy, prevent and alleviate disease, reverse the aging process, detoxify your body, improve your skin, boost your immune system – in essense, to create radiant health – then eat your 'greens.' You've probably heard this said by your grandparents or parents and now, research is supporting their recommendations."
– Susan Smith Jones, Ph.D., in her article, "Superfoods: Eating Greens for Radiant Health" in *Let's Live,* December 1994

# Chapter 14

# Talking Apples and Oranges:

## Synthetic Vitamins and Processed Foods
## Do Not Offer the Same Nutrients as Raw Fruits & Vegetables

*By Michael Dye*

"Green leafy vegetables provide generous amounts of calcium without the animal protein of meaty diets. In fact, green vegetables such as broccoli, collard greens, and kale are loaded with calcium."
– Neal Barnhard, M.D.

Vitamins and nutrition have become hot topics these days. News media, books, health food stores and advertising campaigns are educating us about why we need vitamins and minerals. It is encouraging to see an increased realization of the role nutrients play in preventative health-care and in helping the body to heal itself with a strengthened immune system.

But we are getting a lot of misinformation on this subject from those who profit from the manufacture, distribution or advertising of the multi-billion dollar synthetic vitamin and processed foods industries. Let's take a look at what modern science knows about nutrition, what we are being told about nutrition and what we are not being told.

• The influence from the big business of synthetic vitamins and processed foods has led to a neglect of any distinction between natural vitamins and synthetic vitamins. For example, we are generally not told there is any difference between the vitamin C in a fresh apple or orange versus the vitamin C in a pharmaceutically-manufactured, synthetic pill, or the synthetic vitamins added to "enrich" or "fortify" processed foods, such as white bread and sugar-coated cereal.

• In most of this mass-disseminated information, you also find no distinction between nutrients that are dead and nutrients that are alive. We are told to eat our fruits and vegetables, but we are not told that there is a difference between a fresh, living, raw carrot and one that has been boiled, baked, steamed, radiated . . . or processed, preserved and stored in a tin can on a grocery shelf.

**Co-author Michael Dye is a former newspaper reporter who does the desktop publishing for Hallelujah Acres. He is editor of the Hallelujah Acres newsletter, *Back to the Garden*. Michael has been a vegetarian since 1975.**

• Another closely related point that is overlooked is the essential fact that our body is a living organism made of living cells that are constantly regenerating ... and that living cells need living food to create healthy new living cells. Scientists understand and accept the fact that the life of our body stems from the life of some 100 trillion living cells that are constantly regenerating. It is estimated that 300 million cells are replaced in our body every minute.

We know the food we eat, the liquids we drink and the air we breathe provide the energy and the building blocks for this massive, ongoing rebuilding of cells. We know that raw vegetables and fruits are composed of living cells, and that the cells of these fruits and vegetables contain the same organic minerals, natural vitamins, living enzymes and amino acids (protein) that our human cells need. We also know that cooking, freezing, radiating or processing kills food, stopping its cellular activity ... and that once we have taken the life from food, there is nothing we can do that can restore that life. This irreversible change alters the form of minerals and amino acids and destroys all enzymes and most vitamins.

Contrasting Juice Therapy with synthetic nutrients, Dr. Norman W. Walker states, "One pint of carrot juice, daily, has more constructive body value than 25 pounds of calcium tablets." He notes the calcium in pasteurized milk "is just as inorganic as that used in making cement."

*The result of the influence from the big business of synthetic vitamins and processed food is a neglect of any distinction between natural vitamins and synthetic vitamins. For example, we are generally not told there is any difference between the vitamin C in a fresh apple or orange versus the vitamin C in a pharmaceutically-manufactured, synthetic pill, or synthetic vitamins added to "enrich" or "fortify" processed foods.*

But despite this knowledge, there are those who would like us to believe processed foods are as beneficial to us as raw, living food, and that synthetic vitamins in pills and processed foods are the same as natural-occurring vitamins in raw food. The truth is that modern science knows relatively little about the long-term effects of how man-made chemicals and altered natural substances interact with our bodies on the cellular level. Warnings have been issued about the dangers of high doses of synthetic vitamin C, $B_1$ and A, and similar problems are suspected with synthetic vitamin E. It's possible that some short-term stimulation may be felt from some synthetic vitamins. But let's address the question of whether they can take the place of living nutrients in supplying material for our cells to regenerate new living cells and build a healthy immune system. There appear to be three schools of thought on this comparison between natural nutrients in fresh, raw food versus synthetic vitamins and inorganic minerals.

The first school is characterized by a total silence on the subject of any distinction between natural and synthetic. They'll say a pill has X number of international units of certain vitamins. You may notice that one of these little pills supposedly has a lot more vitamin C than a big juicy, fresh apple or orange. But they make no claim about whether X amount of synthetic vitamin C is as good as the same amount of vitamin C in apples or oranges. They also avoid the subject of whether a person could live healthily on synthetic vitamins alone without ever consuming natural vitamins in food.

*From the Hallelujah Acres mailbag:*

"I believe you are most assuredly on the right track concerning nutrition ... About two years ago I (tried to change my diet)...But now, after reading your book, I can see that my experiences were groping in the dark, compared to what you have laid out. I just think your work there is the greatest and desperately needed to educate people who are killing themselves in ignorance..."
M.B., North Carolina

The second school of thought includes "experts" who recommend synthetic vitamin supplements, but warn we should also eat a balanced diet. These experts acknowledge fresh food is a more "reliable source" of nutrients than vitamins found in pills. But they don't explain the difference, and they still say we should take the synthetic supplements, just in case we don't get enough nutrients in our diet.

*From almost every direction, we are told that cooked, frozen and processed food and synthetic vitamins are equivalent to fresh, raw food. How could we ever comprehend an explanation for this tremendous lapse in mass-disseminated scientific knowledge if we didn't consider the fact that there is more money to be made from selling synthetic vitamins and processed foods than from raw, live food that can be grown in a backyard garden.*

The third school of thought is a minority opinion represented by Hallelujah Acres. This school teaches that there is a major difference between live food and dead food (or live nutrients and dead nutrients), and that the living cells in our bodies are designed to be nourished by live food and live nutrients, rather than dead, processed food and synthetic vitamins. Science has substantiated the superior nutritional value of raw fruits and vegetables, but this emphasis on live foods is still a minority opinion among nutritionists and even in the health food business.

From almost every direction, we are told that cooked, frozen and processed food and synthetic vitamins are equivalent to fresh, raw food. How could we ever comprehend an explanation for this tremendous lapse in mass-disseminated scientific knowledge if we didn't consider the fact that there is more money to be made from selling synthetic vitamins and processed foods than from raw, live food that can be grown in a backyard garden.

For example, if you look at the leading health magazines, you will see that more than 90 percent of their advertising comes from the manufacturers of synthetic vitamins and processed foods. This fact has a tremendous effect on the information these magazines offer and don't offer. Do you think publishers of these magazines – knowing that 90 percent of their advertising revenue comes from synthetic vitamins and processed foods – would publish a story informing people that there is a difference between the nutrition in raw foods versus synthetic vitamins and processed foods?

A book first published six decades ago is more advanced than some of the latest scientific writings on vitamins. Dr. Norman W. Walker wrote *Fresh Vegetable and Fruit Juices* in 1936, with the premise that a deficiency of vitamins, minerals and enzymes is the primary cause of practically all sickness. Dr. Walker was seriously ill in his early 50s when he was encouraged to try natural healing. He went on to develop the concept of healing with fresh vegetable and fruit juices, and lived to be 119 years old, writing his last book at age 115. Dr. Walker taught that all healing and regeneration of the body must come from within. Hippocrates, the Fourth Century B.C. Greek physician who is

*From the Hallelujah Acres mailbag:*

"Thank you so very much for your newsletters. They are so encouraging, especially when we start to waver. Every time something goes wrong we refer to your newsletters, book *(Why Christians Get Sick)*, etc. We look forward to receiving your newsletter every month with great anticipation . . . Thank you very much for your ministry. It has really helped us very much. We have purchased almost all of your listed books and read them. They have been very informative. Thank you also for the product Barley Green. It has been real good for us and the whole family is taking it now. Supplements in pill form just do not hold a candle to Barley Green . . ."
– Merlin & Mary Mesler
Michigan

the Father of Medicine, based his teachings on this same principle. To best nourish our immune system, Dr. Walker taught we should eat a vegetarian diet composed predominately of fresh, raw vegetables, fruits, seeds and nuts. He would agree with nutritionists of today who say it is difficult to get optimal amounts of some nutrients from eating food. Advocates of synthetic vitamins use this as an argument for taking mega-doses of synthetic vitamin pills. Dr. Walker's teachings are more advanced than these modern nutritionists because he recognized the difference between live nutrients and dead nutrients.

Dr. Walker developed Juice Therapy as a means of consuming more nutrients than can be obtained by eating food. In drinking fresh juice, nutrients are available as they occur naturally in live, raw vegetables and fruits, without heating, freezing or other processing that would alter or destroy these nutrients. When juice is separated from the pulp (or fiber), most of the nutrients from these raw vegetables and fruits stay in the juice, while the pulp is expelled and discarded. Without the pulp, the nutrients can go directly to the blood stream and to the cellular level without the time-consuming and energy-depleting process of digestion. And because the pulp has been removed, we can consume a much larger quantity of nutrients than would be possible by eating that same food.

For example, we can consume nutrients from a pound of raw carrots by drinking an 8-fluid-ounce glass of freshly-extracted carrot juice. About 10 minutes after drinking this fresh vegetable juice, its nutrients are already in the blood stream and on the way to our cells. The nutrients in carrots include beta-carotene (which becomes vitamin A in our body), the B-complex vitamins, vitamins C, D, E and K, along with the minerals iron, calcium, phosphorus, sodium, potassium, magnesium, manganese, sulpher and copper, in addition to all eight essential amino acids.

Contrasting Juice Therapy with synthetic nutrients, Dr. Walker states, "One pint of carrot juice, daily, has more constructive body value than 25 pounds of calcium tablets." He notes the calcium in pasteurized milk "is just as inorganic as that used in making cement."

Medical science knows we need calcium to build strong bones, but we also know the inorganic calcium we put into our bodies can form kidney stones, gall stones, tumors and calcium deposits in joints, while leaving our bones deficient in calcium. This paradox could be explained if orthodox medical science would acknowledge the difference between inorganic calcium (which our bodies can't use) and organic calcium (found, for example, in raw carrots or green, leafy vegetables).

Dr. Walker, a doctor of science, was among the first to differentiate between organic and inorganic minerals. He offered an example to explain this distinction simple enough for a six-year-old to understand. Dr. Walker noted the Earth is full of minerals, but the only source of organic minerals our bodies can assimilate is from plants. We know we can't eat a scoop of dirt and get nutrition from minerals in the Earth. That's because these minerals are inorganic. The only means of turning inorganic minerals from the Earth into organic minerals that we can assimilate is through plants and their process of photosynthesis.

Plants take in these dead, inorganic minerals through their roots and transform them into living, organic minerals we can use. Heat from cooking returns these minerals to their dead, inorganic form.

In their book, *Living Health,* Harvey and Marilyn Diamond emphasize: "It is physiologically impossible for your body to use an inorganic mineral . . . Anyone who knows biochemistry and physiology knows this to be true ... chemically an organic mineral is the same as an inorganic one. But there the similarities cease," because inorganic minerals have not been organically processed into a living form by plants.

## Nutrients Don't Work Alone

Modern science is also learning more about the ways that minerals, vitamins, amino acids and enzymes work together, and in relationship with other factors, ranging from pH (acidity and alkalinity) to stress. The more we know about nutrients, the more we realize they don't work on their own as isolated chemical compounds. Minerals in their natural form (in raw foods), are always combined with specific amino acids, and sometimes with vitamins, in a process known as chelation. Our bodies are designed to consume minerals in chelated form.

Amino acids and enzymes also have a vital working relationship. While amino acids (which make up protein) provide building material for our cells, enzymes are the life forces that do the building. Promoters of synthetic vitamins and processed foods don't talk much about enzymes, because they are found only in living organisms (including raw food). Enzymes are a vital element of nutrition. They are the catalyst for all chemical changes in our body, such as digestion of food, sending oxygen from the lungs to our blood and cells, body movement, synthesizing proteins from amino acids to make muscle, and even thinking. Vitamins and minerals work together to help these enzymes function, and are sometimes referred to as "co-enzymes." Those who depend solely on cooked food and synthetic vitamins for nutrition will be deficient in enzymes. (More on enzymes in Chapter 17.)

We also know some nutrients are necessary for the absorption of other nutrients, but modern science has just begun to discover all these interrelationships. So, our goal should be to ensure that our body has a sufficient, balanced supply of all necessary nutrients in natural form, rather than focusing on just one specific vitamin.

## Why Barley Green?

A modern-day medical scientist who has done ground-breaking research in this area is Dr. Yoshihide Hagiwara, M.D., a research pharmacologist who is the inventor of Barley Green and the author of *Green Barley Essence.*

As the owner of Japan's largest drug manufacturing company, Dr. Hagiwara fell seriously ill in 1963 from mercury poisoning, to which he was exposed in his lab work. In the extensive research that led to his recovery, Dr. Hagiwara abandoned the pharmaceutical approach when he found the key to health is nutrition – not drugs – and that the source of nutrition should be natural rather than synthetic. These nutrients are most abundant in the green juices of vegetables, and after researching and testing an incredible number of green vegetables, Dr. Hagiwara found young barley plants to be the most prolific and balanced source of essential nutrients on Earth.

Dr. Hagiwara writes, "I cannot but feel that man has overlooked the power of green in favor of science and technology." To capture the power and the nutrition of this "green," Dr. Hagiwara developed a patented process to extract the juice from young barley plants, and spray-dry this juice into powder. This process involves no heat above body temperature and no freezing, so nothing is done that would destroy the life or vitality of its nutrients. As with other juicing processes, when the juice of barley plants is extracted from the fiber, nutrients in the juice become unstable. To prevent decomposition of nutrients, the juice is spray-dried in a process that takes as little as two or three seconds onto maltodextrin, a water-soluble complex carbohydrate derived from pine nuts and corn. Maltodextrin replaces the role of plant fiber in stabilizing the juice, keeping it from oxidizing. But unlike plant fiber, maltodextrin dissolves in water, allowing the nutrients to be quickly absorbed by the body. This bright green powder is rich in natural vitamins, organic minerals, live enzymes, chlorophyll and assimilable protein. The green color of Barley Green is from the chlorophyll. No artificial colors or flavors are added.

Small amounts of the juice of brown rice powder and kelp are added for additional nutrients. The brown rice adds Vitamins $B_1$, $B_2$, nicotinic acid and linoleic acid, while kelp offers an extremely broad range of the trace minerals, including iodine, that are missing from our diets and our soil.

The finished product, Barley Green, contains an extremely broad and well-balanced spectrum of nutrients, including at least 16 vitamins, 23 minerals and 20 enzymes. Barley Green is also one of the most alkaline substances that can be consumed, which helps balance the acidity found in most American diets.

In *Green Barley Essence,* Dr. Hagiwara writes "minerals, vitamins, proteins, chlorophyll and enzymes are the keys to health. Together, they maintain our cells in a healthy condition and work to correct any abnormal condition that occurs. They do it not like drugs, which are foreign matter within the body, but serve to invigorate natural activities within the body."

Advantages to choosing Barley Green as a means of supplementing our nutritional needs are that it comes from a natural, organically-grown source; it has an extremely broad spectrum of major nutrients and trace minerals; the barley has been juiced to remove the fiber from these nutrients for better assimilation; and it has not been processed with temperatures that destroy or alter the natural vitamins, organic minerals, living enzymes and easy-to-digest protein.

You don't need a Ph.D. to figure out man-made synthetic nutrients are not the equivalent to natural. How much education should it take for a scientist

*From the Hallelujah Acres mailbag:*

"When we came home from attending your seminar, we immediately told our family all about it, and they each one began the juicing and Barley Green . . . Lewis and I both have been helped more than words can say. My arthritis doesn't bother me any more and I have much more energy and vitality. Lewis' arthritis was much more painful … but he has improved greatly. His blood pressure went down almost immediately after starting on the diet and his cholesterol had dropped considerably on his last visit to his doctor. Neither of us take any more drugs whatsoever . . ."
– Lewis & Elizabeth Rice, South Carolina

to know a mega-dose of synthetic vitamin C in pill form is not superior (or even equal) to a smaller amount of vitamin C in fresh, natural food? Regardless of the nutritional claims, how much reasoning is required to know that a tin can of processed and preserved vegetables from a grocery store does not contain the same benefit to your body as live, raw vegetables? Promoters of synthetic vitamins and processed foods expect us to ignore our common sense and scientific fact when they offer man-made or altered products as the nutritional equivalent to the natural foods from which our bodies were designed to be nourished.

Raw vegetables and fruits are the perfect source of the live nutrients our living cells need. The chemical complexities of nutrition on the cellular level are such that it is futile to attempt to duplicate this in a laboratory. Our bodies are not designed to obtain nutrition from synthetic pills, and we are being misled when we are told otherwise. It should be equally obvious that when food has been cooked (killed), processed and preserved, it is not of the same nutritional value as it was when it was alive, despite what the label claims.

So when you are looking for nutrition, look beyond the numbers on a label. You must ensure the nutrients are natural, unprocessed, raw and in a form that can be easily assimilated by the cells of your body. I have found the nutritional program recommended by Hallelujah Acres – a vegetarian diet dominated by raw fruits and vegetables, along with daily consumption of fresh vegetable juice and Barley Green (from American Image Marketing) – is an unsurpassed nutritional combination. In addition to providing the nutrients we need, this diet avoids disease-promoting substances such as meat, dairy, eggs, sugar, salt and white flour. Raw foods provide the fiber we need, while vegetable juice and Barley Green offer more intensive nutrition that is easily assimilated because it has been separated from the fiber. Other barley powder products that have been processed by heating or freeze-drying, or that lack kelp or maltodextrin, do not offer the same nutritional advantages or results as Barley Green.

Since I have been at Hallelujah Acres, I have seen incredible results from people who have switched to this diet. It is common to see those serious about this diet heal problems such as cancer, heart disease, multiple sclerosis, diabetes, arthritis and more. You don't see this kind of healing from synthetic vitamin pills. While the best results come to those who adapt the entire nutritional program recommended by Hallelujah Acres, others see some benefit just by adding the nutrition of Barley Green to a diet that is otherwise deficient in raw foods, natural vitamins, organic minerals and living enzymes.

# Chapter 15

# Protein and Propaganda

*By Michael Dye*

Protein is by far the most widely discussed and publicized nutritional requirement of our body. With all this information available about protein, you might assume that people are pretty well informed on the subject.

Wrong.

The average American consumes over 100 grams of protein a day, which is three to five times as much as experts now say is necessary. We all know that protein is an essential nutrient, but what most of us have not been told is that excessive amounts of protein can be hazardous to our health.

The dangers of a high-protein diet are not commonly known by the general public because we have been fed more misinformation and propaganda about protein than any other category of nutrition. A combination of badly outdated animal experiments and self-serving indoctrination disguised as nutritional education has left most people badly misinformed about our body's protein needs.

"One of the biggest fallacies ever perpetuated is that there is any need for so-called complete protein."
– Dr. Alfred Harper, Chairman of Nutritional Sciences at the University of Wisconsin, Madison, and of the Food and Nutrition Board of the National Research Council

*"In our society, one of the principle sources of physiological toxins is too much protein."* – **Dr. Ted Morter, Jr., in his book *Your Health, Your Choice***

Several generations of school children and doctors were taught incorrectly that we need meat, dairy and eggs for protein. The meat, dairy and egg industries funded this "nutritional education" and it became official U.S. government policy. Much of the evidence used to support the claim that animal products are ideal for meeting human protein needs was based on a now discredited experiment on rats conducted in 1914.

The medical and nutritional establishments have been slow to accept evidence contrary to the status quo of self-serving "nutritional education" promoted by major commercial influences such as the meat and dairy industry. But facing the facts has forced doctors and nutritionists to steer more and more people away from animal products (because of cholesterol, saturated fat, mucous, excess protein, zero fiber, etc.) and to more fresh fruits and vegetables. It has been interesting to observe over the years how expert opinions and official policies have changed, sometimes reluctantly, in the area of health and nutrition. The subject of protein requirements provides a classic example of how experts and official policies have been proven wrong and forced to change.

Nutritionists have drastically altered their thinking about human protein needs since that infamous rat study more than 80 years ago. But this updated knowledge has been very slow to reach the public. Most adults will remember being told repeatedly (and incorrectly) in school about how important it is to get lots of protein. Official U.S. policy on human protein needs has changed so drastically that there is no longer even a minimum daily requirement for protein listed on the latest (1994) nutrition labels.

This new knowledge has left a wide gap between what nutritional experts now say about protein versus what was being taught just a couple decades ago in school. In an effort to fill this wide gap of information as thoroughly and concisely as possible, here is a six-point summary of what we should know about protein.

*1) Modern research has shown that most people have more reason to be concerned about medical problems caused by consuming too much protein, rather than not getting enough.* Protein is an extremely important nutrient, but when we get too much protein, or protein that we cannot digest, it causes problems. In *Your Health, Your Choice,* Dr. Ted Morter, Jr. warns, "In our society, one of the principle sources of physiological toxins is *too much protein."*

It may come as quite a shock to people trying to consume as much protein as possible to read in major medical journals and scientific reports that excess protein has been found to promote the growth of cancer cells and can cause liver and kidney disorders, digestive problems, gout, arthritis, calcium deficiencies (including osteoporosis) and other harmful mineral imbalances.

It has been known for decades that populations consuming high-protein, meat-based diets have higher cancer rates and lower life-spans (averaging as low as 30 to 40 years), compared to cultures subsisting on low-protein vegetarian diets (some with average life-spans of more than 90 years).

Numerous studies have found that animals and humans subjected to high-protein diets have a consistently higher rate of cancer development. As for humans, T. Colin Campbell, a Professor of Nutritional Sciences at Cornell University and the senior science advisor to the American Institute for Cancer Research, says there is "a strong correlation between dietary protein intake and cancer of the breast, prostate, pancreas and colon." Likewise, Myron Winick, director of Columbia University's Institute of Human Nutrition, has found strong evidence of "a relationship between high-protein diets and cancer of the colon."

In *Your Health, Your Choice,* Dr. Morter writes, "The paradox of protein is that it is not only essential but also potentially health-destroying. Adequate amounts are vital to keeping your cells hale and hearty and on the job; but unrelenting consumption of excess dietary protein congests your cells and forces the pH of your life-sustaining fluids down to cell-stifling, disease-producing levels. Cells overburdened with protein become toxic."

Writing in the Sept. 3, 1982 issue of the *New England Journal of Medicine,* researchers Dr. Barry Branner and Timothy Meyer state that "undigested protein must be eliminated by the kidneys. This unnecessary work stresses out the kidneys so much that gradually lesions are developed and tissues begin to harden." In the colon, this excess protein waste putrefies into toxic substances, some of which are absorbed into the bloodstream. Dr. Willard Visek, Professor of Clinical Sciences at the University of Illinois Medical School, warns, "A high protein diet also breaks down the pancreas and lowers resistance to cancer as well as contributes to the development of diabetes."

Anyone successfully indoctrinated by the meat and dairy industry's nutritional education would be puzzled by the numerous studies finding osteoporosis, a calcium deficiency that makes the bones porous and brittle, is very prominent among people with high consumption of both protein and calcium. For example, the March 1983 *Journal of Clinical Nutrition* found that by age 65, the measurable bone loss of meat-eaters was five to six times worse than of vegetarians. The Aug. 22, 1984 issue of the *Medical Tribune* also found that vegetarians have "significantly stronger bones."

> *The dangers of a high-protein diet are not commonly known by the general public because we have been fed more misinformation and propaganda about protein than any other category of nutrition. A combination of badly outdated animal experiments and self-serving indoctrination disguised as nutritional education has left most people badly misinformed about our body's protein needs.*

African Bantu women average only 350 mg. of calcium per day (far below the National Dairy Council recommendation of 1,200 mg.), but seldom break a bone, and osteoporosis is practically non-existent, because they have a low-protein diet. At the other extreme, Eskimos have the highest calcium intake in the world (more than 2,000 mg. a day), but they suffer from one of the highest rates of osteoporosis because their diet is also the highest in protein.

The explanation for these findings is that meat consumption leaves an acidic residue, and a diet of acid-forming foods requires the body to balance its pH by withdrawing calcium (an alkaline mineral) from the bones and teeth. So even if we consume sufficient calcium, a high-protein, meat-based diet will cause calcium to be leached from our bones. Dr. John McDougall reports on one long-term study finding that even with calcium intakes as high as 1,400 mgs. a day, if the subjects consumed 75 grams of protein daily, there was more calcium lost in their urine than absorbed into their body. These results show that to avoid a calcium deficiency, it may be more important to reduce protein intake than to increase calcium consumption.

In his 1976 book, *How to Get Well,* Dr. Paavo Airola, Ph.D., N.D., notes we "have been brought to believe that a high protein diet is a must if you wish to attain a high level of health and prevent disease. Health writers and 'experts' who advocated high protein diets were misled by slanted research, which was

> "When volunteers eat a high protein meal, they lose calcium in their urine. If they consume modest amounts of protein, they lose much less calcium in their urine."
> – Neal Barnhard, M.D.

127

financed by dairy and meat industries, or by insufficient and outdated information. Most recent research, worldwide, both scientific and empirical, shows more and more convincingly that our past beliefs in regard to high requirements of protein are out-dated and incorrect, and that the actual daily need for protein in human nutrition is far below that which has long been considered necessary. Researchers, working independently in many parts of the world, arrived at the conclusion that our actual daily need of protein is only 25 to 35 grams (raw proteins being utilized twice as well as cooked) ... But what is even more important, the worldwide research brings almost daily confirmation of the scientific premise ... that proteins, essential and important as they are, *can be extremely harmful when consumed in excess of your actual need.*"

*It may come as quite a shock to people trying to consume as much protein as possible to read in major medical journals and scientific reports that excess protein has been found to promote the growth of cancer cells and can cause liver and kidney disorders, digestive problems, gout, arthritis, calcium deficiencies (including osteoporosis) and other harmful mineral imbalances.*

Dr. Airola continues: "The metabolism of proteins consumed in excess of the actual need leaves toxic residues of metabolic waste in tissues, causes autotoxemia, overacidity and nutritional deficiencies, accumulation of uric acid and purines in the tissues, intestinal putrefaction, and contributes to the development of many of our most common and serious diseases, such as arthritis, kidney damage, pyorrhea, schizophrenia, osteoporosis, arteriosclerosis, heart disease, and cancer. A high protein diet also causes premature aging and lowers life expectancy."

*2) It is easier to meet our minimum daily protein requirements than most people would imagine . . . with just fruits and vegetables.* Because much of what experts once believed about protein has been proven incorrect, U.S. government recommendations on daily protein consumption have been reduced from 118 grams to 46 to 56 grams in the 1980's to the present level of 25 to 35 grams. In fact, the most recent (1994) nutrition labels for food do not include a minimum daily requirement of protein because nutritionists now know it would be very unusual for a person to not meet his or her protein requirements. Many nutritionists now feel that 20 grams of protein a day is more than enough, and warn about the potential dangers of consistently consuming much more than this amount. The average American consumes a little over 100 grams of protein per day.

Drastically reduced recommendations for protein consumption are an obvious indication that official information about protein taught not so long ago to everyone from school children to doctors was incorrect, but there has been no major effort to inform the public that what we were taught has been proven wrong. So there are large numbers of people with medical problems caused by eating more than four or five times as much protein as necessary, yet their misguided obsession is still to ensure that they get enough protein.

*From the Hallelujah Acres mailbag:*

"I am 85 years old and am in better health than I was 25 years ago when I changed my diet..."
– W. T. Wayman, Florida

A good way of determining which foods provide sufficient protein is to consider recommendations on the percentage of our total calorie intake that should be made up of protein, and then determine which foods meet these recommendations. These recommendations range from 2 ½ to 8 percent. Reports in the *American Journal of Clinical Nutrition* say we should receive 2 ½ percent of our daily calorie intake from protein, and that many populations have lived in excellent health on that amount. The World Health Organization established a figure of 4 ½ percent. The Food and Nutrition Board recommends 6 percent, while the National Research Council recommends 8 percent.

The 6 and 8 percent figures are more than what most people need, and these higher percentages are intended as a margin of safety. But still, these recommendations are met by many fruits and greatly exceeded by most vegetables. For example, the percentage of calories provided by protein in spinach is 49%; broccoli 45%; cauliflower 40%; lettuce 34%; peas 30%; green beans 26%; cucumbers 24%; celery 21%; potatoes 11%; sweet potatoes 6%; honeydew 10%; cantaloupe 9%; strawberry 8%; orange 8%; watermelon 8%; peach 6%; pear 5%; banana 5%; pineapple 3%; and apple 1%. Considering these figures, any nutritionist would have to agree it is very easy for a vegetarian to get sufficient protein.

Two reasons we have such low protein requirements, as noted by Harvey and Marilyn Diamond in *Fit for Life,* are that, "the human body recycles 70 percent of its proteinaceous waste," and our body loses only about 23 grams of protein a day.

**3)** ***The need to consume foods or meals containing "complete protein" is based on an erroneous and out-dated myth.*** Due to lingering misinformation from a 1914 rat study, many people still believe they must eat animal products to obtain "complete protein." And for other people, this fallacy was replaced by a second inaccurate theory that proper food combining is necessary to obtain "complete protein" from vegetables. Both of these theories have been unquestionably disproved, because we now know people can completely satisfy their protein needs and all other nutritional requirements from a good variety of raw fruits and vegetables without worrying about proper food combining or adding protein supplements or animal products to their diet.

In fact, the whole theory behind the need to consume "complete protein" – a belief once accepted as fact by medical and nutritional experts – is now disregarded. For example, Dr. Alfred Harper, Chairman of Nutritional Sciences at the University of Wisconsin, Madison, and of the Food and Nutrition Board of the National Research Council, states, "One of the biggest fallacies ever perpetuated is that there is any need for so-called complete protein."

Protein is composed of amino acids, and these amino acids are literally the building blocks of our body. There are eight essential amino acids we need from food for our body to build "complete protein," and every one of these amino acids can be found in fruits and vegetables. (There is a total of 23 amino acids we need, but our body is able to produce 15 of these, leaving eight "essential" amino acids that must be obtained from food.) There are many

vegetables and some fruits that contain all eight essential amino acids, including carrots, brussels sprouts, cabbage, cauliflower, corn, cucumbers, eggplant, kale, okra, peas, potatoes, summer squash, sweet potatoes, tomatoes and bananas.

But the reason we do not need all eight essential amino acids from one food or from one meal is that our body stores amino acids for future use. From the digestion of food and from recycling of proteinaceous wastes, our body maintains an amino acid pool, which is circulated to cells throughout the body by our blood and lymph systems. These cells and our liver are constantly making deposits and withdrawals from this pool, based on the supply and demand of specific amino acids.

The belief that animal protein is superior to vegetable protein dates back to 1914 when two researchers named Osborn and Mendel found that rats grew faster on animal protein than plant protein. From these findings, meat, dairy and eggs were termed as "Class A" proteins, and vegetable proteins were classified as an inferior "Class B." In the mid-1940s, researchers found that ten essential amino acids are required for a rat's diet, and that meat, dairy and eggs supplied all ten of these amino acids, whereas wheat, rice and corn did not. The meat, dairy and egg industries capitalized on both of these findings, with little regard for the fact that nutritional requirements for rats are very different than for humans.

It was discovered in 1952 that humans required only eight essential amino acids, and that fruits and vegetables are an excellent source of all of these. Later experiments also found that although animal protein does speed the growth of rats, animal protein also leads to a shorter life-span and higher rates of cancer and other diseases. There are also major differences in the protein needs of humans and rats. For example, human breast milk is composed of 5 percent protein, compared to 49 percent protein in rat milk. And a human infant requires an average of 180 days to double its birth weitht, compared to only four days for rats.

To illustrate how ignorant "experts" can be, during the time that high-protein diets were thought to be healthy, many experts felt it was a "mistake of nature" that human females (blame it on the women) produced breast milk of only 5 percent protein.

The "complete protein" myth was given another boost in 1971 when Frances Moore Lappe wrote *Diet for a Small Planet.* Lappe discouraged meat eating, but promoted food combining with vegetable proteins, such as beans and rice, to obtain all eight essential amino acids in one meal. But by 1981, Lappe conducted additional research and realized that combining vegetarian foods was not necessary to get proper protein. In her tenth anniversary edition of *Diet for a Small Planet,* Lappe admitted her blunder and acknowledged that food combining is not necessary to obtain sufficient protein from a vegetarian diet. In fact, Dr. John McDougall warns that efforts to combine foods for complete protein are not only unnecessary, but dangerous, because "one who follows the advice for protein combining can unintentionally design a diet containing an excessive and therefore harmful amount of protein."

*4) Protein is an essential part of our (living) body and there is a difference between protein that has been cooked and protein in its raw (living) form.* We should realize that our body (which is made of some 100 trillion *living* cells) is composed of 15 percent protein, making protein the primary solid element in our body, and second only to water, which composes 70 percent of our body. Protein is composed of amino acids, and amino acids are made up of chains of atoms. These atoms that make up amino acids that make up protein literally become the building blocks for our body.

The problem is that cooking kills food and de-natures or re-arranges the molecular structure of the protein, causing amino acids to become coagulated, or fused together, and it even changes the vibration of the atoms.

Dr. Norman W. Walker emphasizes there is a difference between atoms that are alive and atoms that are dead. Dr. Walker says heat from cooking kills and changes the vibration of the atoms that compose amino acids that compose protein that compose our body. In a human body, Dr. Walker notes that within six minutes after death, our atoms change their vibration and are no longer in a live, organic form. So the difference between cooked and raw protein is the difference between the life and death of the atoms that make up 15 percent of our body.

Dr. Walker writes: "Just as life is dynamic, magnetic, organic, so is death static, non-magnetic, inorganic. It takes life to beget life, and this applies to the atoms in our food. When the atoms in amino acids are live, organic atoms, they can function efficiently. When they are destroyed by the killing of the animal and the cooking of the food, the vital factors involving the atoms in the functions of the amino acids are lost."

You can see protein change its structure immediately when you drop an egg into a hot frying pan. As soon as it hits the heat, the clear, runny, jelly-like substance surrounding the egg yolk turns rubbery and white. Protein is not the same substance before and after it has been cooked. In *The High Energy Diet* video, Dr. Douglas Graham states "protein is destroyed at 150 degrees." At this temperature, he says the chemical bond and structure of protein is "de-natured," and once this happens, there is nothing we can do to "un-de-nature" protein.

But Dr. Graham sends a mixed message on the question of whether our body can get absolutely no benefit from cooked protein, or whether we can assimilate only a small amount of the protein in cooked food. He says both. Shortly after saying protein is "de-natured" and "destroyed" by cooking, and that we "can't get any use out of cooked food" … in the same video Dr. Graham states that "only a small portion of that (cooked) protein is available to human beings."

In *Living Health,* Harvey and Marilyn Diamond send the same mixed messages as to whether cooked protein is unusable or difficult to use. They write that, "When cooked, amino acids fuse together, making the protein unusable." The book also states, "Amino acids are destroyed or converted to forms that are either extremely difficult or impossible to digest."

So, we have three options on how we feel about the difference between raw and cooked protein. We can believe that:

a) our living cells get no benefit whatsoever from the dead atoms, coagulated amino acids and de-natured protein of cooked food;

b) or we can think that surely we must get some small benefit from cooked protein, even if most of it ends up as undigested protein that causes many medical problems (and even if we don't understand how dead atoms can become the building blocks for our living cells);

c) or we can accept orthodox medical and nutritional "wisdom" that still says cooked, dead and de-natured protein is just as healthy as living protein from live, raw foods. (To accept this position, it would be easiest to not think about the difference between life and death in the food we put into our bodies, and to not try to answer the question of how our body can build living cells with dead nutrients).

The first position, which is advocated by Rev. George Malkmus, would be considered the most radical by the medical and nutritional establishment. (Remember, these experts are the same folks who – not so long ago – said people couldn't get sufficient protein from fruits and vegetables, and once recommended levels of protein now known to be a health hazard.)

The second position is a somewhat inconsistent compromise. But the third position, which is currently official government policy, is actually the hardest to defend. Perhaps when the evidence is more carefully considered, this position will change, just as so many other official, orthodox positions on nutrition have evolved. Evidence of the nutritional superiority of raw foods has been available for decades, but information that is contrary to commercial interests is slow to reach the public. For a summary of this evidence:

• All animals in the wild eat raw food, so wild animals kept in captivity have provided a good means of comparing the merits of raw versus cooked food. In the early 1900s, it was common for zoos and circuses to save money by feeding captive animals restaurant scraps. But the mortality of these animals was high and attempts at breeding them were not very successful. When their diets were changed to natural, raw foods, the health, life-span and breeding of the animals improved tremendously. A study of this type at the Philadelphia Zoo was described in a 1923 book by Dr. H. Fox titled *Disease in Captive Wild Animals and Birds.*

• One of the best-known studies of raw versus cooked foods with animals was a 10-year research project conducted by Dr. Francis M. Pottenger, using 900 cats. His study was published in 1946 in the *American Journal of Orthodontics and Oral Surgery.* Dr. Pottenger fed all 900 cats the same food, with the only difference being that one group received it raw, while the others received it cooked. The results dramatically revealed the advantages of raw foods over a cooked diet. Cats that were fed raw, living food produced healthy kittens year after year with no ill health or pre-mature deaths. But cats fed the same food, only cooked, developed heart disease, cancer, kidney and thyroid disease, pneumonia, paralysis, loss of teeth, arthritis, birthing difficulties, diminished sexual interest, diarrhea, irritability, liver problems and osteoporosis (the same diseases common in our human cooked-food culture). The first generation of kittens from cats fed cooked food were sick and abnormal, the second generation were often born diseased or dead, and by the third generation, the mothers were sterile.

• Much of the same pattern can be shown in humans. In his 1988 book, *Improving on Pritikin,* Ross Horne notes, "There is an association between the cooking and processing of food and the incidence of cancer, and conversely, it is a fact that cancer patients make the best recoveries on completely raw vegetarian food ... This shows that when vital organs are at their lowest state of function, only raw foods make it possible for them to provide the body chemistry to maintain health. It follows then, that if raw food permits an otherwise ruined body to restore itself to health, so must raw food provide the maximum benefit to anybody – sick or well."

In his 1980 book, *The Health Revolution,* Horne writes, "Cooked protein is difficult to digest, and when incompletely digested protein enters the colon it putrefies and ammonia is formed." Horne quotes Dr. Willard Visek, Professor of Clinical Sciences at the University of Illinois Medical School, as saying, "In the digestion of proteins, we are constantly exposed to large amounts of ammonia in our intestinal tract. Ammonia behaves like chemicals that cause cancer or promote its growth. It kills cells, it increases virus infection, it affects the rate at which cells divide, and it increases the mass of the lining of the intestines. What is intriguing is that within the colon, the incidence of cancer parallels the concentration of ammonia." Dr. Visek is quoted in *The Golden Seven Plus One,* by Dr. C. Samuel West, as saying, "Ammonia, which is produced in great amounts as a by-product of meat metabolism, is highly carcinogenic and can cause cancer development."

• Cooking food also creates many types of mutagens, particularly with proteins. "Mutagens are chemicals that can alter the DNA in the nucleus of a living cell so increasing the risk of the cell becoming cancerous," Horne explains. "Most mutagens seem to be formed by an effect of cooking on proteins," according to Dr. Oliver Alabaster, Associate Professor of Medicine and Director of Cancer Research at the George Washington University, in his 1985 book, *What You Can Do to Prevent Cancer.* Horne further quotes Alabaster's book as stating, "Broiling hamburgers, beef, fish, chicken, or any other meat, for that matter, will create mutagens, so it appears to be an unavoidable consequence of cooking. Other mutagens are formed by the action of cooking on carbohydrates. Even an action as innocent as toasting bread has been shown to create mutagenic chemicals through a process known as the browning reaction. This reaction also occurs when potatoes and beef are fried, or when sugars are heated . . . Fortunately, extracts of very few fruits and vegetables are mutagenic. In fact, quite the contrary. Laboratory tests have demonstrated that a number of substances in foods (including cabbage, broccoli, green pepper, egg plant, shallots, pineapple, apples, ginger and mint leaf) can actually inhibit the action of many mutagens."

• And the results of personal experience from the many people who have switched to a mainly raw foods, vegetarian diet are even more impressive than scientific laboratory findings. Since Rev. George Malkmus healed his colon

"Cancer growths and sores appear in practically every part of the body and take a long time to heal. Since the body creates these conditions, it is essential to eliminate the foods which feed their development...The most thrilling experience I can recall was to see cancer cells taken from a human body and thriving on cooked food unable to survive on that same food when it was uncooked." – Dr. Ann Wigmore, in her book *Be Your Own Doctor.*

133

# God's Way to Ultimate Health

*From the*
*Hallelujah Acres mailbag:*

"Dear George and Rhonda, Thank you for sharing your time, knowledge and wisdom with us in Lufkin (Texas). That conference served as an energizer for me and my husband. After returning home, we have made some big changes in our diet. We have eliminated meat and increased the fresh fruits and vegetables … Your plan seemed rather radical when we first heard it, but it has not been that difficult at all. We do have some fine-tuning to do, but what we are doing now is a radical change for us and we are feeling better than ever. Thank you again for helping us all to see God's plan for maintaining His temple. May He continue to bless you and the work He has called you to do."
– L.R.,
Texas

cancer and other ailments almost 20 years ago by switching to a diet of raw fruits and vegetables, he has led many others in the same direction. The personal testimonials and letters of many of these people appear in the pages of this book … people who have recovered from cancer, heart disease, multiple sclerosis, diabetes, arthritis, obesity, abdominal pain and more. All this from something as simple as a change to a vegetarian diet of mainly raw fruits and vegetables, with an emphasis on freshly-extracted vegetable juice. (Juicing is important because nutrients in raw vegetable juice can get to the cellular level quicker and more efficiently with these nutrients separated from the pulp, or fiber. This allows the time-consuming and energy-depleting process of digestion to be avoided.)

But George Malkmus was not the first – nor will he be the last – person to get great results from converting to raw foods. The results obtained by Rev. Malkmus and Hallelujah Acres are very consistent with others who have placed an emphasis on nutrition from raw foods and freshly-extracted vegetable juice. Dr. Norman Walker was seriously ill in his early 50s, but healed himself with the juices of raw vegetables, and lived to be 119 years old, writing his last book at age 115. And since the 1920s, the Gerson Therapy developed by Dr. Max Gerson has obtained results with fresh vegetable juices that have been unparalleled by orthodox medical practice. "Incurable" diseases are being healed at the Gerson Clinic, such as lung cancer, spreading melanoma, lymphoma, bone cancer, colon cancer, breast cancer, brain cancer, liver cancer, prostate cancer, multiple sclerosis, severe asthma, emphysema, rheumatoid arthritis, diabetes, lupus and more.

The combination of scientific analysis and real-life experience adds up to strong evidence for the superiority of raw protein over cooked protein. Our understanding of the distinction between the life and death of atoms that become the building blocks of our body, the de-naturing of protein and the mutagens caused by cooking protein all help to explain the real-life medical problems caused by excessive amounts of undigestible, cooked protein, as well as the great results people have seen by switching to a raw foods diet.

*5) Cooked meat is not a good source of protein.* The reason cooked meat is not a good source of protein for humans is both because it is *cooked* and because it is *meat.* As we've seen, *cooked* meat is not a good source of protein for any animal.

And meat in any form is not good for humans. As noted by the Diamonds in *Living Health,* we do not have a digestive system designed to assimilate protein from flesh: We do not have the teeth of a carnivore nor the saliva. Our alkaline saliva is designed to digest complex carbohydrates from plant food, whereas saliva of a carnivore is so acidic that it can actually dissolve bones. Humans do not have the ability to deal with the cholesterol or uric acid from meat. The digestive tracts of carnivores are short, about three times the length of their torso, allowing quick elimination of decomposing and putrefying flesh. All herbivores, including humans, have long intestines, 8 to 12 times the length of their torso, to provide a long transit time to digest and extract the nutrients from plant foods.

134

And all protein ultimately comes from plants. The question is whether we get this protein directly from plants, or whether we try to get it second-hand from animals who have gotten it from plants.

**6) Eating meat – or protein in general – does not give you strength, energy or stamina.** One of the easiest ways to dispel the theory that meat is required for strength is to look at the animal kingdom. It is herbivores such as cattle, oxen, horses and elephants that have been known for strength and endurance. What carnivore has ever had the strength or endurance to be used as a beast of burden? The strongest animal on earth, for its size, is the silver-back gorilla, which is three times the size of man, but has 30 times our strength. These gorillas "eat nothing but fruit and bamboo leaves and can turn your car over if they want to," the Diamonds note in *Living Health*. It would be hard to argue anyone needs meat for strength.

And protein does not give us energy. Protein is for building cells. Fuel for providing our cells with energy comes from the glucose and carbohydrates of fruits and vegetables.

As pointed out by John Robbins in *Diet for a New America,* many studies have shown that protein consumption is no higher during hard work and exercise than during rest. Robbins writes, "True, we need protein to replace enzymes, rebuild blood cells, grow hair, produce anti-bodies, and to fulfill certain other specific tasks … (But) study after study has found that protein combustion is no higher during exercise than under resting conditions. This is why (vegetarian) Dave Scott can set world records for the triathlon without consuming lots of protein. And why Sixto Linares can swim 4.8 miles, cycle 185 miles, and run 52.4 miles in a single day without meat, dairy products, eggs, or any kind of protein supplement in his diet. The popular idea that we need extra protein if we are working hard turns out to be simply another part of the whole mythology of protein, the 'beef gives us strength' conditioning foisted upon us by those who profit from our meat habit." To demonstrate how widely-accepted this seemingly-radical position is in current scientific knowledge, Robbins quotes the "conservative National Academy of Science, an organization hardly renowned for going out on a limb and taking controversial opinions," as saying, "There is little evidence that muscular activity increases the need for protein."

Protein requires more energy to digest than any other type of food. In *Your Health, Your Choice,* Dr. Ted Morter, Jr. writes: "Protein is a negative energy food. Protein is credited with being an energy-producer. However, energy is used to digest it, and energy is needed to neutralize the excess acid ash it leaves. Protein uses more energy than it generates. It is a negative energy source."

A 1978 issue of the *Journal of the American Medical Association* warns athletes against taking protein supplements, noting, "Athletes need the same amount of protein foods as nonathletes. Protein does not increase strength. Indeed, it often takes greater energy to digest and metabolize the excess of protein."

Most athletes are not aware of this information on protein, but there have been attempts to make this warning known. For example, George Beinhorn wrote in the April 1975 issue of *Bike World,* "Excess protein saps energy from

"Animals build larger, huskier and healthier bodies from the amino acids obtained from vegetation, than man does by eating meat. If more proof were needed to refute the farcical claims in favor of meat eating, we could look around for carnivorous animals suitable as beasts of burden – and find none, because they lack both power and endurance. Herbivorous animals, however, from the horse, the oxen to the elephant all have phenomenal strength and endurance obtained from eating raw vegetation."
– Dr. Norman W. Walker in *The Vegetarian Guide to Diet & Salad*

working muscles … It has also been discovered that too much protein is actually toxic. In layman's terms, it is poisonous … Protein has enjoyed a wonderful reputation among athletes. Phrases like 'protein power,' 'protein for energy,' 'protein pills for the training athlete' . . . are all false and misleading."

Robbins gives additional evidence for this claim in *Realities for the 90's* by naming some of the world's greatest athletes, all holders of world records in their field, ***who all happen to be vegetarians:*** Dave Scott, six-time winner of the Ironman Triathlon (and the only man two win it more than twice); Sixto Linares, world record holder in the 24-hour triathlon; Paavo Nurmi, 20 world records and nine Olympic medals in distance running; Robert Sweetgall, world's premier ultra-distance walker; Murray Rose, world records in the 400 and 1500-meter freestyle; Estelle Gray and Cheryl Marek, world record in cross-country tandem cycling; Henry Aaron, all-time major league home run champion; Stan Price, world record holder in the bench press; Andreas Cahling, Mr. International body building champion; Roy Hilligan, Mr. America body building champion; Ridgely Abele, eight national championships in karate; and Dan Millman, world champion gymnast … all vegetarians.

That's a list that would surprise the average American, based on what we have been taught to believe about protein and meat.

***In summary,*** it is difficult to avoid the conclusion that practically everything we have been told about protein is wrong. We don't need as much protein as we have been taught, and consuming excess protein is hazardous to our health. We don't need to eat "complete protein." Our body needs protein from raw foods, because the building blocks for our living cells need to be living instead of dead. Cooked protein contains mutagens that are hazardous to our health, and some nutritional experts say cooked protein is impossible or very difficult to digest. Cooked meat is not a good source of protein. And protein has nothing to do with strength, energy or stamina.

But protein is important. And our best source of protein is from the same raw fruits and vegetables that provide all the other nutrients – vitamins, minerals, enzymes and carbohydrates – we need. The best way to get all these nutrients, including protein, is to eat a good variety of fresh, raw fruits and vegetables. The percentage of calories made up by protein in most fruits and vegetables is equal to or surpasses that of human breast milk, which is designed to meet human protein needs at our time of fastest growth. So don't let anybody tell you that you can't get enough protein from fruits and vegetables.

When you consider the health problems caused by consuming too much undigestible (cooked) protein, it should drive home the point that our body is a living organism made up of living cells. And protein composes 15 percent of our body, therefore the protein we take in should be living rather than dead. Consuming a high quantity of dead, cooked protein is similar to taking mega-doses of synthetic vitamins that we cannot assimilate. We would do better to focus on the quality, rather than quantity, of nutrients, and ensure that the protein (and other nutrients) we consume is in a natural, living form that our body can assimilate at the cellular level and use to build healthy new living cells.

*From the Hallelujah Acres mailbag:*

"Your newsletter (*Back to the Garden*) has made a tremendous difference in our health and I am very grateful. Thank you for your ministry of excellent health."
– Carrie Schauf, Minnesota

# Chapter 16

# Our Health, Disease & "Old Age" Are Formed on the Molecular Battlefield Of Antioxidants vs. Free Radicals

*By Michael Dye*

On the molecular battlefield of our bodies, we have billions of oxidized free radicals out to destroy our cells and alter our genetic material. These free radicals are contributing causes to more than 60 diseases, including heart attacks, cancer, as well as the wrinkles, stiff joints, varicose veins and hardened arteries of "old age."

Free radicals have received much publicity in recent years, as researchers continue to discover more and more diseases and disorders to which they can be linked. Those of you who are unfamiliar with free radicals will soon find a lot of "familiar faces" lurking in the background.

Free radicals have an **unnatural** molecular structure that is caused by **unnatural** forces such as pollution, cigarette smoke, radiation (including that from computers, televisions, microwave ovens, X-rays – and yes, even radiation administered in cancer treatment causes cancer), fried foods, cured meats, stress (mental, emotional and physical), pesticides and other toxic chemicals. Cigarette smoke, including passive smoke, can put billions of free radicals into a person's blood stream. An unnatural environment and lifestyle creates an overabundance of free radicals that play a role in practically every major degenerative disease known to man.

A partial list of the more than 60 diseases and disorders linked to free radicals include: Alzheimer's, Parkinson's, AIDS, cancer, premature aging, collagen deterioration, varicose veins, arthritis, asthma, cataracts, retinitis, angina, rheumatism, cataracts, stress, jet lag, phlebitis, hemorrhoids, heart disease, stroke, senility, swollen extremities, kidney and liver disorders ... just to name a few. So, even if you thought you were unfamiliar with free radicals, you

> "Aging is the ever-increasing accumulation of changes caused or contributed to by free radicals."
> – Dr. Dehnam Harman

> *"Very few individuals, if any, reach their potential maximum life span; they die instead prematurely of a wide variety of diseases – the vast majority being free radical diseases."*
> – **Denham Harman, M.D., Ph.D.**

> "... the life spans of animals are directly related to their ability to repair free-radical damage,"
> – The *Chicago Tribune*, citing research by Dr. Bruce Ames, director of the National Institute of Environmental Health Sciences Center at the University of California in Berkeley.

are very familiar with their causes and their effects. Now let's go back down to the molecular level to take a closer look at how free radicals alter the molecular structure of our body and destroy our cells ... and how our body can defend against this life-threatening attack.

At the molecular level, we find an incredible real-life, high-stakes battle going on inside our body between antioxidant nutrients and free radicals. The drama of our very own molecules makes Star Wars – or any of its Hollywood sequels – seem dull and insignificant in comparison.

A free radical is a molecule or molecular fragment with the spin of one electron that is not paired with a companion electron. This is a very hazardous, unnatural and unstable state, because electrons normally come in pairs. This odd, unpaired electron in a free radical causes it to collide with other molecules so it can steal an electron from them, which changes the structure of these other molecules and causes them to also become free radicals. This can create a self-perpetuating chain reaction in which the structure of millions of molecules are altered in a matter of nanoseconds (a nanosecond is a billionth of a second), wreaking havoc with our DNA, protein molecules, enzymes and cells.

It would be impossible to overstate the role of free radicals in the creation of disease and old age. Dr. Denham Harman, M.D., Ph.D., states, "Very few individuals, if any, reach their potential maximum life span; they die instead prematurely of a wide variety of diseases – the vast majority being free radical diseases." Our immune system has a means of defending against free radicals, but it is very easy for these defenders to find themselves outnumbered. We can take in more than one million free radicals in one breath. To defend against this massive onslaught of free radicals, we need an ample supply of antioxidant nutrients. Our immune system uses antioxidants to stabilize and eliminate free radicals. Antioxidants are able to give free radicals an electron, which becomes a companion to their unpaired electron, thus eliminating the threat of that free radical.

Just as it would be impossible to overstate the potential damage from free radicals, it would be equally difficult to overstate our need for antioxidant nutrients. The most commonly known antioxidants are vitamins A, C, E and beta-carotene (which becomes vitamin A in our bodies). Other nutrients, such as the minerals copper, selenium, zinc and manganese, and certain amino acids, are considered antioxidant nutrients because they invigorate the body's own natural antioxidants.

Bioflavonoids are another significant antioxidant. Bioflavonoids offer numerous benefits to our immune system, because in addition to eliminating free radicals, they also enhance our assimilation of vitamin C, and much more.

The most potent antioxidant ever found is a subgroup of bioflavonoids known as proanthocyanidins. Along with their ability to enhance the benefits of vitamin C, proanthocyanidins have been found in laboratory tests to be 50 times more effective in eliminating free radicals than vitamin E and 20 times more effective than vitamin C. Even more impressive than these lab findings are the actual results from personal experience, medical studies and the reports of

"Recent research into heart disease has found that free radicals give us high blood pressure and make our blood clot abnormally. When they ricochet through the lining of arteries, they trigger the chain of events that permit clumps of cholesterol to build up, block the arteries and cause heart attacks ... Free radicals also create waste products like aldehydes, chemicals that jam together – or 'cross-link' – proteins and other cellular material, much like the tanning of hides. When that happens to collagen, the connective tissue of our bones and muscles, it becomes rigid and doesn't work right – we age."
– *Chicago Tribune*

doctors who have recommended proanthocyanidins to their patients. These results have shown proanthocyanidins to be effective against an incredibly wide range of serious problems.

One reason proanthocyanidins are such a potent antioxidant are their high degree of "bio-availability," a term that takes into account the body's ability to accept, assimilate and utilize specific types of nutrition. It doesn't matter how much nutrition is in a food, powder or pill; if this nutrition is not bio-available, it is useless.

Bioflavonoids, members of the flavonoid family, are plant substances recognized for their antioxidant properties and ability to inhibit inflammation. Bioflavonoids are what bring us the bright colors of pigmentation in fruits, vegetables and other plants. We lose the benefit of many bioflavonoids in our food because their value has been diminished or destroyed by premature harvesting, storage or processing. There are over 20,000 known bioflavonoids, but research in this area now focuses on the subgroup proanthocyanidins, which are nontoxic, water-soluble and highly bio-available. Within 20 minutes of taking proanthocyanidins, most of the proanthocyanidins are absorbed, and can be found in our saliva one hour after ingestion, which shows they are well-assimilated and dispersed. Other types of bioflavonoids are effective in the test tube in fighting free radicals, but are not effective in the human body because they are not as bio-available.

Unlike many other flavonoids and bioflavonoids, proanthocyanidins have proven to be extremely successful in both the test tube and in the human body. In one study of 47 people, a single 100-milligram supplement of proanthocyanidins increased capillary resistance by 140 percent in 72 hours. Those given other flavonoids increased 56 percent, and a placebo group increased only 3 percent. In a German study of 110 people with varicose veins, 77 percent showed a clear improvement on 90 milligrams a day of proanthocyanidins. And of the 41 individuals in the German study that had nightly leg cramps, 93 percent found improvement.

Proanthocyanidins have been licensed in France for years for treating diabetic retinopathy because tests found they have the ability to reduce "microbleeding" of the capillaries in the eye, and improve vision. Varicose veins, leg cramps and diabetic retinopathy are just three problems affected by enhanced capillary strength and resistance.

Capillaries are perhaps the most underestimated part of our circulatory system. Dr. Richard Passwater, Ph.D. emphasizes that in our circulatory system, the capillaries "are where the action takes place." He explains, "The sole function of the circulatory system is to exchange nutrients for waste products. The heart merely pumps the blood and the arteries and veins merely carry the blood. What is important – but usually overlooked – is that the capillaries allow the cells to live by exchanging nutrients for wastes." A significant improvement of capillaries

will help both the nourishment and detoxification of cells, which in turn can help every other function of the body.

Dr. Passwater lists four biochemical properties of proanthocyanidins: "free radical scavenging, collagen (a skin protein) binding, inhibition of inflammatory enzymes, and inhibition of histamine formation."

Collagen is a primary component of all structural parts of our body, including skin, ligaments, tendons, bones, blood vessels and capillaries, and the membranes that hold our body tissues and organs in place. Proanthocyanidins and vitamin C bind to collagen fibers and help form "crosslinks," which keep collagen strong and prevents its fibers from separating. Wrinkled skin is the visible effect of the separation of fibers in collagen. Skin that is easy to bruise or bleed is another sign of weakening collagen.

Many find proanthocyanidins to help with arthritis, partly due to its ability to eliminate free radicals involved in inflammation. Proanthocyanidins are recommended for athletes to improve joint flexibility and minimize inflammation and swelling in case of injuries.

In his book, *The New Superantioxidant – Plus,* subtitled, *The Amazing Story of Pycnogenol, Free-Radical Antagonist and Vitamin C Potentiator,* Dr. Passwater offers a list of the "benefits of proanthocyanidins, demonstrated in many studies and decades of clinical experience." These benefits include: "improves skin smoothness and elasticity; strengthens capillaries, arteries and veins; improves circulation and enhances cell vitality; reduces capillary fragility and improves resistance to bruising and strokes; reduces risk of phlebitis; reduces varicose veins; reduces edema and swelling of the legs; helps restless-leg syndrome, reduces diabetic retinopathy; improves visual acuity; helps improve sluggish memory; reduces the effects of stress; improves joint flexibility; and fights inflammation in arthritis and sports injuries."

Proanthocyanidins are relatively new in the United States, but have been available in Europe and other countries since 1969. Over 1,000 studies have been conducted to document their safety, absorption and bio-availability. More than four million doses of proanthocyanidins are taken every day around the world.

Dr. David White of the University of Nottingham (England) conducted research on the ability of proanthocyanidins to reduce cholesterol. He called proanthocyanidins "the atherosclerosis antidote." In Finland, proanthocyanidins are used widely as a successful means of controlling hay fever. The French are able to purchase proanthocyanidins with health insurance. Many women throughout the world use proanthocyanidins as an "oral cosmetic," to prevent wrinkles and keep their skin soft and smooth. European scientists have dubbed proanthocyanidins as "the youth nutrient" because its free-radical scavenging ability slows the process of cell mutation that brings on old age.

In the fight against cancer, proanthocyanidins have been shown to inhibit tumor production in the skin, reduce cell mutation and guard against some of the carcinogenic effects of cigarette smoke. Dr. Stewart Brown of England found proanthocyanidins' ability to reduce free radicals to be very effective in slowing

"The most dramatic evidence so far linking free radicals to aging has been found in aged gerbils that recovered their ability to remember after they were treated for two weeks with an industrial anti-oxidant called PBN … When placed in a special maze, the PBN-treated gerbils – which previously made 2.5 times more mistakes than young gerbils – now performed as well as the youngsters … When the anti-oxidant treatment was stopped in the older animals, their forgetfulness returned."
– *Chicago Tribune*

cell mutagenesis.

Unlike most antioxidants, proanthocyanidins have the ability to cross the blood-brain barrier, which can improve memory, help reduce mental stress and offer protection against senility. This ability to cross the blood-brain barrier is believed to be the reason why proanthocyanidins have been reported to help some people with Alzheimer's and Attention Deficit Disorder, both of which are considered untreatable.

Proanthocyanidins have another advantage in that they stay in our system much longer than vitamins C and E. Proanthocyanidins stay in our body for about 72 hours, after which they start to be eliminated (along with the free radicals they have neutralized) through urine and perspiration. But rather than arguing about the superiority of one antioxidant over another, many experts in the field emphasize we should provide our body with a wide range of all the known major antioxidants.

Dr. Richard Passwater has studied free radicals for 30 years, and it was he who first brought the terms "free radicals" and "antioxidants" to the public's attention in 1971. He was the first to expose the connection between free radicals and cancer in 1973, and the first to show a link between free radicals and heart disease in 1977.

Dr. Passwater explains the need for an ample supply of all the major antioxidants, and gives a specific example of how proanthocyanidins and vitamins A and C work together in "synergism" to reach their full potential. He writes: "After 30 years, I find that the best protection against the deleterious effects of free radicals is a combination of natural antioxidant nutrients. The various antioxidant nutrients work together. Some antioxidants can protect body components not reachable by other antioxidants. Some antioxidants protect other antioxidants, and in some cases can regenerate other antioxidants. The proanthocyanadin bioflavonoids can protect vitamin C, and vitamin C can regenerate vitamin E that has already been 'spent' by sacrificing itself to free radicals ... Some studies show that these bioflavonoids are more potent free radicals scavengers than either vitamin C or vitamin E, but this is less relevant than it might seem. It is not a matter of potency only, but of complete protection, safety and stability. You need all the important antioxidant nutrients. It would be foolish to rely on vitamin E or vitamin C or bioflavonoids alone. The combination is needed for synergism."

"(Proanthocyanidins), research reveals, have antioxidant properties that protect cell membranes from oxidation, thus reducing muscle damage that occurs during prolonged exercise. A major cause of injuries, pain or muscle cramps is the incapacity of the peripheral circulation to respond to sudden increased demand for oxygen. Circulation can be impaired by free radical damage ... The activation of muscles always demands an increased supply of energy. This demand must be met by tiny capillaries, which deliver fresh oxygenated blood and carry away wastes. Capillaries must be healthy to perform efficiently. When capillaries are weak, they will be damaged by tissue injuries and their ability to carry fluid to and from your injured tissues will be impaired. This could result in pain, swelling, bruising or cramps.

Antioxidant (proanthocyanidins) may be of special value in helping you achieve a higher level of physical performance while safeguarding your body against pain, muscles cramps and strain."
– Arnold Pike, D.C., in *Muscle & Fitness*

141

# Chapter 17

# Enzymes – The Secret to Life?

*By Rob Vaughan*

Of all the major elements of nutrition, enzymes are the least understood, the least written about, and they provide the most underestimated contribution to our life and our health. There are few sources in medical science or nutritional health that offer an in-depth understanding to even begin to thoroughly answer the seemingly simple question of *What is an enzyme?*

But once we review what is known about enzymes, you may want to ask: *Are enzymes the very secret to life itself?*

Everyone has heard of protein, carbohydrates and fats, which are the biggest components in food. Most people also are familiar with micro-nutrients called vitamins and minerals. All of these food components are understood to be important and vital to life and should be supplied in the food we eat.

But how many people have heard of enzymes? And of these people, how many know what enzymes are and how they fit into the nutritional picture?

Are enzymes just another piece in the puzzle of life, like vitamins and minerals?

*NO! Enzymes are what make all the other pieces work. Enzymes are not tangible, physical substances. Enzymes are the very life force that activate vitamins, minerals, protein, and other physical components in our body. Enzymes are the key to understanding the difference between life and death, and between sickness and health.*

Every breath you take, every move you make, every thought you think and every action you take requires enzymes. Enzymes are the work force of the body. No vitamin, mineral, protein or hormone can do work without enzymes.

Enzymes have been studied since the early 1900s, but even today this is a field of research still in its infancy. In 1930, only about 80 enzymes were known to exist. Today, there are thousands of enzymes known, and many reactions have been identified for which the enzymes responsible are not yet known. Every year, more new enzymes are discovered. But even with all its technology, modern science is no closer than it was 60 years ago to knowing what makes an enzyme work. We can only discover the enzyme and give it a name.

Enzymes are still thought of by many to be catalysts. But catalysts work by chemical action only. Enzymes function not only on a chemical level but on a biological level also. The chemical part of the enzyme can be synthesized by chemists, but the biological part cannot be. If this "life principle" could be synthesized, then man could create life. The only way inanimate objects can be brought to life is through God; like when man was created: "And the Lord God formed man of the dust of the ground, and breathed into his nostrils the breath of life; and man became a living soul." (Genesis 2:7)

I choose to see the enzymes in my body – as well as the enzymes in living, raw food – as a gift from God to be cherished and preserved. The enzyme is the difference between *physical* life and death. I believe we have a spirit that lives on when our physical body dies. This spirit is the most important part of us, but we cannot ignore the physical body that God has given us. We are the "temple of God," and the spirit of God does not shine through for all to see in a degenerated body. Without enzymes, our body would be a worthless pile of dust … "dust of the ground."

I hate to break the news to you, but it doesn't matter how much progress is made in scientific research, or how much money we spend on it, we will never understand the creation of life. We can only accept it and have faith that the wonderful body that God made will function properly. Our body will function properly if we give it the proper nutrition – and enzymes are the key to understanding proper nutrition.

The best explanation of enzymes I have found are the words of Humbart Santillo in his book, *Food Enzymes: The Missing Link To Radiant Health.*

> *Every breath you take, every move you make, every thought you think and every action you take requires enzymes. Enzymes are the work force of the body. No vitamin, mineral, protein or hormone can do work without enzymes.*

"It has always been felt that enzymes are protein molecules. This is incorrect. Let me clarify this by giving you an example: a light bulb can only light up when you put an electric current through it. It is animated by electricity. The current is the life force of the bulb. Without electricity we could have no light, just a light bulb, a physical object without light. So, we can say that the light bulb actually has a dual nature: a physical structure, and a non-physical electrical force that expresses and manifests through the bulb. The same situation exists when trying to describe what an enzyme is within our body structure. A protein molecule is a carrier of the enzyme activity, much like the light bulb is the carrier for an electrical current."

In "The Energetics of Juicing" audio cassette Santillo further explains, "An enzyme is the electromagnetic energy that manifests itself in a protein molecule that controls the chemical and biochemical processes of life … Pure Energy. The body needs that energy. The body absorbs energy like it absorbs nutrition, except when the body is depleted of enzymes, when it's depleted of energy, it can't absorb the nutrition. All our lives we have been thinking, 'What vitamins, what minerals should I be taking?' when the bottom line is enzymes because enzymes digest the food, enzymes break the food down, enzymes carry the nutrients to the cells, then the enzymes in the cells take all these nutrients and build the bone, teeth, heart, etc."

But the reason you don't hear much about enzymes from the medical establishment is there is nothing solid that you can put your hands on. It is very hard to explain and impossible to duplicate all their processes. Scientists who fail to recognize the action of enzymes in our body also fail to realize the action of enzymes in food and how they fit into the nutritional picture.

There are three different kinds of enzymes: metabolic enzymes, to keep our body functioning properly; digestive enzymes, to digest food; and food enzymes found in raw (live) food, which also help to digest food in our body. Food enzymes are only found in raw food, which is food that has not been cooked or heated above 118 degrees. According to the research of Dr. Edward Howell, who was a pioneer in the research of enzymes, when enzymes are heated to a temperature of 118 degrees, they are destroyed in a half-hour. You can imagine what cooking temperatures, which start at 212 degrees (the boiling point of water), do to an enzyme. At the temperature of 130 degrees, enzymes are destroyed within seconds.

*"A protein molecule is a carrier of the enzyme activity, much like the light bulb is the carrier for an electrical current."*– **Humbart Santillo in his book, *Food Enzymes: The Missing Link To Radiant Health.***

Since our body makes digestive enzymes to break down food, do we need to have enzymes in our food?

Absolutely, beyond the shadow of a doubt, yes, YES, *YES!* This is the whole point behind what Dr. Howell calls "The Food Enzyme Concept," and this is what I will try to explain.

Our body has an "enzyme potential," which means that there is only a certain amount of enzymes that our body can produce; and if we depend on these enzymes alone, they will be used up just like an inherited bank account that is spent, but not added to.

Our bodies are constantly building and replacing living cells at an unbelievable rate; some estimate hundreds of millions of cells a minute. Within a one-year period, almost every cell in our body will have been replaced. So, since we have a whole new body every year, there is nothing to worry about, right?

WRONG! We have a new body, but whether it is better or not is up to us and how we use our enzyme potential. We can spend this potential making metabolic enzymes to rebuild healthy new cells or we can deplete it trying to digest enzyme-deficient food (in which case, the dead food we eat would be ultimately robbing us of energy rather than giving us energy). Every part of our body has its own metabolic enzymes to do its work. One person found 98 different enzymes in the blood alone. Since metabolic enzymes do the work of repairing body organs and fighting disease, we must make sure nothing interferes with the body making enough metabolic enzymes. This is why eating raw food with enzymes is essential for building a healthy body. If the food we eat contains enzymes, then our body doesn't have to waste its enzyme potential

*From the Hallelujah Acres mailbag:*

"Was at your Juicer Demonstration … on Saturday, February 19, 1994, and bought your book, tape, etc. What I have learned has drastically changed my thinking and my eating habits, and was an answer to earnest prayer for Godly wisdom and knowledge regarding my health … Thank you and may God bless you and Rhonda in your ministry of educating people to God's way to good health."
– Rosalie Smith, Colorado

making digestive enzymes. Our bodies were designed to receive food with enzymes, which means food in its raw form.

The Enzyme Nutrition Axiom of Dr. Howell states: "The *length of life* is inversely proportional to the rate of exhaustion of the *enzyme potential* of an organism. The increased use of food enzymes promotes a *decreased rate* of exhaustion of the enzyme potential."

Human bodies and animal bodies are designed to use the enzymes in food as a means of conserving their own enzymes. A good example of this in the animal world is the cow, which has four stomachs. The first three stomachs secrete no enzymes, which gives the enzymes in the grass a chance to break down the grass, saving the cow's own enzymes for more important work.

Although humans have one stomach instead of four, the relationship between enzymes and digestion is similar. We have two sections in our stomach. Dr. Howell calls the upper section the enzyme stomach, which is where our food stays for 30 to 60 minutes after we eat it. The purpose of the enzyme stomach is to give the enzymes in the food a chance to predigest the food before our body has to work on it. The enzyme stomach does not secrete any enzymes from our body. After passing through this upper section of our stomach, food goes to the lower section, which is where our body secretes digestive enzymes.

If we eat raw, enzyme-rich food, most of the work of breaking the food down is done for us. If we eat cooked food, devoid of enzymes, our body must do all the work. This puts a big strain on our bodies and it is a very inefficient process with a lot of waste. It is such a burden that the immune system is called in to help. This is why the white blood cells of our body multiply when we eat cooked food. They are used to transport digestive enzymes to digest this enzyme-deficient food we have eaten. The main three enzymes that are a normal part of our white blood cells are protease, amylase and lipase. These are the enzymes to digest protein, carbohydrate and fat, which make up the biggest percentage of our food. The white blood cells go to the digestive tract to aid the digestive process. ***In other words, you are weakening your immune system when you eat large amounts of cooked food.***

How can we even be sure if this enzyme-deficient food can be properly broken down by our own digestive enzymes? We can't! In fact, some of this enzyme-deficient food does not get assimilated, which leaves fat and cholesterol clogging our arteries, while undigested protein and carbohydrates cause allergies and countless other problems.

Eskimos are a good example of the difference in eating raw and cooked food. Before civilization invaded the north, early Eskimos lived almost entirely on a raw meat and fat diet, because there was nothing else to eat. Their arteries remained free of fat and cholesterol because they ate their meat raw. This is not to say that I recommend eating this way, because there are other problems associated this with type of diet, but it shows that with enzymes in the raw food, it can be properly broken down, unlike the enzyme-deficient diet most Americans are trying to live on today.

The digestive enzymes produced in our body do as good a job as they can in breaking down our food, but if we eat too much enzyme-deficient food, our bodies can't handle it all. There are also a lot of waste products when breaking down this type of food, which produce a burden for our body to clean up. We also have to consider the expense of producing digestive enzymes in our body. They do not come without a price. Our enzyme potential, the "bank account," is what has to pay the price for the extra work. Since there is only a certain amount of enzyme potential, when we have to produce digestive enzymes, this deminishes our body's capability to make the metabolic enzymes needed for rebuilding and detoxification. When the metabolic enzyme level is low enough that the metabolism suffers, we will eventually die. The good part is that if we notice the problem in time, we can reverse this process by using the enzyme potential for what is intended.

We can choose to eat raw fruits and vegetables, which make superior quality cells, leave no harmful waste products and result in exceptional health and a long life. Or we can continue eating enzyme-deficient food, which produces poor quality cells with a lot of waste that cause physical problems and a premature death.

Dr. Norman W. Walker was an early proponent of the advantages of eating a diet dominated by live foods containing enzymes. In *Fresh Vegetable and Fruit Juices,* published in 1936, Dr. Walker writes: "The basic key to the efficacy of nourishing your body is the life which is present in your food and of those intangible elements, known as enzymes. In other words, the element which enables the body to be nourished and live, that element which is hidden within the seeds of plants and in the sprouting and growth of plants is a life principle known as enzymes."

Dr. Walker emphasizes, "enzymes are not 'substances.' Enzymes are an intangible magnetic Cosmic Energy Life Principle ... which is intimately involved in the action and activity of every atom in the human body, in vegetation, and in every form of life ... ***Where there is life, there are enzymes.***"

So, with all this considered, I ask you again: Are enzymes the secret to life? Decide for yourself. The reason I do what I do is not to fill people's heads with knowledge, but to make people think about what they are doing. This is a concept I learned from one of my professors in college. You don't go to school or read to fill your head with knowledge. You do this to learn how to learn. Another good teacher in high school taught me to think in terms of concepts. Don't worry about the ABC's and formulas – use your brain to learn what will get the results you are looking for.

This is what Hallelujah Acres is all about: RESULTS! We are what you might call truth-seekers. We look at the bottom line, which is, does it work?

What we teach at Hallelujah Acres does work, and people do get results! But, it isn't just eating raw food that does it. It is not what you eat that counts, but what you get to the cell level. By eating raw food, there is a relatively small percentage of nutrients that get to the cell level. According to Dr. H.E. Kirschner, we assimilate from 1 to 35 percent of nutrients from eating raw food, but by juicing, we assimilate up to 92 percent of these nutrients. Juicing is the easiest way to get nutrients to the cell level. Predigestion is the key. Our body doesn't have to expend energy digesting juices like it does with the raw food. The nutrients get to the cellular level within minutes of ingestion. This is why people get such good results.

For so long, we have thought of what vitamin or mineral we need to supplement our diet. We can throw this kind of thinking out the door because it has gotten us nowhere. The first step to correcting a problem is to find the cause and remove it. Then and only then can we think of what to add that will help our body rebuild and repair its cells.

The primary cause of disease is an excess of enzyme-deficient cooked food, which drains our enzyme potential and leaves excess waste in the body. The solution is to eliminate as much cooked food as possible without causing undue stress. Then we can give our bodies some easily-assimilated, enzyme-rich, cell-building, raw food. Raw fruits and vegetables, especially the juices of vegetables and Barley Green, are the best means of achieving this goal.

This is what we practice here at Hallelujah Acres, and the results speak for themselves.

"....I have set before you life and death, blessing and cursing: therefore choose life, that both thou and thy seed may live."
– Deuteronomy 30:19

Explaining the principles of juicing in his book, *Fresh Vegetable and Fruit Juices,* Dr. N.W. Walker writes that it is natural to ask: "'Why not eat the whole vegetable and fruit instead of extracting the juice and discarding the fibers?' The answer is simple: solid food requires many hours of digestive activity before its nourishment is finally available to the cells and tissues of the body. While the fibers in solid food have virtually no nourishing value, they do act as an intestinal broom during the peristaltic activity of the intestines, hence the need to eat raw foods in addition to drinking juices. However, the removal of the fibers in the extraction of the juices, enables juices to be very quickly digested and assimilated, sometimes in a matter of minutes, with a minimum of effort and exertion on the part of the digestive system."

# Chapter 18

# Why Juice?

*By Michael Dye*

Drinking the freshly-extracted juices of vegetables is the fastest way to obtain the nutrients necessary to restore the human body to health. To know why this is true, we must understand what our body is made of, how our body's amazing process of self-healing works . . . and what is the best way of consuming the elements that contribute to this self-healing.

Our body is a living organism made of living cells that require living food (raw food) to function properly. Cooked food is dead food and has very little nutritional value. Cooking destroys about 83 percent of vitamin content, kills all enzymes, de-natures protein and turns organic minerals into an inorganic form that is not usable by our bodies. So, live, raw food has a tremendous nutritional superiority over dead, cooked food. And likewise, it can be shown that there is an additional nutritional advantage in drinking the freshly-extracted juice of raw vegetables.

The most abundant source of nutrients that can be used by our bodies is from raw vegetables. But eating these raw vegetables is not the best way of obtaining this nutrition. The advantage in juicing raw vegetables is that when the juice is separated from the fiber, the great majority of nutrients stay in the juice. The nutrients our body needs are bonded together inside the cells of these vegetables, and the teeth of a masticating juicer rips the cells apart, releasing these nutrients into juice. Because the fiber has been removed, these fresh, living nutrients in the juice can get into the bloodstream and to the cellular level in minutes, without the time-consuming and energy-depleting process of digestion.

When you eat a raw carrot, for example, you must first chew it and digest it. Even if we chew well, this is a less-than-perfect process of breaking down nutrients to make them available at the cellular level. Digestion takes energy, which means part of the energy you are getting from the carrot must be used up to get it. And digestion takes time, which leads to some deterioration of nutrients. And the sicker a person is, the more likely it is that his or her digestive system is not functioning well enough to assimilate raw vegetables. In his book, *Live Food Juices,* Dr. H.E. Kirschner, M.D., notes, ". . . the power to break down the cellular structure of raw vegetables, and assimilate the precious elements they contain, even in the healthiest individual is only fractional – not more than 35%, and in the less healthy, down to 1%. In the form of juice, these same individuals assimilate up to 92% of these elements . . . It is a well-known fact that all foods must become liquid before they can be assimilated."

### *"Juice your vegetables and eat your fruits."*

Although separating juice from the fiber helps us to obtain the nutrients more efficiently, our body does need fiber. In the colon, fiber works as an intestinal broom to help move waste out of our body. If we don't eliminate waste quickly and efficiently, this fecal matter putrefies and becomes a toxic waste that pollutes our entire body (see Chapter 20). So we do need to eat raw fruits and vegetables for fiber, but for maximum nutrition, the rule is, "Juice your vegetables and eat your fruits."

*The advantage in juicing raw vegetables is that when the juice is separated from the fiber, the great majority of nutrients stay in the juice ... Because the fiber has been removed, these fresh, living nutrients in the juice can get into the bloodstream and to the cellular level in minutes, without the time-consuming and energy-depleting process of digestion.*

While juicing vegetables is our best source of nutrients to build and regenerate our body, eating fruit is our best way of cleansing the body. Our body is still in the cleansing stage after fasting overnight, so a juicy fruit of high water content should be the first solid food we eat in the day because it is easy to digest. (Don't waste your energy early in the day by eating food that takes a lot of energy to digest). We can occasionally juice some fruit, but there are two major advantages to eating fruit whole. First, raw fruits, unlike vegetables, are extremely easy for the body to digest (well-chewed fruit enters the stomach practically pre-digested). This makes eating raw fruit an excellent way of providing the fiber we need. And second, juicing fruit concentrates the sugar content to such a high level that this harm to our body can often partially offset the nutritional value we receive from the fruit juice. An occasional glass of fresh fruit juice is wonderful, but due to the high sugar content, drinking fresh fruit juice on a daily basis is not as beneficial as drinking vegetable juice every day.

And please do not assume from all this praise for the benefit of freshly-extracted juice that there is any value whatsoever to be gained from drinking store-bought frozen, canned or bottled juice. There is not. Practically all natural nutrients from store-bought fruit and vegetable juice have been destroyed by heat, because everything in it that is alive – bacteria as well as nutrients – is killed to prevent spoilage during its long shelf life. Anyone familiar with the benefits of juice should understand that processed juice is no substitute for fresh juice. These two different types of "juice" should not even be called by the same name.

*From the Hallelujah Acres mailbag:*

"I saw you interviewed on television recently and I was more than impressed - I was over-joyed and thankful. Forty years ago (I'm 89) carrot and celery juice kept me from being an invalid in a wheel chair ..."
– A.C., California

A vegetarian diet that is high in raw fruits and vegetables – and freshly-extracted vegetable juices – will go a long way in providing the nutrition we need to build and regenerate our living cells, while also helping to efficiently eliminate waste from the body before it causes problems.

The raw foods and juices themselves do not heal. What they do is provide us with concentrated building materials so that our body can heal itself. The first part of our body that will restore when given proper nutrients is the immune system. As the immune system restores, then it seeks out the trouble spots throughout the body and starts to heal them.

---

*One of the earliest promoters of fresh vegetable juice, Dr. Norman W. Walker was seriously ill and dying in his early 50's, but lived to the age of 119 after he discovered the benefits of juicing.*

---

The use of nutrients to enhance our God-given capability of self-healing has proven to be an extremely effective means of helping our body to prevent or heal a wide variety of ailments. The pages of this book are full of testimonies from people who have recovered from cancer, heart disease, diabetes, arthritis and other diseases that have killed and crippled so many people.

If we understand the theory and experience the reality of using nutrition to help our body maximize its own healing capabilities, we will see this is the exact opposite approach of drugs. Drugs are foreign substances to the body that are intended to cover up the symptoms of ill health rather than promote wellness and self-healing.

If we realize that all healing is self-healing, we will see that any healing must come from within the body as we give it the proper building materials to regenerate and heal itself. And if we opt for promoting self-healing through nutrition, experience will show that drinking the freshly-extracted juice of raw vegetables is the most efficient way of obtaining this nutrition. Fresh vegetable juice should be a vital part of the diet of anyone who is serious about using natural foods to build an immune system capable of preventing or curing disease.

### But so much for theory – Now let's consider the results

One of the earliest promoters of fresh vegetable juice, Dr. Norman W. Walker was seriously ill in his early 50s, but lived to the age of 119 after he discovered the benefits of juicing. He was persuaded to try the natural healing approach over the traditional medical route, and went on to practically "invent" carrot juice and the concept of healing with fresh vegetable and fruit juice. After healing himself with the juices he developed, Dr. Walker become a pioneer juicer and an early advocate of natural health, writing his first book in 1936. Dr. Walker wrote his last book at age 115. He attributed his healing and long life to the daily consumption of freshly-extracted vegetable and fruit juices.

In her book, *Make Your Juicer Your Drug Store,* Dr. Laura Newman writes:

"A carrot left in your basement all winter can still be planted in the spring and it will grow. It is a live food. But that same carrot, if cooked, is dead food, and no power on earth will make it grow. What most people are doing is feeding live cells with dead food, and that is one of the reasons why degeneration sets in . . . Above all, raw vegetable juice taken daily by young and old, healthy and ill, is a guarantee that the body is receiving its quota of building materials for all the trillions of cells of which the body is composed."

Perhaps the best-known example of healing with vegetable juice on the international level is Dr. Max Gerson, M.D., who founded the Gerson Clinic, now in Tijuana, Mexico. Gerson Therapy has gained a world-wide reputation for its ability to help people cure "incurable" diseases such as lung cancer, spreading melanoma, lymphoma, brain cancer, breast cancer, multiple sclerosis, lupus, migraines, etc. Dr. Albert Schweitzer was cured by the Gerson Therapy of life-threatening diabetes at age 75, and he called Dr. Gerson "one of the most eminent geniuses in Medical history."

Another impressive example is Rev. George Malkmus, founder of Hallelujah Acres, in Eidson, Tennessee. Rev. Malkmus was diagnosed with colon cancer in 1976 at age 42. He switched from a diet of meat, dairy, eggs and processed food to a raw foods diet, with heavy consumption of vegetable juices, and cured his colon cancer, and every other physical problem he had, ranging from high blood pressure and hemorrhoids to severe sinus and allergies. Rev. Malkmus is now in his 60s with better health and more energy than any time in his life.

These results, along with the many other personal testimonies included in this book, are nothing short of amazing. These are not the kind of results you see from people eating a typical American diet, using synthetic vitamins and taking drugs prescribed by a doctor. The only way to explain these consistently amazing results is to acknowledge that there really is a difference between food that is dead and food that is alive, and to realize that fresh vegetable juice is the most effective means ever developed of getting this live nutrition assimilated on the cellular level of our body.

"I started on the live vegetable juices and was soon off my diabetic pills … Thank you so much. Please send me your book *(Why Christians Get Sick)* as soon as possible. I need your whole program …"
– A.D., Washington

Mae A. Gadpaille

"(At age 87) I was afflicted with arthritis in my knees, hands and toes: on crutches and a cane; in and out of hospitals and taking drugs for pain. It was agony going up and down stairs and walking ... My blood pressure hovered around 210/110, and my hair was thin and falling out daily. After a year of taking Barley Green - although it didn't take that long to show results ... I'm free from arthritis, take no drugs, walk three miles daily, blood pressure normal, lost 20 pounds, hair stopped falling out, growing thicker and taking swimming lessons...I will be 89 years old next July 9."
– Mae A. Gadpaille, South Carolina

# Chapter 19

# Barley Green:

## Vital Nutrients in a Natural, Unprocessed and Convenient Form

*By Michael Dye*

Barley Green was born on the premise that the key to health is nutrition and that the ultimate source of nutrition must be living, natural and uncooked, rather than synthetic and highly processed.

From this starting point, Dr. Yoshihide Hagiwara, M.D., the Japanese research pharmacologist who invented Barley Green, spent years of intense research – including a monumental, methodical trial-and-error process – to develop a form of nutrition that is 100-percent natural, convenient to use, and that contains the widest spectrum of vitamins, minerals and enzymes of any food on Earth.

The challenge to formulating such a potent nutritional source was two-fold. The first task was to determine what source of green vegetation was best suited for meeting our nutritional needs. The second, and more difficult step, was to figure out a way of capturing the nutrients from that vegetation without the use of heat, freeze-drying or any other process that would cause the destruction or deterioration of these nutrients.

The reason Dr. Hagiwara focused his search on green vegetation was that he found the young green leaves of early spring contain the most vibrant energy and nutritional density of any life form on Earth. In addition to reviving our spirit following the cold, dead season of winter, Dr. Hagiwara believes this fresh green growth of spring is also the key to reviving our physical body.

In his book *Green Barley Essence,* Dr. Hagiwara reflects upon the "marvelous vitality of the earth, which expresses itself most profoundly in the cycle of the green leaf . . . I cannot but feel that man has overlooked the power of green in favor of science and technology and modern rationalism . . . Indeed it is no exaggeration to say that since the beginning of life on earth, no animal has been able to live without green."

Dr. Hagiwara believes the prevalent lack of health plaguing modern society is due to a shortage and imbalance of minerals, enzymes and vitamins in our artificial diets, along with chemicals, inorganic drugs and other pollutants. Before devoting his research, and his life, to natural health, Dr. Hagiwara was the owner of the largest pharmaceutical company in Japan. But he came to realize that despite the increasing number of synthetic drugs his profession was mass-marketing, cancer, heart disease and other serious illnesses are on the rise.

That lesson hit him hard in 1963, when Dr. Hagiwara fell seriously ill, from the effects of handling organic mercury in his lab work. His physical and mental health deteriorated, his teeth decayed and fell out, and he began developing red sores and losing his skin. His fellow research assistants, who had also handled the mercury, developed many of the same symptoms.

He sought medical treatment and tried all the drugs, synthetic vitamins and hormones he and his company had developed for these problems, but none helped. He wrote in *Green Barley Essense,* "Frankly, I feel deeply disgusted to realize

*"I cannot but feel that man has overlooked the power of green in favor of science and technology and modern rationalism . . . Indeed it is no exaggeration to say that since the beginning of life on earth, no animal has been able to live without green." – Dr. Yoshihide Hagiwara, M.D.*

what useless things I was making." As his health continued to deteriorate, Dr. Hagiwara changed his approach as he was influenced by Hippocrates, the ancient Greek physician known as the Father of Medicine, and his Chinese counterpart, Shin-huang-ti, an emperor of ancient China who compiled the fundamentals of Chinese medicine. Hippocrates said: "A disease is to be cured naturally by man's own power, and physicians help it," and "Let thy Medicine be thy Food … and thy Food thy Medicine." Likewise, Shin taught, "It is diet which maintains true health and becomes the best drug."

Following this influence, Dr. Hagiwara wrote: "Preventative medicine, intended for improving the constitution of our body, is more necessary now than in any past period in man's history. Wherever possible, we should reduce our use of pharmaceuticals. Instead, we should build a form of natural protection by maintaining nutritionally healthy bodies. Sources of supply must be raw natural foods plentiful in enzymes and minerals."

Realizing that pharmaceutical drugs and synthetic vitamins were of no benefit to him, Dr. Hagiwara re-focused his search toward natural means of preserving and reviving health. He credits the recovery of his own health to this change in attitude, along with a regimen of Chinese herbs and a complete transformation of his diet. "Seeing the success this had, I dedicated the next ten years of my life to the pursuit of health in the pure, natural products of God's own Earth," Dr. Hagiwara writes in his book. He found the types of nutrients needed to provide the nourishment missing in the diet of modern man are minerals, enzymes, vitamins, proteins and chlorophyll, so he began an exhaustive search to find the best natural source of these five essential types of nutrients.

He found these nutrients were most abundant in the green juices of

"We have changed our diet, have been taking Barley Green for 6 weeks . . . our weight is down, high blood pressure gone, no more headaches. We feel great!" – Joanne and Benny Keen, Tennessee

vegetables. As described in his book, *Green Barley Essense,* Dr. Hagiwara did extensive testing on an incredible number of green vegetable juices: cereal grasses such as rice, rye, alfalfa and wheat; nutritional vegetables such as spinach, green pepper, celery, peas, lettuce, cabbage and onion; the leaves from loquat, mango, strawberry and mulberry; along with various herbs, Japanese ivies and other green vegetables from around the world. From all these plants, Dr. Hagiwara selected the young, green leaves of barley as the most prolific and balanced source of nutrients on Earth. He then developed a patented, spray-dried powder from the green juice of the organically-grown, young barley plants, which was introduced in 1969 in Japan under the name of "Bakuryokuso," or "Green Barley Essence." After continuing research, Dr. Hagiwara incorporated small amounts of two additional ingredients that he found particularly beneficial to people consuming an American diet. This improved formula, called Barley Green, contains a small portion of powdered brown rice juice, which is rich in minerals and vitamins (particularly B-vitamins), and acts as a natural preservative, along with a small amount of powdered kelp, which offers an extremely broad range of trace minerals, including iodine, which is needed to invigorate the body's own production of thyroid hormones. Dr. Hagiwara found these trace minerals to be missing from our diet because these minerals have eroded from our soil. (And kelp is grown in the ocean, which is where these trace minerals have been carried.)

Dr. Hagiwara writes in his book that he sees his product as "a kind of antidote for the deteriorated nutrition of the fast-food culture because it is a fast food that is totally natural and yet higher than any other natural food in the essential five ingredients . . . I like to call it the 'Ideal Fast Food' and I believe it can help rescue mankind from the poor state he has let himself fall into."

Although Dr. Hagiwara's research has focused primarily on the physical aspects of health, he notes our mental and emotional habits contribute substantially to our condition. Physical, mental and emotional factors can lead to a "vicious cycle" of imbalances in the body that is not aided by modern medicine. "The starting point in breaking this vicious cycle is to make a commitment to mental and physical habits which contribute to good health and the self-healing process," he writes.

He warns that people have put so much faith in medical technology that, "little by little they give up their personal responsibility for the good health of their bodies." As for the ways in which we are polluting our bodies, Dr. Hagiwara writes: "I hesitate to try to list these fully. I could mention that we drink chemically-sweetened liquids; we eat foods artificially enhanced with vitamins and minerals; we consume substitutes for whipped cream that are 100 percent artificial; we even take chemicals to sleep and stay awake." He estimates "maybe less than 1 percent" of supermarket floor space is for raw vegetables because the priorities of commodity distribution weigh heavier on commercialism than people's nutritional needs.

Dr. Hagiwara notes the nutritional superiority of raw foods over cooked food, because the heat from cooking kills food and renders most of its nutrients unusable by our bodies. And he cites the advantage in consuming the juices of vegetables (after the juice has been separated from the fiber), rather than eating the whole vegetable raw. Much more nutrition can be consumed from the juice of vegetables, with less deterioration of nutrients and less expenditure of energy by our body, because the time-consuming and energy-depleting process of digestion is by-passed. The juice has the most nutritional value, but it is not stable over a long period of time, meaning the juice would have to be dried to powder form. The spray-drying process used to dry the barley juice requires as little as two to three seconds with no heat higher than body temperature. Dr. Hagiwara's patented process converts the juice, which is extracted from the organically-grown, fresh-cut barley leaves, into a "live" green powder, with virtually no loss of nutrients. Until this process was perfected, the problems with deterioration of nutrients during the drying process almost forced him out of business.

"It is the fact that barley juice powder is 'living' that makes the difference," Dr. Hagiwara said. "I can hardly express how happy and excited I was when I succeeded in preserving its nutrients alive." Dr. Hagiwara's patented process is used in the U.S. in the production of Barley Green, which is distributed by American Image Marketing. Dr. Hagiwara says this patented process "makes the essence of young green barley available without causing degeneration or decomposition of the effective components such as proteins, vitamins, enzymes, minerals and chlorophyll." About three grams (one heaping teaspoon) of the resulting powder is the equivalent of about two handfuls, or 100 grams, of the fresh young barley leaves.

Comparing 100 grams of this barley powder to the same weight of other foods, gives a good idea of the wide spectrum of vitamins and minerals in Barley Green. Barley Green is a concentrated food, and is consumed in much smaller quantities than fruits and vegetables, so keep in mind that this a weight-per-weight comparison rather than a serving-per-serving comparison. But there are other dissimilarities in this comparison that weigh in favor of Barley Green. For example, Barley Green is organically grown, it is raw and the barley has been harvested at the peak of its nutritional value and then juiced to separate the nutrients from the fiber. Consider that the nutritional content of fruits and vegetables will vary, depending on whether they are organically or chemically grown, and that this value will diminish if they have aged much or been cooked by the time they are eaten. Also keep in mind that more nutrition can be obtained by juicing raw vegetables than by eating them whole (because the nutrients can get into the blood stream and to the cellular level in just a few minutes without deterioration during the time-consuming and energy-depleting process of digestion.)

With all this in mind, Dr. Hagiwara's book compares barley powder to raw spinach (which is a very nutritional food) and we see that, by weight, barley

Kathy and Jeff Butler

"I have been reading testimonies of others who have tried Barley Green. Now I would like to tell you what it has done for me. For years I have had some sinus problems, but the year 1993 was the worst yet. Every morning I would wake up feeling as though my nose and throat were stuffed with cotton. The doctor I went to told me I needed to take medicine daily for the rest of my life to keep the congestion clear. Not liking this suggestion, I started praying for a better way. At a Sword Conference at Gospel Light Baptist Church in Walkertown, North Carolina, I learned about Barley Green and signed up to receive your newsletter. Upon receiving the first newsletter, I read how you and your wife use Barley Green faithfully. I was very impressed with your testimony. After using Barley Green for approximately 10 days...the symptoms had totally disappeared. I thank God for this natural solution to this sinus problem..."
– Jeff Butler, Kentucky

powder has 18.1 times as much potassium, 11.3 times as much calcium, 3.8 times as much magnesium, 4.8 times as much iron, 1.4 times as much phosphorus, 6.5 times as much carotene, 10.8 times as much B1 and 9.2 times as much B2 as spinach. Barley powder has 6.6 times as much vitamin C as the same weight of fresh oranges, and 11.1 times as much calcium as milk. Barley powder has 94 times as much calcium as wheat grain, and 12.9 times as much potassium; it has 59 times as much calcium as polished rice, and 36.5 times as much potassium.

Because Barley Green is a whole food concentrate, it is more appropriate to compare its nutritional value to foods rather than to synthetic vitamins. The labels on many of these synthetic vitamins list incredibly high "mega-doses," but the issue is not how much of a certain vitamin or mineral is present, but how much of that vitamin or mineral can actually be assimilated and utilized at the cellular level of our body. There are 40 essential nutrients (that we know of) that are necessary to be taken into the body to sustain our energy metabolism and keep our 100 trillion living cells functioning properly. In order to be utilized by our body, most of these nutrients must penetrate two major barriers: first the intestinal wall and then the cell wall.

Generally, synthetic vitamins cannot penetrate either of these two barriers because they are not combined with active transporter molecules that are required to pass through the intestinal wall, enter our blood stream and then be accepted inside a living cell. Most vitamin and mineral supplements are isolated entities that have been extracted or synthesized from petro-chemicals. That is not at all the same as a living nutrient in its naturally-occurring form in raw food, combined with all the other nutrients in that food. When our body's living cells are unable to absorb these dead nutrients from petro-chemicals, it is not uncommon for 100 percent of these "high-potency" synthetic vitamins to be eliminated as waste, providing no benefit whatsoever to our health.

In contrast, Barley Green is a natural, raw food that is literally alive. (Even after a shelf life of three years, the living chlorophyll in Barley Green will undergo photosynthesis if it is exposed to sun light.) Because it is a live food, Barley Green is teeming with chelated (properly bonded) vitamins and minerals in their naturally-occurring state. Dr. Hagiwara explains, "In raw vegetables, minerals are bonded in an organic form to enzymes, proteins, amino acids and sugars." When we understand the difference between the way our body assimilates the nutrients in raw, natural foods and the way our body rejects synthetic vitamins and inorganic minerals, it is easy to see the nutrient content of what we consume is irrelevant unless it can be assimilated on the cellular level and used as ingredients in reproducing new living cells.

Dr. Hagiwara further explains, "Barley Green makes such a difference because it is a whole food. A food such as Barley Green should not be recognized by discussing only the amount of its vitamins and minerals. The era of focusing on a single vitamin or mineral is gone in the field of the most vanguarded research, and much more attention is being focused on biological phenomena."

Dr. Hagiwara's book, *Green Barley Essence,* contains a sampling of testimonial letters from Japan, where Green Barley Essence has been used for more than 20 years. Relief was found by these letter-writers for asthma, eczema, obesity, pimples, skin problems, anemia, sexual impotency, constipation, stiffness, gastritis, gastroptosis, peptic ulcer, diabetes, hypotension, hypertension, heart disease, nephrosis, hepatitis and cancer. "Thousands of letters from people who used Green Barley Essence have now expanded my estimation of its value," he writes.

But he does not see this product as a miraculous cure-all. "What should be regarded as the cure-all is the human body itself. It is we ourselves who effect the cure of our diseased bodies by the right application of nutrients and by the formation of healthful attitudes …"

Dr. Hagiwara has done considerable research and writing to help explain how vitamins, minerals, proteins, chlorophyll and enzymes function in our bodies.

**Minerals** are described by Dr. Hagiwara as "the ring of life." He writes, "The source of life elements in all living organisms resides in the minerals contained in the earth." He notes that if you burn a plant and an animal, "you will get the same minerals from the ashes." The maintenance and balance of minerals is the key to health on the cellular level. Our cells are constantly re-creating themselves in a delicate process upon which our life depends, so our cells need a balanced supply of minerals to properly function and reproduce new living cells. Barley Green contains 23 different minerals, and it provides a better balanced spectrum of our total mineral needs than any one other food of which we are aware, as illustrated by the comparisons on the preceding pages.

Minerals also help maintain the pH balance between acid and alkaline. Dr. Hagiwara warns, "should this balance be upset, the cell metabolism suffers, leading to conditions such as fatigue." He describes potassium as "a source of life activity" as this mineral helps enzymes to function. Potassium is "consumed incessantly within our bodies in the process of energy metabolism." If our potassium supply falls too low, it is replaced by sodium, which can then increase to an unhealthy limit. This upsets a balance, which will affect the functioning of some enzymes. Experiments are cited that show persons submitted to vigorous exercise, fatigue from tension, mental stress or lack of sleep excrete potassium and store sodium in the cells. Dr. Hagiwara notes the reputation for endurance of cattle and horses; they work to exhaustion and then find renewed energy after feeding on grass, "due presumably to potassium and many other nutrients" in the grass.

Perhaps the most important advantage to maintaining an alkaline internal environment is that alkalinity is detrimental to the survival of disease organisms and cancer cells. Dr. Hagiwara also believes alkalinity is a

*From the Hallelujah Acres mailbag:*

Janice McKenzie

"If we could travel with my precious Christian mother to Hallelujah Acres, we would, but we have recently brought Mom home after being in the hospital since Dec. 2 and subacute unit of a nursing home. She was diagnosed with gliobastoma, a brain tumor. We knew nothing of Barley Green and how we wished we did! She underwent her first surgery and a month later had to undergo another brain surgery to REPAIR the damage of a horrible germ she picked up in the operation room. Her fever stayed at 106 too long and that with everything else left her brain-damaged and in a coma. Enter Barley Green into our lives and we praise His name for it. An 87-year-old Christian 'saint' came to the hospital and told us to get Mom on … Barley Green. Mom couldn't swallow, so through unbelievable opposition, her brain doctor approved of the nurses giving it to Mom (through the feeding tube into her stomach). I think he figured she was so far gone that this couldn't hurt her. Well, lo and behold, she began to awaken and respond and SMILE and hug and kiss … All of her liver spots disappeared and she became the best looking 'dead' person many have seen …"
– Janice McKenzie
North Carolina

critical factor in normalizing blood-sugar regulation and the proper functioning of enzymes. A diet in which acidic foods such as meat are dominant will foster a sodium / potassium imbalance, and lead to many other problems that can be helped by dietary changes to make the body more alkaline. We do not know of a more alkaline food than Barley Green. Spinach is considered to be one of the most alkaline of all foods, but Barley Green is more than 50 percent more alkaline than spinach.

**Vitamins** "impart activity to enzymes within the body, thus promoting metabolism," and "assist the body in maintaining health," Dr. Hagiwara writes. There are 16 different vitamins in Barley Green, including the anti-oxidants beta-carotene (which becomes vitamin A in the body), vitamin C and vitamin E, along with a full range of the B-complex vitamins. To be effective, vitamins must come from a natural, rather than synthetic source. High doses of chemical-based vitamins "throw off the balance of the body, leading inevitably to side effects," Dr. Hagiwara writes. He notes the problems caused by high doses of synthetic vitamin $B_1$ and C formulas, and he believes similar problems will be documented with synthetic vitamin E. It has also been reported that excessive vitamin A can have harmful effects by causing hypervitaminosis. Barley Green is a good source of vitamin A because it supplies a healthy dose of beta-carotene. Beta-carotene is classified as provitamin A since it is converted to vitamin A after it enters the body. Unlike consuming vitamin A, provitamin A cannot cause hypervitaminosis, he writes.

> *"In summary, minerals, vitamins, proteins, chlorophyll and enzymes are the keys to health. Together, they maintain our cells in a healthy condition and work to correct any abnormal condition that occurs. They do it not like drugs, which are foreign matter within the body, but serve to invigorate natural activities within the body."*
> *– Dr. Yoshihide Hagiwara , M.D.*

**Proteins** are provided in high quantity by many vegetables, and Dr. Hagiwara says it is a false assumption that meat is a better protein source. (For more information on this subject see, see Chapter 15 on "Protein and Propaganda.") Dr. Hagiwara differentiates between usable protein and crude protein. Meat contains crude protein, whereas Barley Green contains light-weight protein molecules that are more usable by our bodies. By weight, Barley Green is about 12 to 14 percent protein, and it contains 18 different amino acids. It provides all eight essential amino acids, as well as all essential fatty acids ("essential" meaning that they cannot be synthesized within the human body, so they must be obtained through diet.)

**Chlorophyll** is a fascinating nutrient because of its extraordinary similarity with human blood (which is appropriate because chlorophyll is the blood of plants). The structure of chlorophyll and blood "would appear to be twins," Hagiwara writes, with the only difference being that chlorophyll contains magnesium in the position where hemoglobin contains iron. Laboratory tests have found that human cell vitality and renewal are aided considerably by the presence of chlorophyll. Chlorophyll attracted medical attention in 1949 following a *Reader's Digest* article titled "Mysterious Power of Chlorophyll." For awhile, chlorophyll was added to a variety of products, from medicines to toothpastes. But this proved ineffective because the chlorophyll being used was not natural chlorophyll, which can be obtained only from the living leaves of plants. The chlorophyll in Barley Green has powerful anti-inflammatory, deodorizing and germicidal properties.

**Enzymes** are the catalyst for all chemical changes in the body. This includes digestion of food, sending oxygen from the lungs to our blood and cells, body movement, synthesizing proteins from amino acids to make muscle and even the thinking process. (For more on enzymes, see Chapter 17.) Certain enzymes from plant leaves are found in large amounts in red and white blood cells, but are extremely low in cancerous cells. Dr. Hagiwara theorizes this is an indication these enzymes are likely to result in the inhibition of cancer. Another enzyme being studied for its potential effects in preventing cancer is superoxide dismutase (SOD). Hazardous radical forms of oxygen are expelled in the process of respiration and metabolism, and the enzyme SOD works to destroy these oxidized free radicals. Large amounts of SOD have been found in the organs of long-living primates, leading to the belief that SOD can retard the aging of cells. The facts that vitamins and minerals are essential in the functioning of enzymes, and that enzymes work in conjunction with protein, are examples to illustrate that nutrients do not work alone, and that specific vitamins or minerals should not be conceived or consumed as isolated entities.

"In summary," Dr. Hagiwara writes, "minerals, vitamins, proteins, chlorophyll and enzymes are the keys to health. Together, they maintain our cells in a healthy condition and work to correct any abnormal condition that occurs. They do it not like drugs, which are foreign matter within the body, but serve to invigorate natural activities within the body."

*From the Hallelujah Acres mailbag:*

"I agree with you 100% in our need to get back to God's original design. I started on Barley Green 4 years ago when I had cancer. It's gone! Thanks," – Charlie Brown North Carolina

# Chapter 20

# Eliminate Toxins & Disease With a Healthy Colon

*By Michael Dye*

By now, most of us know the nutrition we take into our body is a vital factor in determining our health – how we feel, how effectively our body heals itself and how long we live. On the flip side of that coin there is a factor of equal, if not greater, importance that is sometimes completely overlooked and nearly always underestimated.

This often undiscussed area of health maintenance concerns the elimination of waste and toxins from our body. While it is practically impossible to overestimate the importance of putting good things into our body, it is more likely that we will underestimate the importance of getting the bad things out of our body.

It was Henry Wheeler Shaw who said, "A good reliable set of bowels is worth more to a man than any quantity of brains."

All cells must take in nutrients to maintain their metabolism and their life. As an end result of this metabolism, every one of our approximately 100 trillion cells also produces waste material. To maintain optimal health, we must eliminate this waste efficiently. Every cell and every organ in our body eliminates waste and is effected by waste elimination from the body as a whole.

## The Health of Our Colon Determines the Health of Our Body

It is up to our colon to eliminate the bulk of the most toxic and putrid waste in our body. When we obtain energy from the food we eat, we create a waste product (feces) that should be eliminated within 24 hours or less. But with a meat-based, high-fat, low-fiber diet, the average American has a transit time of 72 to 96 hours, meaning this waste begins a toxic build-up that creates numerous problems for the colon and every other part of the body.

If it is not quickly eliminated, fecal matter in the colon turns into a toxic and putrid waste that is absorbed into the rest of our system. Over the course of time, this affects the functioning of every cell and organ in our body. It poisons the blood, lymphatic system, nervous system and brain, while clogging up the heart, vascular system, lungs and sinuses.

A proper diet is one that provides necessary nourishment for the body, and facilitates proper waste removal and cleansing – from the cellular level to the colon. But the typical American diet featuring an abundance of meat, dairy, fried and over-cooked foods, sugar, starches, salt and artificial chemicals is hard to digest, very little of it can be assimilated as nutrition into our cells, it is high in toxic waste, fat and cholesterol, and slow to move though the colon because it is low in fiber.

### Our Colons – and Our Bodies – Will be Healthier On a High-Fiber, Low-Fat, Vegetarian Diet

We know the body of a dead animal in hot weather creates quite a stench after a couple days. This stench gives us a good idea of what meat does inside the 98.6-degree temperature of the body.

The comparison of a human colon with the colon of a true carnivore, such as a dog, provides strong evidence that humans were not designed to eat meat. The colon of a dog is smooth and straight, like a stove pipe, and takes a short, direct route. In contrast, the human colon turns back and forth along a convoluted pathway with many puckers, pouches, twists and turns. The dog's colon is designed to allow a short transit time for even hard-to-digest meat, cholesterol and fat, without the need for fiber to move things along.

*... most colons have become stagnant cesspools, collecting layers and pockets of toxic and putrid feces and mucus that poisons the blood stream and every cell and organ in the body.*

In *Diet for a New America,* John Robbins points out, "Dogs, cats and the other natural carnivores do not get colon cancer from high-fat, low-fiber, flesh-based diets. But we do ... The toxins from putrefying flesh are not the problem for them that they are for us because everything passes through them so much more quickly." He notes that colon cancer is a killer that affects more than 20 percent of American families, and his book provides an incredible number of statistics and medical studies proving that the more meat, the more fat, the more cholesterol and the less fiber we eat, the more likely we are to die of colon cancer.

Fiber acts as an intestinal broom to sweep things along in the colon while fat clogs up the intestines. It is vital to remember that all animal products – meat, dairy and eggs – have zero fiber, while most are high in fat. In addition to constipation and increased risk of colon cancer, a meat-based, high-fat, low-fiber diet can cause a host of other colon-related problems, including diverticulosis, hemorrhoids, irritable bowel syndrome, spastic colon and appendicitis. These are all problems that can be caused by slow-moving, hard, dry feces, and can be cured by something as simple as a predominately raw foods, vegetarian diet,

*From the Hallelujah Acres mailbag:*

"I have enjoyed your audio tape so much. It is so full of information. I play it every morning going to work and coming home. I can't believe how fast time goes. We use Barley Green and Herbal Fiberblend faithfully. Herbal Fiber Blend saved me from having to go thru a series of colon tests. I was in very bad shape with diverticulitis. NO MORE PROBLEMS..."
– N.S., Nebraska

which is high in fiber, low in fat, and produces soft, moist feces that are easily eliminated.

### A Clogged-Up, Rancid Colon Pollutes Our Entire Body With Toxic Waste

Our colons were designed to act as a smoothly-flowing sewer system to rid our body of waste products shortly after the waste has been separated from usable nutrients. But instead, most colons have become stagnant cesspools, collecting layers and pockets of toxic and putrid feces and mucus that poisons the blood stream and every cell and organ in the body. It has been estimated that the average American colon carries up to five pounds of putrid, partially-digested meat, and another five to ten pounds of toxic fecal matter that has been packed with mucus for years to form a hard lining in deformed folds of the colon.

The colon (also known as the large intestine) is about five feet long, and is the final stop-over for the bulk of the waste from food after it has passed through the stomach and small intestine. The colon begins at the ileo cecal valve (which separates the small and large intestines), and ends at the rectum. The colon is lined with nerves, blood vessels and muscles. These muscles create wave-like motions known as peristaltic waves that propel waste through the colon and out the rectum.

In *Colon Health: the Key to a Vibrant Life,* Dr. Norman Walker notes that in addition to forming these peristaltic waves, the first half of the colon performs two other vital functions.

First, blood vessels lining the colon extract from the waste any available nutrients the small intestine did not pick up. Dr. Walker writes: "Obviously, if the feces in the colon have putrefied and fermented, any nutritional elements present in it would pass into the blood stream as polluted products. What would otherwise be nutritional becomes, in fact, the generation of toxemia ... a condition in which the blood contains poisonous products which are produced by the growth of pathogenic, or disease-producing, bacteria."

The other function performed by the first half of the colon is gathering from glands lining its walls the intestinal flora necessary to lubricate the colon.

But in a typical American unhealthy colon, Dr. Walker notes that hard, densely-packed layers of fecal incrustation interferes with all three vital functions of the colon – the formation of peristaltic waves that move waste

> *Over a period of time, constipation interferes with the functioning of every cell, organ and gland, causes the blood stream and lymph system to become overloaded with toxins, sends poisons throughout the entire body, and clogs much of the system with disease-causing mucus ... Dr. Walker refers to constipation as "the number one affliction underlying nearly every ailment; it can be imputed to be the initial, primary cause of nearly every disturbance of the human system. The most prevalent ailment afflicting civilized people is constipation."*

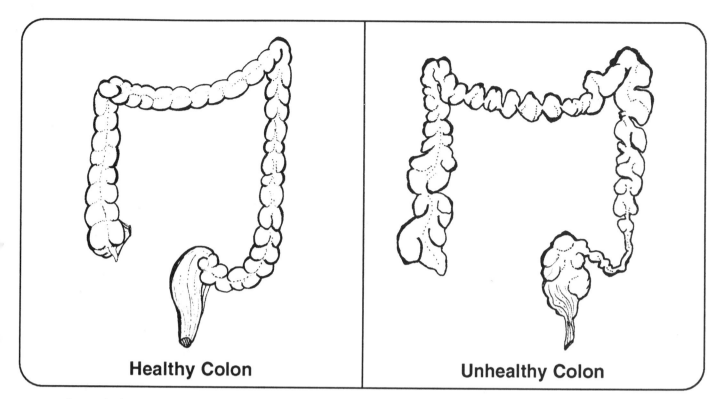

**Healthy Colon**        **Unhealthy Colon**

matter through the colon, absorption of nutrients into the blood stream and the infusion of intestinal flora for lubrication of the colon.

In an effort to minimize toxins absorbed into the blood stream from the colon, mucus is created to encapsulate the waste of certain foods, such as meat, dairy, white flour and other processed foods. This mucus build-up is a natural defense mechanism, and could be efficiently eliminated through the colon if it occurred only rarely. But people who eat mucus-producing foods every day create a toxic build-up of layers and pockets of mucus and decayed fecal matter, remnants of which can stay in the colon for 20 to 30 years or longer.

Dr. Walker's book also explains another way in which the colon has a direct effect on the health of every part of the body. Similar to a foot reflexology chart that shows how certain points on the feet are correlated to specific parts of the body, *Colon Health: the Key to a Vibrant Life* contains a colon chart showing locations on the colon that are correlated to specific organs and glands. "Every time waste matter accumulates in the colon, which results in fermentation and putrefaction, a disturbance takes place both in the afflicted area of the colon and in its corresponding part of the anatomy," Dr. Walker writes. Examples he provides of short-term afflictions resulting from the absorption of mucus and toxic waste from the colon into the rest of the body include pimples, sore throats, colds, hay fever, sinus, eye and ear problems. Afflictions of a more long-term nature caused by a constant influx of toxemia into the body from the colon include degeneration or cancer in vital organs.

In addition to physical ailments, Dr. Walker writes: "It is almost impossible to maintain a clear mind and proper mental and spiritual equilibrium when we allow the colon to go unattended for too long a time."

**Continued in the Right Column of page 165**

Dr. Walker refers to constipation as "the number one affliction underlying nearly every ailment; it can be imputed to be the initial, primary cause of nearly every disturbance of the human system. The most prevalent ailment afflicting civilized people is constipation." He writes "to be constipated means the packed accumulation of feces in the bowel makes its evacuation difficult." He adds, "constipation can also exist when movements of the bowel may seem to be normal, in spite of an accumulation of feces somewhere along the line of the colon."

**Putrid Fecal Matter and Mucus Create Ideal Environment for Parasites**

Over a period of time, constipation interferes with the functioning of every cell, organ and gland. Constipation causes the blood stream and lymph system to become overloaded with toxins, it sends poisons throughout the entire body, and clogs much of the system with disease-causing mucus. This pathogenic mucus, which results from eating and drinking the wrong foods, "is the ideal media for propagating germs, microbes, and bacteria," Dr. Walker writes. If our colon and the rest of our body is free from excessive pathogenic mucus and other putrefactive waste matter, harmful germs, bacteria and parasites will not flourish and cause problems, because there will be insufficient food these scavengers need to survive.

The book, *Cleansing the Body and the Colon for a Happier and Healthier You,* by Teresa Schumacher and Toni Schumacher Lund, states that a clogged-up colon and its parasitic infection is often the undiagnosed root of many physical problems. But, Schumacher writes, the medical profession "does not even agree with the notion of filthy and impacted colons contributing to much American ill health. This may be because there are no patented drugs for quick relief of impacted colons. The only way to cleanse intestines is with natural ingredients, and via a persistent personal hygiene program."

She estimated there are "about 300 different types of parasites thriving in America today," and that more than 80 percent of people in the world are infested. Schumacher quotes parasite expert June Wiles, Ph.D., as saying, "Parasites are vermin that steal your food, drink your blood and leave their excrement in your body to be reabsorbed back into the blood-stream as nourishment." Schumacher's book lists several types of parasites and a variety of ways in which they are caught.

As for parasites in food, Schumacher notes the parasite incubation period is 36 hours. She says once we have eaten a meal we should be able to eliminate the waste from that food within 16 to 24 hours. But, she notes, "it is startling to learn that the average elimination time in America today is 96 hours." If waste is not eliminated within 24 hours, it begins a toxic build-up that provides a breeding ground for parasitic infection. She writes that a clogged intestine with putrid fecal matter and plenty of sugar provides the ideal environment for parasites to thrive. If you want to determine how long your "transit time" is, a good way is to eat some beets (or drink fresh beet juice). The red color will make it easy to tell exactly how long it took to go through your system.

So, it is easy to see how a vegetarian, high-fiber, low-fat diet can affect the health of our colon, and how the health of our colon affects our whole body. Adding fiber to our diet and eliminating animal products and processed foods will greatly assist the movement of waste through the colon, and this will have a major impact on the health of the entire body. Some benefit may be obtained by adding a good fiber supplement to a diet that continues to include fiber-deficient animal products, but this benefit will not be as great as can be found by making a complete dietary change.

At Hallelujah Acres, we recommend a vegetarian diet of at least 75 to 85 percent raw fruits and vegetables. In addition to providing an excellent source of easy-to-assimilate protein, vitamins, minerals, and live enzymes, this high-fiber, low-fat diet will create an improved waste-elimination process, from the cellular level to the colon. Dr. Walker's book recommends the regular use of colonic irrigations to keep the colon clean, but we feel a better approach is to first attempt to cleanse the colon through diet. Dietary changes are a less intrusive approach than colonic irrigations, and we are finding that people are receiving excellent results.

For additional fiber, preventative maintenance of the colon and insurance against parasitic infestations, we recommend daily use of Herbal Fiberblend, which is described in the book *Cleansing the Body and the Colon for a Happier and Healthier You.* Advantages of adding fiber to our diet are well-known as researchers from all around the world have confirmed that populations with high-fiber diets have a much lower incidence of colon cancer, constipation and other colon-related problems. Soluble fibers such as psyllium are also known to help lower cholesterol levels. And because fiber causes starches and sugars to be absorbed more slowly into the bloodstream, this reduces the amount of glucose in the blood, which requires less work from the pancreas in producing insulin.

The 18 herbs contained in Herbal Fiberblend are combined to achieve all these benefits and more. Along with being a great source of additional dietary fiber, Herbal Fiberblend offers insurance against parasitic infections in the colon and preventative maintenance that will benefit the entire body. Herbal Fiberblend is a finely-ground powder that can be taken in juice or water once or twice a day. Some of the ingredients and benefits of Herbal Fiberblend, as described by *Cleansing the Body and the Colon for a Happier and Healthier You,* include:

*Psyllium* is one of the best known sources of dietary fiber, containing more than eight times the bulking power of oat bran. Psyllium acts as a colon broom as it creates bulk to pull putrefactive toxins from the intestinal walls … *Shavegrass* helps to dissolve tumors, expels parasites and kills their eggs. It also strengthens fingernails and hair because it is high in silica … *Black walnut hulls* are known for killing and expelling parasites. They also help regulate body fluids and balance sugar levels … *Alfalfa* is an excellent source of trace minerals because of its deep roots. It contains all eight essential amino acids, the eight essential digestive enzymes and is rich in vitamins … *Oatstraw* stimulates

**Continued from the Left Column of page 164**

tape this past week and I started to eat some raw vegetables and fruit and the swelling in my stomach started to go down!!! I am so grateful and thankful to the Lord for hearing you speak on that tape Brother Malkmus. Thank you from my heart for sharing all that information to the public so it could get into my hands away up here in *Waren, Ontario, Canada! …"*
– Marlene Putman
Canada

the neuromuscular system ... *Pumpkin* seeds contain zinc, an essential trace element. They also help kill parasites and are good for some prostate problems ... *Licorice Root* stimulates enzymes and peristaltic action in the intestines. It is also used to stimulate and regulate the adrenal glands and pancreas ... *Vitamin C* is an antioxidant, and helps the body's absorption of iron ... *Yucca* has been used to reduce inflammation in the joints ... *Marshmallow root* is helpful in removing kidney stones ... *Violet leaves* are a cleansing herb, helping to remove toxins and parasites ... *Slippery elm* coats the digestive tract, helping to heal inflammation and ulcers ... *Capsicum* helps the digestive system, circulatory system and helps to regulate the heart and blood pressure ... *Passion flower* soothes the nervous system ... *Mullein leaves* help with asthma, bronchitis and sinus congestion ... *Witch hazel* helps mucus membranes and the circulatory system ... *Hibiscus flowers* help lubricate the intestinal tract.

Herbal Fiberblend is a professional formulation of the above-named herbs in a convenient, easy-to-use powder that is readily assimilated by the body. Herbal Fiberblend is an exclusive formula, available only through American Image Marketing distributors.

*From the*
*Hallelujah Acres mailbag:*

"I want to express my appreciation for what you have written and your ministry at Hallelujah Acres. We already are faithful consumers of Barley Green (since January) and Herbal Fiber Blend (June). Yesterday, July 4th (Praise the Lord!) we began eating just raw fruits and vegetables. Oh, how I wish we had understood all this long before now. My husband has severe life threatening diseases and I have very debilitating diseases, and we are only 61 and 54 years of age. What a tragedy to have missed your (God's) vital message until now. BUT...how we thank God for it now! I pray God will restore the years of health that the 'locusts and the cankerworms' have stolen from us in our ignorance."
– W.H.,
Georgia

# Chapter 21

# A Word of Encouragement: Giving Up Meat Is Easier Than You Think

*By Michael Dye*

One of the biggest misconceptions about being a vegetarian is that it requires great discipline to refrain from eating meat. Some people who know I have been a vegetarian for over 20 years have suspiciously inquired whether I secretly harbor any lust for a T-bone steak ... or if I ever sneak into a fast-food joint in the dark of night to order a cheeseburger.

No. Those thoughts never even cross my mind and I believe I could safely say the same for the great majority of the hundreds of people I have known who have been vegetarians for a year or more.

That seems to be hard for some to understand. People who have never tried to become a vegetarian have told me they are convinced they could never live without meat, and they find it difficult to understand how anyone could voluntarily endure such a "sacrifice" and "hardship."

Well, for those of you who are considering becoming a vegetarian, or for those who are in that sometimes awkward transition stage, I have good news. It's really a lot easier than you think, once you make up your mind and start doing it. If you have the personal motivation and enough knowledge of how to eat a healthy vegetarian diet, giving up meat can be one of the easiest major transformations you could ever make in your life. It is a step you will never regret. Even if you are one of those who think you could never give up meat, I believe you will find that once your body becomes accustomed to healthier foods, you will have no reason to ever look back with fond memories of eating flesh.

Many people who have quit eating meat due to the influence of Hallelujah Acres have said that they would have never imagined themselves

*Most people are very surprised to find that after a few months on a vegetarian diet, they lose their taste for eating meat, regardless of how much they once loved it.*

becoming vegetarians. (Some have commented that they thought it was just "weirdos" who became vegetarians.) And many have said the dietary change was much easier than they would have ever thought.

Most people are very surprised to find that after a few months on a vegetarian diet, they lose their taste for eating meat, regardless of how much they once loved it. The smell becomes very unappetizing. And if they ever do eat meat again after their body has adapted to a vegetarian diet, there is a very good chance that it will not set well with them. Anyone who has been a vegetarian for very long will tell you that his or her taste buds have changed.

The bottom line is that this is all very good news for those of you who would like to become a vegetarian, but are holding back because you think it would be too difficult for you to give up the taste of meat. If you have not yet made that change, you may think your taste buds will fight against your efforts to quit eating meat. This could be true during the early stage of your transition, but you will find that once you get past this initial stage, your taste buds can actually help you in maintaining a healthy diet. Even if you were once convinced that bad foods taste good and good foods taste bad, after you become accustomed to a healthy diet you will find that good foods can indeed taste good and bad foods will actually start to taste bad. Once this happens, your taste buds will become one of your strongest allies. If you will listen to your body, it will tell you what foods are beneficial and what foods are not beneficial.

The reason most people are not aware of this is that they have never changed the way they eat. Most people will spend their entire life eating approximately the same diet they were brought up to eat as a child. If all a person ever eats is meat, dairy, processed foods, canned vegetables, white flour and white sugar desserts, that will be all his body knows, and later in life something new and unusual like fresh, raw vegetables may taste strange and foreign at first. But after a while, taste buds can change and eventually raw vegetables can taste good even to a person who never liked any kind of vegetables.

I know this from my own experience. As a child, I grew up consuming practically nothing but meat, dairy, eggs, white flour, sugar desserts and a few canned vegetables. As a child, a little bit of fresh fruit was the only decent food I ever put into my body. I wouldn't eat *any* raw vegetables (not even lettuce or tomatoes), and I *never* ate a vegetable salad. I ate hamburgers and hot dogs "plain," with just the meat and the (white-flour) bun. I had two big glasses of milk with every meal – breakfast, lunch and dinner – and more milk with in-between-meal snacks, for a total of at least seven glasses of milk a day. The only green food I ate up until I was 13 years old was canned peas.

I was incredibly finicky. I was the epitome of the kid who hated his vegetables … and I was certainly a very unlikely candidate for vegetarianism.

But when I was 18, I quit eating meat. Once I made the decision to become a vegetarian, I never had the desire to eat meat again. And although it didn't happen overnight, I eventually came to like the taste of practically every fruit and vegetable I have had the pleasure of tasting. Speaking from the perspective of a guy whose diet once included no green food other than canned peas, I can say from first-hand experience that when you change to a natural, vegetarian diet, your tastes can change and it probably will be much easier than you would ever imagine to give up meat.

I realize that not everyone will lose their desire for meat immediately after deciding to become a vegetarian, as I did. In fact, many people will have some difficulty in the first couple months or so. A strong commitment will make this initial transition period go much easier. The commitment that first led me to become a vegetarian was based on my personal views of killing animals. I was uncomfortable with killing an animal myself, so I felt it was philosophically inconsistent (a nice way of saying hypocritical) for me to eat animals that someone else had killed. Other people can develop an equally strong commitment to becoming a vegetarian after they have a heart attack, stroke or diagnosis of cancer, if they are convinced that changing their diet is necessary to save their life. Hopefully more people will become vegetarians *before* they develop a life-threatening illness. And there are many other motivating factors that could lead to the commitment to give up meat. It doesn't matter whether the reasons behind your commitment are philosophical, health, religious or moral, the main thing is that if your commitment is strong, it will make your transition much easier.

Become informed about the subject, because the more you know about meat, the less you will want to eat it. A close reading of this book and *Diet for a New America* by John Robbins will make it much easier for you to become a vegetarian. *Diet for a New America* and Robbins' follow-

*From the*
*Hallelujah Acres mailbag:*

James Hartline

"In March 1993 I (visited Hallelujah Acres and) changed from my regular diet of cooked food, meat, pizza, subs, etc. to a diet of juice from carrots and other raw vegetables with a tablespoon of Barley Green before each meal, plus a large raw salad for lunch and dinner and a little cooked food for dinner. I eat some fruit, mostly apples, bananas and oranges between meals. The following is a list of the problems I had when I changed my eating habits and the improvements which resulted:

1. Every time I brushed my teeth, my gums bled. This cleared up after one week.
2. I had something like grit in my eyes every morning which took several minutes of rubbing to clear. This was gone after one week on this diet and has not recurred.
3. I had a muscle problem in my right eye. After seven months, that problem cleared up entirely. Another eye problem is almost healed after a year.
4. I had a severe case of hemorrhoids ... This problem has cleared up entirely.
5. For a long time, I had a throbbing feeling in the space between my collar bones. This has not occurred since the second week on the vegetable and fruit juice diet.
6. I had constant indigestion. I have not had any indigestion except when I have violated the diet for something I should not have eaten (Turkey dressing and cranberry sauce at Thanksgiving.)
7. I used to get very sleepy after lunch. This ...is no problem.
8. I would fall asleep every time I read for over 10 minutes. I now can read for hours with no difficulty.
9. I had frequent headaches. They have disappeared.
10. I am more alert, can think clearer and have a lot more stamina
11. I had all the symptoms of prostate trouble. I was recently checked by a doctor, and he said there is no longer a problem.
12. I had frequent pains in my kidneys, tiredness and other problems. These too are greatly improved.
13. I had frequent pains that would occur in my legs, so excruciating that I could hardly stand on them. They have not occurred since the second week, except when I got seriously off the diet.
14. I had gotten heavier than I should have been, and lost 30 pounds in the first six weeks after going on the Hallelujah Diet. I have now leveled off at my normal body weight.
15. For years I have had carpal tunnel syndrome, and several fingers on my hands would be numbed by it. It has not shown up since I began this diet.
16. I had a small skin cancer on the bridge of my nose which flared up frequently. It has not shown any sign of activity since I changed my eating habits.
17. After eight months on this diet, neither my wife nor I have had a cold. Neither has been constipated.
18. When I went on the diet, I had 'frozen shoulder' which usually takes three years to clear up, but after eight months, the problem was totally healed.

I guess everyone carries around some minor diet related problem they don't consider serious enough to see a doctor for, but cause discomfort. It is interesting to see how a change in eating habits has changed so much."
–James Hartline,
Tennessee

up book, *May All Be Fed,* give an incredible number of reasons for not consuming animal products. These reasons include a thorough documentation of the dozens of health problems created by meat, startling statistics on the build-up of toxic chemical fertilizers, pesticides and growth hormones in meat, an appalling view of the inhumane treatment of animals in today's modern factory farms, along with an eye-opening view of how our natural resources and environment are being wasted away by society's addiction to meat.

And in *Living Health,* Harvey and Marilyn Diamond give a good explanation of why humans are not well-adapted to eating meat, physically or psychologically: We do not have a digestive system designed to assimilate protein from flesh. We do not have the teeth of a carnivore nor the saliva. Our alkaline saliva is designed to digest complex carbohydrates from plant food, whereas saliva of a carnivore is so acidic that it can dissolve bones. Humans do not have the ability to deal with the cholesterol or uric acid from meat. The digestive tracts of carnivores are short, about three times the length of their torso, allowing quick elimination of decomposing and putrefying flesh. All herbivores, including humans, have long intestines, 8 to 12 times the length of their torso, to provide a long transit time to digest and extract the nutrients from plant foods.

In *Living Health* the Diamonds add that humans are not even psychologically suited for eating meat. As an example, they set the scene of a person strolling through the woods, listening to the birds sing and enjoying the lush scenery. Then a little chipmunk scurries down from a tree. They ask, is the first human instinct to "pounce on it, grab it with your teeth, rip it apart, and swallow it, blood, guts, skin, bone, flesh, and all?" Or is the first human instinct to appreciate the beauty and wonder of the furry little creature. A true carnivore, such as a dog or a cat, would instinctively go after the chipmunk with the intent and ability to kill, even if it had never been trained as a hunter. The same is just not true for a human. The Diamonds prove their point by noting, "Kids are the real test. Place a small child in a crib with a rabbit and an apple. If the child eats the rabbit and plays with the apple, I'll buy you a new car."

And this, I believe, is the ultimate reason that once we become a vegetarian, we lose our taste for meat and junk foods, and start liking the vegetables we once hated. Raw fruits and vegetables were the original diet of mankind, and even today, this is what our bodies will recognize as "natural." We are not physically or psychologically adapted for eating meat, and likewise, the junk food so prominent in American diets does nothing to meet our body's nutritional needs. But society has taught us to eat meat and processed, pre-packaged, unnatural products that bear no resemblance to real food. The only reason anyone thinks of a hamburger, a bag of chips or a candy bar when they are hungry is that is what we have been taught. But even after many years of eating a diet of nothing but unnatural foods, if we change over to a natural, vegetarian diet, and give our body just a couple months to become adapted, natural food will indeed begin to taste "natural" to us.

Personal commitment and a sufficient knowledge of how to prepare healthy foods will be the two key ingredients in the first few months of the transition. Then, and as your body becomes accustomed to a healthier diet, going without meat will become much easier than you would have ever thought possible.

As your tastes change, your body will end up with a totally new concept of what *is* and what *is not* food.

"Greetings from two very happy truckers. We are a husband and wife driving team, who stopped in to see you about 2 months ago, from Seaford, Deleware. On Oct. 15 of '94, we went on your (Hallelujah) diet, **Cold Turkey,** and have had great results! It was a little hard to give up a few things, but we hung in there, and are very glad we did. My husband weighed 301 lbs., and has lost 50 lbs. so far...Now a lady never tells her weight, so I'll just say I lost 25 lbs. & feel great! We both went thru some cleansing & found that to be real exciting ...We have been sharing your tapes & book with so many people. We are on our second case of your book, *Why Christians Get Sick.* Some people are on it also, but some think we are a little crazy: 'You gave up eating meat?' When people think it is too hard to do, we tell them how we do it & that they should try. They have it easy. We are on the road sometimes 2 weeks at a time. But we got a converter for our truck, & we take our Champion (Juicer) along with us & make fresh juice every day. We carry water to wash it up in & buy steam distilled water to take our Barley Green in. We take our crock pot along & plug that into the converter, & kill a few potatoes or other veggies, & I make our salad while we drive down the road. That, along with our 2 ice chests that plug into the cigarette lighter and we eat better meals than you can buy out. It is all in how badly you want to do something. We are so thankful for my husband's sister, who shared your tape with us. We also want to thank you, George & Rhonda, for sharing your knowledge with anyone who will hear it. May God continue to bless you all as you keep sharing what you know to be true."
– Dorothy & Milton Stoltzfus, Deleware

"Nearly 70 percent of Americans are worried about the quality of their drinking water, according to a recent survey. Much of their concern centers on how water looks, tastes or smells. Unfortunately, water that is hazardous to your health usually looks, tastes and smells just fine."
– *Consumer Reports,* January 1990

# Chapter 22

# Water:

## The Precious Fluid that Keeps Us Alive Also has Impurities that can Lead Us to an Early Death

*By Michael Dye*

Since our early years in grade school we have been told that about 70 percent of our body is composed of water, and that no life could exist on Earth without this precious liquid. So, you would think that by now we all appreciate the extraordinarily vital role water plays in maintaining our health and keeping us alive.

Evidently not.

Few people take the effort to ensure that they are drinking pure water, free from inorganic minerals, chemical poisons and other harmful contaminants. Most are willing to drink whatever impurities are in their local tap water ... and our water supplies are becoming increasingly polluted from industrial sources, agricultural run-off, lead pipes, along with sodium fluoride, chlorine and other chemicals added to municipal water supplies. And many people drink water only when soft drinks and other artificial concoctions are not available.

The fact is that very few people are providing their bodies with the pure $H_2O$ that is so vital to our life and our health.

So for most of us, it's been a while since grade school, but perhaps it is time to again be reminded of the elementary – yet essential – fact that *about 70 percent of our body is composed of water and that drinking pure water is one of the easiest and most important steps we can take to improve our health.* Rather than taking this element for granted, we should realize that since water constitutes more than two-thirds of our body, it must be extraordinarily important in the functioning of our body. So, let's examine:

- What does water do in our body?
- What impurities are in drinking water?
- What effects do these impurities have on our health?
- And how can we obtain pure water?

Even a brief answer to the first question should leave you astonished at the incredibly vast and diverse functions water performs in your body. If you are impressed with the wide range of benefits from water, you may be equally amazed to discover the harmful effects that impurities in water can have on your body. And you will see our bodies can obtain pure water from three sources: 1) distilled water; 2) eating live, raw fruits and vegetables; and 3) drinking freshly-extracted juices of raw fruits and vegetables.

### How does water work in our body?

Along with oxygen, water is one of the two most important elements on Earth in sustaining our life. *Everything your body does, it needs water to do it.*

Take just a second to roll your tongue around in your mouth. Imagine how that would feel without water.

Water is the primary ingredient in all bodily fluids, including our blood supply, lymph, saliva, glandular secretions and cerebrospinal fluid. Water constitutes 92 percent of our blood and nearly 98 percent of our intestinal, gastric, saliva and pancreatic juices. While our body contains about five quarts of blood, a 150-pound person contains some 80 quarts of water.

To give just a sampling of the diverse functions of this vital element:

Water helps us to digest food. Water is used to maintain proper body temperature. Water gives our lungs the moisture we need to breathe. Water provides for the form and functioning of our body's 100 trillion cells. When our cells are starved for water, they become parched, dry and more vulnerable to attack by viruses.

Water holds our body's nutrients in solution and acts as a transportation medium to bring them into our cells. And likewise, water holds our waste products in solution and

> *Water constitutes, regulates, flows through, cleanses and helps nourish every single part of your body. But the wrong kind of water – with inorganic minerals, chemicals and other contaminants – can pollute, clog up and turn to stone in every part of your body.*

acts as a medium of transportation to eliminate them from our body. This waste comes from the cellular level, the bowels, blood stream, lymphatic system, and every organ, muscle, bone, connective tissue and piece of flesh.

*Water constitutes, regulates, flows through, cleanses and helps nourish every single part of your body. But the wrong kind of water – with inorganic minerals, chemicals and other contaminants – can pollute, clog up and turn to stone in every part of your body.*

In his book, *Water Can Undermine Your Health,* Dr. Norman W. Walker offers a good account of what water – and its impurities – do in our body.

To start with, everything you eat or drink goes into your stomach and then into 20 to 25 feet of small intestine, he explains. From there, food can go one of two ways: That which can be assimilated is transferred to the liver for distribution to the rest of your system; while most of what cannot be utilized is passed on as waste into the large intestine (colon).

But Dr. Walker notes, "Liquids pass readily through the microscopic blood vessels in the wall of the small intestine," so "whatever the liquid contains in colloidal form goes along with the liquid right into the liver." He defines a colloid as "any substance in such a fine state of particles that it would take from 50,000,000 to 125,000,000 particles to measure one inch." This includes inorganic minerals, the most common of which is calcium (lime).

Once this liquid reaches the liver, he writes, "it is completely divested and cleared of everything whatever that was a component part of the liquid, except only the hydrogen and the oxygen which, together, form the water molecule. Water containing nothing but hydrogen and oxygen is pure water, and this is the only kind of water which the blood and the lymph can use in their work ... Whatever mineral and chemical elements were present in the water when it first reaches the liver, are segregated by the anatomizing processes in the liver and either passed on into the blood stream or are filed away as reserve material."

**What impact do minerals in water have on our health?**

One of the contributing factors to hardened and blocked arteries is the calcium carbonate in drinking water. This inorganic mineral is the same substance that coats the inside of a pan after water has evaporated. The calcium from your drinking water is also a major ingredient in glue and cement. It is also what forms a stalactite inside a cave ... one drop at a time, just as it forms inside your veins.

So, what is the cumulative effect of collecting these mineral deposits in the body? Dr. Walker writes that if a person drinks two pints of water a day, this will total 4,500 gallons of water passing through his body over a 70-year lifespan. *If it is not distilled, Dr. Walker estimates these 4,500 gallons of water will include 200 to 300 pounds of rock – inorganic calcium (lime), magnesium and other mineral deposits – that the body cannot utilize.* He notes most of these inorganic minerals will be collected by the body's water, blood and lymph systems to be eliminated through excretory channels. *But some of this 200 to 300 pounds of rock will stay in the body, causing stiffness in the joints, hardening of the arteries, kidney stones, gall stones and occlusions (blockages) of arteries, microscopic capillaries and other passages in which liquids flow through our entire body.*

It is vital at this point to understand the difference between organic and inorganic minerals. Water flowing through or on the ground collects inorganic (non-living) minerals from the soil and rock through which it passes. These are not minerals that humans or other animals can utilize. Only plants have the capability of transforming inorganic minerals from the ground into living, vital, organic minerals we can use for nourishment. For this reason, we cannot absorb any minerals from eating finely-ground rocks or soil from our garden. We must allow the plants in the garden to take in these inorganic minerals through their roots from the soil and transform them, by the process of photosynthesis, into organic minerals that we can utilize. Inorganic minerals from the earth are absorbed into ground water, so we cannot benefit from minerals in water any more than we could benefit by eating rocks or dirt.

Because these inorganic minerals cannot be absorbed into the cell wall as nutrition, they become distributed elsewhere in the body, causing arthritis in the joints, kidney stones, gallstones, hardening and blocking arteries, etc.

***The most common mineral in ground water is calcium carbonate (lime), which is also a primary ingredient in making concrete and cement. If you have ever seen a large stalagmite or stalactite in a limestone cavern, you can visualize how this hard rock forms, one drop at a time in a cave ... or on the inside of your arteries, a kidney stone, in your joints, etc.*** Another way of actually seeing these mineral deposits is to pour water from your kitchen sink into a pan. Put that pan of water in the sun and let it evaporate. Or if you are in a hurry, boil it. Either way, once the water has evaporated, you will find a solid coat of mineral deposits left on the side and bottom of the pan. These are the same deposits left in your arteries and the rest of your body.

Paul Bragg, an early pioneer of health foods, emphasizes that it is a fallacy of the medical profession to say that hardening of the arteries – known as "arteriosclerosis" – is a result of old age. Actually, he notes, hardening and blocking of the arteries is caused by the consumption of inorganic minerals from water, along with table salt and the waxy saturated fat (cholesterol) and acids from a meat-based diet ... ***not old age.*** (As evidence of this claim, it could be noted that at the age of 95, a physical at Johns Hopkins revealed that Bragg had the arteries of a 20-year-old.)

Bragg adds, "If we examined our arteries closely, we could see that calcium carbonate and its affinities are lining these pipes and making them brittle – beginning to turn our body into stone. "

While water containing minerals is a primary contributor to these deposits, Bragg emphasizes that drinking the proper amount of ***distilled*** water is the way to flush out cholesterol and mineral deposits from our arteries and other body parts. "Remember water is a flushing agent," he notes. If one needs an idea of how effective water is in washing away minerals, look at a river bed ... or the Grand Canyon. The hardest rock in the world is constantly being eroded and washed away by water.

Distilled water helps to cleanse inorganic mineral deposits from the body, but you do not have to be concerned about distilled water leaching away organic minerals that your body can utilize. Explaining this distinction, Dr. Walker notes that living, organic minerals are absorbed into the cell wall for nutrition. He writes, "It is virtually impossible for distilled water to separate minerals which have become an integral part of the cells and the tissues of the body. Distilled water collects only the minerals discarded . . . from the cells, the minerals which the natural water originally collected from its contact with the earth and the rocks. Such minerals, having been rejected by the cells of the body are of no constructive value."

When a person has arteriosclerosis, doctors often recommend by-pass surgery, balloon surgery or some other costly method to replace, clear up or get around the larger blocked arteries that are causing concern.

Both Bragg and Dr. Walker point out the obvious short-comings of this approach. Dr. Walker notes that although the largest artery in the body, the aorta, measures about one inch in diameter, the great majority of our blood vessels are microscopically small capillaries. "The tiny capillaries in your body form a network which, if spread out on the ground, would cover an area of about 1 ½ acres. That's about 63,000 square feet. If all these tiny capillaries were placed end to end, they would make a microscopically tiny tube about 60 miles long," Dr. Walker estimates. So if your arteries are clogged, you should be concerned about the entire 60 miles, not just a few inches that might be temporarily cleared by surgery.

It is the tiny capillaries of the brain that suffer the greatest damage from inorganic minerals, cholesterol and salt. Bragg notes: "Go to the large convalescent and rest homes and see with your own eyes the people who can no longer think or reason for themselves. Many of them cannot recognize their own children and relatives ... *no technique on earth can regain the life of a human brain that is turning into stone.*"

Another very fine passage-way easily obstructed by the impurities in water are the connective tissues that bind, support and protect vital organs, blood vessels, nerves and muscles. Dr. Walker notes these connective tissues form the outer covering of the brain, the membrane of the spinal chord, the cornea of the eyes, and they are involved in the metabolism of cells. He estimates that if the fine membranes forming these connective tissues in a human body were separated and placed side-by-side, they would cover several acres.

"Every piece and parcel of connective tissue is intimately involved in the filtering of water," Dr. Walker writes. "The impurities which circulate through the system with the water and the blood are the villains which clog up the microscopically fine mesh of the filtering membrane ... noticeable in choked varicose veins, coronary occlusions causing heart attacks, etc." Along with inorganic minerals in water, other impurities Dr. Walker blames for obstructing passages in the connective tissues include refined foods such as white flour, sugar, salt, starchy foods and processed carbohydrates that are not water soluble.

### How is Water Distributed Through the Body?

Liquids are transferred wherever they are needed in our body by the process of osmosis, through the microscopic capillary veins of the walls of blood vessels. "Osmosis," Dr. Walker explains, "is the passage of liquids, concentrated solutions and vapors through semipermeable membranes or skin." He warns that when a large amount of water containing inorganic minerals is consumed, "osmotic pressure through the connective tissues is demonstrably decreased, causing the obstruction of functions and activities in the area where it occurs. This interference with the osmotic pressure may result from the mineral matter in the water or from an excessive consumption of salt and starch and sugary foods."

The important function of transferring liquids throughout the body is handled by the endocrine glands, the glands of internal secretion. Dr. Walker refers to the hypothalamus – a small gland near the center of the brain – as "the Emperor of the Endocrine Glands system." The hypothalamus controls our water flow, keeping bodily fluids in balance by determining when we need to replenish or eliminate water. When an organ, mucous membrane or cell in your body needs water, it is your hypothalamus that sends you the message: "I'm thirsty." The hypothalamus also acts as the body's thermostat, so when we get hot, nerve impulses are sent to open pores in our skin. This allows perspiration to moisten and cool our body, helping us to stay comfortable. Or in cold weather, these nerve impulses from the hypothalamus act to close some of these pores, and raise the heat factor in blood circulation, which allows the body to generate and hold in its own heat.

And speaking of nerve impulses, Dr. Walker adds that nerves contain a constant flow of cerebrospinal fluid, which is 92 percent water. So you can see the efficiency of the entire nervous system and glandular system is dependent on the quality of water we consume.

Indeed, Dr. Walker writes, "there is no telling how many millions of people have suffered untold misery and a premature demise by the clogging up of veins and arteries, without their death having been diagnosed as resulting from the accumulation over a lifetime of the inorganic calcium" from their drinking water.

### Chlorine and Fluoride – Poisons Labeled as "Safe" Chemicals

Two chemicals commonly added to municipal water supplies are chlorine and sodium fluoride. Dr. Walker notes the poisonous gas chlorine was first used as a weapon in World War I, before it was used to poison the bacteria in our water supplies. Bragg warns that if the chlorine in drinking water is "sufficient to produce an offensive smell, enough chlorine may enter the intestinal tract to destroy helpful bacteria and thereby deprive us of the important vitamins which they make for us."

An update at the conclusion of Bragg's book, *The Shocking Truth About Water,* states chlorine in water has been linked to heart disease, senility and cancers of the bladder, liver, pancreas, colon and urinary tract. The book quotes Dr. Herbert Schwartz as asserting, "Chlorine is so dangerous it should be banned."

Bragg's book calls fluoride "one of the most potent poisons known to man." The same sodium fluoride used in our water supplies up to 1.2 parts per million is used in a higher concentration as a roach and rat killer and pesticide. Citing a documentary by Peter Gray, *The Grim Truth About Fluoridation,* Bragg says the origin of adding sodium fluoride to water supplies occurred in 1939 when an industry commissioned a biochemist to find a use for the large amount of sodium fluoride wastes produced by aluminum pot lines. Big industry pressured state and local governments to fluoridate their water supplies, and the public was given the sales pitch that fluoride would prevent tooth decay. Bragg

"Now that you know the full extent of the important role water plays in *all* of the operations of your body, by all means make the smart choice in the type of water you drink. There should be only *one* choice – **PURE!** And pure means distilled. By the way, if you have the kind of clothes iron that you fill with water for steam, you know what kind of water is *always* recommended for use. Distilled. Know why? Because if you use other than distilled water, the minerals in it will corrode and destroy your iron. I know people who would no more fill their iron with tap water than they would fill their shoes with glue, yet they drink the very water they wouldn't put into their iron. If nondistilled water will destroy the insides of an iron, what might it do to *your* insides?"
– Harvey Diamond
in *Living Health*

notes any intelligent person knows tooth decay is caused by "poor nutrition, especially the use of refined white sugar," rather than the lack of fluoride in their water supply.

The standard label on a shipment of fluoride is quoted in *The New Drug Story* read: "Warning: Corrosive liquid ... The vapor or liquid material is very dangerous when it comes in contact with the eyes, skin or any part of the body, or if taken internally. When in contact with the skin, it can cause painful and slow-healing burns. Exposure to more than fifty part fumes per million of air is known to be fatal in thirty to sixty minutes. You are dealing with a substance so corrosive that it will eat through a quarter inch steel plate in a few minutes."

*More than 700 chemicals have been found in our drinking water, and 129 of these chemicals have been cited by the EPA as posing serious health risks. Yet the EPA requires that our water supplies be tested for only 14 of these chemicals.*

Commenting on the financial and political overtones of the fluoridation issue, Harvey Diamond in *Living Health* contrasts the publicity given to the AIDS virus versus the publicity given to flouride poisoning: "In the same five years, from 1981 to 1986, that 10,000 people were succumbing to AIDS, a whopping quarter of a million people died from fluoride poisoning. Twenty-five times more deaths and not a word? How come?" (Diamond emphasizes he is not suggesting that victims of AIDS did not merit their publicity, but merely that victims of fluoride poisoning deserved more publicity than they received.)

**And Now for the "UnSafe" Chemicals**

Thus far, we have only discussed inorganic calcium, chlorine and sodium fluoride. These are three of the most common impurities in our drinking water, which an average American may consume every day unless he or she takes the effort to drink distilled water. *It should offer no consolation to know that most public health officials consider these three contaminants "safe."* But there are many other pollutants that, although less common in our water supply, are much more hazardous.

The update to Bragg's book cites an ABC News study revealing that more than 700 chemicals have been found in our drinking water, and 129 of these chemicals have been cited by the EPA as posing serious health risks. Yet the EPA requires that our water supplies be tested for only 14 of these chemicals. Consider these statistics from the July 29, 1991, issue of *U.S. News & World Report*:

• Despite passage of the Safe Water Drinking Water Act in 1974, one in six Americans (40 million people) continue to drink water containing excessive levels of lead, a heavy metal that can impair the IQ and attention span of children. One in six children under the age of six have elevated levels of lead in their blood.

• In early summer, half of the water ways in America's Corn Belt are laced with unhealthy amounts of pesticides.

• A quarter of all private wells in Iowa, Kansas, Minnesota, Nebraska and South Dakota have been found to be contaminated by excessive levels of nitrate, which has been determined to be carcinogenic in animals. The magazine termed current research on the effects of nitrates in humans as "disturbingly incomplete," but said, "Scientists are certain, however, that nitrate in large doses can pose a threat to babies ... In 1986, an infant in South Dakota died after being fed formula made with water from a private well with exceedingly high levels of nitrate."

• The EPA estimates that as many as 17 million Americans may be threatened by excessive levels of radon, a radioactive gas that permeates ground water at the highest levels in New Jersey, New England and the Western Mountain states. Preliminary studies have found that drinking water with radon can double the risk of soft-tissue cancers.

• Waterborne illnesses are on the rise. Municipal water plants use filters and disinfectants such as chlorine to control the spread of microbes, but evidence suggests many microbes are resistant to chlorine and some are small enough to get through filters. Water is both chlorinated and filtered in Carrollton, Ga., but in 1987, water contaminated by a chlorine-resistant parasite led to the illness of 13,000 residents. And Montreal researchers have found one-third of all gastrointestinal illnesses are caused by drinking water.

• Although 70 percent of Americans drink chlorinated water, "its safety over the long term is uncertain," the magazine states. A study by the National Cancer Institute found that drinking chlorinated water may double the risk of bladder cancer, which strikes about 40,000 people annually. Scientists also have discovered that chlorine reacts with organic material in water, such as decaying leaves, to produce hundreds of hazardous chemical byproducts, including chloroform.

• A 1987 study of 1,000 top-priority "Super-fund" hazardous waste sites revealed four out of every five sites were leaking toxins into ground water. Our ground water supplies are being threatened not only by these major Super-fund sites and large chemical plants, but by small businesses such as dry cleaners and service stations. A Congressional study found about 10 percent of the nation's 1.4 million underground gasoline tanks are leaking.

• The *U.S. News & World Report* issue warns, "While assessing the health risks of a single chemical is difficult, evaluating the effects when two or more chemicals are combined is even trickier. In regulating drinking water, officials have looked at the risks from each contaminant individually. But in fact, studies show that some chemicals are much more lethal when mixed together ..."

## So, What About Other Beverages?

If all this makes you lose your taste for drinking tap water, don't think that soft drinks are any safer. In *Water Can Undermine Your Health,* Dr. Walker

" • One in six people drink water with excessive amounts of lead, a heavy metal that impairs children's IQ and attention span.

• In the early summer, half the rivers and streams in America's Corn Belt are laced with unhealthy levels of pesticides.

• Microbes in tap water may be responsible for one in three cases of gastro-intestinal illness.

• Ironically, even the chlorine widely used to disinfect water produces carcinogenic traces when combined with other common substances in water."

– From the article, "Is Your Water Safe?" in the July 29, 1991, *U.S. News & World Report*

includes a 12-page chapter detailing a hazardous list of sweeteners, dyes, artificial flavors, and chemicals used for "fiz," etc., that compose colas and other artificial beverages popular among both adults and children. He warns these chemicals are much more dangerous than the inorganic minerals in tap water. For example:

• Several aniline dyes, usually listed on the ingredients only as "artificial coloring," include Amaranth (red), Bordeaux (brown), Orange I (yellow) and Ponceau (scarlet). Dr. Walker writes that these dyes are derived from compounding nitrogen and benzene, and that benzene is obtained from the distillation of coal. Benzene "is used as a motor fuel, as a solvent for resins, rubber, etc. and … it is an ingredient in coloring beverages. As chemical compounds these dyes are harmful because they afflict the nerve system and the cerebrospinal fluid."

• Caramel, a common ingredient in soft drinks, is obtained by combining sugar, molasses or glucose with ammonia, and heating to more than 350 degrees. "The use of caramel tends to throw the blood out of balance, causing heart trouble which is intensified by the presence of ammonia. When used in excessive amounts it can cause mental and other disorders, particularly in children."

• "Sugar," Dr. Walker writes, "is one of the most harmful ingredients used in the manufacture of soft drinks … Sugar causes irritation and weakening of the mucous membranes of the body and robs teeth, bones and blood of a great percentage of their minerals. Inflammatory diseases of the breathing and digestive organs result from the use of white and brown sugar." Other diseases caused or worsened by the consumption of sugar include appendicitis, diabetes, cancer and poliomyelitis, a painful, crippling disease caused by inflammation of the gray matter in the spinal cord.

Dr. Walker summarizes his argument against these artificial, chemical-laden concoctions (known as "soft drinks") by asking, "If the labels were marked POISON, would you buy them?" He then provides the definition of poison as: "Any agent which, introduced into the organism may chemically produce an injurious or deadly effect. That which taints or destroys purity; to exert a baneful influence, to corrupt."

And in a brief chapter on the hazards of alcoholic beverages, Dr. Walker notes alcohol is the only substance which can pass through the walls of the stomach directly into the bloodstream and to the brain. This has noticeable immediate and long-term ill effects to the brain, eyes and equilibrium. "Of all the beverages best left alone, alcoholic beverages are Number ONE," he writes.

So, we have determined that our body must have liquids to function. But when we analyze the ingredients and effects from three of society's most common beverages – tap water, soft drinks and alcohol – it's enough to kill our thirst. The remaining questions, then, are: From what sources should we obtain water? And how much water do we need?

Bragg writes that the human body "loses about three-and-a-half quarts (of water) daily in perspiration, respiration, urine and defecation." Dr. Walker writes that a person *should* expel a gallon of liquid a day in these functions. Obviously, if we are expelling 3 ½ to 4 quarts of water a day, we must be replacing this water to avoid dehydration and to keep our bodily fluids in balance. To consume this much pure water, Dr. Walker recommends drinking at least one to two pints of steam distilled water a day, "plus as much fresh raw vegetable juices as possible," and eat a diet composed largely of raw fruits and vegetables.

"In their natural raw state, vegetables and fruits, nuts and seeds for man, grains and hay for animals, are composed of from 60 to 95 percent water. This is pure DISTILLED WATER," Dr. Walker explains. As a contrast, he notes, "Processed cereals contain only from 7 to 13 percent water. The average water content of bread is only between 35 and 40 percent … The most dehydrated people on earth are those who live on massive quantities of processed cereals, bread and meat, drinking very little water except perhaps in their coffee or tea and in soft drinks." Food in its natural state (raw) contains a high percentage of pure, naturally distilled water because it takes 15 gallons of water to grow an ounce of vegetation. When a good supply of distilled water is not available, you can replenish your body's water supply by eating fresh, raw fruits and vegetables.

And unlike the harmful, inorganic minerals in water, the organic minerals in raw fruits and vegetables can be utilized by the body for nutrition. Dr. Walker emphasizes the fastest way of providing our cells with the vitamin and mineral nourishment they need is through the freshly-extracted juices of raw fruits and vegetables.

## What Types of Water are Available?

*The Choice is Clear* by Dr. Allen E. Banik offers a good explanation of the many different types of water available. For example:

• Raw water "is water that has not been treated in any way." It may contain inorganic minerals, cancer-causing chemicals dumped into rivers and can be densely inhabited by millions of viruses and bacteria.

• Chlorinated water "kills most germs and viruses, but it can also kills the cells in our bodies," he notes.

• Boiled water kills the bacteria in raw water (if it is boiled for at least 20 minutes). But, Dr. Banik warns "the dead bodies of these germs" are carried into our body when we drink boiled water. These dead germs "furnish a fertilized soil for rapid and lusty propagation of germs already in the body." Boiling water does not remove any inorganic minerals or chemicals.

• Mineral water from certain mineral springs are reputed to have medicinal qualities. The reason for "this so-called medicinal effect is because the body tries to throw off the excess minerals which invade it as intruding foreign deposits … To subsist on this type of water could be detrimental," Dr. Banik writes.

• Filtered water can remove chlorine, some suspended solids and many

"A 1987 review of the 1,000 top priority 'Superfund' sites – the nation's worst hazardous-waste dumps – revealed that four out of every five sites were leaking toxins into the ground water. … While assessing the health risks of a single chemical is difficult, evaluating the effects when two or more chemicals are combined is even trickier. In regulating drinking water, officials have looked at the risks from each contaminant individually. But in fact, studies show that some chemicals are much more lethal when mixed together, according to Daniel Okun, professor emeritus of environmental engineering at the University of North Carolina in Chapel Hill."
– From the article, "Is Your Water Safe?" in the July 29, 1991, *U.S. News & World Report*

synthetic chemicals, but "there is no filter made which can prevent bacteria or viruses from passing through its fine meshes. Each pore of the finest filter is large enough for millions of germs to pass through ... Moreover, decaying matter collects on the bottom of every filter. This forms an excellent breeding ground for bacteria. After a filter has been used for a few days, the filtered water often contains more disease germs than the water which is put into the filter."

• De-ionized water effectively removes minerals, but its resin beds become "a breeding ground for bacteria, pyrogenic matter and viruses ... Furthermore, de-ionization does not remove synthetic chemicals such as herbicides, pesticides, insecticides or industrial solvents," Dr. Banik writes.

• Reverse Osmosis "removes a high percentage of the dissolved solids as well as other contaminants, and when new the result often approaches the purity of distilled water." But the purity varies with the "conditions of the equipment used, much as with filter equipment, and the effectiveness lessens with use. Sometimes drastically!"

• Rain water has been naturally distilled by the heat of the sun. But it becomes contaminated as it "falls through air filled with bacteria, dust, smoke, chemicals, mud and minerals. By the time it reaches the earth as rain water, it is so saturated with decaying matter, dirt and chemicals that its color becomes a yellowish-white." Snow is even dirtier.

### What is Distilled Water?

Distillation is nature's way of purifying water. When the sun heats water, this causes evaporation, an example of distillation on the grand scale. Vapor rises from the surface of water, leaving behind all its impurities. These water vapors rise and cool as air temperature in the upper atmosphere drops, and the vapors change from gas to liquid, becoming water, ice or snow. If our atmosphere were not polluted, each drop of rain or snow would be pure $H_2O$.

The production of distilled drinking water is man's attempt to copy nature's form of water purification. *As with evaporation in nature, distillation actually removes water (in the form of steam vapor) from the heavier materials that are its impurities. Other types of water treatment attempt to remove contaminants from water, rather than removing water from the contaminants.*

In the boiling chamber of the distiller, tap water is heated to 212 degrees, killing bacteria and viruses. The heat produces steam, which rises, leaving behind inorganic minerals, chemicals and other contaminants in the boiling tank. As the water temperature rises, the light gases boil off and are discharged through the gaseous vent. A stainless steel condenser cools the steam, turning it into distilled water. This water passes from the condenser through an optional post carbon filter, and the purified distilled water is collected in a reservoir.

"When the well's dry, we know the worth of water."
– Benjamin Franklin

"If all the earth's water fit in a gallon jug, available fresh water would equal just over a tablespoon – less than one percent of the total. About 97 percent of the planet's water is seawater; another 2 percent is locked in icecaps and glaciers. Vast reserves of fresh water underlie earth's surface, but much of it is too deep to economically tap."
– *National Geographic* Special Edition, November 1993

# Chapter 23

# The Healing Crisis

*By Michael Dye*

Some people are surprised to find that shortly after they change to a healthier diet, they can often experience generally brief but unpleasant symptoms such as headaches, pimples, nausea, cold-like symptoms or loss of energy.

When people give up things like meat and coffee and switch to raw vegetable salads and carrot juice – *and then feel sick* – it may be enough to make them wonder if this natural food is really good for them!

If this happens to you, don't be alarmed and don't turn back. You have just entered the first phase of your healing.

This unpleasant little episode is known as "The Healing Crisis," "Detoxification" or a "Cleansing Reaction," and it is fairly common. Dr. Norman W. Walker refers to this as our body's way of "housecleaning." At Hallelujah Acres, Rev. George Malkmus estimates that about 40 percent of the people who make a major dietary change to natural foods go through some form of healing crisis. About 60 percent of people who convert to a natural diet have no such reaction; about 30 percent will have a mild healing crisis; and about 10 percent will have a more severe reaction, he said.

The healing crisis can be a very discouraging setback to some people if they don't understand what is happening with their body. When we start eating a healthier diet, we expect to feel better, not worse. Some people are so discouraged that they are tempted to abandon their newly-improved diet and return to their old ways at the first sign of unpleasant symptoms. This is unfortunate, because the healing crisis is a classic example of the darkest hour

> "I had a dull head-ache and flu-ish feeling for a week-and-a-half. Then I woke up one morning with the biggest surge of energy I've ever had in my life, and I've felt great ever since then."
> – Dr. Stan Gravely, pastor of Tussekiah Baptist Church in Meherrin, Va., describing his symptoms of "The Healing Crisis" after he went on the Hallelujah Diet, eliminating all animal products, sugar, caffeine and other drugs. Dr. Gravely's testimonial can be found on page 222.

*As our healing begins, we must remember that our body is dealing with toxins that are deep within our cells and vital organs. As our body strives to eliminate these deep-seated toxins, it is very easy to understand how we may feel nauseous or get a headache as these toxins – on their way out of our body – first get circulated a bit in our blood stream.*

"I went on the diet he (Rev. Malkmus) recommended. I went 'cold turkey' . . . no meat, no white flour, no sugar and no dairy," she said. "I felt horrendous after three or four days, but by the fifth day, it was amazing to me to feel the difference . . . no rumbling and gurgling . . . no gas. From that point on, it has been like night and day, as far as how I feel."
– Dianne McKee of Morristown, Tenn., describing her healing crisis and recovery from severe abdominal pain. Before changing her diet, she had seen at least 20 doctors, had four separate surgical operations, had been on numerous medications, but nothing relieved her pain until she changed her diet. Dianne's testimonial is on page 190.

being right before the dawn. This temporary discomfort can be the first sign that our body's natural process of self-healing is kicking into high gear.

As our healing begins, we must remember that our body is dealing with toxins that are deep within our cells and vital organs. As our body strives to eliminate these deep-seated toxins, it is very easy to understand how we may feel nauseous or get a headache as these toxins – on their way out of our body – first get circulated a bit in our blood stream. Or if these toxins are eliminated through the skin in the form of pimples or a skin rash, we should feel relieved to have these impurities exiting at the surface level rather than remaining and accumulating deep in our body.

When the body has accumulated many years of toxic wastes and poisons, this has a degenerative effect, to one extent or another, on every cell and every vital organ in our body. The very first step in our healing process must be eliminating these toxic wastes from the cellular level of our body, and from our vital organs, as we begin to bring in the vital nutrients that our body needs to rebuild its immune system, its 100 trillion living cells and its organs. As we switch to a diet that brings in fresh, living, high-quality nutrients, our body will use these nutrients as building blocks to regenerate new living cells. Because our body now has this new high-quality building material to work with, it will start to discard the old, lower-quality material, including toxins that may have been slowly degenerating our vital organs for years.

So are we happy and relieved to know that these deep-seated toxic wastes are on the way out of our body? Or are we disappointed when these impurities circulate in our blood long enough to let us feel a headache or nausea? Or do we grimace when these poisons are eliminated through the skin in the form of pimples or a rash?

The main thing to remember is that regardless of how bad we dislike these pimples, nausea, fatigue or head-aches, we should realize that it is better for our body to deal temporarily with these symptoms on the surface level rather than to continue holding these toxins deep within our cells and vital organs where they will have a more gradual degenerative effect that could eventually culminate in a serious, life-threatening disease.

Now I realize that pimples, nausea and head-aches are difficult things to feel good about, but if we can comprehend the wisdom of our body's process of self-healing during the healing crisis, we really would appreciate these symptoms of minor discomfort.

Specific symptoms of the healing crisis will vary according to the type and quantity of toxins that need to be eliminated, the health of the organs involved in this elimination, and how abruptly the dietary transition is being made. Other possible symptoms of the healing crisis include diarrhea, constipation, frequent urination, nervousness, irritability and fevers.

Diarrhea and cold-like symptoms are good examples of reactions you may think are bad, but are actually doing good things for your body. The cleansing aspect of fruit can help clean out old, impacted fecal matter from your intestinal walls and flush out this toxic fecal matter in the form of loose stools.

This may seem uncomfortable or inconvenient, but it is very beneficial to your body. Another example of something good that may seem bad is a large discharge of mucus from your nasal passages. This may seem like a bad cold or a sinus attack, but a more accurate explanation is that the dietary change is allowing your body to eliminate excess toxins that have been built up in your mucous membranes.

Since these reactions are part of our body's healing process, experts in natural health recommend against taking pain-relievers or other drugs to mask these symptoms. If we want to learn how to eliminate the cause of our sickness, rather than just continuing to mask its symptoms, we will be willing to tolerate the temporary discomfort of a healing crisis.

But there are some things we can do to minimize these symptoms. Rev. George Malkmus recommends slowing down on the Barley Green and raw foods, while eating more cooked food (such as lightly-steamed vegetables), which will make your body's transition more gradual. Dr. Yoshihide Hagiwara, M.D., the inventor of Barley Green, suggests that "large quantities of fresh water and a stoic approach are the best recourse." Increased quantities of freshly-extracted carrot juice is another means of speeding up the body's process of flushing out these toxins. Rev. Malkmus notes the advantage to using fresh juice, rather than water, is that juice also contains the vital nutrients to help regenerate our body's cells while it is flushing out the toxins. It is also good during a healing crisis to give your body plenty of rest, including your digestive system. This means eating less than normal so you are not overworking your digestive tract while your body is trying to eliminate toxins.

Dr. Leo Roy, M.D., N.D., advises, "If you are worried or confused, call the doctor who helped design your program. Anxiety can drastically slow down healing. Don't get discouraged. Don't quit. If you have not gone back to doing anything detrimental to your health, then you are not going back to being sick … Letdowns can be caused by the dumping of too much disease, dead cells and poisons too quickly. You are healing too fast; your treatment is really working – too well. You may feel worse, but you are not worse."

For most people, a healing crisis does not last more than two or three days. And when it is over, many people report feeling better than they have ever felt in their lives, and have described tremendous bursts of energy. In more extreme cases, symptoms could last a week or so, but they rarely continue for more than 30 days. Sometimes a few days of healing crisis will be followed by feeling great, and then another healing crisis and then feeling better again. With this pattern, generally the extent of each healing crisis gets shorter and less severe, while the periods of feeling good get progressively better and last longer.

Another way of understanding the healing crisis is to remember that certain toxic substances such as cigarettes, coffee, tea, refined sugar, chocolate, soft drinks, alcohol and prescription drugs can be addictive, and when we stop consuming any addictive substance it is common to have headaches or a "letdown" feeling. Most long-term users ("addicts") of nicotine or caffeine will feel terrible during the transitory period in which they are withdrawing from

"While in a period of transition to living foods, it is best to allow your body to accept new food materials into the system, to incorporate new eating patterns so thoroughly that they will become lifetime habits, rather than being discarded as soon as the weight is lost or physical problems overcome."
– Ann Wigmore, D.D., N.D.

cigarettes or coffee. Keep in mind, this terrible feeling is only temporary. In the long run, you'll feel much better. (After all, how could quitting nicotine or caffeine be bad for you?) Withdrawal from meat can also cause a "let-down" feeling in some people, because the large amount of protein in meat has a stimulating effect on the body, even though this type and quantity of protein is unnecessary and not usable by our bodies (see Chapter 15). Again, experts in natural health recommend against taking any painkillers or stimulants to offset the symptoms of withdrawal from these addictive drugs or meat. Part of the withdrawal symptoms people may feel from giving up these addictive substances is caused by the cells of the body beginning to discard toxins such as caffeine, nicotine, chemical preservatives and excess bile and fat that clogs the arteries. The sooner a person can rid their body of these substances, the better off they will be, and any drugs they take to relieve the symptoms will just dump more toxins into their body.

If you consider your overall health to be more important than your brief, short-term discomfort, you won't let the healing crisis tempt you to turn back to your old diet. It may be necessary to remind yourself that although the discomfort of a healing crisis is being felt as you quit consuming harmful substances, the root of the cause of this discomfort was putting these substances into your body in the first place.

"Watch ye and pray, lest ye enter into temptation. The spirit truly is ready, but the flesh is weak."
– Mark 14:38

# Part III:

# An "Amen" From

# People Who Have

# Tried the

# Diet

*From the*
*Hallelujah Acres mailbag:*

John Matthews

"Please add our name to your mailing list. I have been using AIM's Barley Green for the past six years and wouldn't be a day without it. At 64, people have said I should start 'acting my age'! HAH! 'As young as you feel, as old as you decide' is my motto. I feel 34! Blessings to you on your outstanding work!!"
– John Matthews, California

Rev. Gale Galloway, right, lived a medical nightmare for 18 years, battling a half-dozen life-threatening diseases. He had diabetes, prostate problems, toxic poisoning, two heart attacks and went through a four-day coma. Since adapting the Hallelujah Diet, he has enjoyed excellent health.

# Chapter 24

# Testimonials

Elwin Nichols, left, suffered two heart attacks, and doctors gave him little hope for survival. Elwin came to Hallelujah Acres, changed his diet and started exercising. He has cut his cholesterol in half, walks 7 miles a day and is in perfect health.

Pastor Bob East, above, was crippled by multiple sclerosis in the prime of his life. He changed his diet and went on to become a middle-aged mountain climber. Pastor Bob, now in his mid-60s, no longer experiences any symptoms of MS, which medical doctors consider to be an incurable disease that gets progressively worse.

Mary Payne, above, ("before" and "after") lost 112 pounds in 16 months on the Hallelujah Diet. She also found relief for her severe rheumatoid arthritis and several other physical and emotional problems.

188

Edie & Russ Dalson, above, are ages 84 and 92, and they still lead very busy and active lives. They have been vegetarians since they were teen-agers.

Dianne McKee, right, suffered abdominal pain for five years. She had four major surgeries and saw at least 20 doctors, but found no relief until she came to Hallelujah Acres and changed her diet.

Rev. C.R. Williams, above, has seen a major improvement in the health of his church members since a seminar by Rev. Malkmus. Rev. Williams encourages other pastors to invite Rev. Malkmus to their church.

Jim Allen, left, was diagnosed with kidney cancer at age 71 and three doctors told him his left kidney would have to be removed. Jim changed his diet and his body healed the cancer. He still has both of his kidneys, and no sign of cancer.

Carol Cover, above, baffled medical specialists by suffering diarrhea for 22 months. She was on the verge of death, losing down to 78 pounds, when she was introduced to Barley Green. "Barley Green saved my life," Carol said.

# Dianne McKee:
## After Five Years of Pain & Four Operations, It was a Change in Diet that Solved Her Problem

*By Michael Dye*

**Dianne McKee**

When we met April 19, 1993, at Hallelujah Acres, I observed Dianne McKee to be a healthy, energetic and enthusiastic young woman with a smile that revealed her positive attitude toward life.

I would have never guessed that, up until three months ago, she had been in near-constant abdominal pain for the past five years. During these five years. McKee, 46, said she had "seen at least 20 doctors," had four separate surgical operations, and been on different types of medication . . . but nothing helped to relieve the pain. And she said none of the doctors could even say for certain what her problem was.

"I was exhausted, unable to get motivated until at least noon or 1 p.m.," she recalls. "It was controlling my life. Whatever I did was determined by how I felt that particular day." She helps her husband with the family business, but she was months behind on paperwork, and the mother of four was unable to keep up with her housework.

She was suffering from abdominal and stomach pain, but doctors were unable to determine its cause or a cure. In her first surgery, her uterus was removed; in her second and third surgeries, both ovaries were removed (one in each surgery); and in her fourth operation, adhesions caused by the other operations were removed. But still the pain persisted.

After moving from Florida to Morristown, Tenn., about a year ago, McKee went to a Morristown doctor.

"He bombarded me with every test imaginable," she said, "and nothing was found. His only explanation was adhesions (scar tissue that often develops from previous surgeries)."

After five years, 20 doctors, four surgeries and no relief, McKee said, "I decided to just eat right and solve the problem myself."

She saw an ad in a local newspaper and started coming to the seminars at Hallelujah Acres given by Rev. George Malkmus.

> *"Before I started this diet, I had been sick for so long, it had become a constant struggle for me to just get through each day. I was so exhausted at the end of the day, it had an effect on me psychologically." – Dianne McKee*

"I went on the diet he recommended. I went 'cold turkey' . . . no meat, no white flour, no sugar and no dairy," she said. "I felt horrendous after three or four days, but by the fifth day, it was amazing to me to feel the difference . . . no rumbling and gurgling . . . no gas. From that point on, it has been like night and day, as far as how I feel."

McKee said she is now a total vegetarian, with the majority of her diet composed of raw foods, primarily fresh fruits and vegetables. She has a juicer, which allows her to drink a lot of fresh fruit and vegetable juices, and she takes Barley Green every day.

Friends and family members who have seen the difference in her life before and after she changed her diet have been very impressed . . . in fact, so impressed, that many of them have also given the diet a try. Her two oldest children, ages 24 and 25, and her sister-in-law have converted to the vegetarian diet, complete with Barley Green, fresh juices and raw fruits and vegetables. Her mother, friends at church, and a business associate with melanoma are also giving it a try, she said.

McKee said her skeptical 25-year-old daughter told her that if anyone besides her mother had told her this, she wouldn't have believed them. But, her daughter told her, "I know how you were, so I believe it."

McKee admits it was difficult to convince even herself to give it a try. "But," she said, "I was desperate."

"It takes more effort to eat this way, and it takes more time. If people could just take a pill and feel this way, they would," she said.

"Before I started this diet, I had been sick for so long, it had become a constant struggle for me to just get through each day. I was so exhausted at the end of the day, it had an effect on me psychologically.

"I noticed a lot of results after the first week, so that helped me stay on the diet," she said. McKee said she has lost 17 pounds, most of which came off in the first month, and that also helped her attitude.

McKee said she has lost faith in doctors. "They're just not into nutrition or food. They're just interested in treating you with drugs. And if it doesn't show up on an X-ray, they can't help you."

She can't be certain, but McKee said her theory is that her problem was that her colon was sluggish because it was restricted and bound by adhesions (scar tissue from her surgeries). If so, eating meat would have caused the pain because meat is more difficult to digest, causing the colon to work harder, and it stays in the digestive tract a long time.

"I'm so glad I found this place," she said of Hallelujah Acres. "The seminars and the newsletters have been so helpful for me. And there's no charge for the seminars, or the newsletter, so I feel they are rightfully motivated. They've helped a lot of people. Any time I get company, I bring them here. It's a neat experience. There aren't many places like this."

*From the Hallelujah Acres mailbag:*

"Please send 1 copy of *Why Christians Get Sick* - I have loaned mine out and can't get it back - everyone wants to read it...I have also loaned out all my *"Back to the Gardens"* - Can't get them back either - everyone is passing them all around. I would like to give them away, but can't afford it on S. S. I'll be praying for you."
– Arthur Vars, Sr., Connecticut

"I have just read *Why Christians Get Sick - Hallelujah!* Finally in print someone who knows what he is talking about! Praise God! I fully agree with you and will stand with you in prayer."
– Barbara Anne Sutton, New Jersey

# Patsy Stockton
## Reduces Insulin, Relieves Pain, Gains Energy And Loses 48 Pounds on the Hallelujah Diet

*By Michael Dye*

When Patsy Stockton first heard about Hallelujah Acres through a friend at church, she was a diabetic taking 130 to 140 units of insulin in two injections a day, with her doctor saying she needed to increase this dosage.

But based on the recommendation of a friend who had found relief from severe arthritic pain after attending a seminar at Hallelujah Acres, Patsy joined church members in two van-loads who traveled to hear Rev. George Malkmus' seminar on "How to Eliminate Sickness" on Monday, Jan. 25, 1993.

"I started on the diet (the next day) Tuesday morning," she recalled. "My blood sugar was 371 that day. I always check it in the morning. Within three days, my blood sugar dropped from 371 to 112. It hadn't been that low in five or six years."

At the time of this interview, Patsy and her husband – Rev. John Stockton, pastor of Piney Grove Freewill Baptist Church in Hampton, Tennessee – have been on a vegetarian diet of mainly raw fruits and vegetables, and Barley Green for four months. The Stocktons live across the state line in Bakersville, N.C. John has lost 40 pounds and reduced his high blood pressure from 120 / 95 to 105 / 62, but he is more excited about the progress of his wife.

Patsy has reduced her insulin from 130 to 140 units a day to 4 to 6 units per day, and can sometimes go two or three days at a time without insulin. She is looking forward to going off insulin altogether, which her doctor believes will be possible once she loses more weight.

**Patsy Stockton**

> *"I'm not calling this a diet. I call it a new way of living. It's not a diet because I eat as much of the raw food as I like." – Patsy Stockton*

Thus far, she has lost 48 pounds in four months. "I lost quite a bit at first, then I've slowed down to about a pound a week. But I haven't gained one pound of it back. I have lost weight before, but I've always gained it back," Patsy added. "I'm not calling this a diet," she emphasized. "I call it a new way of living. It's not a diet because I eat as much of the raw food as I like."

And when her weight and blood sugar started dropping, it was more than just a change in numbers. "I started feeling better right away. I started having a lot more energy. Before, I hadn't hardly been able to get up in the mornings. I started being able to get up early in the morning. At 6 a.m., I am full of energy and ready to get up. Before, I couldn't get started 'til about 9 or 10."

Patsy – who sings in the Gospel trio, The Heavenly Echos – just finished teaching Vacation Bible School, which included up to 104 children a day. "Four months ago, I couldn't have done it. I was worn out all the time. When your sugar is up, eyesight and kidneys also get bad," she said.

Another symptom of diabetes from which she was suffering prior to her new diet was cracks and sores on her feet. "It was getting to the point that I couldn't hardly walk on my feet," Patsy said. For a diabetic, these cracks and sores can be a serious problem, leading to gangrene and even possible amputation. "The Barley Green and diet solved that too. I have smooth feet now."

She was taking a lot of pain medication, sometimes getting up two or three times a night to take something to relieve the pain. But in the past four months, "I've taken just a couple (pain pills)," she said. The only other medication she now takes is for her thyroid.

"How can you tell kids today, 'Don't take drugs,' when they see you every time you turn around going to the medicine cabinet to take prescriptions?"

Before changing her diet, Patsy said her doctor "was threatening" to either increase her 130 - 140 units of insulin a day with more shots or with a supplemental pill, "but I had such bad allergies, I couldn't hardly take anything. … He changed my antibiotics five times in one week. So many of my medications created other problems, he took me off everything. He told me there was nothing he could do. That totally scared me to death."

Before changing her diet, Patsy also had large spots, which she was told were liver spots, on her arms, and they had spread to her hands. "Within two weeks after starting on Barley Green and new diet, all the spots on my hands were gone. Then they disappeared on my arms too."

Patsy was also suffering from very painful sores on the inside of her mouth, which cleared up within a week after making her dietary change. Other improvements include a reduction in her high cholesterol and high blood pressure, and what her doctor says is a much-improved functioning of her liver.

Patsy said she took literature from Hallelujah Acres to her doctor, "and he's all for it . . . He said when most people come to see him, they just want more pills so they can go home and eat everything in sight, and then come back and get more pills. He said he tells people it (diabetes) is a diet problem, but people just want pills to cure it."

But the diet Patsy is following is very different from the diet doctors recommend for diabetics, which includes three meals and three snacks a day, milk and something from the bread group six times a day. Rev. Malkmus says this diet recommended by doctors – high in meat, dairy and eggs – actually contributes to adult-onset diabetes.

Patsy said several members of her family have followed the pattern of being overweight and developing diabetes at about age 40. Part of the family tradition, she said, is to encourage everyone, even people on a diet, "to eat, eat, eat . . . just a little piece of this cake."

"I agree with George. I believe it's what you eat that makes you sick. I studied nutrition for years, but just didn't put it to use. I really appreciate George sharing what he has learned with everybody . . . A lot of us that have been helped by George are helping others by telling as many people about this as we can."

Patsy said her daughter has lost 30 pounds on the diet, her daughter's young children have seen improvement in their allergies and friends with sinus and stomach problems have also found relief. She made tapes of the "How to Eliminate Sickness" seminar, and she said people who have either heard these tapes, or heard Rev. Malkmus

*"How can you tell kids today, 'Don't take drugs,' when they see you every time you turn around going to the medicine cabinet to take prescriptions?" – Patsy Stockton*

personally, are more likely to stay on the diet "because they understand the whole story."

And, she said, "Everywhere we go, people who see us notice a big difference, especially in me." Rev. Stockton said he did not have as many health problems as his wife, but that he has experienced a noticeable boost in his energy level. "I work a 40-hour job and pastor this church, so I needed some help," he added.

And she said giving up meat has been easier than most people would expect. "I think if people really thought about killing animals, no one would eat meat. We were all just brought up to think we've got to have it to survive."

*From the Hallelujah Acres mailbag:*

"First, let me tell you how much I have gotten out of your newsletters, given me by a friend. I have changed my diet, and have completely cured myself of a congestion in my throat that had kept me from singing for about four years. Music has been an important part of my life most of my life. I had been devastated about my throat. *Now I can sing again, and my energy is back.* I have never been heavy, but I was getting 'different' around the middle. That little extra is gone. My skin has even changed, and I am thrilled, to say the least ... I have been drinking Barley Green for several years ... but what a difference it makes to change the rest of the diet. Thanks so much for everything that you are doing."
– B.W.,
Georgia

# Pastor Bob East:
## "Living Above MS"

*By Michael Dye*

Anyone who thinks he or she has an "incurable" disease beyond all hope should consider the story of Pastor Bob East. Bob went from being unable to walk two steps at a time in the prime of his life because of Multiple Sclerosis to being a middle-aged mountain climber ... and more.

East refers to himself as a "retired" Seventh-day Adventist minister / educator, although he continues in his mid-60s to travel extensively in his own active outreach ministry. Pastor Bob, now living in Rogersville, Tenn., preaches the Gospel and a message of health. And he has a powerful story to tell.

As a young man, Bob was active in outdoor sports and exercise, and taught physical education. But as he entered his late 20s, Bob's health deteriorated rapidly. One of the first signs was difficulty walking up the slight incline in the driveway of his home in rural, northeast Georgia. In the prime of his life, it became a struggle for Bob to stand without a cane or to walk more than a couple feet without falling. He was diagnosed in 1960 by several doctors, including a neurologist, as having Multiple Sclerosis – the crippler of young adults – at age 28.

Doctors who made East's diagnosis of MS did not recommend any treatment. MS is a disease said to have no cure and its victims are expected to get progressively worse with time. Had he gone the standard route, Bob would now be in a wheel chair or his grave.

But an elderly couple from one of the two churches Bob had been pastoring gave him a book (titled *Live Food Juices*) by Dr. H.E. Kirschner on fresh vegetable and fruit juices. Carrot juice became a part of his daily diet, and Bob emphasizes, "The juice therapy is a key factor in me being able to sit here and talk to you today." The fresh juices did not offer immediate relief for his MS symptoms, but it did give him tremendous hope. Within days after starting on a regimen of fresh vegetable and fruit juices, Bob received relief from his painful stomach ulcers. And shortly later, other problems began to vanish . . . constipation, insomnia, headaches, fatigue, "and I noticed I had more energy."

"If it could help all those things in a matter of weeks, I wasn't going to question that it could go even deeper and do more than that," East said. When it comes to nutrition and healing, he said, "A lot of what needs to be done is not

**Pastor Bob East is seen here rappelling the face of North Carolina's Mount Pilot in 1976, 16 years after he was diagnosed with Multiple Sclerosis**

seen. It's going on behind the scenes. Just like a heart attack comes on over a long period of time. Healing and the wheels of nature turn slow. Fortunately, it doesn't take as long to get unsick as it does to get sick. But it's not always something you can look at and see while it is happening. All this can be related to nutritional factors, Barley Green and all the rest," Bob said.

Today, in addition to his daily consumption of fresh vegetable and fruit juices, Bob maintains a low-fat, vegetarian and non-gluten, wheat-free diet, although he occasionally eats some wheat. Bob is also a consumer and promoter of Barley Green.

Bob has gone for more than 25 years without any symptoms of Multiple Sclerosis. He has found a way of – as his book is titled – *Living Above It.* His last MS-related problem came about 1965 or 1966, when, "through negligence, I got busy enjoying the benefits and slacked up on my juicing and my diet." And that, he said, "wasn't an exacerbation. It was mainly physical depletion."

When Pastor Bob presents his lectures on health, he does not aim his message just at those with Multiple Sclerosis. "I'm thinking personally of a larger field, that is people with all kinds of degenerative diseases, which are the plague of America today."

East feels the message of health taught by himself and Rev. George

---

***Looking at the agony created by chemotherapy, radiation, surgical removal of body parts or dependence on a lifetime of prescription drugs that often cause more problems than they solve, East said he finds it somewhat humorous when he hears people say, "Oh, I wouldn't want to have to mess with making that carrot juice."***

---

Malkmus at Hallelujah Acres is one that should catch the attention of any person suffering from a degenerative disease. But East says people who have no major health problems should also see the importance of a healthy diet and lifestyle. It is easier to prevent disease before it strikes than to cure it afterward. Prevention is also much less expensive. Looking at the agony created by chemotherapy, radiation, surgical removal of body parts or dependence on a lifetime of prescription drugs that often cause more problems than they solve, East said he finds it somewhat humorous when he hears people say, "Oh, I wouldn't want to have to mess with making that carrot juice."

East adds, "Any thinking person should not have to be prodded in this direction."

In addition to the juice therapy, which East attributes as the key factor in his recovery, exercise and a positive attitude played vital roles. Along with his daily juice regimen, East fought against being an invalid by struggling every day to walk just a little further than he had the day before.

His experience with MS was steady decline, without remission, until he turned to Juice Therapy. Bob refers to the period of 1958 to the early 1960s as his "low years." He was first diagnosed with MS in 1960. But by 1962 he was able to complete – with some difficulty – a 20-mile hike, and by 1963, he was walking nine miles a day. A photograph on page 195 shows Bob mountain-climbing in 1976. Now in his mid-60s, he still back-packs up to 100 miles at a time.

Describing his experience, East said, "I never got to the wheel chair stage. I could have used crutches, but I chose not to. I used a walking cane. At the worst stages, I was only able to walk a few feet – and this was usually in a falling process – and I'd have to catch onto something. It was mostly leaning against things, holding onto things, sitting down to rest when I had to stop. Falling, oh, many, many times. I tore many suits. My knees, elbows and chin banged on the floor.

"Where was the turning point? Probably a fall I took one time doing my best to hike. I was following Dr. Kirschner's and Paul Bragg's advice. I knew both of them personally, and they advised me. As I was out walking in the cold part of the year, I fell and banged up my elbows and knees and hands. I didn't have gloves on. And for some unbelievable reason, the next morning, I was out again. I was out every day. I kept adding a few feet each day. But I fell again, and hit on the same hand I had hit on the day before. And I lay there on the ground with the blood coming out of my fist. I was about 28 or 29 years old, and I cried. A grown man crying. I said, 'By the Grace of God, I'm going to lick this thing.' "

When asked for recommendations for treating MS, East said, "I think you can relate it to exactly what Hallelujah Acres is all about, in terms of its dealing with the reality of the body being its own best physician." East recommends offering the body a "smorgasbord of natural foods that offer a nutritional variance from the standard American diet."

Many people have found success in dealing with diseases such as MS with diets that avoid saturated fats, meat,

**Pastor Bob East and Rev. George Malkmus enjoy a glass of Barley Green at Hallelujah Acres. Thanks to his change in diet, Pastor Bob, now in his mid-sixties, still enjoys backpacking, canoeing and other outdoor sports – more than 30 years after being crippled by MS.**

dairy, refined sugar, and, for some people, wheat products. This low-fat, non-gluten diet is patterned after a diet recommended by Professor Roger MacDougall, of London, England, as detailed in a six-page typed paper provided by East. MacDougall was diagnosed as having MS in 1953, but recovered to live a normal life and apply his method to thousands of other people in 33 countries.

MacDougall writes, "Multiple Sclerosis is a degenerative condition and it must be attacked by natural regenerative methods. ONLY YOUR OWN BODY CAN REGENERATE ITSELF."

MacDougall says he recovered from MS by using logic and the method of causality. MacDougall drew an analogy between two concepts: "the constant process of cell renewal which is life, and the breakdown of cell tissue which is degenerative disease. Because of this I saw what was required in treating a degenerative disease was very simply to enable the body to build new tissue. My therapy emphasizes the two ways in which this can be done. Firstly, substances which prevent the building of tissue must be removed from the diet. Secondly, nutrients which encourage cell building must be added . . . The body is its own best doctor. Give it the right working conditions and the right tools, and it will get on with the job."

MacDougall says the process can be slow, "but a slow rebuilding is preferable to the slow degeneration which is all the Establishment has to offer." MacDougall says it took him 15 years to "recover completely," and that, "Using myself as my own guinea pig, I made some advances and many mistakes . . . As a result of what I have learned and applied to other people, the first signs of recovery – which appeared after four years with me – can come now in less than four months. I have had many letters to testify to this – at least 500 . . . Progress can be seen in a few months. A year can now bring quite a radical improvement – as witness the results in what amounted to a controlled test at the Cheshire Home in Surrey where, for instance, a man of 74, after just over one year on the therapy, has progressed from total paralysis to the ability to wheel his fellow patients round the ward, and others have experienced similar improvements."

But East notes, "Until a person decides in their own mind that there is hope, there isn't any hope. The first thing you deal with is a mindset. People need to look at the challenge of not being sick ."

East emphasizes that exercise and a healthy diet are "not a way of drudgery. You don't give up anything . . . you gain. The good life is when you are able to enjoy living." Most people don't have the time and freedom to do everything they want to do when they are young. But unless people are careful, by the time they get old enough to find time and freedom, they no longer have their health, he warned.

Because East changed his diet more than 30 years ago, he has had the privilege of watching his children and grandchildren grow up, and he has been able to use his later years to travel extensively. He has seen the pyramids of Egypt, the Aztec and Incan ruins of South and Central America, Hawaii, Europe, Africa and he does frequent missionary work in Alaska. As part of his outreach ministry, Pastor Bob conducts revivals in which he preaches the Gospel and the message of health. He also offers cassette tapes and literature on health.

# Carol Cover:

## After 22 Months of Diarrhea, Weight Loss Down to 78 Pounds & 4 Visits to the Mayo Clinic, "Barley Green saved my life"

*By Michael Dye*

Medical specialists were baffled by the case of Carol Cover of Northfield, Minn. Beginning in May 1990, she became ill with a severe case of diarrhea up to 29 times a day that lasted for 22 months without ceasing. Four trips to the Mayo Clinic provided no clue as to a cause or cure.

Carol's normal weight had been 106 pounds, but she spent most of her 22-month illness weighing in the mid-80's. Following her final treatment prescribed by specialists at the Mayo Clinic, she lost down to a dangerous 78 pounds.

"I lost a quarter of my body weight. People thought I was dying," Carol recalled. "I had a terrible pain in my legs and hands owing to potassium loss, and for a long time, I couldn't get downstairs to cook. I just went from my bedroom to the bathroom, and sometimes I couldn't make that."

After falling ill, she had to quit her job of seven years in the Department of International Studies at St. Olaf College in Northfield. Prior to that, Carol, 59, had been a high school teacher for 10 years.

**Michael Dye interviews Carol Cover**

*After recovery from a condition that caused her to lose down to 78 pounds, it is with no exaggeration that Carol says in her soft-spoken voice, "Barley Green saved my life."*

In addition to diarrhea, Carol also suffered sores in her mouth, throat and tongue so painful she could hardly swallow, her fingernails were breaking, she had excruciating headaches and her hair was falling out. "My hairdresser thought I was dying, based on what my hair looked like," she said.

Her doctors, including a team of medical specialists who treated her four times at the Mayo Clinic, were never able to diagnose the cause of the diarrhea. Carol had traveled to Israel and Turkey in 1989, but tests were negative for any parasites. During her tests at the Mayo Clinic, doctors ruled out all common causes of diarrhea, including a spastic colon, Crohn's disease and gluten intolerance.

In her final treatment from the Mayo Clinic, Carol said doctors prescribed an extremely powerful medication which they told her offered "a 70-percent chance of making me well and a 30-percent chance of making me worse." The powerful medication made her worse. After two months on this treatment, she lost down to 78 pounds, and her family physician advised her to quit taking it. At one point, doctors put her on a supervised three-day water fast, "and even that didn't stop my diarrhea," she said.

---

**"It's an exciting concept, not getting older and sicker, but getting older and better," Carol said.**

---

"My family thought I was going to die. But I managed to live until the next spring (1992) and friends gave me some Barley Green. I was desperate and willing to try about anything, so I asked them to tell me what Barley Green had done for them," Carol said.

"I have lost 25 pounds with Barley Green," one said. His wife added, "I lost 15 pounds." That, Carol recalled, "didn't sound too promising," because weight loss was the last thing she needed. But the couple told her of other cases in which Barley Green had apparently helped to heal everything from pyorrhea of the gums to breast cancer. "So," she said, "I decided to give it a try."

"After my second day on Barley Green, I had my first formed stool in 22 months. After one-and-a-half weeks, my diarrhea was totally gone. On the last Monday in March (1992), I called my doctor and said, 'I'm well.' I had been calling or seeing my doctor two or three times a week for 22 months, so he was quite surprised when I told him that I would see him for my annual physical in June."

After recovery from a condition that caused her to lose down to 78 pounds, it is with no exaggeration that Carol says in her soft-spoken voice, "Barley Green saved my life."

In addition to curing her diarrhea, the Barley Green also took care of the painful sores in her mouth, throat and tongue, and after a couple months, her hair and fingernails were back to normal. During her extended illness, doctors had prescribed potassium supplements, but these supplements never raised her potassium to an acceptable level. But after starting on Barley Green – and trashing the supplements – a recent blood test showed her potassium was normal.

"Northfield is a small town and word travels fast," Carol noted. People who saw her before and after her recovery were quite amazed and wanted to know how she did it. "I had never sold anything in my life," Carol said, but she became a Barley Green distributor in April 1992. "In one-and-a-half years, I have one hundred-plus customers and thirty-plus distributors under me."

With her health problems behind her, Carol took a 3,000-mile automobile trip in the summer of 1992 from Minnesota through Ohio and North Carolina. Carol said she sold a lot of Barley Green on that trip, "but my arthritis went crazy." Her psoriatic arthritis was so painful that she was unable to perform household chores such as vacuuming or wringing out a dish cloth. Initial treatment was unsuccessful so Carol's doctor sent her to an arthritis specialist who put her on methotrexate, a powerful and potentially dangerous medication known as "the drug of last resort" for arthritis. The drug is so powerful it could only be taken one day a week, to avoid liver damage. After taking the drug for five months, from November 1992 to April 1993, Carol and her family physician decided she should quit taking the drug because it was not effective and too dangerous. Carol said while on this medication, she had started getting her headaches again, and that she feared the possibility of liver damage.

It was April 1993 that she attended a Barley Green convention in Oxnard, Calif., and heard Rev. George Malkmus speak about the benefits of a vegetarian, predominantly raw-foods diet. So Carol changed her diet to raw vegetables and fruits, and her arthritis was totally healed within three months. Carol's rheumatologist had given her a book with a chapter called "Ducks that Quack." The gist of that chapter, she said, was that anyone who tells you that a change in diet will affect your arthritis is a quack. But at a check-up in October 1993, her doctor found no sign of arthritis or psoriasis, to which this form of arthritis is related. And her doctor said her iron was the highest it had been in the 10 years since she has been his patient. Her weight has leveled off once again at 106.

She has had to be strict about her diet, she said, because, "If I eat sugar, for the next couple of days, my hands would get swollen."

Carol notes she is an example of how some problems (in her case, severe diarrhea, mouth sores, headaches, hair loss, fingernails breaking) could be cured just by taking Barley Green, but that total health could not be attained without converting to a mainly raw foods diet, and eliminating meat, dairy, sugar, salt and white flour, as recommended by Hallelujah Acres.

Carol's husband, Dick, has also benefitted from the dietary change. He has lost from 180 pounds down to a healthy142, and brought his high cholesterol and high blood pressure down to normal.

And Carol has not kept quiet about her new dietary knowledge. In January 1994, she began teaching a series of 10-week "Let's Be Well" courses, based on the diet recommended by Hallelujah Acres. Carol also is a Health Minister with Back to the Garden Health Ministries.

"It's an exciting concept, not getting older and sicker, but getting older and better," Carol said.

"The truth is that most of the garbage sold in supermarkets isn't really food at all. Some of it is really candy, most of it is really poison. But it's not food. Don't get me wrong – it's not that I want to see the government take all the processed foods off the shelf … Instead, these products should be revealed for what they are, so that people can decide for themselves. For instance, Kellogg's Sugar Smacks, a product that's more than 50% sugar, should not be called a cereal. The word 'cereal' denotes a food made from grain, but Sugar Smacks isn't a food and what little grain is left in it has been robbed of its nourishment. Sugar Smacks is a candy and that's what it should be called. When mothers across the nation find out they've been giving their kids candy for breakfast, Kellogg's – and all the other presweetened breakfast producers – will soon be out of business."
– quoted from Paul Stitt, *Beating the Food Giants*, 1993, in the *Let's Be Well* newsletter published by Carol Cover.
Carol adds to this tidbit by citing information from a video by John McDougal, M.D., that "food manufacturers disguise sugar by giving it different names, so that sugar does not appear as the primary ingredient … (Kellogg's Sugar Smacks) lists sugar, corn syrup, and honey as three of the first four ingredients."

# Elwin Nichols

*By Michael Dye*

In 1982, Elwin Nichols had his first heart attack and quadruple-bypass surgery. In June 1992, Nichols had his second heart attack.

After his second heart attack, doctors told Nichols, who lived in Kokomo, Indiana at that time, that three out of the four bypasses that surgeons had created in 1982 were plugged up. They said he was not a good candidate for another bypass or for opening the arteries by balloon surgery. They changed his medication, but that didn't help. Doctors were pessimistic about his chances for survival. "I couldn't even walk 300 to 400 feet uphill from my house to the barn," Nichols recalled.

After moving to Morristown, Tenn., in the summer of 1993, Nichols went to a cardiologist in Knoxville for another opinion on July 2, 1993. The cardiologist performed a catheter, saw how many arteries were blocked, and informed Nichols

**Elwin Nichols**

that "there was not much hope … He told me there's not much we can do for you. If he operated, he said it would probably make it worse. But he still offered to operate. That guy scared me to death. I got away from him as fast as I could."

"So at that point, I decided to try to solve my problem with diet. I heard about Hallelujah Acres from my daughter, and then I heard about Dr. Dean Ornish, who recommends a diet and exercise program very similar to Hallelujah Acres."

So Nichols came to a seminar at Hallelujah Acres in July 1993. He immediately quit eating meat and dairy products, added a lot of fresh, raw fruits and vegetables to his diet, began consuming three or four glasses of carrot juice and three teaspoons of Barley Green every day. And he started walking.

"I could tell the difference in less than two weeks," he said. He started by working his way up to three-quarters of a mile, "and now I'm walking a little over seven miles every day. " Recalling the hill from his house to the barn that he had been unable to walk up, Nichols said, "I can run up that hill now."

He has lost from 195 pounds down to 162, and Nichols said he has had no more chest pains. His cholesterol had been in the 250 to 300 range, but was down to 143 on Oct. 23, 1993.

Nichols, who is now 63, returned to Indiana a couple months ago for a visit, and went to see his cardiologist, who had been considering him as a possible candidate for another bypass surgery. "My cardiologist told me that anybody who can walk seven miles a day should not be considering any more bypass surgeries. He said, 'Whatever you're doing, keep doing it.' "

Beaming with enthusiasm as he ate a salad at Hallelujah Acres in November 1993, Nichols said, "It's unbelievable what a person can do with three months of his life. Today I'm not the same person I was three months ago. I put up my own hay this year, and I didn't have a bit of trouble." Nichols raises horses on his small farm.

"If I could have been directed this way after my first heart attack, I wouldn't have had to have surgery then. If every one of us would eat like this and exercise, then we'd all feel so much better, and doctors would be out of business."

# Sandy Kureshi

*By Michael Dye*

Sandy Kureshi had devoted more than 20 years of her life to the medical profession, continuing her education beyond a Master's Degree. As a medical records supervisor in California, her career was boosted by a fast-track management training program that gave her prospects of becoming an assistant hospital administrator.

But in June of 1993, while working as medical records supervisor for a large health maintenance organization in California, Sandy was exposed to chemical fumes that she says caused her lungs to crackle like a bag of potato chips when she breathed. She was eventually diagnosed with and treated for severe respiratory problems including pneumonia, chronic asthma and chronic obstructive pulmonary disease.

The end result of medical treatment Sandy received was a toxic reaction to massive amounts of drugs she was prescribed, which nearly killed her. From chemical exposure at her hospital job to a toxic reaction to her numerous prescriptions, the former medical professional says, "Medical science was killing me."

After losing her job, home and health in California, Sandy and her husband returned to Pennsylvania to live with her Mennonite "spiritual family." It was there Sandy was introduced to the Hallelujah Diet with a "How to Eliminate Sickness" tape by Rev. George Malkmus. She began by giving up all meat and dairy, and noticed dramatic improvement in her breathing within two weeks. Then she bought a used Champion Juicer and went on the Hallelujah Diet completely. After 33 days, Sandy had lost 30 pounds, was off all medication and was able to return her breathing machine. With her new diet, there was no need for the anti-depressants she had been prescribed for 18 years. By October 1995, she had lost 90 pounds, down from a high of 260, and is still losing.

Sandy ended her 22-year career in the medical profession and her life is now dedicated to helping people to restore their health through natural diet. Sandy credits Hallelujah Acres with saving her life, so she has completed our three-day training course as a Back to the Garden Health Minister to help her share this message of health with others. Sandy gives her own "How to Eliminate Sickness" seminars throughout the Northeast and into Canada, with as many as 500 people in attendance. She also works in a health food store in the heart of Pennsylvania's Amish Country, where "most of the traffic up and down the road is horse and buggy."

Sandy began her medical career in 1971 in Pennsylvania and continued to advance in that field when she moved to California in 1980. She assisted in surgeries, worked in coronary care and the intensive care unit and then became medical records supervisor for a large health maintenance organization in California. As a medical records supervisor, Sandy supervised over 30 employees, 30,000 medical records and between 450 and 500 appointments per day. "I felt my years of experience had come to fruition. I had a positive attitude, I appreciated the administration and worked with them on a fast-track program, possibly to become assistant hospital administrator," she said.

But then in June of 1993, an accident occurred that drastically changed Sandy's life, health and career. The accident occurred in the Radiology Department. Film developing solutions (from developing X-Rays) were poured down an industrial sink, which began to back up. After being unable to unclog the sink for three days, janitorial services poured a liquid formula down the drain, Sandy said. The mixture of chemicals caused a toxic reaction and a gas that permeated the building. The fumes lingered because the air conditioning system was turned off that day as filters on the roof were

*From the Hallelujah Acres mailbag:*

"Your book *(Why Christians Get Sick)* is a refreshing spring in a dry desert. I loved it and I would enjoy reading more...My doctor... introduced me to your book and I hunger and thirst for more information...May you continue to keep your dream alive for Hallelujah Acres. I thank God for you and may you continue to prosper..."
– Gloria Gumby, California

being changed, she said.

"People had different reactions. Some eyes watered. Others were coughing violently. Some passed out on the floor, including male nurses," Sandy said. A switchboard operator with a history of asthma was hospitalized for two weeks in severe respiratory distress, she added.

"My reaction was dizziness in the head and a burning in the nostrils, like smelling salts were under my nose. I lost my clarity of thinking. I had to prop up my head with my hands," Sandy said. "I asked if we could evacuate the building. We were told it was just a bad smell and that no one was allowed to leave the building."

They stayed in the hospital under those conditions for five hours until personnel from another shift started coming in and noticed the fumes and the physical problems so many people were experiencing. The building was then evacuated and the fire department's hazardous materials team responded, although Sandy notes the administration was not the one who called the fire department. The hazardous materials team, "covered from head to foot" in protective clothing and breathing apparatus, went in and used large fans to blow out the fumes, she said. Even after that, when Sandy and others went back to work the fumes were still present. The building was closed because employees kept complaining and going to the hospital for treatment.

Sandy Kureshi, before and after losing 90 pounds on the Hallelujah Diet. Sandy weighed in at 260 in this picture (top, right) with her husband, Saqib Kureshi and friend Marge Clemons. She was down to 170, and still losing, in this October 1995 photo. Sandy credits Hallelujah Acres with saving her life and has become a Back to the Garden Health Minister to share this message with others.

"The next day in a supervisor's meeting, we learned we had been exposed to gas," Sandy said. Supervisors were asked to turn in reports to OSHA (Occupational Safety and Health Administration), and they were each handed one blank form to fill out and another sheet of paper telling them what to say, she recalled. Sandy said they were told to write in the reports that it had been "a bad smell, foul odor and hysteria, indicating that the people had a hysterical reaction. Nowhere did it state there had been a gas. Nowhere did it state there had been a chemical reaction that released those fumes. They basically denied any and all liability and responsibility for what had occurred, and told us we were to treat our employees as though there were malingerers and they said there was nothing wrong with any of them."

"The administration docked us without pay" for the time spent outside waiting for the fumes to be cleared, she said. Five to seven had been hospitalized, but the administration "assured us they already had a history of weakness in the upper respiratory system, a history of asthma or emphysema."

Sandy said her attempt to tell the truth cost her job and her career in medicine. She couldn't afford to hire lawyers to fight a $5 billion corporation. She could never get an employer reference, and with no job and, of course, no health insurance, Sandy said she went through "two months of self-pity and chronic depression." Sandy and several of her family members had experienced chronic depression for many years. "It ran in the family. My mother was on medication for chronic depression, my sister, aunt and cousins …"

"For this chronic depression I had taken 18 years of benzodiazepine drugs… I also took Prozac," Sandy said. "You see, I was a good student of the medical profession. I learned that if you had a symptom, you took a drug to make it better … I never questioned the prescription drugs I took during those years."

Within two months, Sandy developed the first case of pneumonia she had experienced since shortly after being born as a premature baby. "I thought that was strange. I hadn't had pneumonia since I was born. I hadn't had any upper respiratory problems, other than an occasional cold or sinus, since then." Because Sandy was unable to figure out what caused the pneumonia, she assumed it was stress.

"It lasted several months. I was on lots of anti-biotics and nothing seemed to help it. Finally it went away. I felt a little better but I didn't have all of my energy back. And then I started developing a strange noise in my lungs, a crackling sound. My lungs would crackle." Sandy likened the noise to the crackling sound made by opening and closing a bag of potato chips. She had never smoked and had always worked in a smoke-free environment, so Sandy said she had no clue at that point what was causing her problems. Because she had lost her medical benefits, Sandy said she continued to rely on antibiotics from friends.

Then she developed kidney problems. Her kidneys shut down and she went to an emergency room. "When they catheterized me, they got something (from her kidneys) that looked a lot like motor oil," Sandy said. Doctors were going to admit her, but Sandy said when they discovered she had no money or medical insurance, the hospital sent her home. But doctors were very concerned about her and called her at home every two hours. Sandy was advised to apply for indigent care, which she did. With her county medical benefits, she was examined and referred to another doctor, but that doctor didn't accept county medical benefits.

Then in July of 1994 Sandy heard about a Veterans Administration Hospital looking for subjects for medical testing. The deal was that in exchange for being a subject in the testing of experimental drugs, all subjects would receive free medical care. VA tests found Sandy had only 63-percent of her lung function, and she was diagnosed with chronic asthma and chronic pulmonary disease.

> *"Yes, it's true my lungs were gassed. It's true my lungs were scarred. But what I've eaten since March 18 has radically improved the ability of my body to heal itself.*

The VA hospital gave her an experimental drug for asthma and pulmonary obstructive disease, four different inhalers and two anti-depressants. "But I was getting worse," Sandy said. When she came to the VA hospital, it had been 13 months since her exposure to the chemical fumes. Shortly after starting on the medication given to her by the VA doctors, she developed "giant hives as big as grapefruits from my neck down." Sandy went to an emergency room, where she was given more medication. She returned to the emergency room again and then back to the VA hospital.

"Little did I know I was having a toxic reaction to all the medication. Medical science was killing me," she said. Then VA hospital officials became concerned that Sandy's bad reactions were "throwing off the results" of their tests, so they removed her from their experiment. VA doctors gave her more medication, including nerve medicine, and told her to go home and "sleep it off."

Sandy went home to follow doctors' orders, and when she awoke, her face was hot and she felt like she couldn't breathe. "I looked in the mirror, and from the neck up I was beet red. My eye lids looked like cactus plants. My eye lids, cheeks and ears were filled with fluid. My throat was closing up. My vocal chords were being constricted and I couldn't speak."

As a neighbor took her to the hospital, Sandy felt she was going to die. She had her address book, and began making marks by the names and addresses of people that needed to be notified and told, "Hallelujah, I've gone home to the Lord."

Doctors told Sandy she shouldn't have waited so long before coming to the hospital. They saw she was allergic to many different medications, and felt that a powerful steroid was the one last resort they could try. Doctors told her, "If it doesn't work, there's nothing else we can do," she said.

The steriod reversed the toxic reaction, and Sandy was able to breathe

*From the*
*Hallelujah Acres mailbag:*

"Will you please send me the book *"Why Christians Get Sick"* as mentioned on T.V. on Three Angels Broadcasting Network. I enjoy the show and hope you will be on permanently ... I am 84 and still going strong. With your help I am going to hit 100!"
– Esther Dowd, Arkansas

comfortably again. It was at this point that doctors told her she had a "textbook case of chemical exposure," complete with scar tissue from where the lungs had been burned by chemical exposure. Sandy said this was the first time she realized the hospital accident had been the cause of her problems. Doctors also considered the possibility of multiple chemical sensitivity, fearing something in her home environment may be a complicating factor, so they advised her husband to not take her back to their home. They temporarily moved in with some friends, but Sandy felt she needed to be with her Mennonite "spiritual family" in Lancaster, Pennsylvania. Her doctors warned against the move to a colder climate in her health. But after waiting three weeks to be stabilized, Sandy and her husband drove across country, stopping at three emergency rooms along the way.

Not long after her arrival in Lancaster, the whole family was invited out to listen to an audio tape by Rev. George Malkmus titled "How to Eliminate Sickness." Sandy didn't feel like getting out, but she agreed to go. "I was worn out just from getting dressed," she said, and when she arrived, Sandy had to lie down on the couch to rest while the tape was played.

As she listed to Rev. Malkmus explain why we should give up meat, dairy, eggs, sugar, salt, and processed foods, and nourish the body with raw fruits and vegetables, she was not too excited. Her first reaction was that she really wasn't sure if she even wanted it to be true, because, "I thought there wouldn't be any more fun in life ... But it sounded like it had the ring of truth to it."

So she first decided to just try giving up milk and meat for two weeks. Sandy explains that she had learned the empirical method in school, which meant if she could duplicate the results achieved by Rev. Malkmus and others, then his conclusion would be valid. At that time, Sandy had to sleep with four pillows to keep her upper body elevated enough that she could breathe.

"Needless to say, in two weeks with no milk and no meat, I no longer needed to sleep with four pillows under me at night," Sandy said. She was able to reduce her breathing treatments and started going out again. "I found out there was something I was more hooked on than milk and meat, and that was breathing. And it felt so good to be able to breathe again, it was worth staying off the milk and meats."

She started reading *Back to the Garden* and coming to Mary Glick's health food store, Glick's Natural Products, and she learned that Rev. Malkmus was coming to Lancaster for a seminar at the Harvest House Restaurant. Sandy attended the seminar and decided to go on the entire program. She bought a used juicer and on March 18, 1995, she had her first fresh carrot juice.

"I felt a major transformation in my body," Sandy said. Just 33 days after starting on the Hallelujah Diet, Sandy was off all medication and inhalers, was able to return her pulmonary breathing machine and had lost 30 pounds. "I went from having medication that was killing me to eating food that was healing me," Sandy said. "Yes, it's true my lungs were gassed. It's true my lungs were scarred. But what I've eaten since March 18 has radically improved the ability of my body to heal itself. My chronic depression of 18 years is gone. I'm off of Prozac. The reason for my chemical imbalance was my lack of enzymes that I needed from raw foods. My thyroid now works normally so I can control my weight. I don't have the food cravings like I used to have. I found out within two weeks that my body suddenly liked raw fruits and vegetables."

With her newly-restored health, Sandy has become one of our more active Back to the Garden Health Ministers. When she gives her "How to Eliminate Sickness" seminars throughout the Northeast, Sandy brings an old picture and a box full of the medication she once took, to show people the shape she was once in. Sandy emphasizes, "The solution to sickness is to change your diet. You don't have to be sick."

# Russ & Edie Dalson:
## Vegetarians for 72 and 66 years …
## Still Working Hard and Enjoying Life
## At Ages 92 and 84

*By Michael Dye*

When I first met them, Russ and Edie Dalson were busy renovating their new home … remodeling, cleaning, moving furniture, landscaping, planting flowers, setting out fruit trees and red bud trees, starting a small vegetable garden and planning for their future.

The work they were doing was much the same you would expect of any other couple in the process of starting over again and turning someone else's old house into their new home.

What makes this busy couple unique is that Russ is 92 and Edie is 84 years old.

At a time when most people would either be dead and buried or under the constant care of family members or a nursing home, Russ and Edie are active in their church and community and stay busy working on their house and garden. They both still drive a car (and neither of them has ever had an automobile accident).

Russ mows his own yard, cuts his firewood, and is still handy with a shovel and wheelbarrow, as he has shown by his landscaping work at their new home. Even at age 92, these are things he does without thinking it is unusual to be still doing them. Russ seemed surprised even at the suggestion, for example, that anyone would think that he wouldn't still be mowing his own yard. "If you don't use it you lose it," he added.

Once a month, Edie performs her devotional service by preparing food for students in the school operated by the Seventh-day Adventist Church they attend. She is well-qualified for that task, since she once served as head cook for Andrews University in Berrien Springs, Mich.

Russ & Edie Dalson pause from working on their new home. At 92 and 84, they are more active than some 20-year-olds. The Dalsons have been vegetarians since they were teenagers. As a teenager, Russ decided, "I wasn't going to be an old man when I was 70."

*From the*
*Hallelujah Acres mailbag:*

"Just about a month ago, I was at the end of my rope and really in despair. My immune system was so deficient, I just couldn't seem to stay on top of things without a lot of effort. … As we were traveling the roads of the United States on furlough this summer my body became weaker and weaker and was overtaken with pain. We tried all kinds of 'natural' means to help but to no avail. It was on this particular day that I was ready to give up all hope that we arrived at the home of friends in Tennessee. The Lord, of course, had gone ahead of us in this time of need. The friends we visited had recently been to one of your seminars. They shared with us a copy of the notes they had received as well as telling about the things they had learned … Although we had heard before that a large percentage of the diet should be raw foods, we were never really aware of all that it meant, and we didn't know anything about fresh juices … We thank the Lord for meeting us in the hour of need and for the improvement that has been seen in the past month. A month ago, I could hardly lift my feet to walk, my legs were so painful. Now my husband and I walk about a half hour each morning at a

**Continued in the right column of page 209**

Russ worked from last November to January doing construction on the church's new community center. He worked alongside men a third of his age mixing cement for the steps and doing carpentry work. Russ and Edie also help out once a week at the church's used clothing shop, operated as a community outreach.

"So we're busy," Edie said as a soft-spoken understatement. She said people often see the work she does and tell her: " 'You shouldn't do that.' But I say, 'Why shouldn't I do it?' " She objects to labels such as "old" and "elderly," insisting, "We feel young."

The Dalsons live just a few miles from Hallelujah Acres, and are good friends of Rev. George and Rhonda Malkmus. Russ and Edie bought their 1 1/2-acre home site on Hickory Cove Road in March after living in Eidson, Tenn. for eight years. One reason the couple moved from Eidson to the Rogersville side of Clinch Mountain was so they could be closer to the activities they enjoy in Rogersville, Greeneville and Morristown. "We wanted to be on this side of the mountain. We're 20 miles closer to the things we like to do now," Edie said.

And they're in good health. Edie said it has been about 30 years since she has been to a doctor, and Russ hasn't been much more often himself. The last time Russ went to a doctor was three years ago to have a wart removed from his ear.

Their long lives have allowed them to enjoy their four children (one of whom died in an airplane accident), their 16 grandchildren and 24 great-grandchildren. One of the reasons behind this couple's health and longevity is that they have been vegetarians since they were teenagers. In addition to their healthy diet and lifestyle, Russ and Edie feel it has been a complete trust and faith in God that has allowed them to live such a long and happy life.

Russ has been a vegetarian for 72 years, since 1922, and Edie has been a vegetarian for 66 years. Edie became a vegetarian in 1927, after meeting Russ, and they celebrated their 66th wedding anniversary in June 1994. Even before becoming a vegetarian, Edie didn't eat much meat, because her mother was a Seventh-day Adventist.

"Back when we had cows (and drank milk), Edie used to get strep throat. But since we got rid of our cows, she hasn't had strep throat. And that was about 30 years ago," Russ said.

They eat as much raw food as possible, and use a Champion Juicer to make everything from carrot juice to an all-fruit frozen banana / strawberry "ice cream." Another factor in their health and longevity is that they have never smoked cigarettes or drunk liquor. Russ said, "The hardest thing I ever gave up was chocolate."

Russ and Edie moved to Tennessee 10 years ago. They met in the mid-1920s when they each lived in suburbs surrounding Chicago, Ill., and they later moved to North Dakota and Michigan.

Before meeting Edie, Russ also lived in Wisconsin and Los Angeles, Calif. There were many influences on Russ's decision 72 years ago to adopt a vegetarian diet. He met Paul Bragg, one of the early advocates of health, when

Bragg taught physical education at the Los Angeles Y.M.C.A. This was before Bragg became well-known for his world-wide lecture tours promoting healthy diet and lifestyles. Another big help for Russ was *Life and Health Magazine,* which he began receiving in 1922. This magazine had information about vegetarianism, and Russ, who was raised a Methodist, said he read the magazine for five years before realizing it was published by the Seventh-day Adventists.

But the biggest influence on Russ's decision to become a vegetarian was his own experience of ill health caused by eating meat. He had his first bout with serious illness at age 15, and he didn't like it. As Russ was earning his way through high school working on a farm in Wisconsin, his knees got wet picking strawberries in the mud. He developed a serious case of inflammatory rheumatism from his knees to his hips, and had to stay in bed for weeks at the Wisconsin farm because he couldn't walk. A doctor told him the problem was "too much pork," and sent him home with instructions to not do anything until the swelling went down.

"When I laid on that cot in the dining room, I made a vow to myself that I was not going to be wore out by the time I was 70. I didn't know anything about anything. I didn't know nothing, except that I wasn't going to be an old man when I was 70," he asserted. But at age 19, while working in California, he developed inflammatory rheumatism again in his right knee. He went to an orthopedic doctor, who told him to not eat any meat for one month, and no pork for six months.

Russ made the decision at that point to give up meat, but at age 19 he was puzzled about what there was left that he should eat. His first feeling about vegetarianism was "I felt like I was going to die because I didn't have anything I could eat."

But he learned fast. Even in the 1920s, there were several vegetarian restaurants in Los Angeles, including the Raw Food Cafeteria, which served an all-raw menu that included vegetables, fruits, fresh juices, nuts, soups, pies and wafers baked by the sun.

"You can eat all the raw food you want, and the more raw food you eat, the better off you are," Russ said.

When working for the Los Angeles Bed Springs Co., he did his grocery shopping at the farmer's market, and would bring a big box of raw produce to work every day, eating "whatever fruits and vegetables I felt like eating." At that job for the bed springs company, Russ weighed 145 pounds and was responsible for moving 10,000 pounds of angle iron 100 feet and then had to roll out 10,000 pounds of coil. It was a job that would wear a pair of horse-hide gloves "right off your hands" every two weeks, he said.

"If I could be a vegetarian and do this kind of work, I could do anything," he said.

**Continued from the left column of page 208**

fairly good pace … We thank you for sharing your experience and research with others, and we thank the Lord for friends who cared enough to share, too.
– Lewis and Judy Young, Missionaries to New Guinea

*"You can eat all the raw food you want, and the more raw food you eat, the better off you are," Russ said.*

# Jim Allen
# Uses Hallelujah Diet to Help Heal Kidney Cancer

*By Michael Dye*

When he was diagnosed with kidney cancer at age 70, Jim Allen was told by three different doctors that his left kidney would have to be removed.

Medical science considers kidney cancer to be one of the most difficult forms of cancer to cure. When Jim mentioned the possibility of using a change in diet to help his body to heal the kidney cancer, "the doctor looked at me like I was a fool," Jim recalls.

But after a visit to Hallelujah Acres, Jim did change his diet. And today, at age 71, he still has both kidneys and his medical tests show no sign of cancer. Jim also has no more headaches, no more sinus problems, and has lost 30 pounds. "And I just feel a whole lot better," said the soft-spoken retiree of Eastman Chemical Company in Kingsport, Tenn.

**Anna Lee & Jim Allen of Kingsport, Tenn.**

His wife, Anna Lee, went on the same diet and has been healed of diverticulitis, arthritis, migraine headaches, an irritating skin problem, and she has lost 35 pounds.

One of the interesting things about the Hallelujah Diet, Jim notes, is that a person can start this diet to heal a major, life-threatening disease, and then find that several other unrelated problems also clear up.

This, he adds, is just the opposite of the negative side-effects of prescription drugs and other treatments offered by the medical profession. Jim is speaking from experience here. He said one of his medical treatments for kidney cancer "almost killed me. I thought I was having a stroke. I could not move for seven hours." In addition to the negative side-effects, he said this chemical treatment also caused the cysts in his kidney to spread.

Recalling his feeling when he first learned of his kidney cancer, Jim said, "The doctors left me stunned and in fear. It was the most awful feeling I've ever felt." After his initial diagnosis by a doctor in his hometown of Kingsport, Jim sought a second opinion from a specialist at Duke University Hospital in Durham, N.C. He made six visits to Duke, and was scheduled to have his kidney removed there on Dec. 10, 1993. But Jim decided to get a third opinion from a urologist back in Kingsport.

All three doctors agreed: The kidney would have to be removed. Laser surgery was used in several operations to remove about 40 cysts from his kidney and two from his bladder. The cysts were found to be cancerous, and doctors insisted the cysts would continue returning if the kidney was not removed.

But in the meantime, a couple of friends told Jim and his wife about Hallelujah Acres. They pleaded with Jim to go see Rev. George Malkmus before agreeing to have his kidney removed. The friends told Jim and Anna Lee about several people who had avoided major surgery by healing themselves of various diseases after going on the Hallelujah Diet. The female friend said she had used this diet to eliminate a tumor in her breast, and that doctors were about to remove part of her son's colon before he got on the diet.

They went to Hallelujah Acres that day. After talking with Rev. Malkmus and hearing other people's testimonies, both Jim and Anna Lee decided to get started immediately on the diet.

> *"The doctor came out of the operating room and sat down and told my wife and daughter he could not believe what had happened. The doctor sat there with his chin resting in his hands for a long time, saying, 'I just can't believe it.' He didn't know what to think."*
> *– Jim Allen, describing his doctor's reaction after an exploratory surgery revealed that Jim's body had healed itself from kidney cancer*

Since that day, they have been on a strictly vegetarian diet of about 85 percent raw fruits and vegetables, along with plenty of fresh carrot juice, Barley Green and Herbal Fiberblend.

Jim said Rev. Malkmus and his wife, Rhonda, were both very helpful. "After they explained the difference between the body's means of natural self-healing with proper nutrition versus the doctors' means of surgery and drugs, there was no choice in my mind about which way I wanted to go. They explained about how the body works to heal itself. It just made sense," Jim said. "It wasn't until I was 70 years old that I learned how self-healing works in my body. After starting on the new diet, Anna Lee could see a difference right off. In three weeks or less, I could really tell a difference," Jim added.

After about 90 days on the Hallelujah Diet, Jim's Kingsport urologist wanted to schedule surgery to remove his kidney. This was shortly after 30 to 40 cysts had been removed from the kidney by laser surgery, and the doctor told him the cysts would continue coming back if the kidney was not removed.

During this consultation, Jim said he did not tell the doctor about his new diet, but he did ask if he could postpone surgery long enough to see if his body's immune system could work on the cancer. "The doctor looked at me like I was a fool and he said there's no such thing."

Jim said the doctor told him he would be "taking a chance" if he did not have the surgery, but the doctor agreed to wait 90 days. So on May 18, 1994, the

*From the Hallelujah Acres mailbag:*

"Thanks so much for introducing us to Barley Green and a new diet. My husband has been insulin dependent for 11 years. Within just a few days of Barley Green and more raw vegetables, with very little meat, he has dropped his insulin down and his blood sugar has leveled. We are gradually changing diet and adjusting insulin. Thank so much for new hope and health."
– Anetta Massey, California

doctor went back up into Jim's kidney again. This was six months after he had been eating mainly raw fruits and vegetables, drinking carrot juice and using Barley Green. Much to the doctor's surprise, no new cysts were found.

"The doctor came out of the operating room and sat down and told my wife and daughter he could not believe what had happened. The doctor sat there with his chin resting in his hands for a long time, saying, 'I just can't believe it.' He didn't know what to think." It was after that visit that Jim told his urologist about Barley Green, carrot juice and his new diet. "He said, 'I've never seen anything like it. Just keep doing what you're doing.' "

The doctor scheduled another exam for Jim on Nov. 28, 1994 to check again to see if any cysts had returned. Once again, no new cysts were found. The doctor will continue monitoring Jim's kidney for awhile to ensure there is no re-occurrence, but Jim said he is confident that his diet has eliminated the problem.

"It's just wonderful to know I've still got my kidney. And I'm feeling great," he added. "If it hadn't been for George and Rhonda, I would have lost my kidney."

Anna Lee is equally thrilled … for the sake of her husband and for herself. Her serious medical problems began in 1986 when she had a nervous breakdown. "They kept me doped up all the time. I had to change doctors to get off drugs," she said. "On this diet, I'm not nervous any more. I'm a completely different person."

## "We've stopped going to the pharmacy. Our pharmacist thinks we've left town."
## – Anna Lee Allen

Shortly after her nervous breakdown, she was struck by arthritis and diverticulitis. With the arthritis, Anna Lee said she had trouble walking up and down stairs, and sometimes even walking on level ground was difficult. During this interview, she climbed the steps at Hallelujah Acres with no problem.

She was hospitalized two or three times with diverticulitis, thinking she was having a heart attack. The diverticulitis, for which doctors say there is no cure, made it impossible for her to eat salads. But after a couple months of carrot juice and Barley Green, she was once again able to eat raw vegetables.

Other problems that plagued Anna Lee before her dietary change included migraine headaches and a severe itching on her arms that persisted for 20 to 30 years. She went to several doctors and dermatologists, who were never able to diagnose or cure the problem. "All they could do was give me medication that would knock me out. It was worth a million dollars just to get rid of the itch," she said. "I've seen her scratch the blood out of her arms," her husband added.

With a new lifestyle that includes regular walks along Kingsport's "greenbelt," the Allens prove you are never too old to change. "We've stopped going to the pharmacy," Anna Lee said. "Our pharmacist thinks we've left town," she laughed.

# Chapter 25

# A Pastor Speaks ...

# Lester Roloff:

## A Preacher Ahead of His Time

*By Rev. George Malkmus*

I owe my life to Evangelist Lester Roloff! For it was he, in 1976, who encouraged me to go the nutritional route for the treatment of my colon cancer rather than the medical route which had proved so devastating to my mom. Though Brother Roloff is at home with the Lord today (he died in an airplane accident), I thought our readers would find what he was teaching over 20 years ago to be of great interest.

He wrote two little booklets before he died, *Soul, Mind & Body* and *Food, Fasting & Faith.* He was a preacher many years ahead of his time as he tried to convince Christians and especially preachers to get off the world's diet and back to God's diet. He took lots of abuse from fellow preachers, but he never backed down from what he knew through personal experience and the Scriptures to be the truth. In fact, since starting Hallelujah Acres Ministries, I have had over a half dozen preachers tell me that Brother Lester Roloff had given them a juicer many, many years ago. Some lamented that they had allowed it to gather dust, rather than using it.

Well, what did Evangelist Lester Roloff have to say in the two booklets mentioned above? Let's listen as he speaks through the printed word he left behind for our admonition.

**Evangelist Lestor Roloff**

## Excerpts from *Soul, Mind & Body*

## by Evangelist Lester Roloff:

Lester Roloff suffered more than his share of scorn in response to the burden he felt to tell others of the advantages to a diet of raw fruits and vegetables, with lots of fresh carrot juice.

In his book, *Soul, Mind & Body,* Brother Roloff writes: "For many years, I've been asked by my friends to write this book and give my testimony of what the right kind of food and exercise has done for me. I want it understood that I'm not a doctor, neither do I present any sort of dietary salvation, but I refuse to be pushed out of the field of the physical and the mental because I have found the answer and I'm obligated to give it. After thirty years of illness and fear of being sick, I've found the way of health and I'd be a traitor to my generation if I did not share it. I believe it is a sin to be sick if you could be well, and mighty expensive and discouraging ...

"If I can keep you from getting sick, I can speed you on to a more fruitful Christian life and you can take the money that you'd spend on hospital bills and give it to the cause of Christ or use it for some other worthwhile purpose."

Brother Roloff based his dietary beliefs on a combination of Biblical teachings, scientific knowledge and personal experience. Roloff begins his chapter on The Body by quoting I Corinthians 6:19-20:

*"The secret of a live, clean body is live, clean food – fresh vegetables, juices, fruit, and nice green salads ... I do not live completely without a cook stove, but because of its overuse, it has become the murderer of the human race." – Lester Roloff*

"What? know ye not that your body is the temple of the Holy Ghost which is in you, which ye have of God, and ye are not your own? For ye are bought with a price: therefore glorify God in your body, and in your spirit, which are God's."

In addition to quoting Scripture, Brother Roloff offers the wisdom of dozens of medical doctors, scientists and advocates of natural health in his little booklet. He quotes Jethro Kloss as saying, "God, in His infinite wisdom, neglected nothing and if we would eat our food without trying to improve, change or refine it, thereby destroying its life-giving elements, it would meet all requirements of the body."

Brother Roloff emphasizes, "The secret of a live, clean body is live, clean food – fresh vegetables, juices, fruit, and nice green salads." Noting the heavy price we pay for our cooked food habit, he writes, "Man is the only creature on earth that cooks his food. Man has hundreds of different diseases. I do not live completely without a cook stove, but because of its overuse, it has

215

become the murderer of the human race."

Unlike wild animals who live solely on raw foods, "Man tries to build live healthy cells on dead deficient foods that are lacking in the spark of life … What is this spark of life? A raw carrot has it. When planted, it will sprout. Heat, as employed in canning and cooking, kills this spark of life. A cooked carrot will not sprout. The life is gone – destroyed by heat. All cooked foods are dead foods. Man is the only animal that tries to build healthy live cells out of dead deficient foods … What I want you to get is the fact and the truth that if you can get it (food) just like God and nature finishes it – not stove cooked, but sun cooked – it will be a lot better."

Brother Roloff was not known as a man who pulled his punches or offered a sugar-coated flavoring for his words. For example, he writes: "It's a disgrace to see the poisons that are served around our churches today and the average supermarket is a mausoleum where dead foods lie in state."

He quotes Dr. C.W. Cavanaugh as stating, "The fact is there is only one major disease and that is malnutrition. All ailments and afflictions to which we may become heirs are directly traceable to this major disease."

> *"I do not believe meat was upon God's original menu for man. He had his first serving of meat after the fall. Neither do I believe that we will be meat eaters during the thousand-year wonderful reign of Christ down here."* **– Lester Roloff**

He cites an article in *American Magazine* focusing on the sad commentary that "our hogs are fed more scientifically than our children." Farmers must raise hogs in the most efficient way possible to maximize profit, while the feeding of our children is a "hit or miss" procedure, the magazine notes.

As a man with a soft spot in his heart for children (Roloff founded six homes for homeless, runaway and troubled boys and girls), he adds, "Though you may misunderstand, it ought to really grieve us and we ought to sound a solid protest to the food that's being served in the average school lunchroom or cafeteria. We must get our children away from wieners, lunch meats, cereals, candies and carbonated drinks, greases and starches, if their little bodies are to be sound and their minds clear."

Brother Roloff gives us hope that we can rejuvenate our ailing body as he offers scientific evidence that we literally build an almost entirely new body every year with what we eat, drink and breathe. He quotes Dr. Paul C. Aebersold, director of the Isotopes Division of the Atomic Energy Commission, as informing the Smithsonian Institute, "In a year, approximately 98 percent of the atoms in us now will be replaced by other atoms that we take in in our food, drink and air."

He also quotes Dr. Tom Douglas Spies as informing fellow doctors at the annual meeting of the American Medical Association, "If we only knew enough, all diseases could be prevented, and could be cured, through proper nutrition."

Brother Roloff encouraged people to understand and resolve the cause of their illness rather than just seeking a quick fix for the symptoms. "It seems that some consideration should be given to the cause of our mounting physical disabilities, but instead of going to the root of our troubles – wrong habits of eating and drinking – we rush to the medicine shelf and smother our uncomfortable and distressing symptoms under an avalanche of pills, potions and palliatives."

He adds, "... I believe in divine prevention more than divine healing because the first would prevent the need of the latter ... I not only believe that the Lord is able to get you well, but I believe that He is able to keep you well in obedience to His wonderful way and simple plan of living."

On the subject of meat-eating, Brother Roloff writes: "I do not believe meat was upon God's original menu for man. He had his first serving of meat after the fall. Neither do I believe that we will be meat eaters during the thousand-year wonderful reign of Christ down here."

As for the physiological effects of meat, Roloff adds, "In the colon, meat decomposes rapidly, gives rise to acids and toxins which are absorbed into the blood and distributed throughout the entire body. Meat is toxic to the nervous system and throws an unnecessary and harmful burden on the kidneys and liver."

Brother Roloff sums up the dietary dilemma of the day in one lengthy but eloquent sentence:

"As long as people continue to eat foods that have been prepared of impoverished, ghostly white flour, bleached and sulphured foods, doped and adulterated foods, plaster-like preparations called breakfast cereals; so long as they live on inferior food, material that has been dyed, chemically treated, doctored up so that it will look and feel fresh far past the time when it should have spoiled;

"So long as we live closer to the can opener than to Mother Nature, closer to the baker and the confectioner than to the farmer, closer to the food manufacturer than to the Almighty, closer to the butcher than to the garden and orchard, closer to the drug store than to the health food store, closer to the surgeon than to common sense;

"So long as they try to live on poisoned, overheated preserves, scorched, pressure cooked, fried foods, food that has been altered in its chemistry, disorganized in its molecules by pasteurization, food that has been artificially treated and sulphured until the food juices, vitamins, minerals and other food properties have passed up into the blue sky and there's nothing left but a dessicated lifeless substance sold as food in every grocery store and supermarket in the land and eaten by every man, woman, and child, including the doctors and passed upon as meriting seals of approval by various scientific organizations;

"So long as they mill off, peel off, pare off, and cook away from five to sixteen chemical food elements in the food and eat only the ghost-like starch, food sugar and food fat; so long as they eat food that has stood on warehouse floors and shelves for long periods of time in grime, dirt, dust, heat, moisture, and atmospheric ferments until the food properties have been injured by

*From the Hallelujah Acres mailbag:*

"I listened to some tapes and read some of your material. I agree whole-heartedly with what you are trying to do, but I am not as optimistic as you are. Like Brother Roloff, I don't get much response. However, people in general are getting more health conscious and even science is now acknowledging 'natural' benefits - *But* to get the church to abandon her superstitious faith and become a good steward of the *'life we now live in the flesh'* is a very difficult matter. The church, like the world, waits until crisis directs her actions rather than pleasing God with a motivation born out of gratitude for the love and grace that bought us with His own Blood. I have a Bible teaching ministry which is basically preventive regarding spiritual and physical sickness, and yes they can be related. Therefore, it is good to hear that you are providing help for the casualties. If you will send me a tape with your testimony and the basics of Health Care and permission to duplicate, I will send out several hundred ... I want to keep up with your work and I pray the Lord will be able to prosper it for His Glory and the Benefit of the Church."
W. Joyner Weems, Alabama

*From the*
*Hallelujah Acres mailbag:*

I have praised the Lord daily and given Him thanks for having put in my hands a copy of your #9 issue of *Back to the Garden.* What I read was truly an answer to prayer! I have received so much literature in the mail pertaining to diet, vitamins, etc., etc., - much of it contradictory - I did not, at first want to read any more confusing claims. But, thanks to the good Lord, I did read and knew He had given the Rev. Malkmus the truth about nutrition and His provision. I have been a Barley Green Distributor for 5 years but had not made it a business because, although I had received much benefit from using it, I did not see my health having improved enough to where I could be a walking testimony to potential customers, and my conscience wouldn't permit me to 'push' something I couldn't personally vouch for. I realized after reading #9 issue of BTTG, that there was a lot I still didn't know about nutrition and that I did not have a complete program for myself. I have been suffering for about 10 years with what was finally diagnosed as

Continued in the
right column of page 219

decomposition, toxins, age, vermin, rodents, metallic contamination, and by other agents of decay and corruption;

"So long as they drink bottled goods, soda fountain pop, artificial fruit drinks that have not a drop of fruit juice in them, laboratory fruit juices that contain powdered dope, dyestuffs, preservatives, and glucose; so long as they eat cold storage meat that may have been put in storage when the market price was low and kept for months or even years and doped, doctored, and embalmed to be sold when the market price was high; so long as they drink chocolate, cocoa, coffee and tea, or eat cream puffs and grease-filled doughnuts and sweet rolls;

"As long as they eat decomposed, rancid, lifeless, adulterated, fumigated, corrupt, foodless food material; so long as they eat fritters, fudge, syrup, soda crackers, cookies, candy, creamless ice cream, starchy noodles, pickled food, pig's feet, puddings, and all such meals of demineralized and devitalized food products presented by the food manufacturers and technicians more interested in how their wares will perform in their assembly line food processing machines than what their ware will do for your stomach;

"So long as they continue to procrastinate and postpone obtaining the flood of health that can be released to them through the daily use of nature's fresh, vibrant and vital plant juices – that long will they continue to be half alive and sick. That long will undertakers be in demand early in life; that long will they continue to sacrifice long before it's time the greatest miracle of the universe – human life."

Brother Roloff quotes Leviticus 17:11, "The life of the flesh is in the blood," and notes that "the blood must have good circulation, which comes, of course, from proper exercise." He also notes, "Good blood cannot be made of white bread, embalmed beef, sausage, potatoes, gravy, doughnuts, pie, cake and coffee."

He recommended pure water and "daily faithful exercise," especially walking and jogging. He added, "Everybody ought to try to get real hot at least two times a week to sweat out as much of the impurity as you can through the millions of sweat pores. If you don't exercise your body, you cannot have good health."

Brother Roloff was widely known for his fondness of carrot juice. In a "radical statement out of the conviction of my soul," he writes, "If you were to offer me one hundred thousand dollars for my vegetable juicer that travels with me everywhere I go and I could not get another, it would be no temptation to sell it. That's how strongly that I recommend that you get one and faithfully use it. Do not get a cheap juicer because it will not hold up cutting through those big California carrots."

Describing his diet, Brother Roloff writes, "I drink from a quart to two quarts of juice, either vegetable or fruit or both, every day. I eat a big salad made out of fresh vegetables for lunch. I take a walk and many times will jog a mile. I sleep on a real hard bed and if I can't find one, I get on the floor. I eat a lot of grapes, pears, apples, persimmons, nuts, raisins, dates, figs, and whatever I can get in season, including watermelons, cantaloupes, and honeydew melons."

Brother Roloff's message was a simple one, and he repeated it more than once. In his conclusion, he wrote:

"Now here is a summary: Get a vegetable juicer, and I didn't say a liquidizer or a pulverizer, but the best juicer you can get and use it every day ... And then move away from the cookstove and eat some big raw salads ... And whatever you do, remember that you are not to eat all you can hold, but just all you need because that's all the Lord said that He would provide for us. Philippians 4:19 ... The right kind of food and the right kind of exercise will bring the right kind of natural rest ... Get plenty of fresh air, exercise, and natural rest, and some good sunshine. And when you properly mix that with the food we have mentioned along with the Scripture, prayer, and faith, you'll have life and have it more abundantly.

"Take God's Word as it is, eat God's food as He gives it, and live accordingly and I believe you will find the pot of gold at the end of heaven's rainbow."

And Brother Roloff warns readers in his conclusion: "Remember one thing, good health is found nowhere along the line of least resistance and you had better deal gently with me in what I've said until you've proved that what we've said won't work. And remember, 'To him that knoweth to do good, and doeth it not, to him it is sin,' James 4:17."

**Continued from the left column of page 218**

fibromyalgia, complicated by osteoporosis (I am in my 75th year) and, of course, related afflictions - chronic fatigue, digestion & skin problems. To make a long story short, I am determined to do everything suggested in the Hallelujah Acres nutritional program and am slowly, but surely, cleaning out all the 'junk' from my freezer, refrigerator and pantry and have started the raw fruit and vegetable regime as well as increasing my Barley Green intake from one teaspoon daily to one Tablespoon three times a day. In a few short weeks I have already experienced marked improvement in my health...My thanks to you and to Almighty God for your ministry..."
– Virginia C. Aylor, Virginia

# Evangelist Dr. Nathan Meyer:

## Hallelujah Diet Gives His Preaching Career A "Major Extension" at Age 76

The following letter, printed in its entirety, is part of the application of Evangelist Dr. Nathan M. Meyer of Salem, Virginia, to become part of our Back to the Garden Health Ministry.

At age 76, Dr. Meyer maintains a very active ministry as an evangelist and is best known as a Bible prophecy preacher. He has been in the ministry for more than 46 years and publishes a twice-a-year newsletter with a circulation of 12,000.

Rev. Meyer's recent schedule has brought him to churches in Ohio, Pennsylvania, Indiana, Kentucky and North Carolina.

According to his application to become a Back to the Garden Health Minister, Rev. Meyer first heard about Hallelujah Acres when "a lady in a church in Ohio gave me a copy of *Back to the Garden*." His letter states:

**Dr. Nathan Meyer**

"For 35 years the study of health and nutrition has been a hobby of mine. I have accumulated a whole library of health books and magazines. I thought I was doing reasonably well.

I was taking every vitamin and mineral supplement imaginable, everything from Vitamin A to Co Q 10 and from (proanthocyanidins) to Fortified Flax. I also had medical doctors give me special treatments like Chelation and Hydrogen Peroxide infusions. I slept on a mattress pad of magnets and walked on magnets in my shoes. Everything for a reason and everything helped, I do believe, but there were no cures. Maybe it was just part of growing old?

Then a friend gave me a magazine called *Back to the Garden* published by Hallelujah Acres. I was also given two books: *Why Christians Get Sick* and another definitive book on distilled water called *The Choice is Clear*. Suddenly I was absorbed in an informational revolution. These materials were absolutely the best I had ever read. They made my whole library on the subject obsolete. Finally after all these years of searching, I found answers that had eluded me all my life.

For over two months I have been experimenting with this revolutionary diet called the Hallelujah Diet. It has meant a drastic change in lifestyle and it has not been easy. However, preliminary results are extremely encouraging in that they have indicated a major victory.

At age 76, I thought that my very fruitful and satisfying preaching-ministry of more than 46 years was about to end. Now I believe that I have been given a major extension.

Ever since 1991, when I was suddenly afflicted with what the doctor calls "intrinsic asthma," my voice has been getting weaker on various expensive drugs including Ventolin, Serevent, Asmacort, Theodur, Phenylprop / Guiaf and Prednisone – all of which can have serious side effects. Even so, every few months I would cough up mucous from my bronchial tubes. To overcome these infections the doctor would always prescribe a round or two of antibiotics. Even with the antibiotics, it was getting to the point where it seemed I was losing the battle. As I write this, I have just recovered from such an infection without using antibiotics. I believe my immune system has been greatly strengthened by my new diet.

*"For over two months I have been experimenting with this revolutionary diet called the Hallelujah Diet. It has meant a drastic change in lifestyle and it has not been easy. However, preliminary results are extremely encouraging in that they have indicated a major victory."* **– Dr. Nathan Meyer**

After nearly 3 months on the Hallelujah Diet, I am happy to report:

My voice is stronger again – like old times.

My nasal passages are now clear most of the time.

My 'incurable' Psoriasis is almost gone.

My energy level is definitely up.

I'm off all medication except Serevent and Theodur.

I've lost 30 pounds without trying and I'm feeling very good.

My Asthma and Arthritis have improved but it appears they heal more slowly. I have high hopes that within a year they will be totally and permanently cured."

> Nathan M. Meyer
> Virginia

*From the Hallelujah Acres mailbag:*

"Thank you so much for your prompt response to my request for a book *(Why Christians Get Sick)*. The next day my husband was telling one of our friends about the book when she was in the store and she said, "I would like to read that sometime." So he said, "Here, take it along," even though I hadn't even had a chance to look at it at all. A few days later she called and said she would like two copies - one for herself and one to share around with others. The day after that she said she needed three, because her mother wanted one also. So I am ordering six copies, and hopefully I will get a chance to look at one! Just thought you would enjoy that little scenario. Also, I gave away the newsletter to a friend whose father just found out he has cancer. . ."
> – Ruth Meyer,
> West Virginia

# Dr. Stan & Jodie Gravely
## Are Helping to Spread the Word in Virginia

Dr. Stan and Jodie Gravely of Meherrin, Va., have seen a tremendous improvement in their health since coming to Hallelujah Acres, and they have carried this message to their congregation and other churches in the region.

Stan has been offering seminars to his congregation at Tussekiah Baptist Church every six weeks and has recently been taking this message of health into other churches throughout Virginia, wherever he has received an invitation. These seminars have had an impact on the lives and health of people in his congregation and from other churches.

**Rev. Dr. Stan & Jody Gravely of Tussekiah Baptist Church in Meherrin, Va.**

The Gravely's were first exposed to the teachings of Hallelujah Acres in February 1993, when they read *Why Christians Get Sick* by Rev. George Malkmus. They came to Hallelujah Acres for a seminar in spring 1993 and invited Rev. Malkmus to their church to give a seminar in September 1993.

One reason that Stan's seminars have had a powerful impact is that people have seen changes in the life and health of Stan, Jodie and their three children since their change in diet. Stan's health improvement has been the most noticeable.

At a height of 5'7", he is now a fit and trim 140 pounds. But three years ago, Stan topped out at 197 pounds. He also suffered from hemorrhoids, severe sinus and allergy problems, frequent colds, flus, tonsillitis, strep throat … and he said, "I had very little energy."

"Every time a cold or flu came around, I got it," Stan recalled. He was a heavy consumer of more than a half-dozen prescription and over-the-counter remedies, which he would alternate, because the effectiveness of any one drug would lessen once he built up a tolerance to it. Although these "remedies" would never remedy the problem, "they would mask the symptoms and drug me to sleep," Stan said.

At this time, the Gravely's were eating the typical American diet of meat, dairy, eggs, white flour, sugar, etc. Stan consumed four cups of coffee and two diet soft drinks with caffeine every day.

Before learning about Hallelujah Acres, Stan first lost some excess weight by going on a nationally-known diet plan that encouraged eating just fruit for breakfast, limiting meat and proper combining of food, such as not mixing meat and starches in the same meal. With this program and exercise, Stan lost from 197 to 165 pounds, but his health problems remained unchanged.

"Then I got a-hold of George's book," he said. "When I read *Why Christians Get Sick,* I thought, 'Now, this makes sense!' I used the other program just as a plan to lose weight. The Hallelujah Diet is more of a lifestyle than just a weight-loss plan."

When Stan went on the Hallelujah Diet, eliminating all animal products, sugar, caffeine and other drugs, he went through a healing crisis similar to what many others experience when they cleanse a polluted body. "I had a dull headache and flu-ish feeling for a week-and-a-half. Then I woke up one morning with the biggest surge of energy I've ever had in my life, and I've felt great ever since then."

In the first month, he lost another 25 pounds, down to his current ideal weight of 140. "And I have had no colds, flus, sinus flare-ups or anything, and my

> *"And (since going on the Hallelujah Diet) I have had no colds, flus, sinus flare-ups or anything, and my hemorrhoids went away," Stan said. "I have energy to do things with the kids that I haven't been able to do in years. I used to sleep all Sunday afternoon. Now I'm outside playing softball and doing things with the kids out in the sunshine."*

hemorrhoids went away," Stan said. "I have energy to do things with the kids that I haven't been able to do in years. I used to sleep all Sunday afternoon. Now I'm outside playing softball and doing things with the kids out in the sunshine."

Stan and Jodie have three children, Luc, Matthew and Noelle. Before their diet change, Jodie said "every month we were taking one of our kids to the doctor for colds, ear infections, etc. They haven't had to go to the doctor since we've changed."

As an adult, Jodie has always weighed about 100 pounds and looked healthy. But, until their dietary change, she said, "I had suffered since childhood with irritable bowel syndrome, PMS and for three years with painful lumps from fibrocystic breast disease." The PMS and bowel problems cleared up almost immediately, and the lumps on her breast went away about two months after going on the Hallelujah Diet. But, she adds, the lumps reappeared on occasions when she ate meat or sugar at other people's homes, so, "You had better believe that I don't 'cheat' and eat unhealthy things anymore!"

It was after seeing these changes in their personal lives, the lives of their children and in their congregation that Dr. Stan and Jodie Gravely extended their Christian ministry into the realm of helping people to regain their health through proper diet and lifestyle. In their letter to Rev. Malkmus, expressing a desire to help this cause, the young couple wrote: "We, like you, see nutrition as a part of our God-given ministry now. It is such an essential part of the Gospel Message."

*From the Hallelujah Acres mailbag:*

"Dear Ones: I lost my eyesight completely on dead food (meals on wheels). Praise the Lord, now on live food for one week I can see again, even read my name. Thank you so much. Please send me another jar of Barley Breen..."
— A.D.,
Washington

# Rev. Hal Kirk:

## "Heart problems gone ... Hiatus hernia gone ... Colon problem gone ... Prostate problem gone ... Today I walk around pain-free."

*By Michael Dye*

"I just couldn't envision myself with heart problems," said Rev. Hal Kirk, the 54-year-old pastor of Bridgeport Freewill Baptist Church, near Newport, Tenn. "I was the one who went to the hospitals to visit other people with health problems."

But after suffering what doctors believed to be two mild heart attacks, Rev. Kirk was warned last October by his cardiologist that he was "a prime candidate for a trip down the road in an ambulance." Following doctor's orders, he had to briefly quit preaching at the church he has pastored for the last 10 years in his rural community 50 miles east of Knoxville, Tenn.

His Knoxville cardiologist diagnosed the problem as blockages in the upper and lower parts of the heart, and hardened arteries. At that time, Kirk said he was unable to walk the 71 steps from his carport to the mail box without stopping to catch his breath. Rev. Kirk also had a hiatus hernia, colon problems, prostate trouble and a circulation problem in his left foot.

In December, he was referred by a friend to Rev. George Malkmus. On his first visit to Hallelujah Acres, Rev. Kirk bought a Champion Juicer, water distiller and started taking Barley Green. "I noticed within three days my energy level began to rise," Rev. Kirk said. "I would go to bed at 11 or 11:30 and get up at 4:30 looking for something to do."

Now, he said 65 to 70 percent of his food intake is raw fruits, vegetables and freshly-extracted vegetable juice. After first changing his diet, Kirk would still occasionally eat chicken in social situations, but he said he has now become a total vegetarian. "And it was easier than I would have thought. I have no craving for meat, whatsoever."

Although he was unable to walk 71 steps to his mailbox without

**Rev. Hal Kirk**

*When you take George's advice and get on his program, it can turn your life around," Rev. Kirk said. "People with heart problems need to know that you can reverse these problems with this diet."*

stopping in October, "Today (less than six months later), I can run two to three miles at a time. Heart problems gone ... hiatus hernia gone ... colon problem gone ... prostate problem gone ... Today I walk around pain-free. I don't know where to lay all the credit, but I know after starting in on Barley Green, carrot juice, and raw fruits and vegetables, all these problems are gone."

"It's incredible that something so simple can be so good for your heart. When you take George's advice and get on his program, it can turn your life around," Rev. Kirk said. "People with heart problems need to know that you can reverse these problems with this diet."

As an initial treatment for his heart disease, Rev. Kirk chose chelation therapy, which he felt was the best option offered by the medical profession. Before learning about Hallelujah Acres, Kirk took 20 three-hour treatments of chelation therapy, and started walking to increase his stamina. He lost 35 pounds, but despite this initial improvement, he said the weight loss and chelation therapy "sapped me of all my strength. After the treatments, I was too tired to get up."

*"It's not a sacrifice, especially when you measure how you feel before and after," Rev. Kirk said about converting to the Hallelujah Diet. "Just to see the sun rise in the morning means more to me than it ever did. I feel better than I have in 20 years or longer. It would be hard for a person who has never been sick to understand the difference."*

Since starting on the Hallelujah Diet, Rev. Kirk has lost an additional 20 pounds and greatly increased his energy level. He describes carrot juice and Barley Green as "instant vitality."

"If I had gotten on this program (in October), I don't believe I would have had to take the chelation therapy," he said. "God gave us the ability for self-healing, but we've gotten away from it."

With this newfound knowledge about health, "I have a whole new way of helping people. And I'll talk to anybody that will listen to me. I am constantly in the hospital ministering to people who are sick. I buried a dear friend yesterday. A big strong man. I married him 20 years ago and I buried him yesterday. These are the kind of people who need to hear this message, for their sake, their family's sake and for service to God. It all ties together, the physical and the spiritual."

"Our body is the temple of God. When you harm it, you're doing wrong. How can you have much of a spiritual life if you don't feel well. It's hard to serve God when you're sick. It's hard to serve God from a hospital bed."

Rev. Kirk said there are several members of his congregation on the Hallelujah Diet. "We have some people who are doing great with it. And I think they will stick with it." He feels once these people have been on the program for six or eight months, "others will see ... I hope in the future we're able to tell even more people about it."

"One lady in the church has lost 12 pounds and feels terrific. She's just as excited as I am. Her daughter had low blood sugar and constant headaches.

They were so bad she used to have to come home from work. Just three days after starting in on the Barley Green and carrot juice, she quit having these problems. And the woman's husband has also lost a lot of weight, and said he feels like a 16-year-old. I don't know how old he is, but I know he is considerably older than that," he said.

Rev. Kirk said his wife, Nancy, also has benefited from the diet, by losing weight and getting relief from her headaches.

Rev. Kirk enjoys his new diet, and emphasizes, "It's not a sacrifice, especially when you measure how you feel before and after."

"Just to see the sun rise in the morning means more to me than it ever did. I feel better than I have in 20 years or longer. It would be hard for a person who has never been sick to understand the difference," Rev. Kirk said.

# Rev. C.R. Williams

## Hattiesburg Church and Pastor
## Find Renewed Health on Hallelujah Diet

The health and outlook on life at Central Baptist Church in Hattiesburg, Miss., will never be the same again following a "How to Eliminate Sickness" seminar last March by Rev. George Malkmus.

Pastor C.R. Williams estimated 25 to 35 percent of his congregation who heard Rev. Malkmus' seminar are now on the Hallelujah Diet "to one degree or another." Williams' church has a Sunday School attendance of 700 to 800, and more than 500 turned out to hear Rev. Malkmus' seminar.

A large number have found great benefit from Barley Green and carrot juice, and quite a few have also made major changes in their diet, Williams said.

"I'm surprised at some of the people who have gotten on the program. We had a very good response and there has been no adverse reaction or resistance that I'm aware of," Pastor Williams said.

In just a few short months on the new diet, members of the Central Baptist congregation have reported numerous cases of increased energy and weight loss, along with relief from cancer, breast lumps, allergies, arthritis, back pain, diverticulitis and gout. On just two day's notice, Pastor Williams gathered the 14 statements listed below, which we print in their entirety, without editing.

And although he isn't on the Hallelujah Diet 100 percent, Pastor Williams said he has been using Barley Green and fresh juices for three months. "My energy level has jumped sky-high. I feel better than I've ever felt in my life and I'm 72 years old. I have more nasal freedom, and improved memory and eye sight. My vision has improved so much I have to take my glasses off to drive," he said.

Rev. C.R. Williams
of Central Baptist Church in
Hattiesburg, Miss.

### Testimonials from members of Central Baptist Church

*These are unedited statements of church members we received in writing from Pastor Williams:*

"I have been taking the Barley Green, drinking the carrot juice and eating about 60% right for five months. The most noticeable improvement was that my energy level doubled in just a few weeks. My arthritis, allergies, low blood sugar and my eye sight have all improved. I can use a pair of glasses that were too weak for me two years ago." – H.B.

227

"Feel much better after taking Barley Green. Quit vitamins. Also changed eating habits and lost 15 pounds without really trying." – I.W.S.

"I was first introduced to Barley Green in February of this year. I also changed my diet somewhat, to more vegetables and fruits. Along with this I began to add fresh juices to my diet. Immediately I began to notice a rise in my energy level. I seemed to have boundless energy! I believe this was due to the Barley Green and the change in my diet. I thank God for showing me how to better care for my body so that I can serve Him better!" – T.A.

"I have taken Barley Green for some three months now. Also, I have taken carrot juice 3 - 4 times weekly. I have more energy than at anytime during the past few years. I have to give the above health items the credit for having done this for me. I highly recommend them to anyone. Thanks!" – J.G.

"The greatest change has been in renewed physical strength. Less pain in lower extremities from a chronic problem called neuropathy (nerve damage) caused from a back injury and subsequent surgery about 30 years ago. Swelling has decreased also. Recent blood work was all normal." – N.G.

"For months I suffered from some kind of allergic reaction. The cause was unknown. I began on the Barley Green, carrot juice and raw diet. Within a few weeks I no longer had these allergic reactions." – M.W.

"My energy level is better and arthritis has improved." – L.D.

"I started taking Barley Green in January 1994. I noticed an increase in my energy level in just a few days. I have had a problem with diverticulitis in my colon for years. This restricted my eating many raw foods, especially salad. After taking the Barley Green and drinking carrot juice daily for about three months, I am able to eat any raw fruits and vegetables I want to eat." – J.A.B.

"I've had lumps in my breast for 40 years and had surgery once but to no avail. Since January 15, I've been taking Barley Green and the lumps are all gone. My eyesight has actually improved." – E.J.

"Since taking Barley Green and carrot juice, my energy has increased and my physical strength has improved. My eyesight has also improved." – F.B.

"Having been plagued with allergies (cosmetics and jewelry mostly) for years, Barley Green is a real blessing! I was on a line of cosmetics from the health store after many attempts at other lines and began having allergic reactions – eye lids swelling, etc. It was very frustrating as I work in the public and enjoy a little enhancement from makeup. I was introduced to Barley Green at that time and immediately got some relief from the itching and burning. After several months of Barley Green and carrot juice which I've added, I'm enjoying my makeup and have lost down to the size I was when married 34 years ago (128 pounds)." – H.E.

"My doctor told me, after a series of tests, that I had cancer cells. I

*From the Hallelujah Acres mailbag:*

"Dear Brother Malkmus: You surely captured our attention when our sister sent your book *Why Christians Get Sick*. She had seen you on 3ABN Television and immediately started making changes in her diet. We are deeply indebted to the Lord's leading in your life. Your book (*Why Christians Get Sick*) is easy to read and understand and we truly appreciate it! Since we received our book, it has been on loan ever since we finished reading it. Our Baptist neighbors have it at the present time. Praise the Lord for truth. Truth will come out! … Thank you so much for your ministry..."
– David & Dorothy Kulisek, Oregon

started with Barley Green and carrot juice. My last check-up revealed no cancer cells. Also, I have more energy since being on this diet." – G.G.

"I have been taking Barley Green for five months now. I do things with more energy and pep. I have also lost ten unwanted pounds." – S.C.

"I don't have gout anymore since being on Barley Green and juicing fruits and vegetables." – H.M.

**Rev. Williams wrote the following open letter to fellow pastors, encouraging them to invite Rev. Malkmus to bring his Biblical-based message of health to their church.**

## Central Baptist Church

Dr. C.R. Williams, Pastor

Telephone: (601) 544-0186
5402 U.S. Hwy. 49
Hattiesburg, MS 39401

Dear Fellow Pastor:

I am writing to say a personal word about Bro. George Malkmus. He was with us on March 5th, and 6th for three wonderful messages. His emphasis is on "Health", and he is a walking testimony of the fact that God does want us to have good health unless of course, we are suffering for the glory and honor of God, as was Job and the Apostle Paul. Bro. Malkmus is a disciple of Bro. Lester Roloff and has written a book on "Why Christians Get Sick". It is an excellent book. I believe that God wants His people to have good health so that they will be able to serve Him more and for a longer time. I believe we are our worst enemy in the matter of health. He says the same. He was a tremendous blessing to our people.

I have lived, to some small degree, by sound, Bible health principles for years. The results have been that I have had above average good health. I've only missed one Sunday in the pulpit because of illness since I surrendered to preach in 1951.

I am convinced that Bro. Malkmus would be a blessing to any church or people as their eyes would be opened to what the Bible has to say about good health. I believe that God wants His people to have good health so that they can win more souls and be more effective in their witness. It will also keep them out of the "Egyptians", doctor's clinics and funeral homes with the unsaved or the "Egyptians". In Exodus 15:26, God told His people in that day, that if they would abide by certain principles and precepts, He would put none of the diseases on them that the Egyptians had. Surely, that will hold true today. Of course we must know what the principles and precepts are in order to obey them. Bro. Malkmus clearly shows principles that will give us immunity from these diseases. He was very helpful to our church. I highly recommend him and am convinced he will be a blessing to any ones or church if you see fit to invite him to come.

In Christian love,
*C. R. Williams*
C. R. Williams

P.S. Many of our church people are rejoicing in better health because of the nutritional diet Bro. Malkmus helped them to adopt and begin to use.

*Churchwide Soul Winning • Missions • School • Singles • Youth • Senior Citizens • Bus • Deaf • Radio*

# Rev. Gale Galloway

## Baptist Pastor Recovers from a Half-Dozen Life-Threatening Illnesses With a Change of Diet

*By Michael Dye*

For the past 18 years, Rev. Gale Galloway of Lindale, Texas, has lived a medical nightmare, more than once on the verge of death and with little that doctors could do to help him. But after struggling for survival in the face of more than a half-dozen life-threatening diseases, Rev. Galloway is now able to continue his ministry in great health at age 58, while looking forward to many more quality years.

All he did was change his diet after reading a copy of *Back to the Garden.* After converting to a vegetarian diet of about 85-percent raw foods, plenty of fresh vegetable juice and Barley Green, Galloway has amazed doctors with his recovery.

"This is the best shape I've ever been in," Galloway said. "I'm 58 years old and I can do more now in a day's time than when I was in my 30s."

He said his renewed health will allow him to continue carrying "tons of Bibles to foreign lands." Rev. Galloway is the pastor of Central Baptist Church in Lindale, Texas, which he described as "a very missionary-minded church, with 78 missionary projects around the world." In recent years Galloway's ministry has taken him to Russia, Guatemala, the Phillipines and Cayman Islands.

To fully appreciate where he is now, you have to understand where he has been. Since age 40, Rev. Galloway has struggled against severe osteo-arthritis that led to two hip transplants, toxic poisoning from prescribed medications, two heart attacks, a blood clot that destroyed a quarter of his left lung and a four-day coma from which he was not expected to awaken. He was overweight, carrying as much as 246 pounds on his

**Rev. Gale Galloway and his wife, Betty**

5-foot, 9-inch frame. And Rev. Galloway's ailments continued to mount last summer as he was battling a "terrible combination" of diabetes and serious prostate trouble when he first read a copy of *Back to the Garden* in late May of 1994.

He immediately went on a vegetarian diet of 85 percent raw fruits and vegetables, with plenty of fresh vegetable juice, Barley Green and Herbal Fiberblend. He eliminated all his health problems in a matter of weeks. As Rev. Galloway attended the Oct. 20 – 22, 1994 training for Back to the Garden Health Ministers here at Hallelujah Acres, he was able to tell his fellow Health Ministers that his doctor had given him a clean bill of health on all these former ailments. And after less than five months on the Hallelujah Diet, Galloway had lost 78 pounds, weighing in at 164 at the October Health Ministers meeting.

In a one-sentence summary of his medical history, Galloway said, "It's been a nightmare." As he begins to detail the long chronology of his medical problems, Galloway notes he grew up on a farm, eating mainly cooked vegetables, very little meat, but lots of dairy. He wasn't sick much in his younger years, but he said he had little energy and endurance.

> *"After four weeks on the Hallelujah Diet, all infection (from diabetes) was gone and my prostate problem was all gone. My soreness in the urinary tract was gone for the first time in two years ... Going on this diet has been the greatest thing that has ever happened to me."*
> *– Rev. Gale Galloway*

But by the time Galloway turned 40, he had developed a severe case of osteo-arthritis. "At age 45, I couldn't hold a knife to cut a steak," he recalls. This first affected his hands and feet. At 45, Galloway had to have surgery to replace his right hip. "My hip joint was dead," he explained.

Doctors had him on cortisone, a powerful steroid prescribed for extreme cases of arthritis, and 16 aspirin a day. From these drugs, Galloway developed toxic poisoning. This led him to try to avoid all prescription drugs, so he went to a health food store to get information about natural ways to heal arthritis.

Based on this reading, in about 1983, Galloway said he went on a cleansing fast, began eating more vegetables, started drinking distilled water and gave up milk. This was the first of his attempts to change to a healthier diet, but it wasn't enough.

A short time later, he suffered congestive heart failure, with two blocked arteries causing a 35-percent blockage of blood flow to his heart. He spent 2 1/2 days in intensive care. Based on this experience, he decided to give up red meat, but he continued eating fish and chicken. (Fish and chicken have the same levels of cholesterol as red meat, as well as other contaminants, such as growth hormones in chicken and toxins from water pollution in most fish.)

Two years later, Galloway had another heart attack. Doctors said his main heart valve was deformed. Surgeons removed this valve and replaced it with a St. Jude's Carbon Steel Valve.

In the meantime, he had hip surgery. While in recovery, a portion of skin on his stomach about the size of a large saucer turned black. The dead flesh had to be removed to a depth of about 1 ½ inches. Doctors said it was medication from the hip surgery, given to prevent blood clots, that caused his skin to die as a bad side-effect. Doctors said this reaction indicated the medication did not achieve its desired effect of preventing blood clots.

This was verified as Galloway's next emergency was a blood clot that destroyed one quarter of his left lung. He went into a coma for four days. Doctors thought he was about to die, and all his family was called to the hospital. Galloway recovered from the coma, but spent 31 days in the hospital.

*As one might expect, these health improvements have not gone unnoticed by Rev. Galloway's congregation. "My people have wondered what has happened. They know what I've been through. All this has really made a big difference in the health of the people in this church."*
*– Rev. Gale Galloway*

After recovering from the coma, he had a bad reaction to heart rhythm medication. "I didn't have the strength to walk into the hospital," Rev. Galloway recalls. He spent another 10 days in the hospital recovering from this reaction, and realized that any medication he took in the future could cause him serious problems.

Galloway's next trip to the hospital was for replacement of his left hip at age 55, ten years after the replacement of his right hip.

Less than two years later, he was rushed to the hospital again, thinking he was having a stroke because the left side of his body went numb. "I couldn't even function enough to write my name, and I passed out in the emergency room," Rev. Galloway recalls. At this point, doctors discovered Galloway was a diabetic, and told him he should start by taking insulin in pill form, and then later would need to take injection insulin.

Because of his previous bad reactions to medication, Galloway said, "I refused to take the pill." Instead, he attempted to control his diabetes by losing weight. "But with every diet I tried, I could never get below 220."

Then about a year later, he developed serious prostate problems. He said "diabetes and prostate trouble are a terrible combination" because the burning urine and infections caused by diabetes are aggravated by prostate problems, which required him to get up every 20 minutes to urinate for six months. His prostate trouble also led to locked bowels, which required an enema to unblock.

Doctors told him, "You've got to do something because you're in serious shape." But Rev. Galloway said he refused to take any medication for his prostate trouble "because three or four days before I got ahold of a copy of *Back to the Garden*." He read the newsletter and the book *Why Christians Get Sick* by Rev. George Malkmus, and immediately cut out all meat and went on a vegetarian diet of about 85 percent raw foods, with fresh vegetable juice, Barley Green and Herbal Fiberblend.

*Back to the Garden* gave him hope, he said, because, "I read the testimonials and it sounded like these people were getting some help." And now Rev. Galloway's own life has become one of these testimonials. In less than two weeks, he saw a major improvement in all symptoms. "And, after four weeks on the Hallelujah Diet, all infection (from diabetes) was gone and my prostate problem was all gone. My soreness in the urinary tract was gone for the first time in two years ... Going on this diet has been the greatest thing that has ever happened to me."

When he returned to his doctor two months after starting on the Hallelujah Diet, blood sugar was normal, there was no sign of prostate trouble, and his cholesterol, triglycerides and thyroid all were normal. His blood sugar had topped out at the dangerous level of about 300, but after two months on the diet, it was at 94 (below 100 is considered good). His triglycerides had reached 323, but after two months, they were at 118 (50 to 150 is considered safe). His cholesterol had once hovered around the 300 level, but after two months, his LDL (bad cholesterol) was 104, with total cholesterol at 144. By that time, Galloway had lost down to 197 pounds and said he was "feeling great."

Two months later, he came in for another check-up, which showed continued improvement in every category, and the loss of another 21 pounds. "My doctor sat me down and said, 'I want to hear everything you're doing.'" Galloway said he told him about the diet, fresh juice and Barley Green, and the doctor commented, "Well, it's working."

After eight months on the diet, Galloway said in late January that he has had no re-occurences of any of his previous medical problems. He has leveled off at below 160 pounds. He now takes proanthocyanidins (see Chapter 16), which he said has given him added strength.

Rev. Galloway's wife, Betty, has also benefitted greatly from the Hallelujah Diet. In the past six months, Betty has lost from 150 to about 117 pounds. Galloway notes that his wife had a bad cholesterol problem and was "on the verge of having a stroke." She was unable to reduce her cholesterol on medication. But since changing her diet, Betty has reduced her cholesterol to the normal range and has quit taking cholesterol medication.

As one might expect, these health improvements have not gone unnoticed by Rev. Galloway's congregation. "My people have wondered what has happened. They know what I've been through. All this has really made a big difference in the health of the people in this church. There were 46 people at the first seminar I gave on diet and Barley Green. This one woman in the church has been able to reduce her insulin and she expects the doctor to take her totally off insulin in her next visit."

Rev. Galloway and his wife have opened a small health food store in a 12-by-20-foot building between their home and the church. Rev. Galloway offers nutritional counseling in the health food store, and said his plans for the

*From the Hallelujah Acres mailbag:*

"I very much appreciate your ministry. I am interested in helping spread the message of nutrition as well as the Gospel. I believe this may be a ministry where the Lord can use me ... I would like to start a ministry of offering seminars, educational materials, juicers, distillers, and Barley Green to the public ... I would appreciate any advice you could offer as well as any resources for learning you would recommend ... Since adopting your health program I can tell a tremendous difference in my over-all health."
– Olin Idol, North Carolina

future include spending more time "teaching people from the pulpit on health, and holding more seminars, including a weekly support group." He adds, "The Health Ministry training session (at Hallelujah Acres) was very helpful because I learned more details on how to explain all this and answer people's questions."

# Chapter 26

# Back to the Garden Health Ministries

In the summer of 1994, we announced the beginning of a new ministry called *Back to the Garden Health Ministries.* This ministry makes it possible for individuals all over the world to become a part of Hallelujah Acres so they can share with people in their community the good news – "You do not have to be sick!" The response has already been overwhelming, far beyond our most optimistic expectations. We receive letters and calls daily from those who want to be a part of this exciting ministry.

Those responding come from all walks of life and all educational backgrounds. Some from foreign countries. Most have college degrees, some are doctors, some are old and some are young. Some are already in the health field and some are starting out with very little knowledge in this area. But one thing they all have in common is their desire to minister to others and share the message of Back to the Garden.

This ministry allows those who have a burden to help others to do just that by sharing the good news with people in their communities. It becomes their own personal Ministry. They can do it through seminars in their church, in public places or meetings in their home. Those who are good at public speaking

*From the Hallelujah Acres mailbag:*

"... Since I have a real burden for our country and the state of affairs, do you see me as a possible candidate for your **Back to the Garden Health Ministries?**... As you know, I have been taking Barley Green, eating more fruit and vegetables, cutting out meat, drinking more water ... and walking four miles a day. I have lost over 20 pounds, reduced cholesterol reading from 240 to 181, and have lost symptoms of gastritis, too much uric acid, and concern about my health. All of this helped me better communicate with the people of East Tennessee during my recent race..."
– Larry Gaudet,
Past candidate for Congress,
Tennessee

**An enthused group of Back to the Garden Health Ministers listens to Rev. George Malkmus at the Oct. 20 – 22, 1994 training session at Hallelujah Acres.**

can use their talent here, while others may prefer to show a video or share an audio cassette. Personal testimonies of what a changed diet has meant for different people can be shared. Literature and tapes can be loaned out. They can make information available for sale in the form of books, audios and videos, along with juicers and distillers.

For those of you with a burden to share the health message with others, ***Back to the Garden Health Ministries*** provides a vehicle to make it happen in your own community. We will train you, provide educational materials and health products in the form of books, audios, videos, juicers, distillers, etc. The products will be purchased from us at wholesale so that those who become a part of this Ministry can potentially support themselves. We will help you, and even support you with regional seminars throughout the country. We will list the names and phone numbers of those who join us in our newsletter, *Back to the Garden,* so people in your community will know where they can find support and encouragement in this new and healthy way of life.

> *"I have seen in my work (as a nurse), that people really don't get any better with the present methods of giving drugs. And the things they do to cancer patients are really atrocious! Actually, I am glad to be retired, and be able to teach a different way of healing …"*
> *– Gretta VanDerLoon, Ontario, Canada*

As this book is going to press, this ministry is still in its infancy, but we already have 86 Health Ministers spread out across the United States, as well as into Canada, Hawaii and Puerto Rico. And we are preparing for our fourth training session here at Hallelujah Acres. We envision a time when we will have thousands of people all around the world becoming a part of ***Back to the Garden Health Ministries.*** Listen as some of these people share their reasons for joining us:

***Richard Woodside***, a Pastor and Missionary from Millville, Penn., writes: "I have felt a burden to help those suffering from sickness here at home just as a 'medical missionary' does overseas. I felt that if we could help meet people's real physical needs, we would have greater opportunities to give them the Gospel as well."

***Morris Watson,*** a missionary to Germany now living in Spencer, Ind., states: "After my wife and I had bouts with serious illnesses (and getting little or no help from the medical establishment) we concluded that we could be of little help to others or have a good Christian testimony while being sick. This prompted us to seek the answers to this and find the root causes. We believe we have found the answers in the ministry of Back to the Garden. We have studied it quite thoroughly, have put into practice what we have learned with significant benefits in a short time … In six months I have recovered from prostatitis and a severe arthritic condition. Now we are sharing these truths with others."

***Gretta VanDerLoon,*** a retired Registered Nurse from Ontario, Canada, writes: "I have seen in my work (as a nurse), that people really don't get any better with the present methods of giving drugs. And the things they do to cancer patients are really atrocious!  Actually, I am glad to be retired, and be able to teach a different way of healing … My friend Sara (Sara VanAkker, also a retired R.N.) and I will work the ministry together.  We have been vegetarians for 21 years."

*James Stokes,* a missionary from Grand Rapids, Mich., states: "I am interested in being used by God to bring revival to the body of Christ in the U.S.A., and the whole area of health and nutrition is crucial in accomplishing this and most neglected."

*Wesley and Alma Stillwell,* Health Ministers in Grandview, Wash., write: "A big thank you to each of you for making our visit to Hallelujah Acres such a special time.  Our new ministry is already helping others to better health.  I am down 40 lbs. from my heaviest weight of 328."

*Eli Slabaugh,* a Mennonite Pastor and Evangelist from McGaheysville, Va., wants to be a Health Minister "for the very same reason you are – to help people (along with ourselves) *It works!*  I weighed 220 pounds and now weigh 196. … We have seven children and one by one they are going on Barley Green, carrot juice and the whole ball of wax. Praise God!"

*Elaine Robitzach* of Macon, Ga., writes: "The improvements in my health are worth telling … My depression has lifted, *gone* after 15 years of misery.  I am very excited and anxious to tell the world this wonderful news, 'God's Marvelous Self-Healing Body' *really does heal itself!!!*  I am living proof.  I can hardly wait for the doctor to check my blood chemistry – triglycerides were high and I weighed 165 lbs. last January; I was told to lose 30 pounds by giving up fats but I craved sugar and sweets and was addicted to chocolate.  This caused drastic mood swings and rapid personality changes and I had never gotten a good night's sleep.  *Now, all* my physical symptoms have vanished.  I sleep well, wake up with energy to walk a mile every morning PLUS the added reward of *feeling good*, like a 25-year-old and my age is 57.  My arthritis has improved in 5 weeks and I have lost 15 lbs!  I think more clearly and my memory has improved … So … that is why I am ready to minister to everyone I meet.  *I know it works!!!*"

*John Peters,* a Chemical Engineer from Pittsburgh, Penn., says: "God has blessed me in so many ways and has been preparing me to be a Health Minister for many years. My Christian faith; my scientific background; my experience as a Dale Carnegie Instructor, my illness and now my recovery.  All of this came in focus when I heard Rev. Malkmus' message … His message to treat the <u>cause</u> instead of the symptoms was like turning on a light on my problems … I had large cell lung cancer.  After surgery and radiation, I began to fade.  When the doctors talked about open chest surgery a second time, I went on the Gerson program and began to recover in about one month … my health is good now … Thus, I am eager to be in your training program, so I can learn to use my talents to the highest good – To become a channel for God's good – and to help others be healthy.  There is too much suffering in the world today, and I want to help eliminate it."

*Diane Patterson,* supervisor of 60 employees for Los Angeles County,

*From the Hallelujah Acres mailbag:*

Margaret Chamberlain

"What a paper! *Back to the Garden* is truly a blessing…Thank you for taking the time and all the hours to help others … which is truly what the Christian life is all about!"
– Margaret Chamberlain, Minnesota

living in Los Angeles, Calif., writes: "I was writing 'Why Christians Get Sick' when I saw Rev. Malkmus' book! He said what was in my heart. Every word is true ... I am so happy to find out that there is an organization that has its focus on God's Word and how to eat so as to regain and maintain our health. After a year on a 100% raw diet I feel better than I believed a human being could feel ... Totally joyous, friendly, loving, able to cope with anything, energetic and radiant."

*Nicasio Ortiz,* Pastor of a Presbyterian Church in Carolina, Puerto Rico, states: "Last August, while I was in Mexico, somebody loaned me your book *Why Christians Get Sick,* and I believe it was God answering a question I had for a long time ... 'Why, if we have a wonderful, merciful God and healer ... Why are so many Christians sick?' Your book was clear and direct, so here I am. I believe in your Back to the Garden Ministry and want to pass on the information to others that 'you do not have to be sick!' "

*Angie Olson,* a housewife and church worker in Hastings, Minn., states: "I am an active Christian working with children at our First Baptist Church in Rosemont, and I see many Christian people sick ... mostly because of what and how they eat. I want to help get the message out that people don't have to be sick! ... Since going on the Hallelujah Diet: my arthritis is gone ... Backache much, much better (have had three car accidents) ... Have lots of energy! ... Heartburn totally gone ... We are using our Champion (Juicer) every day, eating less, drinking no more coffee, eating lots of salads, planted a garden after many years of excuses not to."

*Jane Jennings,* a pharmacist from Winston-Salem, N.C., states: "Because I have had to search so hard for material to inform me about correcting my own health, I would like to be a part of a ministry that has the information. A ministry that teaches others in a clear, simple and concise manner. It took me years, traveling through the writings of many, to finally reach Rev. Malkmus' ministry."

*Fred and Janet Huhn* of Salisbury, Md., write: "Since being introduced to the Hallelujah Diet several months ago, we have experienced renewed health and vitality. Janet suffered from asthma for years but has been able to drastically reduce her need for medication and can even jog several miles – 35 pounds lighter. Fred has had heart problems but is now exercising regularly and feeling fit and trim 40 pounds lighter – cholesterol has dropped 60 points – to 177 without medication ... We believe our bodies are the temple of the Holy Spirit and that we honor God when we take care of them."

*Ann Gentry*, a Registered Nurse, from Tempe, Ariz., writes: "As a nurse I have witnessed such abuse of patients with drugs and chemotherapeutic agents and radiation with no attempt made toward prevention. I am no longer willing to stand by and watch. Many people come to me asking what to do about their degenerative diseases of all types ... I need the tools to get them interested (in a changed diet)."

*Dr. Jana Boggs,* who lives in Kamuela, Hawaii, has a B.S. in Nutrition and is a Doctor of Nutrition. She writes: "I have long had a dream of helping

*From the
Hallelujah Acres mailbag:*

"It was a pleasure meeting you this past Monday and having the privilege of enjoying a good meal at Hallelujah Acres. We appreciate so much what you are doing in the line of health reform. This is the work that the Seventh-day Adventists were given to proclaim to the world, but sad to say, we've fallen down on the job. Hopefully you'll be the inspiration to revive us in proclaiming it again."
– H.M. Cherne, M.D. Tennessee

Christians with their health. We must use the talents God has given us for the equipping of the saints for ministry, and for strengthening the body of Christ (the Church). I wrote a paper in college called 'The Calling' in which I spoke of this as my life's goal. I feel that I have been being prepared and am now ready to do this."

*Heide Brown,* a Kindergarten Teacher in Wilson, N.C., writes: "God has used this (Hallelujah Diet) to help me regain my health. It seems so logical now to eat fruits and vegetables, mostly raw, that I am surprised to have found this so late in life … I am very enthused about this Health Ministry and would like to (eventually) do it full time."

*Pierre Buch*, a retired anesthetist from Moneta, Va., with a BS in nursing and a Masters in Public Health, writes: "I believe the health message is the right arm of the Gospel … I want to keep active as long as life lasts by helping others improve health so they can enjoy the abundant life."

*Nancy Fitzmorris,* a mother of five from Covington, La., says: "Because of the difference in my children's health (after changing our diets), including a change in my hyper child, I have wanted to share it with others … With the Lord's help I hope He can use me …"

*Larry & Janet Horton* live in Marion, Mass. Larry is a businessman while Janet is a full-time mother. Their reason for becoming a part of Back to the Garden Health Ministries: "In order to better serve our fellow Christians with good health information and products … working together part time until we can make this a full time career/ministry."

*Dr. James Hostetler* of Dalton, Ohio, has had a professional Chiropractic practice for 12 years and studied health-related subjects since 1976, including Pre-Med / Nursing. He has a B.S. in Human Biology and is a Chiropractic physician. After 20-plus years of study he has arrived at the same conclusions as taught by Back to the Garden Health Ministries: "We don't have to be sick" if we will nourish our bodies God's way! Dr. Hostetler writes: "I believe God has been preparing me and my family for this Health Ministry to the body of Christ … Our heart is more toward a 'temple' oriented focus, bringing believers to maturity and thereby honoring the reputation of our Lord Jesus Christ."

*Olin Idol,* a businessman from Mocksville, N.C., writes: "I obtained a degree in religion with the intent of entering the ministry … I have always been interested in a healthy lifestyle and helping others. This would be a ministry where God could use my talents and interests."

*Karen Martin,* office manager and administrative assistant in Searoy, Ark., writes: "I know that I have a calling on my life to minister to God's people and to the lost that they can be healed and live in victory … complete in spirit,

> *"Last August, while I was in Mexico, somebody loaned me your book Why Christians Get Sick and I believe it was God answering a question I had for a long time … 'Why, if we have a wonderful, merciful God and healer … Why are so many Christians sick?' "*
> *– Nicasio Ortiz, Puerto Rico*

soul and body ... Now God has marvelously revealed to me yet another of His hidden secrets, through you, how we can be healed and live wholly in the body. I am excited about this new revelation in my life and want to share it with others."

*Dr. Rowen Pfeifer,* after two years of Pre-Med, changed to a Chiropractic College and graduated with a D.C. degree. He has been a Chiropractic Physician for over seven years. Dr. Pfeifer writes: "I have been, as has George Malkmus, an avid student of health principles, nutrition, holistic health, etc., for the last 19 years ... One thing I have learned; all the answers to the nutrition subject are deceptively simple ... The bottom line is that the simple truths of nutrition are constant – and all the experts with all their research only ultimately prove these simple truths. We don't need to wait for the next research project to prove this or that. The truth has always been with us ... It is my mission in life to help teach others how to keep themselves well, to be able to beat the odds, and to understand that illness is not normal."

---

*"...Everywhere I look, I see and hear people in pain. Each in their own way crying out for health. I have always wanted to help these people ..."*
*– Margaret Irwin of Louisville, Kentucky*

---

*Dave Luwemba* of Berrien Springs, Michigan, writes: "The approach as taken by Back to the Garden Health Ministry is an answer to much of the world's problems - physical, mental, spiritual, economic as well as social. To me, it will be an opportunity to be a part of a group that God has called at this time through the experiences and work of Pastor George Malkmus to share a philosophy of life and style of living that makes sense from both the religious as well as true science point of view ... I will begin the ministry as a part-timer and eventually move it into a full time ministry before taking this health ministry to Malawi, Africa, within the next three to four years ... "

*Mary Truitt* of Carson, California, writes: "I desire to have the best knowledge, information and products available to inform and instruct people that they indeed do not have to be sick and that they can raise healthy, happy children. Of all the products, companies and sources of information that I have ever come across; I believe that you are the closest to the truth and that you are right on track. I am a born again believer and I know that God wants the best for His people; and the more I research and discover, all our health, vitality, and longevity can only be based upon God's Word. I need to learn how to reach more people and I desperately need to be connected with people who are like-minded ... I am around so many people who are killing themselves with their forks. The need is so great."

*Gay Tall* of Port Republic, Maryland, writes: "I feel called to help spread the word that you do not have to be sick and feel that God has guided me to Back to the Garden to glorify His name in my Community..."

*Ann Dean* of Waxahachie, Texas, writes: "My personal quest for health began about seven years ago and has brought me to such wonderful knowledge, not to mention better health, that I have a tremendous desire to share this information. I would personally like to see everyone take advantage of this newfound information to improve their health and increase their productivity. Ill health is so needless and the word must be spread. Your approach is clear-cut and to the point and offers all who will listen and heed the chance to improve their quality of life..."

*Carol Cover* of Northfield, Minnesota, writes: "Dick (my husband) and I believe in, practice, and share the principles of Back to the Garden with everyone who will listen. An amazing number of people are listening. We have seen lives irrevocably changed by following these principles..."

*John Winstead* of Charlotte, North Carolina, writes: "I believe the message Back to the Garden Health Ministries is trying to convey to people is the answer to their health problems. My research over the years has led me to the same conclusion . . . Your ministry is a great opportunity to reach more people in need, that would otherwise continue to suffer without ever being told the truth and shown a healthier option..."

*Margaret Irwin* of Louisville, Kentucky, writes: "...Everywhere I look, I see and hear people in pain. Each in their own way crying out for health. I have always wanted to help these people but all I could do was listen and offer an encouraging word. This ministry is putting before me an opportunity to do more than only listening and encouraging, but a way to really help. I am excited about this ministry."

*Dwight Dennis* of Pampa, Texas, writes: "I agree with you and your ministry 100%. I love people! I have had many of my friends and family that have died needlessly. I have many friends and family that are sick now. I really want to help educate people into the Biblical way of being healthy..."

*Charlie Brown* of Charlotte, North Carolina, writes: "I want to help people 'see the light' about getting back to God's original diet so they can get well and stay well. The seminars and the 'truth' George is preaching would give me a vehicle to do this."

*Perry Hedger* of Auburn, New York, writes: "Being actively involved in God's work for over 50 years, I have hundreds of friends and acquaintances who need to hear the message of Back to the Garden Health Ministries and I would like the opportunity to tell them. I believe in what you are doing!"

*Don Prewitt* of Orlando, Florida, writes: "Having observed several instances in recent months where people were sick and dying who should have had many years of good health and noticing that I too could be in that condition, I started to search for a way to change my eating habits. After I heard the Rev. Malkmus, I started to change my diet and immediately began to see a change in weight, energy, and better rest when sleeping. At this point I have lost 25 pounds..."

*David Miller* of Rifle, Colorado, writes: "My wife and I strongly believe that a great need exists for teaching people how to eat a proper diet, especially in the church where a common fellowship meal is coffee and doughnuts..."

*Leola Fier* of Kansas City, Missouri, writes: "In the past two years, my father has had gout, clogged arteries, poor circulation, surgery, amputation,

*From the Hallelujah Acres mailbag:*

"... Since I have not written in to Back to the Garden prior to this, may I say that we are being blessed in a manifold fashion as we move into our eighth month on the Hallelujah Diet. After years on blood pressure medication, both of us are experiencing very beautiful blood pressure readings. Gone is our arthritis and so is the medication. As well, we no longer take allergy medications and most symptoms have disappeared. For years I had to go to a Dermotologist for the removal of pre-cancerous spots on my hands and ears. I will not need to go this year - I have no spots. I could go on and on as we realize new blessings almost every week. Thank you for sharing this good news and for your gracious ministry to us. It is indeed a privilege to now be yoked with you and Rhonda and the rest of the staff as Health Ministers. We look forward to many years of ministry as we anticipate many people getting serious about the proper care of their body - God's Temple..."
– Pastor Brice Casey, Tennessee

*From the*
*Hallelujah Acres mailbag:*

"It was a pleasure to meet you and hear your presentation at last weekend's Pennsylvania Natural Living Convention; I have been working with live foods for 17 years and am very excited about your work. As you may recall, we discussed the possibility of your speaking at our upcoming Whole Foods Expo honoring National Nutrition Month on Sunday, March 26, 1995. Your message of healing through God's natural laws will be of great inspiration to those in attendance. The event drew about 400 persons last year and promises to be even more popular this year. It will be held in the Grand Ballroom of the Holiday Inn, City Line and Presidential Boulevard, in Philadelphia, from 10:00 a.m. to 4:00 p.m. ..."
–Susan Silberstein, Ph.D., Executive Director, Center for Advancement in Cancer Education, Pennsylvania

bedsores, feeding tube, stroke and wheelchair, etc.— an enormous amount of medical intervention with no progress ... I want to bring some answers to our family that have lasting results for better physical and mental health. So many people I know suffer from pain and obesity. I want to help them!"

*Bev Cook* of Houston, Texas, writes: " I am interested in Back to the Garden Health Ministries because I am a Christian and have a burden to help people in a valuable way ... My heart breaks at all the unnecessary illness and misinformation."

Aren't they great! And that is only a sampling of the responses. Although many of them once had serious physical problems, they are now free of most of these problems as a result of changing their diet and lifestyle.

We envision thousands of Christians joining us from all over the world. Not only will many individuals want to become involved, but every church should become a part, not just for their own membership, but also to help those in their communities. Many churches already carry our literature, audios, videos and Barley Green in their book stores and some offer juicers and distillers. Many pastors and evangelists are starting to incorporate the health message into their ministries. It is all very exciting!

If you are interested in learning more about how to become a part of this exciting Health Ministry, write or call us to request our "Health Ministry Information Pack." Please address all requests for information to: Back to the Garden Health Ministries, P.O. Box 2388, Shelby, NC 28151.

# Part IV

# Recipes and Tips

# on How to Prepare

# Natural Foods

"Whether therefore ye
eat, or drink,
or whatsoever ye do,
do all to the
glory of God."
– I Corinthians 10:31

# Chapter 27

# Why the Hallelujah Diet?

*"Beloved, I wish above all things that thou mayest prosper and be in health, even as thy soul prospereth."*
(III John 2)

*By Rhonda J. Malkmus*

So often, people fail to see the need to change their diet and lifestyle until a crisis arises. I acknowledge that change is often very difficult unless we understand the reason why. So, it is my prayer that as you read through this book you will understand the reason why and that you will allow God to get hold of you so that you might see what the **Standard American Diet** (**SAD**) is doing to you and those you love.

My goal in writing this chapter is to give you guidelines as you seek a healthier lifestyle. Here at Hallelujah Acres we do not teach an all-raw diet (although that is the ideal). Many find it too difficult and thus will not stick with an all-raw diet. However, we do strive to maintain at least an 85% raw diet. The cooked food portion included in these recipes are to assist those in the process of changing to the Hallelujah Diet and to provide help for the 15% of the evening meal that does allow for some cooked food.

Perhaps the questions most often asked are: "Why a *vegetarian* diet? What is wrong with animal products?" My answer to those questions is that when we look at the anatomy of man, we find that we were never designed by God to be carnivores (meat eaters). We do not have the teeth to rip and tear animal flesh. We do not have the high hydrochloric acid content in our stomach to break down and digest this flesh. Also, our digestive tract is too long, with too many bends and twists, which produce monumental problems in our colon when flesh foods are consumed.

As you probably already know, George became a vegetarian in 1976 due to a potentially life-threatening physical problem in a desperate attempt to save his life. My problems were not life-threatening, although they certainly did affect my quality of life. My prayer is that you will not have to have a serious physical problem before you are ready and willing to make changes in your diet and lifestyle required for a healthier and more productive life.

Prior to changing our diet and lifestyle, George and I were both, in ignorance, on the **SAD** American Diet, and we had been all of our lives. We had to learn the hard way that animal products, sugar, salt and white flour products were harmful to our health and potentially deadly.

Another question I am frequently asked is: 'What about protein?' Well, the first thing we need to know about protein is that the body utilizes protein for maintenance and repair and what is left over is stored as fat. What few people realize is that when meat is cooked (heated above 160 degrees), the protein molecules are altered, thus rendering the protein unusable and unassimilable by the body. Because the body cannot use the now-altered protein, it rots in the digestive system causing body odor and all kinds of colon problems.

Contrary to popular opinion, the vegetarian diet provides sufficient and complete protein. Protein is found in all green leafy vegetables and, in fact, in all living plants. George often asks people in his seminars: "If man has to eat the flesh of the cow to get protein, what does the cow eat that produces that protein?" And of course the answer is grass! I have found that many of the

*... over 65% of our adult population and over 20% of our youth (those under the age of 17) already have chronic diseases and are on medication. If that does not make you angry, it should! We need to wake up and take back the control of our bodies before the foods of this world destroy us.*

things I had been taught through my life about nutrition are just plain wrong, and I have had to re-program my mind.

We are often told that we need to consume animal products in order to get vitamin $B_{12}$, yet this vitamin is produced in the healthy body from such foods as green leafy vegetables and sea vegetables.

Green leafy vegetables are the primary foods needed to feed our body. They are also the most healing of all the foods God has given us. Watch an animal when it is sick and you will find that the only thing it will eat is grass. This grass is jam-packed with enzymes, vitamins, proteins, organic minerals, chlorophyll, anti-oxidants, and much more. George and I use Barley Green with amazing and exciting results! (I personally think it tastes better than grass.)

The **SAD** American Diet of today is lacking in nutrition! The nutrients our body needs cannot be found in the dead, devitalized, manufactured products we buy in cans, bottles, jars, boxes and packages found on our supermarket shelves. As George so often says: "Once you leave the fresh produce department in your supermarket, there is practically zero nutrition in the rest of the store."

Fast food restaurants are slowly destroying the health of those who patronize them. The foods found in these establishments are full of fat

*From the Hallelujah Acres mailbag:*

"Thank you - thank you for giving of yourselves at our Convention in Alexandria, Minnesota. You left us with a wealth of information, inspiration and challenge. We really appreciate you! God bless your ministry!"
– Ralph & Phyllis Peterson, North Dakota

(lard), salt, sugar and other harmful substances and are a major cause of the heart attacks and cancers experienced by such a large percentage of our population.

But even after people purchase raw foods from their produce markets, they usually cook that food before eating it. In the Bible we find that God gave mankind the Ideal Diet in Genesis 1:29. Here God is telling us that He has supplied all the nutrients we need in the fresh, raw fruits and vegetables without cooking our foods or consuming the flesh of another animal!

When we cook our food, almost all nutritional value is destroyed. When we put this heat-altered and thus nutritionally-deficient food into our bodies, our bodies have to work overtime to digest and dispose of it. By God's design, we were meant to eat our food raw just like all of the rest of the animal kingdom that God created.

But why eat our food raw? By eating foods just as close to the way God designed them, all of the nutrients and enzymes are available to the body to nourish and maintain or even regain health. Since the human body was designed to eat raw food, these raw foods digest very quickly, usually in 30 to 60 minutes – rather than the hours or even days required by many of the cooked foods or cooked flesh products.

Raw foods are certainly more economical than flesh and processed foods and require much less effort and time to prepare. In fact, if a person has an area where they can garden, they can produce their own food for pennies while enjoying healthy exercise. And when it comes to clean up – how much easier it is to simply rinse off a plate that has contained a raw meal than the clean-up required from the grease on dishes and pots and pans after a meal based on the **SAD** American Diet.

Raw foods help the body's weight to normalize and keeps the body's appetite control in check. It is almost impossible to overeat on a raw, whole-foods diet. Amazingly, when we eat food the way God designed, degenerative diseases do not occur; in fact, these diseases usually reverse and disappear if they already exist. People often report that they have more energy, rest better at night and do not require as much sleep. Mood swings usually disappear and even the need for a deodorant or breath fresheners stop. Problems with PMS and menopause usually disappear and even the mind becomes clearer while improving memory and concentration.

Americans need to realize that the average supermarket has its shelves piled high with thousands of manufactured, processed, non-food items that do not nourish our bodies. These manufactured products are not only all cooked, but also are full of chemicals and other toxins our bodies were never designed to have to deal with. Consequently, over 65% of our adult population and over 20% of our youth (those under the age of 17) already have chronic diseases and are on medication. If that does not make you angry, it should! We need to wake up and take back the control of our bodies before the foods of this world destroy us. I know it is not easy, but thousands are doing it each day and so can you. My Bible says: ***"I can do all things through Christ..."***

*From the Hallelujah Acres mailbag:*

Linda Clifton

"Greetings from Hong Kong – A friend sent me your book and it is fantastic. Enclosed is my order for 50 *Why Christians Get Sick ...* to share here. So many missionaries are burning out because they are not living by God's principles for wholeness ... I reach a wide audience here because I recovered from Epstein-Barr on natural remedies ..."
– Linda Clifton, Hong Kong, China

May God guide you, bless you, strengthen you and help you to do that which you know in your heart is right for your own body and your loved ones. My prayers are with you!

*"I beseech ye therefore, brethren, by the mercies of God, that ye present your bodies a living sacrifice, holy, acceptable unto God, which is your reasonable service. And be not conformed to this world; but be ye transformed by the renewing of your mind; that ye may prove what is that good, and acceptable, and perfect, will of God."* (Romans 12:1&2)

"I don't understand why asking people to eat a well-balanced vegetarian diet is considered drastic, while it is medically conservative to cut people open or put them on powerful cholesterol-lowering drugs for the rest of their lives."
– Dean Ornish, M.D.

*From the Hallelujah Acres mailbag:*

"I am a retired physician and interested in your ministry. My daughter introduced me to your Health publication and many in our family are trying to adapt this better way of eating. Thank you for making this publication available to so many."
– Dr. William Graves, M.D., Tennessee

# Chapter 28

# How to Set Up Your Own Natural Foods Kitchen

*By Rhonda Malkmus*

It was in January 1991 that I attended my first "How to Eliminate Sickness" Seminar. At that time I was very overweight (wore a size 20 dress) and I had arthritis (the result of a train striking my automobile on a rail road crossing in 1981) in almost every joint in my body. My arthritis was so bad that I had to put hot water on my hands to be able to use them each morning. I had a degenerated spine from spinal meningitis at age 7. I had very little energy ... and just didn't feel good.

After attending George's "How to Eliminate Sickness" seminar, I started to change my diet and my physical problems started to go away and today, every physical problem I had is gone. You can read my testimony on page 31. George and I were married in April of 1992 and I had to learn how to prepare vegetarian meals, something in which I had absolutely no prior training or experience. It has been fun learning and experimenting, and the benefits have been wonderful.

**Rhonda makes a salad in her well-equipped kitchen.**

But it was not easy in the beginning. I remember the difficulties I experienced in learning a whole new way of preparing and serving meals. So, I feel it will be helpful if I share a few things I have learned that will help others get started in this new way of life.

One question I am often asked is, "How do I begin changing my kitchen so that I can prepare the foods I will be feeding my family with this new lifestyle? What do I need to eliminate and what should I keep? What about my old cookbooks? What about my canned and frozen food?" Sound familiar?

Let me begin to answer that question by quoting Dr. Dean Ornish, M.D.: "When people make only moderate changes in diet and lifestyle, they have the worst of both worlds. They have the sense of deprivation because they're not able to eat and do everything they want, but they're not making changes big enough to make them feel much better or to have much effect on their weight, their cholesterol, or their health. On the other hand, when people make comprehensive changes in their diet and lifestyle, they begin to feel so much better so quickly that the choices become clear and, for many people, worth making."

Dr. Ornish reflects my personal experience also. The easiest way to change your diet and lifestyle is to jump right in and make it happen. Don't look back.

There are some very basic essentials to setting up a natural foods kitchen and they are as follows:

1. As finances allow, we recommend the purchase of a Champion juicer (seen at the left in the picture on page 248), which we consider to be the most valuable machine in the kitchen. It can be used for making baby food, nut butters, soft banana/fruit ice cream, apple sauce as well as many wonderful juice combinations. It can also be used to grind nuts or shred cabbage, beets, carrots, etc. for salads.

> "What we put in our mouths strongly determines the daily and long-term quality of our lives."
> – Rita Romano,
> *Dining in the Raw,
> Cooking in the Buff*

## *The easiest way to change your diet and lifestyle is to jump right in and make it happen. Don't look back.*

We recommend only two juicers - both of them are of the "masticating" type. The Champion, which currently retails for under $300 and the Norwalk Press ($2,000). Both of these juicers break open (masticate) the cell structure of the vegetables or fruits being juiced to release the nutrients. This method yields up to four times more vitamins, enzymes and trace minerals than a "centrifugal" type juicer. Any juicer with a spinning (centrifugal) basket can not do the same job and will not produce the same results. Nor can they make the baby foods, soft fruit creams, nut butters, etc.

For the money, the Champion is your best deal. The Champion is dependable, easy to use and easy to care for. It has a $1/3$-horse power, heavy-duty motor so you need not worry about putting it to heavy use. Many have told us of daily using their Champion juicers for over 20 years. A commercial model is available with an even heavier motor.

And remember, the very purpose of a juicer is to *remove* the pulp. With the pulp removed, the nutrients are literally pre-digested and no digestion is necessary. Thus, up to 90 percent of the nutrients reach cell level in a matter of minutes. Anyone who is interested in exploring the tremendous health benefits of juicing should know to avoid a well-known, nationally-advertised machine that blends food into a mushy mix, similar to the texture of applesauce. Water must be added to this mixture if you want to drink it. This does not produce the

• • • same benefits as drinking fresh juice, because the fiber or pulp has not been
• • separated from the juice. Even after the fruit or vegetable has been blended and
• mixed by this machine, it still must go through the digestive system. This requires energy and time, and it means that most of the nutrients will have deteriorated during the one- to two-hour process of digestion. (For more information on juicing see Chapter 18.)

2. We would also highly recommend that a Water Distiller be a part of your new kitchen. We believe that distilled water is the only water that should ever be consumed. Our bodies need minerals but not in powdered rock form as found in all ground water sources (spring, river, well, etc.). These minerals can cause many problems for the body such as arthritis, gall stones, kidney stones, hardening of the arteries etc. (See Chapter 22.)

A distiller is filled with ordinary tap water, which is heated to 212 degrees. This heating process kills the bacteria, germs and viruses that the water may contain. Light gases are removed by a gaseous vent and some have a post charcoal filter. As the water turns into steam, the inorganic minerals, salts, chemicals and other pollutants are left behind. Unlike other forms of water purification, a distiller separates water from the pollutants (by evaporation), rather than trying to separate the pollutants from the water.

Distilled water also can be purchased in plastic containers in most grocery stores, but you have less knowledge about and control over the purity of store-bought water than water you distill in your own home. If you buy distilled water in plastic jugs at a store, make sure the label says "Distilled Water," rather than Spring Water, Mineral Water, Drinking Water, etc. If the water tastes like plastic, don't drink it. Plastic can leach into the water if it is stored in the sun.

3. A food dehydrator is a machine that allows food to be preserved by a low-heat process, which leaves the enzymes intact. It is of vital importance that the dehydrator have a thermostat which can be set down to 105 degrees or lower. Some models come with a fan and this is preferred.

Drying food is a good way to maintain its nutritional value because of the low-heat process. No chemicals or additives are needed to preserve the foods.

---

## The Dangers of Aluminum

Many studies have linked aluminum exposure to Alzheimer's disease, a condition that results in loss of reasoning, memory, and language. Alzheimer's disease affects an estimated four million Americans and is the fourth leading cause of death among the elderly after heart disease, cancer, and stroke.

"...The evidence is strong enough that the prudent person will eliminate all food and cosmetic sources of aluminum, and will use aluminum cooking utensils only if they are coated," suggests Gary Price, MD., author of *Nutrition, Health, and Disease*....Scientists suspect that aluminum does its damage as it slowly accumulates in long-lived cells such as nerve cells, where it acts as a neurotoxin causing degenerative damage in the brain.

"Diet is probably the most common means by which aluminum enters the body ... To reach the brain, aluminum must pass the blood-brain barrier, an elaborate structure that filters the blood before it reaches this vital organ. Elemental aluminum does not readily pass this barrier, but certain aluminum compounds found in processed foods and drugs do. For example, if you use orange juice to wash down aspirin, which is commonly buffered with aluminum hydroxide or aluminum glycinate, the citric acid in the juice transforms the aluminum in the aspirin to aluminum citrate. This form is up to five times better able to surmount the blood-brain barrier. If the aluminum in food combines with maltol, a sugar-like additive that is used in many baked goods as a flavoring agent, its capacity to pass into the brain increases by as much as 90 times.

"...The amount of aluminum from aluminum cooking vessels is meager when compared to the amount of aluminum being ingested through food additives," Todd notes. Aluminum compounds are widely added to foods to adjust acidity, make foods lighter in texture, and to keep processed fruits and vegetables firm. The most common aluminum additive is sodium aluminum phosphate, an ingredient in baking powder, cake mixes, and self-rising flours. Even salt, whether iodized or non-iodized, contains aluminum in the form of sodium aluminosilicate, which serves as a desiccant and anti-caking agent.

Other notable sources of aluminum include antiperspirants, antacid tablets, toothpastes, infant formulas, cosmetics, and dental amalgams... Aluminum-containing antiperspirants are designed to be absorbed,

**continued – please see right column, page 251**

Dehydrated foods are easy to store and can be used when traveling, hiking, camping, or re-hydrated in meal preparation. Remember that conventional dehydrated foods are full of additives and preservatives and we do not recommend them.

Dehydrators can also be used to preserve fresh herbs, make seed patties and other treats for your families.

4. Remove all aluminum cooking utensils or any items on your shelves which contain aluminum. Aluminum leaches or is dissolved into the food and has been linked to Alzheimer's and cancer. (See sidebars.)

5. As you are able, replace all items which have been purchased in cans with fresh produce or food which has been prepared by you. Home canned and frozen items have little nutritional value, but can be used in the 15% cooked food portion of your diet.

6. Go through your favorite recipes and see if the harmful ingredients can be replaced by something less harmful. i.e.. white sugar with honey or maple syrup, white flour with whole grain flours or unbleached white; white pastas with whole grain pastas, etc. If you are unable to figure out revisions at this time, set them aside until you have learned more. See additional substitutes on pages 255-257.

7. Remove from your kitchen the microwave oven. Many tests have proven they are hazardous to our health.

8. Other items you may find useful in your kitchen include:

A. A large cutting board. Because wood is natural, a wooden cutting board has certain advantages over a plastic cutting board. But wood provides a more fertile environment for bacteria and germs. A wooden cutting board should be cleaned periodically with a solution of lemon juice and baking soda.

B. A good blender used for making blended salads, sauces and dressings.

C. A food processor saves time when chopping, shredding, grating, and making bread dough.

D. A good quality set of sharp knives, including a chopping knife and hand steel for sharpening.

E. Stainless steel or glass saucepans, skillets, kettles and a stainless steel wok if you can afford one.

**continued from left column, page 250**

and studies show that regular use of these products can raise the risk of Alzheimer's by as much as three-fold. Regular use of antacids, to treat ulcers, for example, can be a major source of aluminum. 'A normal dose of Tums will give you 5 grams of aluminum hydroxide a day,' according to Elizabeth Jeffery, a research scientist at the Intsitute for Environmental Studies at the University of Illinois. This amount is several hundred times greater than that normally obtained from food sources. And even toothpaste may be a significant source, since many brands contain aluminum compounds.

Typically, the most prominent source of aluminum is our municipal water supplies, most of which are treated with alum (aluminum sulfate) to get rid of murkiness. At least seven separate studies have shown that people drinking water high in alum are more likely to develop alzheimer's than people drinking water low in alum.

By themselves, studies of alum-treated water are inconclusive, but that may be because of the role fluoride plays in aluminum toxicity. Aluminum researcher Jeffery has found evidence that fluoride interferes with the body's ability to get rid of aluminum. 'My research indicates that fluoride readily combines with aluminum in the blood, and that aluminum fluoride, once formed, is very poorly excreted in the urine,' says Jeffery. He believes that the aluminum then becomes highly concentrated in the bones, where it may be slowly released over time.

Albert Burgstahler, a professor of bio-chemistry at the University of Kansas, has found that the transfer of aluminum across biological barriers, such as the blood-brain barrier, can be significantly enhanced when it travels in the form of aluminum fluoride. Ironically, 143,000 tons of fluoride are pumped into the nation's reservoirs yearly, most of it in the form of recycled sodium floride, an industrial byproduct of aluminum refiners.

Until all the questions about aluminum's role in Alzheimer's disease have been satisfied, the best advice is to play it safe. Avoiding sources of aluminum and fluoride may be the best way to prevent Alzheimer's disease. *Canned drinks, including non-carbonated ones, can also be a significant source of aluminum, which...may cause degenerative damage of the brain. The acidic beverages dissolve aluminum during storage. The EPA Secondary Maximum Contaminant level of aluminum for water: 50 ppb. Coca-Cola Classic soda in aluminum can: 6,160 ppb. "*
– *Natural Healing*, May/June 1993.

F.  2 and 4-cup glass measuring containers, and a set of ¹/₄, ¹/₃, ¹/₂ and 1-cup measuring cups.

G.  Scissors for snipping fresh herbs.

H.  Hand juicer for squeezing citrus juices used in dressings and sauces.

I.  Oven-proof casserole dishes, and glass, earthen ware or ceramic dishes for lasagna, braising vegetables, etc.

J.  Steamer for vegetables.

K.  Peeler for carrots, potatoes, broccoli stalks, etc.

L.  Spatulas, measuring spoons, garlic press, hand grater, potato masher (which works great for avocados), melon ball tool, colander, vegetable scrubber and a funnel are a few of the items that you may also find useful.

When preparing a recipe, it is best to:

A.  Assemble ingredients
B.  Preheat oven, if required
C.  Do chopping
D.  Measure carefully
E.  Follow directions
F.  Cook as directed, if required

When increasing the size of a recipe, do not increase the seasoning automatically. Taste after adding the regular amount of seasoning to see if more is required.

Herbs can replace salt and pepper and make your meals delightful, but it is important to remember they are to add sparkle to your dishes, not to bury the natural flavor of the food!  Following are a few of the herbs and how you might use them in your kitchen:

**Basil** - Sweet and full flavor - improves the flavor of pasta, salads, soups and dressings.  Also good with tomatoes, eggplant, squash, mushrooms, etc. Fresh is best.  Used in many Italian recipes.

**Bay Leaves** - Fragrant and pungent - Add depth and a sweet peppery scent - use in soups, stews, sauces and tomato dishes.

**Cardamom** - Enhances the flavor of  vegetables  such as sweet potatoes, pumpkin and winter squash.  Used in Middle Eastern and Scandinavian dishes.

**Chervil** - Aromatic herb - used in soups, stews and salad greens - Use like parsley, has a similar flavor, but milder.  Used in French recipes.  Add at end of cooking time to preserve flavor.

**Chives** - Similar to the taste of scallions only milder - use with potatoes, tomatoes, mushrooms, steamed vegetables, grains, dips, spreads, herb butters, etc.

**Cilantro** - Used in East Indian, Central and South American and Asian dishes. Much stronger dried than fresh. Cannot be replaced or substituted for because nothing tastes like cilantro.

**Coriander** - nutty flavor with a delightful aroma, tastes like lemon peel and sage blend - use with cauliflower, mushrooms, rice, in stir fry, curry sauce and salads. Use sparingly because it tends to dominate. Use in Mexican dishes.

**Cumin** - Gives aromatic taste to stews, vegetables - Mexican and Indian cookery - has warm, robust flavor. Use sparingly. Used in curry and chilies.

**Dill** - aromatic foliage and seeds - use with potatoes, tomatoes, cucumbers, mushrooms, in sauces, dips, dressings and salads.

**Garlic** - Whole garlic in soups and sauces and soups - gives a mild fragrance and flavor. The flavor of garlic when sautéed is half as strong as pressed garlic. Raw garlic is the strongest flavor. $1/8$ tsp. of powder equals 1 tsp. of fresh. Garlic becomes bitter if burned.

**Ginger** - Pungent flavor, golden color. Use root in stir fries or other middle eastern dishes. Grate or slice thinly. Leaves can be used in soups.

**Marjoram** - Member of the mint family - Sweet herb with mild flavor, best added toward the end of cooking time in soups, stews and stuffing. May also be used in salad dressings. Goes well with tomatoes and onions.

**Mints** - there are many kinds of mint – peppermint, pineapple, chocolate, orange, spearmint, etc. They make wonderful herb teas and also enhance the flavor of beets, carrots, grains, peas, potatoes pilafs, chutney, stir fries, sauces, dips and dressings. Mints go well with other herbs.

**Oregano** - strong, similar to marjoram. Use sparingly with basil, garlic, olive oil, tomatoes, potatoes, eggplant, summer squash, in marinades, herb vinegars, pizza, Greek and Italian dishes. Oregano is a member of the mint family.

**Parsley** - mild flavor - use with cauliflower, lima beans, summer squash, potatoes, pilafs, tabouli, dips, marinades, soups, stews, sauces and pasta. Blends well with most other herbs. Makes a nice garnish.

**Rosemary** - aromatic shrubby mint with a strong pine taste. Use with cauliflower, lemon, mushrooms, parsnips, peas, potatoes, tomatoes, in marinades, soups, stews, etc. Use sparingly as it can easily dominate.

**Sage** - aromatic and spicy. Use with beans, grains, pasta, potatoes, stews, dressings, soups, sauces and marinades. Can be domineering, so use sparingly.

**Savory** - aromatic, grasslike smell with a mild peppery flavor. Assertive. Use with green beans, salads, cabbage and soups.

**Tarragon** - use in salads and with vegetables. Fresh tarragon has a taste similar to licorice. Great alone or mixed with parsley, chives and chervil.

**Thyme** - heavy aroma and spice taste - use with asparagus, carrots, eggplant, leeks, mushrooms, nutmeg, onions, parsley, peas, potatoes, tomatoes, soups, stews, sauces, herb butters, marinades and bean dishes.

**Turmeric** - adds slight flavor and yellow color to curries and rice dishes.

When buying spices in the market place, be sure they are non-irradiated.

For soups and stews, if not using soup stock, tie the following herbs in a bag: 1 Bay Leaf, 1 tsp. each fresh thyme, parsley, marjoram, sage and rosemary

"Next to nothing is currently known about the human toxic effects of almost 80 percent of the more than 48,000 chemicals listed by the United States Environmental Protection Agency. Fewer than 1,000 have been tested for immediate acute effects, and only about 500 have been tested for their ability to cause long-term health problems such as cancer, birth defects, and genetic changes. A National Research Council study found that complete health-hazard evaluations were available for only 10 percent of pesticides and 18 percent of drugs used in this country."
– Debra Lynn Dadd, *Nontoxic, Natural, and Earthwise*

or your favorite herbs.  Remove before serving.

Instead of salt, use Bragg Liquid Aminos or try combining fresh herbs such as parsley, chives, chervil and tarragon.

There are other items you may not be familiar with.  I get calls all of the time inquiring about what these items are, where to obtain them and how to use them.  I will attempt to give you some assistance and I hope that you will try some of these products.  Most of them should be available at your local health food store.  If they do not carry them regularly, they can probably be special-ordered for you.

**Agar Agar Flakes** - Colorless, natural gelatin derived from a sea vegetable. Use to replace gelatin from animal sources, for example to make aspics.  Also comes in flakes, blocks or cakes. Use 1 teaspoon powdered or 2 teaspoons flakes to 1 cup of liquid.  Can be used to thicken pies, etc. It must be added cold and then heated to thicken.

**Apple Cider Vinegar** - organic, raw, unfiltered vinegar.  Use wherever vinegar is called for in recipes.  Never use white vinegar in food preparation. It is not a healthy option.

**Arrow Root Powder** - Made from West Indian arrow root plant. As a thickener, use instead of corn starch.  Blend with a little liquid before adding to hot dishes to prevent clumps from forming. It does not have to be heated to thicken.  Store in cool, dry place.

**Basmati Rice** - is a long grain brown rice. This rice is very flavorful, enhancing anything else that is prepared with it.  Organically grown Basmati rice is the only rice George and I use.

**Bragg Liquid Aminos** - or "Braggs" as it is often referred to, is a product developed by Paul Bragg. It looks like and has a taste similar to soy sauce. Braggs is not fermented and contains no additives or preservatives.  I use it anywhere I would use salt in meal preparation and at the dinner table.  It gives food a salty taste.  It does contain sodium but no sodium chloride.  Some have found putting it in a small bottle with a mister distributes it over the food more evenly.  I wouldn't be without it in my home, however, we use it sparingly.  One tablespoon of Braggs equals one teaspoon of salt.

**Bulgur Wheat** - is made from whole wheat kernels that have been cracked and toasted.  It has a nutty flavor and can be prepared in about 15 minutes.  It is delicious in pilafs and salads and can be used in place of rice.

**Couscous** - is made from the whole grain of durum wheat. It is light and fluffy when cooked and can be prepared in about 10 minutes.  Can be served as a side dish or in combinations with vegetables.

**Mayonnaise** - commercial mayonnaise is made from eggs and oil. It has many additives and is high in cholesterol.  In your health food store you should be able to find "mayonnaise" made from cold pressed oil that is cholesterol free. Mayonnaise should be used very sparingly.

**Millet -** is an ancient grain, originally from Africa and Asia, that can be used in place of rice. It is a small yellow grain which has a slightly nutty but mild flavor. Millet can also be used to make stuffing and vegetarian burgers.

**Molasses -** is a residual product of sugar refining and contains only minimal nutrients. Unsulphered molasses is best.

**Nutritional Yeast -** golden in color. *Do not confuse with baker's yeast, which should never be consumed raw, or brewer's yeast, which has a bitter taste.* Nutritional yeast is 50% protein, and comes in powder or flakes. Nutritional yeast adds a rather cheesy taste to dishes. Add toward the end of cooking time. Can be used on salads, in soups, main dishes or sauces.

**Olive Oil -** first pressing or extra virgin olive oil is the best oil to use for dressings or food preparation. The body can digest it, and it adds a wonderful flavor. Store in cool, dry place. Buy in small quantities unless you use it often.

**Pasta -** made from flour and water with salt often added. Vegetable pastas are available at health food stores and are preferable to those made with white, bleached flour. Products that are called "noodles" almost always contain egg or egg whites.

**Quinoa -** originally from South America. A delicious grain that has a subtle, pleasing flavor, and can be prepared quickly. It is alkaline so the body can digest it easily. Quinoa should always be rinsed well in hot water to remove the saponin that protects it from birds and pests. Pilafs are wonderful when made using quinoa.

> "In most cases, impaired health is more the result of indulgences and practices that are absolutely harmful, than it is the result of omissions. Most sick people are very anxious to find out what they can do to get them well. What they fail to ask is, 'What can I stop doing that is making me sick?' "
> – Dr. Ralph Cinque

*Remember that once you leave the produce department of your supermarket, there is practically no nutrition found in the rest of the store.*

**Rolled Oats -** are hulled oats from which the bran has been removed. They have been steamed and flattened into flakes by large rollers. Rolled oats are less processed than quick-cooking oats and they take longer to prepare. Quick-cooking oats often have added ingredients such as salt, caramel color, etc.

**Tahini -** is made from ground sesame seeds. Good quality tahini has most of the nutrients from the sesame seeds remaining intact. It contains vitamins, minerals, protein and essential fatty acids that the body needs. Use in sauces, dressings, dips, etc.

**Tamari -** a fermented soy sauce similar in taste to Bragg Liquid Aminos. In recipes calling for Tamari, I use Braggs. Tamari contains salt.

**Tofu -** made from soybeans, is often bean curd. It is white in appearance and has very little taste, however, it takes on the flavor of whatever it is mixed with. Tofu is a refrigerated item that comes packed in water, and must be drained before use. Use sparingly as it is very high in protein. Tofu can be baked, braised, broiled, marinated or steamed.

**SUBSTITUTIONS: Try some of the following to convert traditional recipes to healthier foods. Replace all animal products, including poultry,**

> *From the Hallelujah Acres mailbag:*
>
> "We are looking forward to meeting you. God bless you - your work is as precious as gold."
> – D.S. & B.S., Tennessee

*From the*
*Hallelujah Acres mailbag:*

**fish, eggs and cheese:**

Meat stock can be replaced with vegetable soup stock, see page 270.

"Dear Staff of Hallelujah Acres:

GOD BLESS YOU! Your ministry has completely changed my life. And as a result, my experience has completely changed the lives of my family and many of my friends.

Allow me to elaborate. A little over a year ago, I had to have my gallbladder removed – I was only 26! I have spent a lifetime completely abusing my body, going on every fad diet that came along trying desperately to lose weight, only to end up gaining more and more each time. I had finally given up. My weight stabilized at about 215 lbs. (I am 5'6" and am NOT big-boned.) I began having gallbladder attacks and ended up in the hospital with pancreatitis. I vowed to take better care of my body. The problem was, I was still ignorant – I didn't know what to do differently. I began to pray for wisdom and discernment in this area. Little did I know how God would answer this prayer so dramatically.

My health problems continued after I made some initial changes in my diet and had lost some weight. Now, I began having very mysterious dizzy spells. I went to an ear doctor who originally had the right idea, but he was only about half-right. He put me on a very low-salt diet thinking that the fluid in my inner ear was fluctuating. I took this diet to the extreme, eating almost nothing – it's very difficult to stay below 2,000 mg of salt a day! Our non-food American diet is loaded with sodium. Needless to say, this didn't work.

I went to another doctor who did a complete work-up on my blood. He said my weight loss was screwing up my electrolytes and that I needed to drink more water. Again, good advice, but not whole advice. My symptoms were still very aggravating and getting worse. I felt tipsy, my balance was not good, I was constantly fatigued and had completely stopped exercising. On to yet another doctor.

That's when things really got scary. The ear doctor told me that maybe I had MS and they just hadn't caught it yet. I was devastated. I couldn't work, I couldn't eat. I was completely debilitated by my fear.

I went to a neurologist who tested me for a variety of neurological disorders. He did an MRI and found nothing – no MS, no tumor, nothing. I was completely relieved and frustrated at the same time. What in the world was going on? The neurologist thought that maybe I had a problem in my neck. I was having a lot of neck pain and some loss of motion in my neck. So it was on to a chiropractor. Do you see a pattern developing here?

I spent several months going to a chiropractor who actually did help to alleviate some of my symptoms, but at $53.00 a visit, I had spent every penny I had and could no longer afford to go. This is after spending thousands of dollars on an MRI, neurologist, internest, otolaryngologist, blood work-ups, prescriptions, and on and on. My parents had to pay my rent some months!

I felt doomed. That I had to just sit back and wait for MS to strike me down. I felt completely hopeless.

It just so happens that I am a professional singer and sing in my church, Grace Community, quite often, and so even though we are a very large church, people know me quite well and many were watching me go through all of these problems. I was to the point of believing that I might not be able to hold down a job because I was so fatigued and frightened all the time – I couldn't concentrate. One day, as I was walking off stage at

**continued – please see right column, page 257**

In yeast breads, try leaving out the eggs.

Use crumbled tofu instead of cottage cheese.

Replace traditional pork and beans with vegetarian baked beans.

Replace eggs when used for liquid in recipes by adding one of the following substitutions: 2 tablespoons of another liquid such as lemon juice or water, half of a ripe banana, 1/4 cup of raw apple sauce or ground zucchini.

To replace eggs when used as a binder try using mashed potatoes, quick cooking oatmeal, or fine bread crumbs.

To cream soups add rice that has been cooked and then pureéd or add some potatoes and allow them to cook down.

Replace buttermilk with tofu milk to which 1 tablespoon apple cider vinegar has been added.

Replace cow's milk with rice milk or soybean milk.

Replace white rice with brown rice and wild rice.

Bake potatoes instead of frying them.

Replace ground meats with lots of cut-up vegetables or try tvp (texturized vegetable protein) if you are just changing your diet. You will find that after being on a mostly raw diet that you will no longer need meat substitutes.

In baked goods, replace fat with applesauce, mashed bananas, pumpkin or ground zucchini. Bananas, applesauce and pumpkin will add flavor; zucchini will not.

Try using honey or maple syrup instead of sugar. Use sparingly as these are *concentrated sweeteners.* Forty gallons of sap are required to make one gallon of maple syrup.

Sauté without oil. Use lemon juice (or other citrus juices), vegetable broth or braggs aminos, to which you may add minced garlic, finely chopped onions and/or your favorite herbs. This method is preferred to using oil.

When planning your menus ask yourself the following questions:

1. What can I serve my family that is raw and delicious?
2. What new taste treat can we try?
3. What is easy to prepare for the cooked food portion of the family meals.

Plan ahead, and make your meals attractive. Eye appeal is very important.

***When grocery shopping, avoid all refined foods. Select natural foods that provide you and your family an adequate intake of vitamins, minerals, trace elements and amino acids. Remember that once you leave the produce department of your supermarket, there is practically no nutrition found in the rest of the store.***

Be adventuresome. Try adding new and unusual items to your diet. If you aren't sure how to prepare them, ask a clerk that works in the produce department. Add fresh greens to your diet. Try collards, spinach and leaf lettuce.

Pick fresh fruits and vegetables when available. Before serving, vegetables should always be cleaned with a non-toxic, biodegradable soap and rinsed well.

If fresh fruits and vegetables are not available and you must buy frozen, make sure you buy those with no sugar, salt or preservatives added.

**Seeds and nuts -** If you must eat them, use sparingly. Almonds are the least harmful. Peanuts should be avoided. They are a legume, not a nut, and do

**continued from page 256**

church, a friend of mine who plays trombone in the orchestra and who has literally been on death's door several times with colon cancer, grabbed me by the arm and said, 'You are just too good to be sick. I know with a voice like that, God has big plans for you. We are just going to have to get you well.'

It was this friend who introduced me to Barley Green. He told me that he believed it literally saved his life. I tried it begrudgingly, thinking, well, I've tried everything else. What could it hurt? My energy returned in five days. In less than a month, I felt like someone had given me my life back. Then this same friend gave me your newsletter on 'Living Above MS.' My hopeful spirit had been restored. I decided at that time, that even if I didn't have MS, changing my diet was something I really needed to do and I proceeded to eliminate dairy, eggs, and cooked food from my diet. I had one month of feeling almost completely normal!

Then I slipped a little in my diet. How easily we fall back into old habits! My symptoms returned, only this time they were worse. I was having a lot of trouble walking, I felt so unsteady on my feet. Then one evening, I had another terrible dizzy spell, only this time, I completely lost hearing in my right ear. It came back over the next few days, but needless to say, being a professional singer, it scared me to death.

While I was sitting in the waiting room, waiting to see the ear doctor again, I was praying in the name of Jesus that I would be provided resolution and solutions. I placed my hand over my ear and imagined how Jesus would place his hand over my ear and fill me with His healing spirit.

When I told the ear doctor about my last episode, this time, he got a little smirk on his face and said, 'Well, this hearing loss is the symptom we've been waiting for. Sometimes, it takes a while to rear its ugly head but I can confidently diagnose you with Endolymphatic Hydrops.' It was a completely answered prayer! I called everybody – my parents, my prayer partner, my friends and church, everybody who had been praying on my behalf for a year!

Now, you may be asking, what in the world is Endolymphatic Hydrops? It is a balance disorder of the inner ear for which there is no cure and in my case, no known cause. The solution to managing my symptoms is – you guessed it – diet! Low sugar, low salt and lots of water, which translated means, raw fruits and vegetables and purified water – and of course, my Barley Green.

Case closed.

I don't think I would have made it through this 'Year of Fear' as I have so affectionately donned it, if it had not been for your ministry. Reading the stories about the MS patients and others who had found hope again through changing their diet and lifestyle turned on the lights for me and really helped me to cope with my fear. Please keep this letter on file, write to me, call me in the middle of the night if you have to – I will always be here to testify to the impact of your ministry. And of course to testify to the infinite grace and mercy of the Lord, Jesus Christ."

– Elizabeth Kelly,
Tennessee
P.S. I've lost around 45 lbs. and am slowly taking the rest of my excess weight off!

not easily digest. In seeds and nuts about 80 - 90% of the calories come from fat.

**Grains** should be used sparingly as they are acid forming in the body, and our bodies should maintain an alkaline pH. Of the grains, millet and quinoa are the least acid forming.

There are two types of fat, saturated and unsaturated. The difference between the fats are:

**Saturated fat -** those that harden at room temperature also harden in the body. Found in animal products, coconut and palm kernel oils. These fats cause your cardiovascular system great problems and should be avoided.

**Unsaturated fat -** those fats that are liquid at room temperature. There are two types of unsaturated fat; monosaturated which is olive, almond and canola oil and polyunsaturated which are found in corn, safflower, and cotton seed oils.

# Chapter 29:
# Recipes from Rhonda

Make it a point to always keep plenty of fresh, ripe, raw fruits and vegetables around the house for handy consumption. On the Hallelujah Diet, you and your family will soon get in the habit of making a meal out of fresh, raw fruits or vegetables, because it's so incredibly quick and easy.

# Fruit Dishes

## Avocado Fruit Salad

1 banana, sliced
1/2 avocado, diced
3-4 dates, cut into small pieces
1/4 cup raisins, organic, soaked

Serve as is or on a bed of fresh leaf lettuce

**A Tip:** Eat melons alone or leave them alone. They do not digest well with anything else.

## Fresh Fruit Salad

8 dates, cut into small pieces
3 bananas, sliced
2 apples (Granny Smith), diced
1 pear, diced
3/4 C raisins, organic
3/4 C apple juice, organic

Prepare all fruits and combine with apple juice. Stir, cover and chill before serving.

## Raw Apple Sauce

Scrub or peel about two medium apples for each person. Then quarter and remove seeds. Using your Champion Juicer (with the solid plate instead of the screen in place), simply run the apples through the machine. Out of the front of the machine will come beautiful, raw, nutritious, apple sauce! A small amount of cinnamon can be added for more flavor. You can also add raw, pitted dates for a wonderful taste sensation. Just place a date or two in the hopper with every four quarters of apple and run them through the machine together. Two or three almonds can be run through with every four quarters of apple for another delicious taste treat. Let your imagination have some fun as you try your own combinations.

# Juice Recipes

Freshly extracted, raw vegetable juices are the fastest way we know of to get the largest amount of nutrients to the cellular level of the body. This is because with the fiber removed nutrients can be easily and quickly absorbed into the bloodstream without going through the process of digestion. (This is not true of any juice found in a can, bottle, or container. All processed juices have been heated to kill the enzymes so they will not spoil on the store shelf. This processing destroys almost all nutritional value.) The fresh, live juices brings to the body natural vitamins, minerals, protein, enzymes and so much more.

Carrots should comprise at least 60% of any vegetable juice mix you make. It takes approximately one pound of carrots to make 8 fluid ounces of juice, which allows you to consume the nutrients of an entire pound of carrots in one serving of fresh carrot juice. The body cannot assimilate more than 8 to 10 ounces of juice at one time, so drink one serving and then wait one hour before drinking additional juice.

Buy organically grown produce if you can. If pesticides are a concern, you can peel your carrots and soak other vegetables.

Here at Hallelujah Acres, we do not recommend any juicer that has a spinning basket. These juicers leave too much of the nutrients in the pulp. The Champion Juicer is the one we recommend as the best buy for the money.

Vegetable juices can be used as mid-morning or mid-afternoon pick-me-uppers or as an appetizer 30 minutes before a meal. (Never drink juice or any other liquid with a meal as it dilutes the digestive juices and makes digestion very difficult.) Here are a couple of recipes for juicing you might like to try for yourself and your family:

### Carrot / Apple Juice

For every 8 to 10 carrots you run through your juicer, add one apple (Granny Smith or Gala are best for juicing). This is the only exception to not mixing fruit and vegetable juices together. It's delicious!

### Carrot / Vegetable Juice

Run 5 to 6 carrots, 1 beet, 1 stalk of celery (cut into 1 inch pieces), along with some green leaves from spinach, kale, lettuce or cabbage through the juicer. You can vary the number of vegetables and the quantity to create many different flavors. Experiment to decide which combinations you like the best. The juices you make will be alive and full of nutrition, rather than the cooked and dead juice found in cans and bottles at the supermarket.

# *Salads*

## ── How to Build a Salad ──

Back when we operated Hallelujah Acres as a Natural Foods Restaurant, people would often rave about our raw vegetable salads, saying things such as: "This is the best salad I have ever had in my life!" Actually, building a salad is really quite easy once you have the ingredients assembled. And it does take more than iceberg lettuce and a tomato to make a salad. Here is how we do it here at Hallelujah Acres:

Start with deep green leaf lettuce (*Never use iceberg lettuce. It has practically no nutrition!*) Make sure it is washed well and completely drained. This can be accomplished by washing and loosely rolling in a towel. Then place in the refrigerator still rolled in the towel for a half hour or so to chill while you prepare the rest of the vegetables. (Never use paper towels for drying. Some are coated with formaldehyde.) Use a clean dish towel to dry or store food like spinach or lettuce.

While the lettuce is crisping in the refrigerator, clean and prepare the rest of the vegetables. After the vegetables have been prepared, you are ready to build your salad. The first thing you do is tear your crisped lettuce into small, bite sized pieces, and fill salad bowl half full with the lettuce. Next, add in layers the following vegetables ...

1. Small broccoli florets.
2. Small cauliflower florets.
3. Finely diced celery.
4. Finely diced red and/or green peppers.
5. Finely chopped *sweet* onion (if desired).
6. Top salad with grated carrots (California grown).

This is how we did it at our restaurant, but there is no end to where your creativity can take you. Have fun and enjoy your own creations!  And don't be afraid to try new or unusual vegetables in your salads, like raw asparagus, raw corn off the cob, raw cubed summer squash, raw grated sweet potato, cucumbers, etc.  Also, you can add sunflower seeds to your salads or sprinkle with grated raw almonds. Now add your salad dressing and enjoy!  Your salads do not have to be boring nor bland!  The variety and combinations are endless. This is the salad George and I share together each day and it is the high point of our eating experience.  Our salads are very large and totally filling and often serve as the complete meal.

Serve with your favorite dressing, but not with the super market dressings that are full of sugar and preservatives.  Most health food stores carry a nice line of salad dressings, or you can create your own.

## Hallelujah Acres
### Cabbage Salad

2 large apples, grated
1 cup carrots, grated
2 cups cabbage, grated
2 stalks of celery, chopped
1/2 cup organic raisins

Grate apples, carrots and cabbage, chop celery, and add raisins. Mix with the following dressing, refrigerate and allow flavors to blend for one hour.

Dressing – combine & mix well:
1/2 cup cold-pressed mayonnaise
1/2 tsp. dried onion
2 Tbsp. honey
1/2 tsp. minced garlic
2-3 Tbsp. organic apple juice

## HEALTH TIP:

Wash fruits and vegetables thoroughly before you eat them. I use a product called BRONNER'S SAL SUDS. There are other fruit and vegetable cleaners on the market. Use recommended amount in a basin or sink of water. Wash fruits and vegetables with a vegetable brush if appropriate. Don't leave fruit in water; wash it quickly to minimize discoloration. Never soak vegetables for more than a few minutes. Rinse thoroughly. Dry with a cloth towel.

*From the*
*Hallelujah Acres mailbag:*

Lillian Schultz

"I am deeply enjoying the latest issue of *Back to the Garden* (#9). What would we do without Rhonda's beautiful, life-saving, recipes? 'Thank-You' Rhonda!"
– Lillian Schultz, Florida

## Blended Salad

One of George's favorite ways to fix a salad is to blend it into a coarse or fine cold soup. He learned this method of preparing salads at the Shangri-La Health Resort in Florida. There it was used for people who had difficulty chewing. But it is a delicious variation of salad preparation for anyone. This salad does require a blender. Here is how it is made: Gather all the ingredients together before you begin …

| | |
|---|---|
| 1 medium tomato | 2 cups leaf lettuce or spinach |
| 1/4 of a cucumber | 1 stalk of celery |
| 1 ripe avocado | 1 tsp. Bragg Liquid Aminos |
| 1/4 cup broccoli & cauliflower florets | 1/2 tsp. herb seasoning |

Blend tomato, cucumber, avocado, Bragg Liquid Aminos & seasoning to make the dressing. Then add remainder of ingredients except for celery. As you push the veggies down into the blades with the celery stalk, quickly turn the blender on and off until all veggies are in the dressing. Then continue turning the blender on & off until desired consistency is reached. If the dressing is too dry, a little distilled water may be added. (If you turn your blender on and leave it on instead of pulsing it on and off rapidly, your salads will be too fine.)

# Salad Dressings

*From the Hallelujah Acres mailbag:*

"Praise the Lord! *Your ministry has changed our lives!* My husband and I are in our early thirties and I have always struggled with my weight but in the last three years I have lost the battle completely … my eyes have been opened to the single greatest lie Satan has been telling for centuries … that we inherit our physical problems. Think about it. When do people question God the most? That's right … when their family members, friends or they themselves are sick and dying. With this one belief, we have cursed ourselves. Although I have feared the cancer, diabetes, gout, high blood pressure, kidney problems and heart disease of my parents, I believed they were inevitable. And though I have always heard that you are what you eat, I figured … why bother! With the food industry, all magazines and nutrition classes telling us that proper nutrition includes the basic 4, we couldn't get past the lie. *Thank God you did!* How could we as Christians be so blind? As with everything, the blueprint to health has always been there for us to read … *'and be not conformed to this world'* didn't just mean in morality, politics, etc. but in our eating. Now

**Continued in the Right Column of page 265**

---

**Cashew Dip**

Blend until smooth:
- 1 C cashews, raw and unsalted
- 1 C water, distilled
- 2 Tbsp. dehydrated minced onion
- 1/2 tsp. paprika
- 1 garlic clove, minced
- 1 Tbsp. lemon juice
- 1 Tbsp. parsley

Add slowly, while blender is running:
- 1/4 C extra virgin olive oil

Optional: 2 Tbsp. sesame seeds or nutritional yeast for a cheesey taste. Another option is to add your favorite herb seasonings or Bragg Liquid Aminos.

**Avocado-Tomato Dressing**

Blend in a blender, 1 medium or 2 small ripe tomatoes with one ripe avocado adding a teaspoon (to taste) of BRAGG LIQUID AMINO (can be found in most Health Food Stores) for flavor enhancement. You can also add celery to thicken if desired. Then add your favorite herbs for additional flavor.

**Cucumber Dressing**

In a blender, combine the following ingredients:
- 1/2 avocado
- 1 large cucumber, peeled, seeded & chopped
- 1/4 cup green onion, chopped
- 1 tsp. dill weed
- 1 clove garlic
- 1 tsp. honey or maple syrup

If too thick, add distilled water. If too thin, add more avocado.

# Main Dishes

## Sweet Potato Delight

Wonderful for the holidays or anytime you want a special treat.

      4 sweet potatoes, peeled and cut in 1" chunks
      1 large green apple, peeled and diced
      1/4 cup raw cranberries (optional)
      1/2 cup of raisins
      2 Tbsp. raw, unfiltered honey
      1/2 cup fresh orange juice

Preheat oven to 350 degrees. Place sweet potato chunks in a large baking dish. Top with diced apple, cranberries and raisins. Drizzle with honey and pour orange juice over all. Cover and bake approximately one hour, or until sweet potatoes are tender.

Health Tip: Aluminum cookware leaches aluminum into our food and our bodies. We recommend only glass or stainless steel.

## Veggie / Rice Medley

| | |
|---|---|
| 2 C cooked and seasoned Basmati rice | 1/2 tsp. sweet basil |
| 2 Tbsp. olive oil | 1/4 tsp. ginger |
| 7 garlic cloves, pressed | 1/3 cup Braggs |
| 5 large onions, sliced thin | 1 C bean sprouts |
| 2 celery stalks, sliced diagonally | 1 C water chesnuts |
| 1 green pepper, diced | 1 C carrot, sliced diagonally 1/8-inch thick |

Heat oil in large pan. Add garlic, onions, celery, pepper, carrots and oil. Sauté 5 minutes. Add other vegetables. Simmer on low heat stirring occasionally until vegetables are al dente (tender but firm). Add Braggs and other seasoning. Serve over seasoned rice.

Continued from the Left Column of page 264

I am no longer dieting to lose weight. I have changed completely what I put into my (God's) body. And it isn't nearly as difficult as I thought it would be. *Thanks to your wonderful ministry I now have that new attitude I have been searching for and the weight loss is just one of the many bonuses!* Please pray that we can spread this message through our own lives as examples and save our families and friends from the misery of illness. We don't have to be sick!!!"
– Linda Crawford, Kentucky

## Wild Rice Dressing

4 cups vegetable broth
1 tsp. Braggs
¾ cup Basmati rice
¾ cup wild rice
2 Tbsp. olive oil
1 small onion, chopped
1 lb. fresh mushrooms, cleaned & sliced
½ cup fresh chopped parsley
1 cup diced celery
¼ tsp. sage
⅛ tsp. marjoram & dried thyme
1 cup pecan halves, broken length-wise

Bring water to a boil; add rice; reduce heat to lowest temperature, cover and cook until tender (about 30-40 minutes).
Pre-heat oven to 350 degrees.
In a large skillet, heat oil and sauté onion and mushrooms until onion is transparent. Add parsley, celery and cooked rice, seasoning and pecans. Add Braggs to taste; stir to mix. Cover and bake 15 minutes.

**Hint for dressing up your baked potatoes:**

Try topping your baked potatoes with any of the following veggies that have been sauted in a small amount of extra virgin olive oil, or lightly steamed: chopped green pepper, chopped red pepper, finely chopped broccoli, finely chopped cauliflower, chopped celery or chopped onion. Add Bragg Liquid Aminos and herb seasoning for a wonderful taste treat. It will delight your taste buds!

*From the Hallelujah Acres mailbag:*

"I enjoy the materials I receive from you. I have lost 65 pounds since last August ... I feel much better and can work hard without getting tired..."
– Ernest Gignilliat, Georgia

## Stuffed Tomatoes

*Stuffed Tomatoes* can be absolutely scrumptious! Just take a large, ripe, tomato and core out the stem end. Cut the tomato (stem-end up) into 8 wedges – but stop about a half inch from the bottom. If the bottom is rounded and will not sit flat, flatten it by cutting a little off. Place on plate on top of a large piece of leaf lettuce (not head lettuce). Stuff with your favorite stuffing and serve with celery and carrot sticks, red and/or green pepper rings, etc.

For *Taboule* stuffing, place in small mixing bowl: 1 cup bulgar wheat soaked in 2 cups of distilled water a half hour before adding the following ingredients:

2 Tbsp. fresh parsley (or 1 tsp. dry); 2 Tbsp. each of chopped onion, celery and pepper; 1 tomato chopped; 2 Tbsp. cucumber, chopped fine; 1 Tbsp. Braggs Liquid Aminos (purchase in Health Food Store); 1 to 2 Tbsp. Extra Virgin Olive Oil; ¼ cup fresh lemon juice; 2 Tbsp. fresh mint (or 1 tsp. dried). Toss lightly. Refrigerate at least one hour before stuffing the tomato. You can change the flavor of Taboule by adding or omitting different vegetables or seasonings. Taboule can also be served on a bed of lettuce without being stuffed into a tomato.

You can also use quinoa, couscous or brown rice cooked according to directions in place of the wheat in the above recipe.

*Another stuffing* for the tomato would be to chop your favorite veggies into small pieces - as great a variety as desired. Saute till desired tenderness in vegetable broth, distilled water or small amount of Extra Virgin Olive Oil. (Add some Bragg Liquid Aminos and herbs while sautéing if desired.) Place into prepared stuffing tomato as explained above. Top with a sauce made from two blended tomatoes, three garlic cloves, Bragg Liquid Aminos and your favorite herbs - eg. basil, oregano or mixed herbs.

Still another excellent stuffing for tomatoes is the guacamole recipe on page 268.

## Seasoned Basmati Rice

This is one of our favorites on a cold winter evening after we have had our Barley Green and salad. This is the only kind of rice we use and the aroma of this rice cooking will tantalize your taste buds

> 1 cup Brown Basmati Rice, rinsed and set aside
> ½ cup of celery, chopped
> ¼ cup onion chopped
> ¼ cup red and/or green pepper
> 3 cups distilled water

Sauté the celery, onion and peppers in water, vegetable soup stock or olive oil, until onion is translucent. Add rice and saute a few minutes (do not let it burn). Then add 3 cups of distilled water and bring quickly to a boil. Cover, reduce heat and simmer for 30 minutes. Turn burner off and allow to sit covered an additional 15 to 30 minutes. Do not lift lid. Stir, season with Bragg Liquid Aminos and herbs to taste. Serve alone or use as a base on which to place stir-fried or steamed vegetables.

## Pasta Primavera

1 cup chopped broccoli
1 cup chopped cauliflower
1 cup carrots, sliced in thin diagonals
3 Tbsp. olive oil
¼ cup diced red pepper
2 cups snipped fresh chives or basil, if available
5-6 cherry tomatoes or 1 roma
2 Tbsp. minced parsley (fresh is best)
½ cup onion, diced
½ pound angel hair pasta

Bring large pot of distilled water to boil.
Blanch broccoli, cauliflower, carrots and onions for 3 - 5 minutes or until tender. Remove veggies with slotted spoon, rinse in cold water and pat dry.
Return vegetable water to a boil. Add 1 Tbsp. olive oil. Add pasta and cook until al dente (tender but firm), about 3 - 5 minutes.
While pasta is cooking, heat remaining olive oil in large skillet. Add blanched vegetables, red pepper, seasoning and tomatoes. Saute 3-5 minutes.
Drain pasta and transfer to large bowl. Toss with vegetables. Season with Bragg Liquid Aminos and herb seasoning.

# Quick & Healthy Meals

---

*From the*
*Hallelujah Acres mailbag:*

"My wife and I have been users of Barley Green and Herbal Fiberblend since 1989 with some results – but now we know why not totally - We didn't do the other half of the program – eliminating meats and getting on a vegetable and fruit diet. Please put us on your mailing list – *Back to the Garden* is now a must..."
– Joseph Stolarz, Mississippi

---

## Avocado Salad Pita Pocket

Pita pockets are wonderful! One of my favorites is this live, all-raw recipe:

Spread pita bread with mashed avocado and stuff with your favorite fresh veggies ... diced tomatoes, sprouts, lettuce, cucumber, shredded carrots, etc. Add favorite salad dressing.

---

## Health Tip
### – Avocados –

Avocados are usually hard when purchased. They are not ripe until they give slightly to the touch. Sometimes it takes a little experience to determine just when an avocado is ripe. Once ripe, they remain in useable condition at room temperature only for a couple days, but can be kept in the refrigerator for up to a week.

---

## Guacamole Dip

2 very ripe avocados
2 Tbsp. onion, chopped fine
1 clove garlic, minced
$\frac{1}{2}$ red pepper, cut fine
$\frac{1}{2}$ green pepper, cut fine
1 medium ripe tomato, peeled and chopped
2 stalks celery, chopped fine
1 Tbsp. lime or lemon juice

Halve the avocados, remove pits and scoop flesh into a glass container. Mash with a fork and blend in remaining ingredients. Serve as quickly as possible. Serve w/ fresh veggies.

## Fresh Vegetable Platter

Cut equal amounts of the following fresh, raw vegetables into serving pieces:

Red, green & yellow peppers
Celery sticks
Carrot sticks
Broccoli
Cauliflower

Arrange attractively on a platter and serve with an avocado-tomato dressing/dip or the Cashew Dip found on page 264 or the Salsa recipe at the right.

## Hallelujah Acres Potato Salad

4 C boiled, diced potatoes, peeled
$1/8$ C chopped sweet red & green pepper
1 C diced celery
$1/4$ C chopped onions
$1/8 - 1/4$ C parsley flakes

Boil potatoes and cool. Dice potatoes, chop pepper, celery, onions & add parsley. In a separate bowl, combine the following dressing:

1 Tbsp. cider vinegar
1 tsp. celery seed
1 T Braggs Liquid Aminos
1 tsp. honey
2 tsp. poupon mustard
$1/2$ C mayonnaise or 1 avocado, mashed
1 Tbsp. herb seasoning

Stir until all ingredients are mixed well. Add to potato mixture and toss lightly. Chill several hours before serving.

## Salsa

1 C chopped tomatoes (peeled if desired)
2 Tbsp. dehydrated minced sweet onion
$1/2$ C minced red bell pepper
$1/2$ C minced green bell pepper
$1/2$ C corn, if desired
$1/2$ C cucumber or celery
1-2 Tbsp. extra virgin olive oil
1 Tbsp. minced cilantro
1 tsp. basil
1 tsp. oregano

For a creamy texture, combine half of the tomatoes, red pepper, celery and onion in blender. Blend until smooth. Mix this in with the remaining ingredients, chill and serve.

Tip: Eat foods just as close to the way God made them as possible.

"Our cancer research is misdirected, inefficient, and inadequate. We have almost as many people living off the disease as are dying from it. The government spends billions on cancer research, but at the same time allows known carcinogens in our processed foods, subsidizes cigarettes, and continues to develop new radiation, surgical, and chemotherapy techniques when burning, cutting, and poisoning have already proved largely unsuccessful. Physicians have not been trained in preventive medicine and, not having experience or knowledge of preventive medicine, they continue the outmoded but orthodox approach of treating symptoms rather than the entire body ..."
– Richard O. Brennan, M.D., D.O., from *Coronary? Cancer? God's Answer: Prevent It!*

*From the
Hallelujah Acres mailbag:*

"Dear Brother Malkmus:
You surely captured our
attention when our sister
sent your book *Why
Christians Get Sick*. She
had seen you on 3ABN
Television and
immediately started
making changes in her
diet. We are deeply
indebted to the Lord's
leading in your life. Your
book (*Why Christians Get
Sick*) is easy to read and
understand and we truly
appreciate it! Since we
received our book, it has
been on loan ever since we
finished reading it. Our
Baptist neighbors have it
at the present time. Praise
the Lord for truth. Truth
will come out! ... Thank
you so much for your
ministry..."
– David & Dorothy Kulisek,
Oregon

# Soups

## Vegetable Soup Stock

Every cook knows the secret to any good soup is the soup stock from which it is made. Here is a recipe that will give your soups lots of extra flavor and body:

8-10 cups distilled water
2 onions, cubed, leave skins on if clean
2-3 cloves of garlic
3 carrots, chopped
3-4 stalks of celery, chopped
2 potatoes, scrubbed & quartered,
    w/skin

$^1/_2$ - 1 cup parsley
1 bay leaf
1 tsp. thyme
1 tsp. basil
2 cups broccoli pieces (stems are fine)
2 cups cauliflower pieces
$^1/_4$ cup olive oil

Chop all vegetables into 1-inch pieces. Place in stock pot or large stainless steel kettle, and add seasonings. Sauté in $^1/_4$ cup olive oil. Cover with distilled water, bring to a boil, and reduce heat and simmer over low heat for 45 minutes to one hour. Cool and strain twice to remove all debris, and discard vegetables. Stock may be frozen or will keep in refrigerator up to one week. Use for soups or stews.

## Gazpacho Soup

3 C ripe tomatoes
2 C cucumbers, peeled & diced
2 stalks celery, diced
$^1/_2$ green bell pepper, seeded & diced
1 red bell pepper, seeded & diced
3 green onions, sliced or 2 Tbsp dry
onion flakes
2 Tbsp. extra virgin olive oil
$1^1/_2$ – 2 Tbsp lemon juice
2 tsp Bragg Liquid Aminos
herb seasoning to taste
$^1/_4$ C soup stock, optional

Place $1^1/_2$ tomatoes, $^1/_4$ cup soup stock in a food processor and pureé. Place in a glass container, add remaining vegetables, stir in olive oil, lemon juice, Braggs and All Purpose Seasoning to taste. Cover & chill. Do not heat. This soup is served cold. Garnish each bowl with a few parsley flakes.

## Raw Carrot Soup

2 C hot vegetable soup stock or
    distilled water
$^1/_2$ C cashews (raw, unsalted)
1 C fresh parsley or 1 Tbsp. dried
2-3 Tbsp. Bragg Liquid Aminos
$^1/_4$ C finely chopped scallions,
    green onions or chives
1 C shredded carrot

Blend first four ingredients, add carrots. Pulse blender to chop carrots to desired consistency. Pour into bowls, garnish with green onions before serving. A garden salad and soup make a wonderful meal.

## Minestrone Soup

For that cold winter evening, a thick, full-bodied soup with homemade whole-grain bread can be a welcome treat following your large green salad. (Remember to start each meal with either Barley Green or fresh vegetable juice at least 20 to 30 minutes before the meal.)

    8 cups of vegetable soup stock
    1 1/2 cups of garbanzo beans, cooked & drained
    2 cups of red kidney beans, cooked & drained
    1/2 cup of carrots, diced or chopped
    1/2 cup onion, chopped
    1 cup cabbage, chopped
    1 clove garlic, crushed
    3 medium tomatoes, peeled & finely chopped (or one 14 oz. can
        of unsweetened and unsalted Italian tomatoes with juice)
    1/4 teaspoon oregano
    3/4 teaspoons basil
    1/4 teaspoon thyme
    1/2 cup fresh parsley (or 1 tablespoon dried)
    2 tablespoons Bragg Liquid Aminos (add slowly to taste)
    1 package spinach noodles - prepare according to directions
        and set aside.

Chop carrots, onion, celery and garlic and sauté in water, soup stock or olive oil over medium heat until the onion is translucent - about 5 minutes. Stir in kidney beans, garbanzo beans, tomatoes and herbs. Bring to a simmer, then turn heat down and simmer about 10 minutes. Stir in cabbage and parsley and simmer with lid partially on for about 15 minutes or until cabbage is tender (be careful not to burn). Soup will thicken. Add more tomatoes or soup stock as needed. Serve over spinach noodles. This was the most popular soup at our restaurant.

## Split Pea Soup

| | |
|---|---|
| 1 Tbsp. olive oil | 1/2 C parsley flakes |
| 1 med. onion, chopped | 1/8 tsp. cayenne |
| 1 tsp. garlic powder | 2 C uncooked split peas |
| 1 tsp. ground cumin | 2 qts. soup stock |
| 3 Tbsp. Bragg Liquid Aminos | 1 medium potato, cubed |
| 3 stalks celery, chopped | 2 carrots, shredded |

Soak peas overnight. Drain & rinse, set aside. Sauté onion and spices in olive oil for 1 minute. Add Braggs, peas and soup stock. Bring to boil, simmer for one hour. Add potatoes and celery. Cook additional hour on low until peas have reached a creamy consistency. Stir often to prevent soup from sticking.

"The Department of Agriculture's promotional posters used to list milk as the first group and meat as the second. Grains got a group, and fruits and vegetables had to share a group. Because livestock products were assigned two of the four groups, menus developed under this plan were often loaded with fat and cholesterol. That is how an entire generation learned to eat, and how they, in turn, raised their children. The results are tragic. There are 4,000 heart attacks *every single day* in this country. The traditional four food groups and the eating patterns they prescribed have led to cancer and heart disease in epidemic numbers, and have killed more people than any other factor in America. More than automobile accidents, more than tobacco, more than all the wars of this century combined."
– Dr. Neal Bernard, M.D. in his book *Food For Life.*

# Breads

## Hallelujah Acres Cornbread

In first bowl, combine the following:
3/4 C Corn Meal
3/4 C Unbleached White Flour
1/4 C Rye Flour
2 tsp. Rumford <u>Aluminum-Free</u>
    Baking Powder
1 tsp. Italian Seasoning
1 Tbsp. Onion Flakes

In second bowl, combine the following:
1 C Water
1 1/2 Tbsp. Honey
1 Tbsp. Apple Cider Vinegar
1 Tbsp. Bragg Liquid Aminos

Spray muffin tin with Pam. Mix wet ingredients well until honey is dissolved. Add dry ingredients. Mix quickly & pour into a 6-muffin pan, filling each 1/2 full. Bake 20 min. in 350-degree oven. Let cool 5-10 min., remove from muffin pan and cool on wire racks. Store covered in refrigerator.

Tip: Use only an aluminum-free baking powder, ie. Rumford

## Hallelujah Acres Date Nut Bread

1 cup organic pitted, whole dates,
    cut into pieces
1 cup organic raisins
1 1/2 cup boiling distilled water
1 cup whole wheat flour
1 cup unbleached flour
1 tsp. baking soda
1 tsp. aluminum-free baking powder
2 slightly beaten egg whites or egg replacer
1 tsp. vanilla
1/2 cup chopped pecans

Place cut dates and raisins in small bowl and pour boiling water over them. Set aside to cool while preparing remainder of recipe. In a large bowl, stir together flour, baking soda and powder. Stir in pecans. Add vanilla to egg whites and blend. Add date and raisin mixture and egg white mixture; stir until well blended. Mixture will be thick. Spread evenly into a lightly oiled 9x5x3-inch loaf pan. Bake 350 degrees 35 to 40 minutes or until it tests done. Cool in pan 10 minutes. Remove from pan and cool thoroughly on wire rack. Best wrapped and stored overnight before serving.

# Desserts

## Hallelujah Acres
## Fresh Strawberry Pie

**Pie Shell:**

1 cup raw almonds (or ½ cup almonds and ½ cup cashews)
1 cup soft, pitted dates
½ tsp. vanilla

Grind the nuts in a food processor until finely chopped, add the dates and vanilla, and **blend well.** Press thinly into a pie plate (from center to the outside rim) to form the shell.

**Binder:**

7 or 8 **large** ripe strawberries
5 soft dates, pitted
2 bananas, fairly ripe
1 Tbsp. fresh lemon juice

Blend all ingredients in food processor or blender until well mixed.

**Fruit Filling**

Cut 2 pints of fresh strawberries into quarters, fold into binder and fill shell. Decorate with approximately ½ pint of quartered strawberries.

Cover with plastic wrap and store in refrigerator. Chill before serving.

## Frozen Banana
## Smoothie

This treat was frequently ordered at Hallelujah Acres, and loved by those who tried it. A tasty, all-natural drink with nothing to harm the body. Your family will love it.

1 ½ - 2 frozen bananas
8 oz. organic apple juice
2-3 frozen strawberries
or other frozen fruit

Pour apple juice into blender. Start machine and add strawberries and bananas in pieces until desired consistency is reached. (Note: peel bananas before freezing.)

## Pritikin French Apple Pie

**CRUST:**
Moisten 1 cup Grape Nuts cereal with
3 Tbsp. frozen apple concentrate, thawed.
Pat into bottom of pie plate.

**FILLING:**
Peel 5 - 6 large Red and Yellow Delicious Apples
Cut Core and slice half of the apple slices into pie, sprinkle generously with cinnamon, add remaining apple slices and sprinkle again with cinnamon. Do not skimp.
Cover with foil.
Bake approximately 50 minutes at 350 degrees.

**Remove from oven and make glaze.**
In saucepan, heat & stir 'til clear & thickened:
½ cup (or a little more) frozen apple juice
½ cup water, distilled
2 heaping Tbsp. cornstarch
Pour over top of apples, covering **all** of them. Cool, cover with clean plastic wrap and refrigerate. Serves 8.

"Your choice of diet can influence your long-term health prospects more than any other action you might take."
– Former Surgeon General C. Everett Koop

"Men dig their graves with their own **teeth** and die more by those fated instruments than by the weapons of their enemies."
– Thomas Moffett, 1600

# Chapter 30:

# In Conclusion: The Two Most Important Issues in Life

"And be not conformed to this world; but be ye transformed by the renewing of your mind, that ye may prove what is that good and acceptable and perfect Will of God."
– Romans 12:2

*By Rev. George Malkmus*

As I write these final words, I have lived on planet earth for well over half a century. Recently, I was thinking back over my life and asked myself a question that brought me to some very interesting conclusions – and here they are: Based on my personal experiences over these many years my conclusion is that all of life boils down to knowing the answers to two basic questions.

The first question that needs answering after we enter this physical world is: HOW DO I PROPERLY NOURISH THIS BODY/TEMPLE WHILE HERE ON EARTH SO THAT IT WILL FUNCTION PROPERLY AND NOT BE SICK? That sounds like a very simple question and yet my parents did not know the answer to that question and thus I had all kinds of physical problems as a child. My first recollection was having my tonsils removed at age 3, then there were the colds, flu, and pneumonia, headaches, upset stomachs, ear aches, swollen glands, all the childhood diseases (I even had mumps and measles simultaneously), along with terrible teeth problems. When I was around 12 or 13 years old, I had over 40 cavities with the resulting fillings during a one-to-two-year-period.

As I grew older and left home, I still did not know how to properly care for my body/temple and so my physical body continued to deteriorate. There was not only the continuation of most of the physical problems that had begun as a child, but now I needed eye glasses, false teeth, I developed hypoglycemia, dandruff, body odor, hemorrhoids, severe sinus and allergy problems, high blood pressure, fatigue and finally at age 42 was told I had a tumor in my colon area the size of a baseball.

All the physical problems I experienced up until this point in my life I had just accepted as normal, and then I had accepted the current medical methods of dealing with them as mother had taught me to do throughout my childhood. (My mother was a Registered Nurse.) However, the medical treatments for colon cancer had been so traumatic for mother that I could not accept them for myself. It was at this point in my life that I started searching for an alternative way to deal with my physical problems.

And so it was at the age of 42, because of a serious physical problem, that I started seeking some answers as to WHY I was getting sick, instead of just trying to treat the symptoms of these physical problems as mother had when I was a child and as I had up until this point in my life. What I learned as a result of that intensive search finally gave me the answer to that most basic question to life: HOW DO I PROPERLY NOURISH THIS BODY/TEMPLE WHILE HERE ON EARTH SO THAT IT WILL FUNCTION PROPERLY AND NOT BE SICK? How sad I had to suffer so many physical problems for so many years before learning the answer to this most basic question.

The second question I feel is so basic and essential to life is: HOW CAN I BE PROPERLY PREPARED FOR THE NEXT LIFE, WHEN THIS EARTHLY LIFE HAS COME TO AN END? Though I went to church on a fairly regular basis as a child, this question was not answered in my life until at the age of 23, I attended a Billy Graham Crusade Meeting in Madison Square Garden in New York City in 1957. It was on that night, that I learned for the first time in my life that I was a sinner in need of a Saviour. And so on May 29, 1957, at the age of 23, I asked Jesus to come into my heart, forgive me for my sins and become my Saviour. Thus, it was on that night, the Great Creator became my Saviour and I had the answer to the second most basic and essential question pertaining to life.

As I was thinking about what I considered the two most basic questions pertaining to life, I started feeling sorry for myself. First, because of all the physical suffering I had experienced during the first 42 years of my life because I had not known the answer to that first and most basic question regarding the body/temple and secondly because it had taken me 23 years before I met my Saviour. Yet, on further reflection, I quickly stopped feeling sorry for myself when I considered the multitudes that live and die without ever knowing the answer to either of these questions.

And so my friend, as we conclude this book, do you know the answer to these two most basic questions pertaining to life? This book answers the first question in abundant detail and I trust you will accept and apply what has been shared in this book so that you can experience health and life to the fullest while in your physical body while here on planet earth.

But what about the second question: HOW CAN I BE PROPERLY PREPARED FOR THE NEXT LIFE, WHEN THIS EARTHLY LIFE HAS COME TO AN END? If you do not know the answer to this second question, please consider that you can apply all the principles of this book and live a long, healthy life, yet spend eternity separated from God and heaven. If you would like additional information on how to answer this second question, write me and I will send some literature that I think will help.

> "Enter ye in at the straight gate: for wide is the gate, and broad is the way, that leadeth to destruction, and many there be which go in thereat: Because straight is the gate, and narrow is the way, which leadeth unto life, and few there be that find it."
> – Matthew 7:13,14

# Appendix:
# Our Newsletter: *Back to the Garden*

*Back to the Garden* is a bi-annual newsletter published by Hallelujah Acres. *Back to the Garden* offers the benefit of over 20 years experience and research by Rev. George Malkmus into the causes of sickness and how we can eliminate sickness from our life by changing our diet and lifestyle. And in *Back to the Garden,* Rev. Malkmus' experience is combined with the writing of editor Michael Dye to produce informative and inspirational information on natural health care.

Since May 1993, when the first issue of *Back to the Garden* was pubished, this newsletter has been on the leading edge of genuine health care reform by showing people how to put this healthful knowledge to use in their own home. *Back to the Garden* teaches health from a Biblical perspective, backs it up with scientific and medical findings and offers great recipes in every issue. This newsletter also provides testimonials from real people – with real names, addresses and pictures – who have healed themselves from cancer, heart disease, arthritis, diabetes, obesity, diverticulitis, spinal meningitis, multiple sclerosis, emotional depression and more.

Each single issue can – and has – changed people's lives, as the powerful letters from our readers clearly show:

"I appreciate and enjoy your newsletter *Back to the Garden*. It is very encouraging and uplifting. I read it from cover to cover. The information is great."
> Grace Sulkowski,
> New York

"Could you please put my aunt on your mailing list to receive *Back to the Garden* … She just found out she has cancer … Thank you very much!! I look forward to every newsletter. ***You have changed my life!***"
> Heidi Suhl,
> Minnesota

" ...I am a Barley Green Distributor and promote Herbal Fiber Blend because these products definitely made a difference in my life. I have been interested in natural ways for over 20 years, but no one has ever taught me how or why until I have been receiving *Back to the Garden*..."
> N.S.,
> Nebraska

"Some weeks back (friends)...sent me some issues of *Back to the Garden* - what fantastic reading! I have read several books on nutrition from our local library but they didn't give me the information for which I was searching. I could write on and on, but I have started to apply your sound advice on diet and I can feel a big improvement with my rheumatoid arthritis. Today has been the most pain free day that I have had in the last six months. God bless you and keep up the good work."

Leonard Brackitt,
Massachusetts

"Congratulations on your May 1993 issue of *Back to the Garden*. I thoroughly agree with its precepts and concepts ... I have been taking college courses in nutrition for some five years or so. From being a big meat eater, I am now a vegetarian ... In 1961, I weighed 206. In nine years I soared to 233. In 1970, I had a massive stroke ... Subject to my nutritional studies I changed my eating habits. Forsaking meat and going the raw route on vegetables ... Today I am 75 and weigh 145 ... Please ensure that I am on the mailing list for future issues of *Back to the Garden.*"

H.P. (Pappy) Neal,
Florida

"Thank you so much for your newsletter. I devour every word of it."

Dr. E.G.
North Dakota

"Read a copy of your Back to the Garden. It is a great publication. Could you please put me down for subscription?"

Dr. Thomas H. Smith, N.D.,
Nevada

"I love everything I have read thus far in the newsletters *(Back to the Garden)* ... It seems that although you do not have a clinic per se, you have nevertheless been able to counsel and educate hundreds in how to improve their health through preventive approaches; and also in the administration of therapies which have resulted in remissions and even cures in chronic and degenerative disease, including cancer. More power to your divine work, George..."

Jack Tropp, Ph.D.,
California

"...I have lots of Health Books and papers, but *Back to the Garden* is my ***favorite!***"

Wanda Bennett,
Kentucky

"This is the best Health Newsletter I have ever read."

Bob Derby,
California

**For a free subscription to *Back to the Garden,* write or call Hallelujah Acres at:**

| | |
|---|---|
| **Hallelujah Acres** | **(704) 481-1700** |
| **P.O. Box 2388** | **FAX: (704) 481-0345** |
| **Shelby, NC 28152** | **http://www.hacres.com** |

*From the*
*Hallelujah Acres mailbag:*

Charlene Momeyer

"Recently a friend of mine showed me your May/June issue of *Back to the Garden*. I would very much like to be put on your mailing list...I have just begun taking Barley Green and am studying nutrition. This all evolved out of a desire to lose weight and because I was extremely tired and experiencing daily headaches. After just a few weeks on Barley Green and eating things that are nutritionally good for me, I am feeling better than I can ever remember feeling and my headaches are gone! I am discovering a whole new world ... Thank you for making *Back to the Garden* available to others. May God continue to bless you in wonderful ways!
– Charlene Momeyer, Arizona

# *God's Way to Ultimate Health* **Bibliography**

John Thomas, *Young Again.* Kelso, Washington: Plexus Press, 1994.

Don W. Cubbison, *Divine Healing and Natural Health.* Lexington, South Carolina: Professional Printers, Ltd., 1992.

John A. McDougall, M.D. and Mary A. McDougall, *The McDougall Plan.* Clinton, New Jersey: New Win Publishers, Inc., 1983.
------------ *A Challenging Second Opinion.* Clinton, New Jersey: New Win Publishers, Inc., 1985.

Jerry Hoover, N.D., *Natural Medicine.* Anaheim, California: KNI Printers, 1993.

Ross Horne, *Health & Survival in the 21st Century.* McMahons Point, Australia: Margaret Gee Publishing, 1992.
------------ *Improving on Pritikin.* Avalon Beach, Australia: Happy Landings Pty Ltd., 1988.
------------ *The Health Revolution.* Avalon Beach, Australia: Happy Landings Pty Ltd., 1985.

Arthur M. Baker, M.A., *Awakening our Self Healing Body.* Los Angeles, California: Self Health Care Systems, 1993.

Jack Tropp, *Cancer: The Whole-Body Approach to Cancer Therapy.* Los Angeles, California: G.R.D. Clinic, 1980.

Yoshihide Hagiwara, M.D., *Green Barley Essence.* New Canaan, Connecticut: Keats Publishing, 1985.

Bob Owen, *Roger's Recovery from AIDS.* Malibu, California: Davar, 1987.

Deepak Chopra, M.D., *Ageless Body, Timeless Mind.* New York, New York: Harmony Books, 1993.

Richard Yerby, *Creature Versus Creator.* Vernon, Alabama: Christ Is All.

Elmer Cranton, M.D., *Bypassing BYPASS.* Trout Dale, Virginia: Medex Publishers, Inc., 1993.

Elmer Cranton, M.D., *Bypassing BYPASS*. Trout Dale, Virginia: Medex Publishers, Inc., 1993.

Keki R. Sidwa, N.D., D.O., *Medical Drugs on Trial? Verdict "Guilty!"* Chicago, Illinois: Natural Hygiene Press, 1976.

Frank A. Oski, M.D., *Don't Drink Your Milk!* Brushton, New York: Teach Services, 1983.

Dr. Edward Howell, *Enzyme Nutrition*. Wayne, New Jersey: Avery Publishing Group, Inc., 1985.

Humbart Santillo, B.S., M.H., *Food Enzymes – The Missing Link to Radiant Health*. Prescott, Arizona: Hohm Press, 1987.

Dr. Hans Diehl, *To Your Health*. Loma Linda, California: Lifestyle Medicine Institute, 1987.

John Robbins, *Diet For A New America*. Walpole, New Hampshire: Stillpoint Publishing, 1987.
------------ *Diet For A New World*. New York, New York: William Marrow and Company, Inc., 1992.

Ronald L. Seibold, M.S., *Cereal Grass*. Lawrence, Kansas: Wilderness Community Education Foundation, Inc., 1990.

Dr. Mary Ruth Swope, *Green Leaves of Barley*. Phoenix, Arizona: Swope Enterprises, Inc., 1987.

Teresa Schumacher, *Cleansing the Body and the Colon for a Happier and Healthier You*. St. George, Utah: Health is Wealth, 1987.

Dr. Allen E. Banik, *The Choice is Clear*. Kansas City, Missouri: Acres U.S.A., 1971.

Dr. Norman W. Walker, *Water Can Undermine Your Health*. Prescott, Arizona: Norwalk Press, 1974.
------------ *Fresh Vegetable and Fruit Juices*. Prescott, Arizona: Norwalk Press, 1936.
------------ *Colon Health: The Key to a Vibrant Life*. Prescott, Arizona: Norwalk Press, 1979.
------------ *The Vegetarian Guide to Diet & Salad*. Prescott, Arizona: Norwalk Press, 1940.

Paul C. Bragg, N.D., Ph.D., *The Shocking Truth About Water*. Santa Barbara, California: Health Science.

# Index

## Quantity Discounts for *God's Way to Ultimate Health*

| Quantity | Price |
|---|---|
| 1 – 3 books: | $18.99 |
| 4 – 16 books: | $15.19 |
| 17 books (case): | $13.29 |
| 51 books (3 cases): | $11.39 |

## Additional book, video and audio cassette by Rev. George Malkmus

<u>RECIPES FOR LIFE... FROM GOD'S GARDEN</u> by Rhonda J. Malkmus is the perfect companion piece to *God's Way to Ultimate Health* because it begins where the theory and rationale for the diet leaves off. With more than 400 nutritious and delicious recipes, this huge 8 1/2 by 11-inch spiral bound book proves that healthy food tastes great! Includes detailed index of recipes. ($24.95 plus 6% North Carolina sales tax, for in-state residents)

<u>WHY CHRISTIANS GET SICK</u> by Rev. George Malkmus is especially helpful in introducing Christians to a natural diet and lifestyle. Letters are received daily from all over the world from people helped by this book. *Why Christians Get Sick* helps you understand the cause of disease and how you can eliminate sickness from your life. This book is written on a solid Biblical foundation with over 150 Bible verses. ($8.95 plus 6% North Carolina sales tax, for in-state residents)

<u>HOW TO ELIMINATE SICKNESS SEMINAR ON VIDEO</u> This 2 1/2-hour professional quality video includes a full-length "How to Eliminate Sickness" Seminar by Rev. Malkmus. This seminar contains a powerful summary of everything Rev. Malkmus teaches. *A Must-See Video!* ($24.95 plus 6% North Carolina sales tax, for in-state residents)

<u>HOW TO ELIMINATE SICKNESS SEMINAR ON AUDIO CASSETTE</u> This is an updated 3-hour recording of Rev. Malkmus' seminar. It covers the basics of why we get sick and how to restore our health. It will change your thinking forever as to what is nutrition and what is not. Two tapes in jacket. *A powerful presentation of the health message!* ($12.95, plus 6% North Carolina sales tax)

## *QUICK ORDER FORM*

**Mail to: Hallelujah Acres  P.O. Box 2388  Shelby, NC  28151**

*For credit card orders, call (704) 481-1700 or Fax at (704) 481-0345*

Name (Please Print) _____

Address _____

City _____ State _____ Zip _____

Telephone (including area code) _____

☐ Please send me a free issue of your newsletter, *Back to the Garden*

Please send me:

____ copies of *God's Way to Ultimate Health* @ $ _____ = $ _____

____ copies of *Why Christians Get Sick* @ $ _____ = $ _____

____ videos  of How to Eliminate Sickness @ $ _____ = $ _____

____ audios  of How to Eliminate Sickness @ $ _____ = $ _____

6% sales tax (N.C. only) $ _____

Shipping $ _____

Total $ _____

**Shipping**: $5.00 for orders under $50.00; 10% of orders over $50.00

North Carolina residents add 6 % sales tax

| Method of payment: ☐ Check ☐ Money Order ☐ Visa ☐ Mastercard ☐ Discover |
|---|
| Card Number: ☐☐☐☐☐☐☐☐☐☐☐☐☐☐☐☐ |
| Signature _____ Card Exp. Date _____ |

*Visit our web site*
*www.hacres.com*

## Quantity Discounts for *God's Way to Ultimate Health*

| Quantity | Price |
|---|---|
| 1 – 3 books: | $18.99 |
| 4 – 16 books: | $15.19 |
| 17 books (case): | $13.29 |
| 51 books (3 cases): | $11.39 |

## Additional book, video and audio cassette by Rev. George Malkmus

**RECIPES FOR LIFE... FROM GOD'S GARDEN** by Rhonda J. Malkmus is the perfect companion piece to *God's Way to Ultimate Health* because it begins where the theory and rationale for the diet leaves off. With more than 400 nutritious and delicious recipes, this huge 8 1/2 by 11-inch spiral bound book proves that healthy food tastes great! Includes detailed index of recipes. ($24.95 plus 6% North Carolina sales tax, for in-state residents)

**WHY CHRISTIANS GET SICK** by Rev. George Malkmus is especially helpful in introducing Christians to a natural diet and lifestyle. Letters are received daily from all over the world from people helped by this book. *Why Christians Get Sick* helps you understand the cause of disease and how you can eliminate sickness from your life. This book is written on a solid Biblical foundation with over 150 Bible verses. ($8.95 plus 6% North Carolina sales tax, for in-state residents)

**HOW TO ELIMINATE SICKNESS SEMINAR ON VIDEO** This 2 1/2-hour professional quality video includes a full-length "How to Eliminate Sickness" Seminar by Rev. Malkmus. This seminar contains a powerful summary of everything Rev. Malkmus teaches. *A Must-See Video!* ($24.95 plus 6% North Carolina sales tax, for in-state residents)

**HOW TO ELIMINATE SICKNESS SEMINAR ON AUDIO CASSETTE** This is an updated 3-hour recording of Rev. Malkmus' seminar. It covers the basics of why we get sick and how to restore our health. It will change your thinking forever as to what is nutrition and what is not. Two tapes in jacket. *A powerful presentation of the health message!* ($12.95, plus 6% North Carolina sales tax)

## QUICK ORDER FORM

**Mail to: Hallelujah Acres   P.O. Box 2388  Shelby, NC  28151**

*For credit card orders, call (704) 481-1700 or Fax at (704) 481-0345*

Name (Please Print) _____

Address _____

City _____ State _____ Zip _____

Telephone (including area code) _____

☐ Please send me a free issue of your newsletter, *Back to the Garden*

Please send me:

____ copies of *God's Way to Ultimate Health*    @ $ _____ = $ _____
____ copies of *Why Christians Get Sick*    @ $ _____ = $ _____
____ videos  of How to Eliminate Sickness    @ $ _____ = $ _____
____ audios  of How to Eliminate Sickness    @ $ _____ = $ _____

6% sales tax (N.C. only) $ _____
Shipping $ _____
Total $ _____

**Shipping**: $5.00 for orders under $50.00; 10% of orders over $50.00
North Carolina residents add 6 % sales tax

Method of payment:  ☐ Check  ☐ Money Order  ☐ Visa  ☐ Mastercard  ☐ Discover

Card Number: ☐☐☐☐☐☐☐☐☐☐☐☐☐☐☐☐

Signature _____  Card Exp. Date _____

*Visit our web site*
*www.hacres.com*